BETWEEN GOD AND THE SULTAN

KNUT VIKØR

Between God and the Sultan

A History of Islamic Law

OXFORD
UNIVERSITY PRESS

OXFORD
UNIVERSITY PRESS

Oxford University Press, Inc., publishes works that further
Oxford University's objective of excellence
in research, scholarship, and education.

Oxford New York
Auckland Cape Town Dar es Salaam Hong Kong Karachi
Kuala Lumpur Madrid Melbourne Mexico City Nairobi
New Delhi Shanghai Taipei Toronto

with offices in
Argentina Austria Brazil Chile Czech Republic France Greece
Guatemala Hungary Italy Japan Poland Portugal Singapore
South Korea Switzerland Thailand Turkey Ukraine Vietnam

Published by Oxford University Press, Inc.
198 Madison Avenue, New York, New York 10016
www.oup.com

Library of Congress Cataloging-in-Publication Data
Vikør, Knut S.
Between God and the Sultan : a history of Islamic law / Knut S. Vikør.
p. cm.
Includes bibliographical references and index.
ISBN-13: 978-0-19-522397-2 (cloth : alk. paper)
ISBN-10: 0-19-522397-7 (cloth : alk. paper)
ISBN-13: 978-0-19-522398-9 (pbk. : alk. paper)
ISBN-10: 0-19-522398-5 (pbk. : alk. paper)
1. Islamic law. 2. Islamic law--Methodology. 3. Islamic law--History. I. Title.
KBP144.V55 2005
340.5'9--dc22
2005015491

1 3 5 7 9 8 6 4 2

PREFACE

Today's discussions on Islam and the place religion should have in society often end up being about the Sharīʿa, the Islamic law. Those who work for a political role for Islam demand that 'the Sharīʿa must be applied' in their country, while those who criticise Islam use the law as proof of how 'medieval' the religion as such is. Islam is sometimes, not quite justly, called a 'religion of rules', and the rules of Islam are the Sharīʿa.

But it is often hard to find out exactly what this law is in more practical terms. Asking those who favour it or those who oppose it may only lead to greater confusion. Both a rule and its exact opposite can simultaneously be said to be 'what the Sharīʿa says' and what God asks of the believer. It may even be questioned if there is any Sharīʿa at all in the mundane world, or whether it is just an ethical ideal, or an ethereal body that only God can know. At the same time people may be stoned or mutilated in the name of this same law.

The key is the concept of 'religious law'. This is almost a contradiction in terms in our modern conception of the world; 'religion' is something we consider internal to the human soul, a faith in a non-material force of some kind, while 'law' is external to us, something that society has established in order to regulate the material needs of the community.

We may perhaps say that it was not like this 'before', in the pre-modern period when God was more present in the everyday life of the believers. But the contrast between 'religion' and 'law' has been continuous throughout Muslim history. The Islamic law has always existed in a tension between these two forces: on the one hand God, who gave the law, on the other the state, the 'sultan', who represents society and is to implement the law. This tension and dynamic has created a very particular history for the law, both in how it was formulated and by whom, in its theoretical basis and its actual rules, and in how it was practised in historical reality from the time of its formation until today. That is the main topic of this book.

We will discuss this in four different parts, each spanning three or four chapters. The first and last parts of the book focus on the law itself, while the two in the middle discuss the 'law in history', its practice and relation to political authorities.

Part I draws up the fundamentals of the methodology of the law and its transition from a revelation from God, through a formulation into rules by means of various methods, to its confirmation as practicable law by the consensus of scholars. Part II presents the historical formations of the 'schools of law' and their practical application in courts. Part III shows how the state and the sultans influenced the field of practised law, through the establishment of separate courts outside the Sharīᶜa system, and the development of the legal system through the Ottoman and colonial periods until today's demands for 're-application' of the Sharīᶜa. Part IV, finally, presents some illustrative examples of Sharīᶜa rules in the fields of criminal law, family law and some areas of economic activity.

This is probably the first introductory textbook to the history of Islamic law to appear in English since 1964. Given the rapid expansion of research in this field over the last decades, this fact is a lasting testimony to the two great works that appeared in that year, Neil Coulson's *History of Islamic Law* and in particular Joseph Schacht's magisterial *Introduction to Islamic Law*. The lasting quality of these works has made it difficult to consider the need or indeed possibility for any replacement to them. Nor is the present book intended to be seen as any replacement for Schacht's *Introduction*. However, there may be need for a less demanding work for the student that comes fresh to the field of Islamic law. It can perhaps function as an 'introduction to the *Introduction*'.

The aim of this textbook is also slightly different, as its focus is primarily on the *history* rather than the content of the law. It presents how the development of the law appears in the light of recent research, carried out by a younger generation of scholars, on whose work this presentation relies. The contrast to Schacht's great work may indeed make it necessary to point out this obvious fact, that this is a *textbook*, not a monograph presenting original research, as his *Introduction* was. What is presented here relies completely on the research of other scholars. The study of the Sharīᶜa has exploded over the last decade, approaching the topic from many angles; as history, law, religion, anthropology, philosophy or sociology. This research is exciting, often controversial and conflicting, and the way it has been merged here into a continuous narrative is my responsibility alone. It is also a continuing process, and another textbook in ten years may well have to revise many of the assumptions made here, but such is the nature of historical surveys; their shelf-time may always be short.

The intended reader is the student who wants to go beyond the few pages afforded to Islamic law in standard introductions to Islam, but before going into the detail of the books of Schacht and other specialized works. However, we hope that the book will also be of interest to the general public who seek a general introduction to this theme, so hotly debated with so little insight today, an introduction that tries to bring out both the diversity of the law and how it depends on history, while giving an impression of the main lines that define it.

The present book is a revised edition of one published in Norwegian in 2003, for which I received welcome comments from Jakob Skovgaard-Petersen, Kåre Lilleholt and Endre Stiansen, and for the English edition from Maribel Fierro, Robert Gleave and in particular Aharon Layish. I thank them all for their help in improving the quality of this work. Of course they have no responsibility for the errors and shortcomings that still persist, or for the choices I have made in my presentation of the material.

Bergen, June 2005 KNUT S. VIKØR

CONTENTS

Part III. THE HISTORY OF THE LAW

1

INTRODUCTION
DOES ISLAMIC LAW EXIST?

The first question to be answered in a book on Islamic law is, does such a law really exist? It is quite possible to answer, 'No, and that is why studying it is so exciting'.

Such a paradox may sound a bit off-putting. But it is more than a play on words. It is also a warning to the reader to try to put aside any pre-conceived notions she may have about the theme. We continuously hear on the news that 'Islamic law has been introduced' in this or that country, entailing barbaric punishments, the oppression of women and the crushing of liberties as a result. How can something that does not exist have such dramatic consequences? Is this not Islamic law then?

The answer, as is so often the case, is both yes and no. There is no such thing as *a*, that is *one*, Islamic law, a text that clearly and unequivocally establishes all the rules of a Muslim's behaviour. There is a great divergence of views, not just between opposing currents, but also between individual scholars within the legal currents, of exactly what rules belong to the Islamic law. The jurists have had to learn to live with this disagreement on and variety (in Arabic, *ikhtilāf*) in the contents of the law.

Yet these differing opinions have one thing in common: that the law should be the expression of God's will for mankind and be based on His revelation. The Revelation is in its nature one, as it exists with God. But it is not unequivocal in appearance to man; the Revelation must go through a human intellectual process before it can become a cohesive legal system for society.

Thus the Islamic law both does and does not exist, through the many, different and often conflicting views and individual rules that Muslim scholars have developed on the basis of this shared divine Revelation. Questions like 'What does the Sharīᶜa say about such-and-such' may be partly meaningless, because Islamic law is no more than a body of sources of revelation and a methodology for making rules from these sources. How successful this methodology has been in articulating God's will in each matter is something to be decided by the Muslims, and in particular the Muslim scholars. Thus, what we read in the newspapers as the 'introduction of the Sharīᶜa'—almost invariably about criminal laws—may or may not be *part* of the Sharīᶜa, depending on the scholars' views, but it is never *identical* to the Sharīᶜa. Thus our suggestion to the reader is: put all preconceptions about what the Islamic law 'is' aside for the moment.

So far, we have partly spoken of 'Islamic law', partly used the Arabic word, 'Sharīᶜa'. This term is used in slightly different ways. Some, in particular younger Muslim scholars, tend to use 'Sharīᶜa' as a name for the divine will as only God knows it; an abstract divine law only perceived by Him.[1] Mankind has only been given glimpses of this divine will through the Revelation, as far as God has willed it. But what the jurists have on the basis of this Revelation formulated through their reason is only 'law' as a science, *fiqh*.[2] This science is human and contestable, while the Sharīᶜa is of God and cannot be subject to any lack of clarity. However, defining 'Sharīᶜa' in this way makes it only a religious ideal, something that cannot impinge directly on the human experience.[3]

It is more common to use 'Sharīᶜa' as a name for the Islamic legal rules that we actually see applied in our human existence. Then one distinguishes between *fiqh* as the science used to derive the legal rules from their sources and the Sharīᶜa as the result of

1 In the same way as 'the Koran' may also refer to a methaphysical 'book' that only exists with God and that only He can know and fathom; the physical book that we humans have is only a mundane copy, a *muṣḥaf* of the immaterial Message.

2 But the distinction between 'Sharīᶜa' and *fiqh* is often unclear among the theoreticians, and one may find *fiqh*, 'the Sharīᶜa' and *furūᶜ* used interchangeably regarding the actual rules of law, often in the same work. A believer will of course consider these specified rules to be an expression of God's will, so which of the three terms is most apt may depend more on context than content.

3 A variant, and a natural consequence of this, is to distinguish the five *ḥudūd* rules of the criminal code, which we will discuss further in Chapter 14, as the 'real' Sharīᶜa, as these five are based directly on the text of the Revelation. Thus 'God's Sharīᶜa' may be reduced to these five crimes. This is not uncommon among the Islamists of today, who tend to see these as symbols for the 'application' of the Sharīᶜa. However, other jurists will point to the fact that these five rules were also formulated through human *fiqh*.

this endeavour, the actual body of laws or rules in all their variations and internal inconsistency. It is also common to divide *fiqh*, jurisprudence, into two parts, the science of the methodology (*uṣūl al-fiqh*, literally 'the roots of jurisprudence'), and the science of the actual rules and legal fields (*furūᶜ*, literally 'branches').

Different parts of the legal system

The Sharīᶜa is thus not based on any decision from a parliament or council, but is the result of individual efforts by the scholars working with God's revelation. It is God who is the 'legislator'. This also affects the division of the law into different parts. In Western law, we often distinguish between what we call 'public law' and 'private law'. While the former is concerned with the individual's relations to the state, or matters internal to the state, and contains areas such as criminal law, rules for state administration, and so on, the latter deals with the affairs individuals have with each other.

Islamic law has a similar division, however, here it is not between the individual and the state, but between the individual and God. The main distinction is thus between man's affairs with man, *muᶜāmalāt*, and man's affairs with God, *ᶜibādāt*. These last mostly consist of rules that we in the West do not consider appropriate to law, such as how to perform religious rituals, but also some areas we see as legal, thus in Islam a part of the criminal law is seen as crimes against God. The distinction between these two types of rules runs throughout the system, so that certain legal principles that apply for inter-human relations do not apply in the affairs of God. But the general methodology, *uṣūl*, is on the whole the same for both, and Muslims consider both indivisibly to be part of the Sharīᶜa, though purely religious and ritual matters do not generally appear in court. In this book, which is mostly concerned with the role of the Sharīᶜa in society, we will therefore focus primarily on the inter-human, *muᶜāmalāt*, parts of the law.

We can see another element here: Relations that are not infractions against God are seen as conflicts between individuals. Islamic law does not in principle recognize public prosecution and the state's responsibility to initiate legal proceedings against criminals.[4] The reason for this is historical, and we will discuss it later. But this means that every case in court is based on one individual party, the plaintiff, making a claim against another individual, the defendant, both presenting their own cases, without lawyers or public prosecutors. This is true even if the end result may be a punishment carried out by the state authorities. If fines are to be paid, they are most often paid to the injured party, not to the state. These factors tend to reduce the difference between 'private' and 'public' law as we know it.[5] Thus there are no separate courts for 'private', 'public' or 'criminal' cases in the Sharīᶜa system, and the procedures that the court follows is by and large identical whether the matter at issue is a breach of contract or a murder.

Still, differences exist. When later on we see how law is actually practiced, we will find that we can clearly distinguish separate areas of law, such that we can talk of 'criminal law', 'family law', 'economic law', and so on as separate legal areas.[6] However, in this work, we will when a specific distinction has been made, discuss all these areas as one, as they are all built on the same basis.

Where is the Islamic law?

There is thus something factual that we may call 'Islamic law'. But how and in what form does this law exist? Or, when a judge sits in his court and attempts to find a resolution to the case in

4 At least in general. There exist, as we shall see in Chapters 9 and 10, procedures and courts where the society, the public, may promote the interests of the commonality by the judge representing it as 'the injured party'. But these are adaptations to actual social needs and subsidiary to the main principle that the court is to resolve conflicts between two equal parties.

5 One way to locate 'public law' in Islamic law is to look for those areas that are considered 'the rights of God' (*ḥuqūq Allāh*), which include e.g. the *ḥudūd* rules (see Chapter 14). Thus the interests of the public and those of God coincide, in contrast to 'civil' matters that only concern the two parties to a dispute; see Bernard G. Weiss, *The Spirit of Islamic Law,* Athens, GA 1998, 182-3.

6 It should still be noticed, particularly for those versed in Western law, that the distinctions used there between 'private' and 'public' law do not really apply in Islamic law, so that the rules treating crimes (murder, theft, etc.) are treated as belonging to 'private law'.

front of him, where does he turn to find the legal norms that he is to apply?[7]

In Western or European law, there are basically two different types of answer to this; one typical for continental Europe, one specifically Anglo-American.

Codified law

In one system, the judge will look to one specific clear source for his deliberation: a law book consisting of a systematic presentation of rules and their application, organized in laws, chapters, paragraphs and sub-paragraphs. This law-book, or *law code*, has been decided upon by a body that is independent of the judiciary: a legislative body such as a parliament or national assembly. The code may be open to interpretation by the judge when applied to actual cases, but the principle is that it should be as clear, univocal and complete as possible. This is thus known as a *codified* law,[8] and the most famous law code of modern times is probably the Code Napoléon,[9] still valid in France and very influential in countries under French inspiration; including many Muslim countries. In the nineteenth century, this law was seen to be so complete that it covered all possible cases; no judge could claim that a case could not find its solution in this code. But the code was, of course, in spite of this faith in its perfection, originally given by a legislator that had and has the liberty to change it when need arises.

Common law

The other system is that known as common law, which dominates to a varying extent in Britain, the United States and countries influenced by the English. The basis for the common-law system is that law is expressed through the established legal practices of

7 Michael Bogdan, *Comparative Law*, Stockholm 1994.

8 Also called 'civil law'—a term with many meanings—both terms come from the Roman law code 'Corpus juris civilis', which was written in the Byzantine empire in the sixth century. This law book, which became one of the foundations for laws in many countries of Medieval continental Europe (alongside various types of customary law) is therefore called 'Roman law'.

9 There were five such codes in all, Code Napoléon is the commonly used name of what was formally called 'Code civil'.

society, that is the courts. It may thus be described as a sophisticated system of the customary law that is often found in stateless societies. In these, the legal authority, be it headman, religious elder or the community of free man, seeks what has earlier been the established custom in society and attempts to reproduce this in the case at hand. The headman or elders did not believe that they *created* the law, they summed up and applied the custom that the members of society knew and accepted.

Similarly, in the British courts, it is the custom of society that the judge applies, here refined and expressed in what earlier courts and judges have ruled, that is, precedence. The courts, originally subservient to the King and partly to the Church, asserted their independence by applying a 'common law' for all of England (as opposed to feudal Europe, where the law could differ from county to county). This system has been modified over the centuries, in particular through the addition of a separate legal body called 'equity', but is still dominant in Britain (while the United States only applies the common law principle in certain areas of law).

Here, then, a judge when searching for the legal rule, looks at precedence. If a case similar to the one at hand has been decided earlier by a court on the same hierarchical level, the judge is bound to give an identical verdict; he cannot change an established rule by himself. Of course, judges do precisely that, laws must develop as time passes. But this is mostly done through the fiction that the case at hand does not in fact correspond to anything that has ever come before a court. If that is so, the judge is free to judge as he likes and set precedence, which other judges later have to follow. This system may be called *casuistic* in that the law is defined through individual cases, rather than through over-arching basic principles as in a codified system.

In addition, Parliament does of course pass laws, or *statutes* —thus 'statutory law'—but these are, strictly speaking, anomalous to the system. Therefore, British judges will, once such a parliamentary-based law has been enacted, tend to wait until it first comes up in a court case, before using that judgement as a source for precedence for future cases.

Juristic law

Islamic law stands for a third, perhaps *the* third model of law;

some historians talk of division into three; codified, common-law and Islamic law.[10] As in customary and common law, Islamic law does not have any code, any over-arching law book where the rules are specified in paragraphs and sections. But it is not, as in customary law, earlier social practice that determines the law. Judges cannot decide what is right or wrong, nor can they look at the precedence of earlier decisions. That would make the judge into the legislator, and in Islam it is not the judge, society or any assembly that lays down the law, it is God.

But as God has not given us any indisputable law-code, humans must step in to clarify the law for our use. That is not the judge's task; he, the *qāḍī*, has to *apply* the law in actual cases as in any other legal system, but he can no more here than in any other system *formulate* the law. He is bound by another party: the jurist, the legal scholar. The legal scholar, *muftī*,[11] does not take part in the procedures of the court and has no knowledge of the proofs or claims in the cases at hand. His task is identical to that of the law-book in the codified system and of precedence in common law; he clarifies what is the legal basis on which the judge has to make his decision.

This point has been passed over lightly by many historians of law, who have accepted too easily a description given by Max Weber, where the *qāḍī* from his own inclination and quite informally metes out right and wrong, something he called *Kadijustiz*.[12] An English judge once wrote, when he was uncertain on a point, that he had been 'put in the position of a cadi under the palm tree. There are no principles on which he is directed to act. He has to do the best he can in the circumstances, having no rules of law to guide him', or as an American judge, Frankfurter, once put it, 'This is a court of review, not a tribunal unbounded by rules. We do not sit like a kadi under a tree dispensing justice

10 Knapp, *Základy srovnávací právní vědy*, Prague 1991, 52-3 & 58, quoted in Bogdan, *Comparative Law*, 87.

11 The general term for a specialist in law is *faqīh*, we are here more concerned with the specific role played in the judging process, where the term *muftī* is used. We will discuss this in greater detail in Chapter 8.

12 Weber did of course know of *muftī*s, but considered both the *muftī* and *qāḍī*'s work to be basically haphazard, unsystematic and subject to the will of the 'patrimonial' sultan, not the realization of a systematic Islamic legal system; Bryan S. Turner, *Weber and Islam: A Critical Study*, London 1978, 107-21. See further on '*Kadijustiz*' below.

according to considerations of individual expediency'. The actual *qāḍī* thus also has a position quite different from this 'kadi under a tree'.[13]

Because of the central role of the jurist, the Islamic legal system is thus often called a 'juristic' system. But the legal scholar cannot of course make the rules up on a whim. As God is the legislator, the scholar's task is to find out what God meant the law to be in each particular case. This may look similar to a common-law system, where society or its custom is the actual 'legislator', and the judge must *discover* what this lawgiver has said, through his particular methodology, precedence.[14] In the same way, the Islamic jurist must use a particular method to discover what legal rule, *ḥukm*, God has assigned to the case at hand. The legitimization of the rule as God's thus lies in an acceptance of the methodology and of the scholar's ability to use it.

The muftī as focal point

The basic system is thus: A case is brought before a judge. He establishes the facts of the case. Then he, or one of the parties in the case, goes to a *muftī* and asks what kind of legal rules exist for this type of case. The *muftī* consults his source, in the last instance the Revelation, uses the appropriate methodology, and determines that in this type of case God's rule is such-and-such. This he sums up in written form in a statement called a *fatwā*, which then forms the basis for the judge's decision.

Thus the *muftī* only makes a statement of principle. He has no responsibility for the actual case that caused the request or the facts within it; that is the judge's job, and the judge must himself determine whether the *fatwā* statement is at all relevant to the case. The *fatwā* is no verdict and the *muftī* no judge; all that is the work of the *qāḍī*, the judge in the court. But every judgment shall in theory be based on pre-established legal rule as expressed in a *fatwā*. And in theory, a *fatwā* has no validity beyond the moment

13 Both quoted from Lawrence Rosen, *The Anthropology of Justice: Law as Culture in Islamic Society*, Cambridge 1989, 58. See also Noel J. Coulson, *Conflicts and Tensions in Islamic Jurisprudence*, Chicago 1969, 40, and Haim Gerber, *State, Society and Law in Islam, Ottoman Law in Comparative Perspective*, Albany, NY 1994, 10-12.

14 Lawrence Rosen, *The Justice of Islam: Comparative Perspectives on Islamic Law and Society*, London 2000, 38-68.

it was expressed, Islamic law does not know the principle of precedent, any more than the European codified system does.

Of course, this is theory.[15] If the case is unproblematic and the judge feels he knows the legal basis, he will not bother going to a *muftī*. He will only do so if he is in genuine doubt, or if the case is so important that he wants the extra authority that an external *fatwā* can give. (However one or both of the parties to the case can go privately to a *muftī* to have their position evaluated.) On the other hand, this theory puts the complete responsibility of knowing God's law on the individual *muftī*, assuming his total competence in establishing it in a perfectly unequivocal way so that no other scholar could disagree; as God's law cannot be one in Cairo and another in Damascus.

Clearly, no human of the real world can have such complete competence; so in reality a legal scholar can and should rely on what other and greater scholars have done before him. He has at hand a large body of legal literature of various levels of complexity and disagreement, and as we shall see, a real-life *muftī* will stay within the boundaries of this established literature when he makes his statement.[16] To what degree he can act independently of established practice is one of the great debates in the history of the law, and we shall see in greater detail how this is played out.

Among the various types of law-books written over the centuries are short, pointed summaries of commonly applied rules called *mukhtaṣarāt*. Some historians believe that these, in conjunction with *fatwā* collections, form a kind of semi-codified system, so that we can say Islamic law moved in the direction of codified law.[17] If so, this is only in a very rudimentary way, and it is doubtful whether it is meaningful to use such a term. The basic

15 And it must be noted that in the classical theory the *qāḍī* and the *muftī* could be the same person, who should be fully versed in the law and then did not need to seek outside opinion (a *qāḍī-mujtahid*). But, as is detailed below, these two roles in the judicial process increasingly came to be seen as separate.

16 The *muftī* may in the historical reality become more involved in the actual processes of the courts than this classical and theoretical sharp division would indicate, in particular from the late Middle Ages onwards; more on this in Chapters 8 to 10.

17 Mohammad Fadel, 'The social logic of *taqlīd* and the rise of the *mukhataṣar*', *Islamic Law and Society*, III 2, 1996, 193-233. See more on this in Chapter 8.

principle is in any case that the law must in the last instance always refer back to God, the legislator.

Schools of law

The development of this 'practised' Sharīᶜa has historically taken place within systems known as 'schools of law' (Arabic, *madhhabs*). In the majority Sunnī current of Islam, there are today four such schools, while the different Shīᶜī and other minority theological currents each have their own *madhhab*. These schools are more than just currents of thought or traditions; they are fully parallel legal systems, each with their own methodology and rules; most often with separate courts and judges.[18] Still, the actual rules and basic methodology of these four show great similarity, the difference is most often only in the detail. In the last century, the tendency has been to diminish the difference between the four Sunnī schools, such that they can often only be discerned in some variations in the performance of prayer (which is of course also directed by the Sharīᶜa and is thus divided along the schools' opinions).

Some would therefore today prefer to call these religious 'rites' rather than legal schools; but historically the division between them was fundamental; every legal scholar had to belong to one and only one *madhhab*, and most ordinary Muslims also identified with one school, such as in his selection of which mosque he visited and in how he was trained in performing the prayer.

The four Sunnī schools, each named after the scholar said to have founded it, are mainly distributed geographically. One way of describing their respective areas is to imagine three circles that meet up in Egypt. If you draw a huge circle with a centre in the Sahara and with Cairo on its outer perimeter, you will have drawn the area where the Mālikī school dominates: North and West Africa, going as far east as the Sudan and the southern parts of Egypt. The Mālikī school, named after the eight-century jurist Mālik b. Anas, also has some followers in the Arabian Gulf, and

18 This is, of course, a matter of definitions. Some scholars would insist that there is only one Islamic law, but that it exists in different *variations* in the four schools. In the historical section, we shall see in more detail how the different schools interacted.

formerly dominated Islamic Spain (al-Andalus) before this country was conquered by the Christians.

Another circle with a centre slightly north of the Caspian Sea, encompassing the Balkans on its western periphery and stretching to Pakistan and northern India, would indicate the area of the Ḥanafī school, named after Abū Ḥanifa.[19] This school is all-dominant in the Turkish-speaking areas as well as in those regions where Islam was introduced by Turks and Mongols, that is south-Eastern Europe and Central and South Asia. Where they had power, the Ottoman empire made the Ḥanafī school into a 'state law', so that in parts of the Middle East (Syria, Egypt and North Africa through to Algeria), many people had one *madhhab* privately, while another was used in the courts of law. We will look into how that worked in more detail later on.

The third circle, which isn't quite circular, has a centre somewhere in the Indian Ocean. The Shāfiᶜī school has its strength on the coast of East Africa and in South-East Asia, but also adherents in central Arabic areas, such as northern Egypt, the Arabian peninsula, Syria and parts of Iraq. Iran was mainly Shāfiᶜī before it turned Shīᶜī in the sixteenth century, and the school has some adherents in coastal areas of India. We shall hear a lot about the eponymous 'founder' of the school, Muḥammad b. Idrīs al-Shāfiᶜī, because his theoretical work on the methodology of law has laid the foundation for all schools, not just his 'own'.

The fourth and last of the Sunnī schools is also the smallest and does not require any circle to be described. The Ḥanbalī school, named from Aḥmad b. Ḥanbal, did not have any exclusive geographical domain until the middle of the eighteenth century, but it has since, due to the expansion of the Wahhābī reform movement, dominated most of the Arabian peninsula (Saudi Arabia and Qatar). However, Ḥanbalism was always present among the scholars of the great centres of learning, and was always counted among the four established schools, even before the Wahhābīs built a state power around it.

Thus the history of these schools of law is central to the history of Islamic law, and we will discuss them in greater detail in several chapters to come.

19 'Ḥanafī' is the adjectival form of 'Ḥanīfa' in Arabic, thus 'Abū Ḥanīfa-ian'.

The methods for studying Islamic law

With the single exception of Saudi Arabia, this classical court and legal system, with *qāḍī*s querying *muftī*s, is not in use in any Muslim country today. Still, the Sharīᶜa is important to the law of most countries, albeit in different ways. Parts of the Sharīᶜa's rules may have been introduced into the otherwise 'Westernized' laws of each country, or the Sharīᶜa may be equated with 'traditional practice' which the judges may or must take into account. This is particularly the case in family law, in many countries the 'preserve' of the Sharīᶜa, but also in other legal areas.

Many countries also have some general formulation that the modernized law shall be 'inspired' in some way by the Sharīᶜa. However, what the content of this 'inspiration' is, or to what degree the classical rules have survived in the modern legal system, varies greatly from country to country and between the different fields of law. Thus, there is much disagreement on whether what we see today is actually 'the' Sharīᶜa, or only empty references to the divine law.

Not only do Muslims themselves differ on how to apply the Sharīᶜa, but also Western scholars disagree on its nature. The debate over the last century has at times been heated on quite basic questions. Has the Sharīᶜa actually ever been in use? Is it a 'law' at all, or only a set of moral exhortations for the believer? Was there any historical developments of note after the formative period ended, or was what followed only a continuous decline of an ossified and impracticable orthodoxy? And is there really any historical truth at all in the Muslim sources on which we base our knowledge?

Until about 1880, all Western historians tended to accept the Muslim historiography of the law at face value. The Sharīᶜa, they said, grew out of the prophet Muḥammad's own actions (his *sunna*), which was summed up in the Traditions (*ḥadīth*) of his sayings and doings, and which was formulated into legal rules by the great scholars, the school founders, about three to four generations after the Prophet's death.[20] This was a straight-

20 Harald Motzki, 'Introduction' in Motzki (ed.), *The Biography of Muḥammad: The Issue of Sources*, Leiden 2000, xi-xvi.

forward and coherent account, well documented with extensive biographical and historical source material. Still, at the end of the nineteenth century, some Orientalists started to doubt this story. Others defended it, although some have done so by developing new methodological tools to evaluate the historical veracity of the Muslim sources for early Islam. In summing up the different currents of Western studies, as far as they relate to legal history, we can perhaps group them into three broad currents.

One of these is most commonly know as the *revisionist* trend. Those who follow it, reject to various degrees the Muslim historiography, and cast doubt on its sources. The dominant name in this current, as in the modern history of Islamic law in general, is Joseph Schacht (d. 1969). Primarily, he criticised the contents of the legal *ḥadīth*, which he claimed did not relate events of the Prophet's own time, but were constructed one or two centuries later to support views arising then.[21] Thus they were fakes, although they give us information about legal disputes of that later date.

Like many other Orientalists, Schacht emphasized the religious nature of the Sharīᶜa, which for him was more an ethical norm for good behaviour than a coherent body of laws.[22] The Sharīᶜa did not really play any dominant role in the Muslim courts, he said; judgements were rather made on the basis of secular needs and local custom.[23] Sultans and other rulers decided what the law should be according to their own wishes, and the courts and judges were the sultans' willing helpers.

21 Joseph Schacht, *The Origins of Muhammadan Jurisprudence*, Oxford 1950.

22 This is also a view expressed by scholars of Western law, to emphasize the difference between Islamic law and the 'normal' fashion of the legal process in Western societies. They assume that it is the judge's own conscience that guides his judgement, not reference to any actual texts in a 'neutral legal literature'. Such a view may echo what some Sharīᶜa judges themselves present as the religious foundation for the verdicts, see in particular Frank Vogel's study from Saudi Arabia, *Islamic Law and Legal Systems: Studies of Saudi Arabia*, Leiden 2000. Cf. also the discussion of morality in Weiss, *Spirit of Islamic Law*, 145-71.

23 Cf. a criticism of this in Baber Johansen, 'Die sündige, gesunde Amme: Moral und gesetzliche Betimmung (*ḥukm*) im islamischen Recht', *Die Welt des Islams*, XXVIII, 1988, 264-82 (and in Johansen, *Contingency in a Sacred Law: Legal and Ethical Norms in the Muslim* fiqh, Leiden 1999, 172-88).

Schacht here followed the lead of Max Weber, whose theory of *Kadijustiz* meant exactly that, that the judges made their own rulings independent of any fixed and formal law.[24] The Sharīᶜa had, according to him, 'an inadequate differentiation of ethical, religious and legal norms and a low level of systematization'.[25] Both Weber and Schacht based this view in the belief that there were no noticeable developments in the law after the schools were formed in the Islamic Middle Ages (tenth-twelfth century). Thus the Sharīᶜa had become rigid and could no longer answer the needs of the ever-changing society. Therefore, to regulate its affairs, society had to have recourse to ad-hoc rules outside of the Sharīᶜa, exactly the opposite of what is expected of a systematic legal system. The voluminous works we find that later authors write on aspects of Islamic law were not intended for any practical application. They were only intellectualism, 'in what amounted to a jurist's ivory-tower, free from the practical demands of courtrooms, the scholars preserved a legal tradition which was ironically irrelevant to the practical needs of ordinary Muslims', as Weber put it.

In recent years, other aspects of established chronology have come under revisionist-inspired scrutiny. Particular attention has been paid to the early 'paradigmatic' jurists, the assumed founders of the four schools of law. Some scholars believe that the development of these schools took quite a bit longer than traditionally believed,[26] and that the eponymous founders did not in fact play the crucial role in their establishment with which they have later been credited. We cannot really speak of such 'schools', certainly not with any fixed body of law, before two centuries or more after their time, according to these critics.[27]

24 Cf. Mohammad Hossam Fadel, 'Adjudication in the Mālikī madhhab: A study of legal process in medieval Islamic Law', Ph.D., University of Chicago 1995, 2-5 & 22-5, for a discussion of this view as expressed by Weber and Schacht.

25 Turner, *Weber and Islam*, 111. Cf. also Fadel, 'Adjudication', 3.

26 Norman Calder, *Studies in Early Muslim Jurisprudence*, Oxford 1993. Cf. an overview of this discussion in Vikør, '"The Truth about Cats and Dogs": The historicity of early Islamic law', *Historisk Tidsskrift* [Norway], LXXXII, 1, 2003, 1-17.

27 Some extreme revisionists, in particular John Wansbrough, have also questioned the history of the Koran itself. He believes that it must have been edited much later than in Muḥammad's lifetime; probably in Iraq in

All these revisionist rewritings of early history have of course been severely attacked by Muslim scholars, because they attack the very authority of the Muslim revelation.[28] If the Traditions did not in fact originate with the Prophet, then they cannot possibly express the divine will; and if that is true, then much of the basis and legitimacy for practiced Islam evaporates. The same, although less dramatically, can be said for re-dating the history of the schools. Much of the authority of the *madhhab*s' rules lies in the fact that they were formulated by the great and acknowledged founders, not by anonymous scholars two centuries later.

But Western historians have also attacked the most extreme forms of revisionism.[29] These anti-revisionists have found methods for textual criticism that 'saves the reputation' of many, if not all, of the traditional sources. They believe that, although not all details need be historical, the main body of the historical facts they present are probably true. The most important contribution of this generation of scholars, which we can perhaps call 'historians of practice', has been the study what actually took place in the courtroom in much greater detail than was possible in Schacht's time, with the appearance of large amounts of new textual material.[30]

---

the tenth century. This view is not accepted by most historians of Islam, but several known historians of the Koran, such as Andrew Rippin and Gerald Hawting must be considered to be influenced by revisionism. Cf. John Wansbrough, *Quranic Studies: Sources and Methods of Scriptural Interpretation*, London 1977 and *The Sectarian Milieu: Content and Composition of Islamic Salvation History*, Oxford 1978.

28 Among others M.M. Azami, *Studies in Early Hadith Literature*, Beirut 1968 and *On Schacht's Origins of Muhammadan Jurisprudence*, Riyad 1985, and Yasin Dutton, *The Origins of Islamic law: The Qur'an, the Muwaṭṭa' and Madinan ʿamal*, London 1999.

29 Harald Motzki, 'Quo vadis, Ḥadīṯ-Forschung? Eine kritische Untersuchung von G.H.A. Juynboll: "Nāfiʿ the mawlā of Ibn ʿUmar, and his position in Muslim ḥadīṯ literature"', *Der Islam*, LVIII, 1-2, 1996, 40-80 & 193-231 and 'The Prophet and the Cat. On dating Mālik's *Muwaṭṭa'* and legal traditions', *Jerusalem Studies in Arabic and Islam*, 22, 1998, 18-83; Gregor Schoeler, *Charakter und Authentie der muslimischen Überlieferung über das Leben Mohammeds*, Berlin 1996; Miklos Muranyi, 'Die frühe Rechtslitteratur zwischen Quellen-analyse und Fiktion', *Islamic Law and Society*, IV, 2, 1997, 224-41, and Wael B. Hallaq, 'On dating Malik's *Muwatta'*; *UCLA Journal of Islamic and Near Eastern Law*, I, 1, 2001-2, 47-65.

30 Among these are Wael Hallaq, Christopher Melchert, David Powers and

They believe, for one thing, that Schacht was mistaken when he claimed that the Sharīᶜa had become ossified and showed no further development. In fact, the law did develop continuously, but using other methods than those of the formative period. The famous expression that the 'gate to reinterpretation (*ijtihād*) was closed' is wrong, they said, it was always open.

Furthermore, the Sharīᶜa was in fact used in practice. It was not the only source for court decisions, and it is true that rulers often disregarded its rules and followed their own whims. But such practices outside the letter of the law were often a result of an accepted adaptation of the Sharīᶜa, or of its acceptance that the judge had discretion. The Sharīᶜa courts would, in most cases that we can study, both acknowledge and, as far as it could, try to follow the rules and procedures of the law. The scholars' books were not divorced from social reality, they were most often a distillation of actual cases and meant to be applied in later ones.

As it happens, the classical Orientalists seem to have found allies among modern Post-Modernists and anthropologists. Many of these share Schacht's basic assumption that the Sharīᶜa is an 'external' theory with little impact on what takes place in the court. They put greater emphasis on the contextual factors, the actors in the court dramas, which they see as strategic negotiations between the parties.[31] The judges do not make their verdicts from some pre-defined law text, but from their view of who the parties 'are', and how basic ethical or social goals can be achieved. The Sharīᶜa is thus at best a tool, but more often a hindrance, to achieve these desired goals, a hindrance that the judge will ignore when he so wishes.

This 'actor-oriented' or 'processual' view is logically linked to attacks on an 'essentialist' view of Islam. Following post-modernist thought, they will criticize the conception of Islam as a total entity with an 'essence' that manifests itself in a similar fashion across centuries and social borders. One cannot find Islam

---

Ruud Peters, cf. the Bibliography and later chapters for detail. Several of these historians also challenged the traditional Muslim chronology, and are thus 'revisionists' themselves, but they are primarily critical of the historization proposed by Schacht and his generation.

31 In particular Rosen, *Anthropology of Justice* and *Justice of Islam*; also June Starr, *Dispute and Settlement in Rural Turkey: An Ethnography of Law*, Leiden 1978.

by chasing such an 'essence' in the sacred texts, they say; Islam is to be found in a practice, what the Muslims at any moment do. In this case; what they do in the court room.[32]

This debate is still continuing, and both revisionists, historians of practice and processual analysts are publishing research results based on their respective paradigms. To some extent, these are only different perspectives and approaches that can be unified into the same reality. But some viewpoints are also empirically in contrast, so that only one can be true. As for the revisionist approach, their claims can probably be evaluated on an empirical basis. If the anti-revisionists do find a basis in the sources that re-establishes the classical chronology, then that must be considered true and the revisionist view wrong. But if such a critical source study does not produce this evidence, then the fact that a description has been repeated from the eleventh to the twentieth century cannot be proof that it actually represents events that took place in the seventh and eighth.

When it comes to the 'law in practice', what went on in the court room, there is a similar gap between the ideals that are expressed in Muslim traditional historiography and what we can now consider proven 'actually took place'. However, the gap is not so wide here as in the question of historicity of the early sources, nor is the issue as normative. Concerning the 'classical' period, the first four or five centuries of Islam, we mostly have access to normative works that tell us how the judges *should* behave as much as informing us of what they actually *did*. From the eleventh century onwards, we start getting a few glimpses of actual historical practices that may correct and adjust this, and give some greater surety of historical facts. From the Ottoman period (fifteenth-sixteenth century) and onwards we can actually start to map a known historical development.

These records show us that the actor perspective can be an important contribution to understanding actual practices both in these earlier times and today. The criticism of essentialism is necessary and correct. Classical Orientalism and Islamic studies have far too easily created an ideal of 'Islam' on the basis of the

32 The Muslim historiography, which Schacht criticized, is precisely one of the 'great stories' that post-modernism tries to deconstruct and transform into instances and moments; each case in court becomes an ad-hoc-based process.

texts, and seen all practices deviating from this 'normative' Islam as non-Islamic custom or influences from other religions.[33] Such notions obscured the view of a wide and rich regional variation that in fact was and is genuinely Islamic, and by focusing on the 'kernel' as an ahistorical and eternal existence also tended to lose sight of changes in Islam.[34]

But at the same time, these anti-essentialists have often too easily accepted the Orientalist view of the Sharīᶜa texts as monolithic and frozen. When the full span of writings and viewpoints within the Sharīᶜa is considered, it can be seen that actions of local judges, that at first sight seem to contradict one or another Sharīᶜa rule, do in fact fall within the wider area of variation accepted in the law-books and literature. Court records show that the judges were aware of this and referred to, or stayed within, what the texts state. Although this does not exclude the possibility that these records may be a post-edited version of what actually took place in the court room, it shows that the Sharīᶜa was far from ignored in the process.

Thus it is by putting aside this idea of an 'essence' in the Sharīᶜa that we can see how the contextualized courtroom practice and the literary textual practice of the jurists in fact interpret and redefine the law, under cover of merely continuing what the pious forefathers, the *salaf*, had said based on the Revelation itself. This made the law more flexible while continuing the fundamental tenets that had been passed down since classical times. In the understanding of all parties, this *is* the Sharīᶜa, based on a written literature they all had access to and which laid down the

33 Cf. e.g. the discussion between the Islamologist Aharon Layish and the anthropologist John Davis in the introduction to Aharon Layish, *Legal Documents on Libyan Tribal Society in Process of Sedentarization.* Vol I *(with an Anthropological Critique by John Davis),* Wiesbaden 1998, 1-20. The works of Chr. Snouck Hurgronje from South-East Asia may be a typical example of such an idealization of what the Sharīᶜa 'is', seen in contrast to the actual practice that he saw around him; cf. e.g. his *Oeuvres choisies*, Leiden 1957.

34 Evidently influenced by the views of Muslim believers, they are of course precisely 'essentialists' in that they consider the eternal core to be God's revelation to Man. How far Muslim scholars consider regional differences as variations within the genuinely Islamic or as deviations from it will vary, but the 'fundamentalists' will tend, like the Orientalists, towards the latter position.

boundaries for what was and was not possible to do.

Only in the last century or so, has this flexible development come under pressure, partly from the external influences of Western law, partly from forces that try to adapt society to an apparently fixed and frozen, but in fact new and 'modern' understanding of the 'true' Sharīᶜa, rather than to adapt the law to society. This is the result of political and historical developments that may lead in different directions, and we cannot say today which course it will take. But whatever the direction, the future development of the law and of Muslim society is likely to display its heritage in the theoretical and social development of the Sharīᶜa over the last millennium and a half.

PART I. THE THEORY OF THE LAW

2

FROM PRACTICE TO METHOD

The rules of the Sharīᶜa are thus, in Muslim historiography, based on the Revelation that God gave to His prophet Muḥammad until his death in 632. Most of our specific knowledge of this period is based on this historiography, but it is also reasonable to assume that early Muslim society to a large extent continued the practices of the pre-Islamic period.[1]

There is no necessary contradiction in this. Muḥammad himself had to build his new society from the customs that existed, adapting them to his new message. Beyond this, one must also remember the time horizon that was in play. Muḥammad and his contemporaries believed that the end of time was nigh, the Day of Judgement would come soon after this revelation of God's last message to Mankind.[2] Even if the Prophet himself did not live to see the Day, it would come in the near future. Thus, there was no need to establish a detailed social system for this short period.

It was only after a few years had passed and the Muslim society settled and became normalized, that it became evident to the Muslims that they had to start planning for a society on earth without direct divine guidance. By that time, their rule had stretched far beyond the core area in Arabia and included many provinces that had either been under Roman or Persian control. Initially, the new Arab governors largely maintained the practices of the previous rulers in relation to the original non-Muslim

1 Josef Schacht, 'Pre-Islamic background and early development of jurisprudence', in Majid Khadduri and Herbert J. Liebesny (ed.), *Law in the Middle East: [1:] Origin and Development of Islamic Law*, Washington 1955, 28-56; Émile Tyan, *Histoire de l'organisation judiciaire en pays d'islam*, Leiden 1960, 17-100, and Noel J. Coulson, *A History of Islamic Law*, Edinburgh 1964, 21-35. For a historiographical analysis of this period in Western Orientalisme, cf. Harald Motzki, *The Origins of Islamic Jurisprudence: Meccan Fiqh before the Classical Schools,* Leiden 2001, 1-49 and his alternative hypothesis, p. 295-7.

2 S.D. Goitein, 'The birth-hour of Muslim Law? An essay in exegesis', *Muslim World*, L, 1, 1960, 24.

inhabitants, while the immigrant Muslim Arabs were governed by new rules established according to need, when direct commands were not to be found in the divine message itself.

The example of the Prophet's behaviour was no doubt important to these early Muslims. The governors were aware that they were building a new community based on the new revelation, and that Muḥammad as the prophet and first leader of that community was an example to be followed. But if there was no precise knowledge that Muḥammad had ordered a particular course of action, which was probably the case for many of the day-to-day issues encountered when administering a foreign province, the established Roman or Persian way of doing things could be sufficient,[3] and if not, then new rules would have to be created as best they knew how.

Thus, different local practices, or *sunna*s, appeared.[4] The term *sunna* was probably already being used in the later meaning of 'the Prophet's practice', but not exclusively so. It could also mean 'the way we do things here'.[5] At this point, there cannot really have been any cohesive 'law' at all in these new provinces, so the question of whether there was an 'Islamic' as opposed to merely a 'Muslim' law (a secular law created by Muslims) is probably anachronistic.

Law or tradition

In this first century of Islam, few people probably cared much about the increasing differences in administrative practices of the provinces; they were still trying to find their feet after the rapid expansion of Arab rule. But from the mid-eighth century, it became apparent that a problem was brewing. The Abbasid

3 Patricia Crone argues that it was not Roman law itself, but the law developed in the Near Eastern provinces, which included elements of but was not identical to Roman law proper, that was the basis for much of Islamic law; *Roman, provincial and Islamic law: The origins of the Islamic patronate*, Cambridge 1987.

4 G.H.A. Juynboll, 'Some new ideas on the development of *sunna* as a technical term in early Islam', *Jerusalem Studies in Arabic and Islam*, X, 1987, 97-118.

5 A usage of *sunna* as 'normative custom' that probably goes back to pre-Islamic times.

revolution of 750 moved the centre of the empire to Iraq, but its most important effect was a greater centralization of the state around a strong caliph. This meant that the different provinces also needed to have a unified system of government. At the same time, the Arab immigrants had over the generations become permanent settlers and started to merge with the autochthonous populations who increasingly turned to Islam and lost their non-Arab distinctiveness. Thus maintaining the original differences between those regions that had been Roman and those that had been Persian or otherwise became more and more pointless. The same rules should apply everywhere, the time for local *sunna*-practices had passed.

At the same time, there evolved a specific class of scholars, the *ᶜulamāʾ*. In the course of the eighth century, these started to specialize in different branches of science, particularly related to religion. One such religious science was knowledge of the Prophet's deeds and actions, *ḥadīth*. We do not know when exactly this came to be considered a separate science: Muslim tradition links it to the immediate aftermath of the Prophet's death, when people of good memory started to relate stories of his deeds, while modern revisionists date the appearance of this as a separate form of normative literature only three to four generations later.[6]

Both views may be right, at least in part. There is no reason to doubt that stories of the Prophet were told from the very earliest times, by those who had seen him alive, to youngsters or other later Muslims who had not had that privilege. But the formalized science of *ḥadīth* is probably a ninth-century development. The early stories of the Prophet probably had a fairly simple form. Some of those who told them mentioned the name of the person they had heard it from and perhaps his source

6 Azami, *Studies in Early Hadith Literature*; Muḥammad Zubayr Ṣiddīqī, *Ḥadīth Literature: Its Origins, Development, Special Features and Criticism,* Calcutta 1961; Alfred Guillaume, *The Traditions of Islam: An Introduction to the Study of the Hadith Literature*, Oxford 1924; John Burton, *An Introduction to the Ḥadīth,* Edinburgh 1994, and G.H.A Juynboll, *The Authenticity of the Tradition Literature. Discussions in Modern Egypt.* Leiden 1969, *Muslim Tradition, Studies in Chronology, Provenance and Authorship of Early Ḥadīth*, Cambridge 1983 and *Studies on the Origins and Uses of Islamic Ḥadīth*, Aldershot 1996. Cf. also Vikør, 'Truth about Cats and Dogs' and the sources quoted there.

too, in a more or less complete 'chain' of transmitters (an *isnād*), while others only told the story as an anecdote on its own merit. Some stories concerned the Prophet himself, others the actions of his companions or contemporaries.[7] Over time this relation of *ḥadīth* had acquired the status of a separate branch of knowledge, complete with a methodology of separating the true from the spurious, and culminating with the great collections of al-Bukhārī and Muslim around 870.[8]

Some scholars felt that Muslims had to follow *only* the practices laid out in the Koran and by Muḥammad, nothing else. There was no need for any law beyond what was stated in the Book and the Traditions; in these God has given us all necessary knowledge. This current, normally called the 'Traditionists' (here used with a capital T), *ahl al-ḥadīth*, developed in Iraq and particularly in the town of Kufa, which was an intellectual centre at this time.

Others believed there was a need for a more developed body of rules for Muslim behaviour, what we may start to call a law, formulated by qualified scholars. These scholars also transmitted *ḥadīth* and emphasized the example of the Prophet, but *ḥadīth* was not the beginning and end for them. This body of literature was still too amorphous and unwieldy to be used as a guide for behaviour. Instead, they summarized what they thought must be correct solutions to the problems they encountered based on what Muslims generally did, what the Prophet had done when that was clearly known, and what logic told them must be the extension and conclusions from these sources. These scholars came to be known as *ahl al-raʾy*. By *raʾy* was meant 'sound practice', 'what is commonly done', based on local *sunna*. This approach was present among scholars in various centres, both Kufa, Baghdad and Medina. But what actually was 'commonly done' was not necessarily the same in Kufa as in Medina; and perhaps not even the same in all groups in Kufa. Thus the *content* of these rules based on *raʾy* came to differ.

7 The anti-revisionist Motzki accepts Schacht's statement that the early *ḥadīth* more often represent the practices of the early caliphs or other 'Successors' than those of the Prophet himself, but points to the existence of a number of *ḥadīth* on the Prophet himself that were already in circulation in the very early period; Motzki, *Origins*, 296.

8 To be presented in Chapter 3.

Thus geography played some part in the differences between different currents of thought. In particular the Medinese put an emphasis on location; theirs was the city of the Prophet, thus their customs must be those most closely reflecting what he would have done had he been alive. Some observers thus started to speak of the 'Kufa group' and the 'Medina group' of scholars (*ahl Kūfa, ahl Madīna*), and later biographers were keen to attach individual scholars to one or other of these groups. In modern times, some historians have called them 'geographical schools of law', that is, groupings of scholars established around local practices, ancestors to the later four schools of law in Sunnī Islam.[9]

However, it is doubtful whether we can talk about 'schools of law' in this early period. These were not in any sense cohesive groups of lawyers, nor was geography really the dominant factor. They were more like informal circles where a scholar might share the opinions of one set of colleagues on some questions and with another on others.[10]

These currents or circles also spanned several cities. One could find 'Kufa people' in Baghdad, Basra and other major centres of learning, while there were many scholars in Kufa who did not agree with the 'Kufans'. The name was simply used to refer to a certain set of opinions that was shared by some dominant scholars living in the city in question. Although some such colleagues might agree on a certain number of points, they were not fixed entities. A student or a scholar of law could go from a teacher who was identified with the 'Kufa group' to one who was among the 'Medina group' without any sense of changing identity or loyalty, as such a move would come to mean in later times, when converting from one school of law to another was a major upheaval for a learned jurist.

9 Schacht calls them 'the ancient schools of law', before the later schools named after the four major jurists developed; *An Introduction to Islamic Law*, Oxford 1964, 28-37 and *Origins*, 6-11.

10 Christopher Melchert, 'How Ḥanafism came to originate in Kufa and traditionalism in Medina', *Islamic Law and Society*, VI, 3, 1999, 318-47 and 'Traditionist-jurisprudents and the framing of Islamic Law', *Islamic Law and Society,* VIII, 3, 2001, 383-406; Nimrod Hurvitz, 'Schools of law and historical context: re-examining the formation of the Ḥanbalī *madhhab*', *Islamic Law and Society*, VII, 1, 2000, 37-64, and Wael B. Hallaq, 'From regional to personal schools of law? A reevaluation', *Islamic Law and Society*, VIII, 1, 2001, 1-26.

Lawyers in Kufa and Medina

Although those who practised law mostly based their decisions on local *sunna* and logical *ra'y*, the opinions of the *ḥadīth* people won support. It was an attractive idea to have a fixed basis for the rules of law in the example of the Prophet, and it was well suited to the general trend of centralizing practices in the empire. Possibly as an answer to this trend, the *ra'y* people started to link their viewpoints to particular named authorities. Rather than saying that 'this is the correct rule because it is the sound practice [here]', they started to say, 'this is the correct rule, because such-and-such eminent jurist has said so'. Among the names used to support legal viewpoints among the Kufans were Abū Ḥanīfa (d. 767), Abū Yūsuf (d. 798) and Muḥammad al-Shaybānī (d. 804). Thus, when later historians talked of the Kufans, they came to mean those three and their colleagues. Now the Kufans could say, 'well, this is the way Abū Ḥanīfa did things, and do you really think your own knowledge is superior to that of the great Abū Ḥanīfa?'

As it must have been easier to establish these figures as great authorities after their death, it was probably only a generation or two later, in the first half of the ninth century, that this development took place.[11] In later times Abū Ḥanīfa became the leading figure of these three, but the three were independent of each other. However, they do seem to have shared some basic points of methodology, which does make it natural to group them together.[12]

This was thus a fairly decentralized current of thought, focused on the idea that the law must be based on established practice, the *sunna* of the region. The three terms *ra'y*, *sunna* and *fiqh* ('understanding') were used more or less interchangeably for this legal view based on established practice.

The three pioneers in Kufa were not the only ones who were used as sources of authority in this fashion. In more or less the

11 Jonathan Brockopp has named it 'the great shaykh theory': persons that had acquired a high status and perhaps, in the eyes of the common man, had a direct channel to God, could easily turn into personal authorities without reference to the Revelation; 'Competing theories of authority in early Mālikī texts', in Bernard G. Weiss (ed.), *Studies in Islamic Legal Theory*, Leiden 2002, 3-22.

12 Hallaq, 'From regional to personal', 8.

same period some scholars in Medina and Egypt started to refer to the jurist Mālik b. Anas (d. 795) in the same way. Mālik is today known as a collector of *ḥadīth* and for his knowledge of the example of the Prophet, but this is an image that is partly a later construction. Mālik certainly did transmit *ḥadīth*, but while he would include the Prophet's example in his legal opinions when he knew it, he did not necessarily follow it. His conclusions were based more on the local views in Medina at his own time, thus his own *raʾy*.[13] He could introduce a *ḥadīth* into a discussion, but conclude that, 'however, we do it in this other fashion' and the latter was thus the determinate factor. Thus, the practice of his community in Medina, the local *sunna*, was for Mālik of equal or higher value than the revelation of the *ḥadīth*.[14]

The main contradiction was thus between the law as it was actually practised in contemporary society, the *fiqh* of the *ahl al-raʾy* scholars, and a theoretical reaction pointing to the Traditions of the Prophet that were being transmitted, but had not yet been formulated into any law. Indeed, the Traditionists rejected any attempt to formulate these *ḥadīth* into (humanly expressed) legal rules, nor did they yet have any proper methodology to distinguish true *ḥadīth* from false. Even that seemed to them to be a dangerous human vetting of the divine message. How could any man evaluate what was divinely ordained? However, since the amount of *ḥadīth* material grew rapidly and became increasingly

13 Cf. Mālik b. Anas, *Al-Muwatta of Imam Malik ibn Anas: The First Formulation of Islamic Law* (trans. Aisha Abdurrahman Bewley), London 1989.

14 This is also accepted by the Muslim Mālikī scholar Yasin Dutton. He believes, however, that Mālik's aim was still to follow the Prophet's *sunna*. But the science of *ḥadīth* was at that time still so rudimentary that one could not distinguish true from false *ḥadīth*. Thus, it was rather in the continued practice of Medina, the Prophet's own town, that one could find the best source for what the Prophet had done. Thus, there was for Mālik no distinction between the Prophet's *sunna* and the *sunna* of Medina; Dutton, *Origins of Islamic Law*. This presentation has been criticised for being too uncritical; for a perhaps better image of how the early Mālikī current was constituted, see Jonathan E. Brockopp, *Early Mālikī Law: Ibn ʿAbd al-Ḥakam and his Major Compendium of Jurisprudence*, Leiden 2000. A more hagiographic presentation of Mālik's life according to Muslim tradition can be found in e.g. Mansour Hasan Mansour, *The Maliki School of Law*, San Francisco 1995, 1-19. We will pick up the story of these nascent 'schools' in Chapter 6.

contradictory, it soon became clear that no law could be built on such an unsteady basis.

Al-Shāfiʿī

An answer to this problem was formulated soon after by the scholar Muḥammad b. Idrīs al-Shāfiʿī (d. 820). He is later known as one of the founders of a school of law, but his recognition only came long after his death. It was probably only in the mid-ninth century that other scholars started to notice the contribution he made to methodology, and much later that some started to consider themselves as belonging to his 'school'.[15] But eventually his book *Risāla* came to introduce a revolution in Islamic legal science, by uniting the two counterpoints, *raʾy* and *ḥadīth*, while rejecting the existing interpretations of each in the legal field.[16]

However, he was not a neutral middle-man. His sympathies were clearly with the *ahl al-ḥadīth*, but he saw that their lack of flexibility made their position impracticable. Instead, he developed a methodology that was intended to lead to a common, practicable and practised law throughout the Muslim community, based on a common basis: the Traditions from the Prophet. His aim was thus a 'Traditionalizing' of *fiqh*, in the sense of making the Prophetic Traditions the foundation for human endeavours.

He accomplished this by using the same terms as the *raʾy* people used, but redefining them so they all referred to the texts of the Revelation. For example, *sunna*, which meant any sort of established practice, whether of each community or the historical one of the Prophet, for Shāfiʿī had only the latter meaning; what the *ḥadīth* told of. This came to be the only meaning of the term '*sunna*'.

15 Wael B. Hallaq, 'Was al-Shāfiʿī the master architecht of Islamic jurisprudence?', *International Journal of Middle East Studies*, XXV, 4, 1993, 587-605 and *A History of Islamic Legal Theories: An Introduction to Sunnī uṣūl al-fiqh*, Cambridge 1997, 16-35.

16 Muḥammad b. Idrīs al-Shāfiʿī, *al-Risāla fī uṣūl al-fiqh: Treatise on the Foundations of Islamic Jurisprudence*, ed. & trans. Majid Khadduri, Cambridge 1961. As pointed out in later studies, the *Risāla* is not a consistent work of theory, nor the 'beginning' of *uṣūl al-fiqh*, but it represents in its way of conceptualization a new era in the history of methodology; Hallaq, *History of Islamic Legal Theories*, 30-1.

Similarly, *fiqh*, the rational exposition of the law, was torn free from *raʾy*, opinions. This last term became the great bogeyman, and came to mean personal views of the latter-day scholars divorced from the divine Revelation. *Fiqh* thus acquired the generalized meaning that it now has: 'study of the law', the discovery of God's will through work on the scripture. Thus, Shāfiʿī appeared to use terms from both sides of the debate, but always in such a manner that the work was based on Revelation. We will later see several examples of these adaptations.

Although it took some time before the other scholars took notice, the views expressed by Shāfiʿī eventually became the acknowledged norm. This did not put an end to the division of opinions, but the *raʾy* people could no longer refer only to local custom or to individual late lawyers. Instead, they also 'Traditionalized' their rules, by discovering and emphasizing *ḥadīth* that supported the views that they already held. The content of their rules did not necessarily change, only the manner in which they supported them in the legal debates. As time passed they also accepted Shāfiʿī's basic contention that the final authority had to be the Koran and *sunna*. When we read the early law books, we find that this was not necessarily carried through, many rules are still only based on the say-so of the founders or early scholars of the schools, but in theory, everything is based at some level on Revelation. Thus there was a transitional period, of which we can still see the effects, when not all practice was explicitly based on *ḥadīth* or could even contradict it, when it was based on the views of great authorities who by later assumption only worked on the basis of Koran and *sunna*. At the same time, the *madhhab*s based on these currents developed methodological exemptions that allowed them to introduce more pragmatic and in effect *raʾy*-based rules into their laws, but without using this term or openly opposing the Shāfiʿī-based theories.

We do not yet know the details of how this developed through the ninth century. Shāfiʿī himself was not primarily a practising lawyer, nor a collector of *ḥadīth*, he was a theoretician. Thus, he did not 'found' the school that carries his name, it arose in Baghdad much later.[17] Nor did he always practice what he

17 Christopher Melchert, *The Formation of the Sunni Schools of Law: 9h-10th Centuries C.E.*, Leiden 1997, 48-68. See further Chapter 6.

taught; when he introduces examples in his book, he does in some cases apply the *ra'y*-based method that he has rejected in theory. Similarly, the actual rules that his followers and other supporters of *ḥadīth* develop, are often almost identical to those that had earlier been practised by the *ra'y* people, only the justification was different. There is nothing peculiar about this, the *ḥadīth* positions were primarily about justification and authority, more than the rules themselves. As long as a rule did have the prescribed authority in the divine message, the fact that it was already practised by the Muslim community was of course no reason to oppose it.

But still, the main contradiction that dominated the debate and the development of the concepts throughout this formative period, was always between those whose main and only emphasis was on the Prophetic example and those who wanted to temper this by referring to actual practices formed on a different basis. This contradiction lasted until the process of 'Traditionalizing' had been completed, and the two had merged so that all actual legal practice was, or at least was considered to be, authorized through the Koran and *sunna*. The result was that both ended up with a methodology that was based on Shāfiʿī's concepts and a legal practice that mainly continued the precedence of the *ra'y* scholars. Still, the difference never went away completely. Even after the schools had become fully established several centuries later, one can still find some variations in methodology that show the origin of some currents in the *ḥadīth* people and some in the *ra'y* group.

Consolidation through traditionalizing

From a modern perspective, this debate between *ra'y* and *ḥadīth* can easily appear to be one between 'good' pragmatism (*ra'y*) and 'bad' religious dogmatism (*ḥadīth*). Such a dichotomy is probably off the mark when looking at the historical context. The law that Shāfiʿī and the *ḥadīth* people were trying to create was to be a law common to all the provinces and regions where Muslims were living. They rejected the situation where each province or town, or even each court, had its own law, one for Kufa, another for Damascus and a third for Medina.

Such a communality in matters of law could only be based on something that the regions had in common. And what they had in common was the religion, Islam. There is thus a connection between the law being 'common' for the empire and it being linked to Islam, a specifically *Islamic* law that took its authority from the same source as the religion did, God's revelation to Muḥammad.

Thus the central factor was that the law was common and had the proper authority, not necessarily what it said. Consequently, it was not a problem for Shāfiᶜī to include rules that the *raʾy* people had already propagated, as long as they were meant to be valid only in *one* town or for one group of Muslims. Evidently, the system also had to be internally consistent, a more serious crime earning a more severe punishment; to clarify this was part of the jurists' work.

The Islamization of the law thus contributed to its unification throughout the known world as a coherent system, linked to the legitimacy of the empire itself. This, then, is not the result of dogmatism, but a natural corollary of the integration of the provinces into one empire that took place at the same time, symbolized in particular by the Abbasid's ascent to power in 750. We will see that this development also had an important impact on the development of the court system, and that it marks an important departure for the history of the empire. The first century, that of the Umayyads, was mainly one of expansion, when the regions were still largely ruled as before the conquest. As the Abbasids took power, the time had come to consolidate the conquered domains into one community.

In this perspective, the *raʾy* tendency belonged to a time that had come to an end, it was no longer practicable. It was thus Shāfiᶜī who was the pragmatist and created a system that could work. That is why his theoretization survived and became the foundation even for his opponents' methodology. The *raʾy* current could only survive by becoming 'Traditionalized', linked to *ḥadith*, as Shāfiᶜī defined it. This is also the reason the various legal traditions turned out to be as similar as they did, in spite of the basic ideological differences that can be found in their early history; they developed under the same historical conditions.

3

THE KORAN AND *SUNNA* AS SOURCES

Four sources or three levels

The classical methodology for the law from Shāfiᶜī is most often summarized into 'four sources' of the Sharīᶜa. They are, beside the Koran and the *sunna*, the derivation of rules by analogical extensions of rules already established (*qiyās*) and the acceptance as law of 'what all Muslims agree on' (consensus, *ijmāᶜ*). Recent studies actually show that Shāfiᶜī never did formulate this idea of 'four sources', and probably would not have appreciated it if he had heard it. His attitude to consensus as a legal source was dubious; it was the Koran and in particular the *sunna* that was the paramount source for the law.[1]

This idea of 'four sources', although commonly expressed, is probably not the best way to explain the development of the legal science. It may be more helpful to think of three different *levels* in the process of establishing the law, as the classical theorists described it.

The first level, and actually the only real 'source' to the Law, is the Revelation, expressed in the Koran and *sunna*. These sources must go through a process of understanding, in which one draws out of them what is relevant for the law. The Revelation is only the raw material, on which human effort must be applied in order to read it correctly. What is then drawn from the Koran and *sunna* as true and legally relevant divine revelation, is what can be called 'the Text', *naṣṣ*.

On the basis of this Text, the lawyers must then formulate the actual legal rules. This process is called *ijtihād*, which generally means to develop rules of law, that is, on the basis of the legal material of the Revelation. The most well known and extensive method of this systematization is the process of *qiyās*, which is

1 Joseph Lowry, 'Does Shāfiᶜī have a theory of four sources of law?', in Weiss, *Studies in Islamic Legal Theory*, 23-50, and Susan Spectorsky, '*Sunnah* in the responses of Isḥāq b. Rāhwayh', in *ibid*, 51-74. See also the previous chapter.

both more and less than the 'analogical deduction' it is most often translated as. But there are many other methods used in this process of formulation, some by all *madhhabs*, some only by one.

The result is then a *potential* legal rule. But the number of legal scholars are legion, and there are many possible and often contradictory ways to formulate a rule on the basis of the same text of revelation. Not all variants can become law, at least not if this law is to be applied in society. Thus, some of these competing views must be singled out as *the* formulation that is considered the best and correct and what Muslims must follow, rather than the competing expressions. Those who decide this are the legal scholars of each *madhhab*, and this is thus the third level in the process of expressing the law and the real meaning of consensus, *ijmāᶜ* within the *madhhab*: A *confirmation* of a subset of the formulated rules into an applicable law.

In this and the following two chapters we will discuss these three levels of the establishment of the law.

The Koran

The basis for the law is thus to be found in God's revelation to the Prophet. Muslim tradition came to accept it as expressed in two ways: In the Koran, which contains God's own words; and through the Prophet's *sunna*, Muḥammad's normative sayings and doings expressed in *ḥadīth*. Both are revelation, but they are different in nature. The Koran has an established and certain content; there is no disagreement among Muslims over its actual words, but it needs to be read correctly to be understood. The other source, however, the *sunna*, does not have such a clear delimitation. It must go through a dual process; it must first be determined whether each individual *ḥadīth* is actually a true expression from the Prophet before one can draw any normative inferences from its text. But both the Koran and true *ḥadīth* are equally valid expressions of God's revelation.

In principle, everything in the Sharīᶜa is linked to the Koran, it is the source of the rules, *ruʾūs al-aḥkām.*[2] All chapters of *fiqh* can be related to the Koran. Not so that each rule can be derived

2 Mohammed Hashim Kamali, *Principles of Islamic Jurisprudence,* Cambridge 1991, 14-44 & 86-123.

directly from a verse, of course, too few of them have a direct legal content for that. The *sunna* is far more instrumental in justifying individual rules; the Koranic basis appears mostly through general commands to 'follow the example of the Prophet' and those appointed over the community, or similar. Furthermore, a distinction is made between general and specific rules. The Koran is specific in matters that are eternal, and general in matters that may change.

All Muslims agree on the basic text of the Koran. There exist some minute variations of certain vowels, often called the 'seven readings', but there is no complete agreement on what these seven are, and they are not considered to have any impact on the meaning of the text.

There are 6,200 verses in the Koran, of these some 350 are considered to be relevant for the law.[3] These concern:

— 140 on ritual matters
— 70 on issues of marriage: whom one can (not) marry, divorce also inheritance, endowments etc.
— 70 on trade, contracts etc.
— 30 on matters of crime and punishments
— 30 generally on justice, evidence, the rights and duties of citizens, etc.
— 10 on other economic and social matters, poverty, rights of workers etc.

Of these 350 verses, 180 are *qaṭī^c*, that is to say absolutely certain and not open for debate, the rest are *ẓannī*, 'probable' or 'assumed', that is, there may exist disagreement on how they should be understood.[4] For example, the Koran says 'God will not take you to task for a slip (*laghw*) in your oaths, but he will take you to task for such bonds as you have made by oaths', the penalty for this is to feed ten poor persons, clothe them, set free a slave, or fast for three days [5:92]. The rule is clear and must be followed. But what is meant by this word 'slip'? Some believe it refers to an honest mistake; something the oath-giver believed to be the case turned out not to be so. Others think it refers to an

3 Kamali, *Principles,* 19-20. Others speak of about 500 verses relevant for the law; Hallaq, *History of Islamic Legal Theories*, 12.
4 Kamali, *Principles*, 21-9

oath made without the intention of swearing. Also, the 'three days', are they to taken as consecutive, or on three different occasions? Both interpretations are possible, even if the nature of the verse as a general command for Muslims is clear. When such uncertainty arises, the answer might be found in the *sunna*, the Prophet may have given an authoritative explanation in a *ḥadīth*.

A precondition for understanding the Koran is an adequate competence in language. The text was given in Arabic as it was spoken at one particular place, the Hijaz, at one particular time. The jurist lives in another time at another place, where the words may have changed their meaning. Thus, grammar is an important ancillary science for law.

Further, one makes a distinction between *tafsīr*, to find the evident meaning of the words, and *taʾwīl*, to find any intended meaning behind the words.[5] Both are necessary and accepted ways of elaborating the meaning, but any *taʾwīl* must restrict itself to what is 'commonly accepted', not venture into improbable or unreasonable interpretations of what the text may mean.[6]

An important part of deriving rules from the Koran is to distinguish between those verses that are 'general', *ᶜāmm*, and those that are 'specified', *khāṣṣ*.[7] A rule may apply to all Muslims forever, or only for some Muslims or those in a particular situation, such as those in the same context as that in which the rule was revealed. Again, it is the *sunna* that can explain what this context was. A specified, *khāṣṣ*, rule outweighs one that is *ᶜāmm* and is considered *qaṭīᶜ*, definitive, while a general rule is considered to be probable, *ẓannī*, and open to further discussion. If one verse can be read as a general rule for all Muslims, and another rule specifies different behaviour in a certain context, then the specific one is always the correct one for those in that context, since that verse is then definitive.[8] A *khāṣṣ* rule cannot be subject to *taʾwīl* interpretation.

A similar distinction exists between those verses that can be

5 It is said that *taʾwīl* brings out the most probable (*ẓāhir*) understanding; Hallaq, *History of Islamic Legal Theories*, 47.

6 Kamali, *Principles*, 88-9.

7 Kamali, *Principles*, 26, and Hallaq, *History of Islamic Legal Theories*, 42-58.

8 The Ḥanafīs also consider that a general rule is *qaṭīᶜ*, and thus see the possibility of a conflict between an *ᶜāmm* and a *khāṣṣ* verse.

understood independently from the rest of the Koran, and those that are 'dependent' on another verse; *muṭlaq* and *muqayyad*. One example is the issue of witnesses to a sale. One verse says that you should bring two witnesses when you make a contract (2:282). Another verse, elsewhere in the Koran, says that one should bring two trustworthy witnesses ('men of equity') when one rescinds a divorce (65:2).[9] Are these verses, discussing two different topics, unrelated or should they be understood together, so that the issue of trustworthiness also applies to contract witnesses? The accepted answer is yes, the verses are to be read in conjunction, so that 'witnesses' in 2:282 must be understood to mean 'trustworthy witnesses' as in 65:2.[10]

Sometimes, the specialists had to determine the actual meaning of a word that was no longer in common usage. Thus, *ribā* is banned (2:225), but this word did not exist in standard Arabic when the text was to be explained.[11] The Koran specialists then had to figure out what it meant. Beyond this, they had to determine whether a word was intended in its direct, every-day meaning, or was used in a more precise, technical sense, and if so, what that was in Muḥammad's days.

Meanings of Koranic terms may also be *mafhūm*, implied, or *majāz*, allegories. Some verses in the Koran are clearly meant allegorically, which adds to the uncertainty of the import of the verse, both whether the words are allegorical, and if so, allegories of what.[12]

9 Koran 65:2. On the revocation of divorces, reversible *ṭalāq*, see Chapter 15.

10 Kamali, *Principles*, 26 & 68. The jurists do however consider, independently of this issue, that a contract is valid even without any witnesses at all, but this has little practical significance since witnesses are necessary to prove the existence of the contract if any dispute arises. The Ẓāhirīs alone believe that a transaction without any witness is invalid in itself, on the basis of the text of the Koran.

11 The literal meaning is 'growth', but it is in context understood as 'usurious rent' or interest in general. See further in Chapter 16.

12 One example is a verse that requires a believer to perform a new ablution before prayer if he has 'touched women' (4:43). The Shāfiᶜīs take this literally to mean each time a Muslim has touched a woman (outside the family), the Ḥanafīs consider it a metaphor for sexual intercourse; only then do they need to perform a new ablution before the next prayer; Kamali, *Principles*, 119, and Laleh Bakhtiar, *Encyclopedia of Islamic Law: A Compendium of the Views of the Major Schools*, Chicago 1996, 21.

Can a rule that has clearly been expressed in a certain context be generalized? A verse specifies a particular penalty for the unintentional killing of a slave, but says nothing of an intentional one. Should the penalty established for the specified case of unintentional death then apply to all killings of slaves? The accepted view is that this is the case, rules must be transferred from the specific case to the general one, when there is no other rule formulated for the general one.

Types of rules

There are two types of rules, those that tell us *how* to do a certain thing, and those that tells us *whether* we should do them (of course, a 'how' rule can also be formulated 'whether it is correct to do it in such-and-such a fashion').

These 'whether' rules can be grouped into five categories:[13]

(1) The required, *wājib*, that which it is a sin to omit. Another term for this is *farḍ*, which can be subdivided into two:[14] That which is required for every individual to do, is a *farḍ ᶜaynī*. Prayer and fasting are clearly among these. When it is sufficient that someone, but not all, in the community performs the duty, it is known as a collective duty, *farḍ kifāʾī*. These include ensuring the existence of knowledge about Islam in society: Not everyone needs to be a scholar, but the society at large must contain scholars. *Jihād* is normally considered to be a *farḍ kifāʾī*.[15]

13 Kamali, *Principles*, 34-5. One definition of what the Sharīᶜa 'is' focuses on these categories that God has divided all acts into and says that the Sharīᶜa is the sum-total of these divine categorizations; Weiss, *Spirit of Islamic Law,* 18.

14 This categorization is of course the result of the scholars' *fiqh* work. The Ḥanafī school distinguishes between *farḍ*, which is based on a secure text of Revelation and which it is unbelief not to perform, and *wājib*, duties which are open to some doubt, and which it does not constitute unbelief not to do. The Shāfiᶜīs contest this view and makes no such distinction; A. Kevin Reinhart, '"Like the difference between Heaven and Earth": Ḥanafī and Shāfiᶜī discussions of *wājib* and *farḍ*', in Weiss, *Studies in Islamic Legal Theory*, 205-34.

15 *Jihād* is (in normal language) an armed conflict between the Muslim society and a non-Muslim enemy. It is the duty of all Muslims to defend their society, but this is normally delegated to the ruler, the 'imam'. Only if the society has no legitimate Muslim ruler does the duty pass to each Muslim as an individual duty. The *jihād*ists of today claim either that today's rulers are infidels, or not able to defend the society against the

(2) That which is recommended, but is not a sin to omit, is *mandūb*. Prayer beyond the required five times a day is such an act.

(3) That which is neither recommended nor disapproved is *mubāḥ*, neutral.

(4) That which is disapproved of or 'repulsive', but not directly a sin to commit, is *makrūh*.

(5) That which it is a sin to do, is forbidden, *ḥarām*.

The opposite of *ḥarām* is *halāl*, allowed. This includes acts on the first three levels. There is some dispute over whether the 'repulsive' is also *halāl*; it is certainly something that good Muslims should avoid. However, of these five levels, only the first and the last have any legal significance. The law specifies what is required and what is forbidden; the other categories ultimately remain a matter between each believer and God.

This categorization is the jurists' domain. It is their job to position each disputed act into this schema, and in particular to decide where the limits for what is forbidden and what is required go. And where there are jurists, there will be disagreement. Some acts considered to be *ḥarām* by some authors, may be merely *makrūh* for others, and vice versa.

As mentioned, only some thirty verses, less than one in ten of those with legal import and half a per cent of the Koran in all, refer to crime and punishments. They deal with five issues that have, or are considered to have, specified punishments meted out in the Koran, and we will meet them later as the *ḥudūd* rules.[16] They concern theft, highway robbery, drunkenness, marital infidelity and false witness of infidelity. The rest of criminal law is left to society.

This does not mean that the Koran is much more specific when it comes to the relation between man and God, the *ᶜibādāt* rules. Most of the Muslim rituals are based on observances of the Prophet, recorded in *sunna*. The Koran is mostly specific on a few issues such as those relating to family matters; what kind of kinship prevents marriage, the distribution of inheritance, and similar topics. The Koran is also often expressly imprecise, it has formulas of the type 'Do not ask about things which, if they were

---

'enemy', and that it has thus become a duty for every Muslim. Notice a struggle between two Muslim countries can never be a *jihād*.

16 Kamali, *Principles*, 10. Seen more in Chapter 14.

revealed to you, would cause you trouble' and 'God desires ease for you, not hardship'.[17]

Ḥadīth

Given the lack of detailed rules in the Koran, other sources were needed to determine God's will as a basis for the Sharīᶜa. As the law had to go through a human elaboration, it was all the more important that this interpretation could be firmly based in a text that had the same level of authority as the Koran and was a result of divine revelation. This more extended source was the *ḥadīth*, the stories told about the Prophet and his community, his *sunna*.

Not all *ḥadīth* actually talk about the Prophet, and not all stories about the Prophet are *ḥadīth*. There are several genres of such stories. Some are merely biographical (*sīra*), or they relate the events of his military campaigns (*maghāzī*). These may be important for pious Muslims who want to emulate the Prophet, but they are technically relating the history of the Prophet's 'human' endeavours, where he acts in his own capacity. It is the *normative* stories, those that are meant to be important for how later Muslims should act and where Muḥammad transmits directly or indirectly God's intention and will, that are given the name *ḥadīth*, and are thus subject to the detailed methodology that separates true from false.

Some *ḥadīth* tell of acts carried out by the Prophet's contemporaries and companions without his own input being referred to. These evidently have less impact than those telling about Muḥammad himself, but can still carry normative power; these were exemplary Muslims who lived with the Prophet and saw what he did, thus they were better sources for what he might have done than the practices of later generations.

Ḥadīth studies

Clearly, the early uncritical acceptance of anything that called itself a *ḥadīth* had to be abandoned once the mass of this literature had grown to an immense body of contradictory statements all claiming to come from the Prophet. Evidently many or most of these stories had to be false. But which ones? To presume to

17 K 5:101, 2:185, etc.

discuss the validity of a *ḥadīth* based on its content was problematic since it was, if true, of divine origin and thus beyond human capacity to question. Man cannot evaluate the correctness of God's will. Also, since most of the purported *ḥadīth* functioned as supports for arguments in a debate, it was not very convincing if those supporting the opposing view rejected the *ḥadīth* just because it was 'illogical'.

Instead, those who developed into a separate class of *ḥadīth* specialists started to evaluate the presumed *ḥadīth* stories according to criteria that were external to the text itself, by looking at the human element in them, not the potentially divine content.

A simple *ḥadīth* may look like this:

> Muḥammad b. Salām told us, he said that Abū Muᶜāwiya told us, from al-Aᶜmash from Shaqīq, who said,
>
> I sat with ᶜAbd Allāh and Abū Mūsa al-Ashᶜarī [who started to discuss using sand for ritual ablution when water was unavailable]. Abū Mūsā said, 'Did you not hear ᶜAmmār say to ᶜUmar b. al-Khaṭṭāb, "God's messenger sent me out on a mission. As I was ritually impure and could not find water, I rolled in the sand as a donkey rolls around. When I came to the Prophet, he said, 'This would have been sufficient', and struck the palm of his hand once on the ground, then shook it and pulled the palm of his left hand over the back of the right—or over the palm of the left with the back of the right—and then pulled both hands over the face".'[18]

Here, we can see that the *ḥadīth* is divided into two, first a 'header' containing the name of the man who is the source for the story (in this case Shaqīq) and of those who told it from him, in a chain of transmitters reaching from the Prophet's generation down to the time it was written down. This chain of transmitters is known as an *isnād*. Then follows the actual text, *matn*, which tells of the event and what the Prophet said or did.

The example also shows the function of a *ḥadīth*. The Muslims at this point knew the basic features of the prayer ritual, that one should pray five times a day and that prayer should be

18 Bukhārī, *Ṣaḥīḥ*, 'Tayammum' 8 (edn. Beirut 1982: I, 152-6:13), trans. El-Bokhâri, *Les Traditions islamiques*, transl. by O. Houdas and W. Marçais, Paris 1903, I, 131; cf. in other collections: Muslim, 'Ḥayḍ' 110-3; Abū Dāwūd, 'Ṭahāra' 121; Nasāʾī, 'Ṭahāra' 195 & 198-202; Ibn Māja, 'Ṭahāra' 91-2, and Ibn Ḥanbal, *Musnad*, IV, 264-5, 315, 319 & 396-7.

carried in a state of ritual purity, achieved by washing oneself in a precise manner. But a problem arose: What if there was no water available when the time of prayer arrived? A verse in the Koran answered this: The believer should take fine sand ['wholesome dust'; 5:5] onto the hands and feet instead of water; but did not explain further the details of how this was to be performed.

The *ḥadīth* first presents a potential way of doing this washing with sand, to 'roll around as a donkey'. This is then presented to the Prophet who instead presents a simpler ritual as the prescribed way of using sand for ablution. Thus, a new rule is created for how this *tayammum* procedure is to be performed.[19] In this way, the *ḥadīth* is used to make the law more sophisticated. As new problems or conflicts between different rules appear, a *ḥadīth* can be used to give authority to the solution found. This is used both for ritual issues like the one here, or others where the Prophet's example lays down the line.

Categorizations

When a scholar evaluates which *ḥadīth* are true and which are false, he cannot then directly reject the content which may have come from God. Instead, he looks at the first part of the story, the 'header' with the list of names. In this example we see four different names in the chain, which must have started in the first generation after the Prophet (Abū Mūsā met the caliph ᶜUmar b. al-Khaṭṭāb, d. 644), and ended when the *ḥadīth* was written down sometime in the mid-800s. Is this believable? Could Muḥammad b. Salām actually have heard it from Abū Muᶜāwiya, or was he perhaps born after Abū Muᶜāwiya had died? Had that been the case, there would have been a 'gap' in the chain. Such a gap does not invalidate the *ḥadīth*: maybe it was just the later transmitters who had forgotten the name of the person who was between the

19 The *ḥadīth* about *tayammum* is actually mostly about whether verse 5:5 is applicable at all, as ᶜAbd Allāh claimed that this would make 'everyone come and say that this water is too cold', thus questioning the authority of the Koran. The first part of the *hādīth*, not included here, supports the use of the Koranic text, that sand may only be used if there is no water present at all. Then it adds the specification of what this means. Notice the variant included in the *ḥadīth*, probably added by the *ḥadīth* collector, on whether it is the left or right palm that the Prophet pulled over the back of the other hand. This variant was clearly not so important that the collector wanted to split the story into two separate *ḥadīth* texts.

two. But it could also be that this Muḥammad b. Salām had simply invented the story himself; a gap certainly does not help credibility.

But even if these people could have met, that does not mean the story is true. This Aᶜmash in the chain, is he known as a credible source? Or does he rather have the reputation of a fanciful storyteller who often made up or embellished stories on his own account? Or was he a drunkard? Someone with a notoriously bad memory? Or perhaps a sectarian who could twist a story out of shape for his own purposes? Any or all of these things could be used to discredit the story itself, even if only one of the transmitters was so criticized, and such problems had to be resolved before the *ḥadīth* could become normative.

However, that did not have to be the end of the debate. Most *ḥadīth*s were told in more than one version. Various transmitters could relate the same basic event with greater or smaller differences in wording or content, or with different names in the *isnād*s. Some stories only had a few variants, others could be related in dozens of different versions. This was perfectly understandable, each person who heard of such a saying from the Prophet could have passed it on, and on each occasion have had many listeners or students who again transmitted it to many others. Since all transmissions of these stories were initially done orally and based only on the memory of the story-tellers, it is not surprising that each story could appear in different wordings.

Thus, the *ḥadīth* specialists had a body of material that they could compare critically. Generally they did not try to 'edit' the stories into one standard version, as they saw themselves as transmitters, collectors who did not have the authority to change a text that in origin was divinely inspired. Instead they sorted out those variants they concluded must evidently be false, and then included the remaining variants alongside each other, each with its own *isnād*, and mostly without giving any indication of which they found to be most trustworthy. Then later scholars were free to evaluate and categorize the *ḥadīth* according to how believable it is that it actually represents the *sunna* of the Prophet. Such an evaluation can designate a *ḥadīth* as 'sound' and true, *ṣaḥīḥ*, or weak and less trustworthy, *ḍaᶜīf*.[20]

20 Burton, *Introduction to the Ḥadīth,* 110-16. Cf. also Guillaume, *Traditions*

The most general basis for this division is one that divides all *ḥadīth* into two groups. One consists of those that have been told by so many known and trustworthy persons based on original direct observation, that they cannot be false; not all of these persons can have lied or transmitted falsely. Therefore these *ḥadīth* are certainly true, and form a certain basis for the law. The term for these is *tawātur*.[21]

Those *ḥadīth* that have not reached the status of *tawātur*, are normally called *aḥād*. These are not certainly true, they can only be considered to be probably (*ẓannī*) true after a scholarly exercise of verfication.[22] These form the vast majority of *ḥadīth* and as a consequence legal rules based on them are necessarily also only *ẓannī*. How many must be involved for the *tawātur* level of certainty to be reached is a matter of discussion. Some say as little as five is enough, others put the number as high as 300.[23] We will discuss the term *tawātur* later in the context of consensus, which is based on a similar type of argument: If everyone or the large majority agree that something is true, then it cannot be false.

A significant distinction is between *ḥadīth* which are assumed to be transmitted word by word (*lafẓī*) from person to person, and those in which only the meaning is transmitted (*bi'l-maᶜnā*). The former are evidently better for legal purposes, but there is disagreement on whether it is a requirement that the transmitter knows the legal consequencces of the expressions that he transmits.[24]

Thus, there is a finer structuring of the 'proof value' of a *ḥadīth*. Among the terms used to categorize it are

— The best grades are those of *thābit*, trustworthy, *mashhūr*, well known, and *ḥasan*, good.

— Those *ḥadīth* which are known as *mawsūl* or *muṭassil*,

---

of Islam, 86-8, with its much finer categorization based on al-Jurjānī.

21 Aron Zysow, 'The Economy of Certainty: An Introduction to the Typology of Islamic Legal Theory', Ph.D., Harvard University 1984, 11-24 and *passim*, and Weiss, *Spirit of Islamic Law*, 47-52.

22 Technically, *aḥād* means 'singular'; that is a *ḥadīth* which exists in only one version or with one *isnād* chain *A ḥād* may be used in this more restrictive sense, but the normal usage in *uṣūl al-fiqh* is the wider of any *ḥadith* that does not have *tawātur* distribution.

23 Hallaq, *History of Islamic Legal Theories*, 61.

24 Hallaq, *History of Islamic Legal Theories*, 64-5.

'connected' are also valued highly. They have a continuous *isnād* without any 'gap' between transmitters.

— *Ḥadīth* that do have such a gap are known as *maqṭū*ᶜ or *munqaṭi*ᶜ, 'cut off'. These lack one link in the middle of the chain, while one that is *mursal*, 'transmitted', lacks the first link, the original eye-witness to the Prophet's action.[25]

— Even less valued is a *ḥadīth* which is *munkar*, disliked.

Thus, it is doubtful whether a *ḍa*ᶜ*īf*, weak, *ḥadīth* should be taken into account at all. However, some would say that even a weak *ḥadīth* is better than just *ra*ʾ*y*. Others would accept *ḥadīth* with a singular complete chain, but none of any lesser probative value, and some would say that a rule based through proper *qiyās* on a sound *ḥadīth* must be a better representation of divine will than a rule based directly on a *ḥadīth* that may be quite false. Thus, there is room for conflict, not only between the evaluation of different *ḥadīth*, but also between their role in the hierarchy of methodologies for the law.

The ḥadīth collections

As Islam never had any final theological authority figure who could decide which *ḥadīth* were true or false, it was up to the competent reader to decide which ones to use. Thus, there was never any unified Muslim 'Talmud' which encompasses all authoritative *ḥadīth*. There were dozens of collections made by different *ḥadīth* collectors from the eighth to the tenth century, some also later. But by general consent, six collections are considered to be 'canonical', those that most Muslim theologians and jurists consider the most authoritative. They can be grouped into three.

Most valued are the collections of Muḥammad b. Ismāᶜīl al-Bukhārī (d. 870) and Muslim b. al-Ḥajjāj (d. 875). Both normally carry the title *Jāmi*ᶜ *al-ṣaḥīḥ*, 'The collection of sound [*ḥadīth*]',[26]

25 On the different views of *mursal* traditions, see Zysow, 'Economy of Certainty', 49-60.

26 The two are together called '*al-Ṣaḥīḥān*', 'The two true *ḥadīth* collections'. These collections were probably all copied, and later printed, with somewhat varying titles, where it is the author/collector's name that distinguishes them. But the separation implicit in calling these two *Ṣaḥīḥ* and the others *Sunan* also imply an evaluation. This may be seen in that the

and a *ḥadīth* included in both of these will be accepted as true by virtually every scholar. Slightly less authoritative are the collections of Muḥammad b. ᶜĪsā al-Tirmīdhī (d. 892) and Sulaymān b. al-Ashᶜath Abū Dāwūd (d. 888). They are mostly printed with the title *Sunan*, 'Collections of *sunnas*'.[27] The fifth collection is that of Aḥmad b. ᶜAlī al-Nasāʾī (d. 915), but there is some disagreement on which is the sixth canonical collection. Most scholars take it to be that of Muḥammad b. Yazīd Ibn Māja (d. 887), but some consider ᶜAbd Allāh b. ᶜAbd al-Raḥmān al-Dārimī (d. 869) as more authoritative than Ibn Māja.[28]

All these six works are organized according to (legal) themes, and are thus called *muṣannaf*, 'ordered'. Another collection which, while not among the six, still has great authority, is organized by the names in the *isnāds*; a *musnad*. This is the collection of Ibn Ḥanbal, who, as we have seen, also has a school of law named after him. Still, he preferred to use the *musnad* form to avoid undue human intervention and editing in his presentation of *ḥadīth*. The major legal work by Mālik, another founder of a school, the *Muwaṭṭaʾ*, is also considered to be a *ḥadīth* collection, as it contains many *ḥadīth* in addition to Mālik's own decisions. Dozens of other *ḥadīth* collections are also regularly used by scholars to this day.

In conjunction with the *ḥadīth* collections, a science of transmitters, *rijāl*, also developed. This gathered information of those who were cited in the *isnāds*, and categorized them according to trustworthiness.[29] This was evidently an important aid for the later evaluation of *ḥadīth*. But a full consensus could not be reached on the status of the individual transmitter, indeed many of them were almost or totally unknown except for their names. Later transmitters or editors also often confused different early transmitters with similar names. All of which was of course a

---

most trustworthy of the four others, that of Tirmidhī, is also sometimes published under the name *Ṣaḥīḥ*.

27 Burton says this name comes from the four being more concerned with legal *sunnas* that the two *Ṣaḥīḥs*; *Introduction to the Ḥadīth*, 126.

28 Burton, *Introduction to the Ḥadīth*, 129-30, and Ṣiddīqī, *Ḥadīth Literature*, 115. The collection of ᶜAlī b. ᶜUmar al-Darāquṭnī (d. 995) is also important. More on this in Chapter 6.

29 Even Bukhārī is to have written one such, *Kitāb al-ḍuᶜafāʾ*. This evaluation of personal integrity did not only take place in the early period, *rijāl* criticism was an active genre as late as the seventeenth century.

basis for later debates on the re-evaluation of individual *ḥadīth*, and thus the legal rules that used them for justification.

Topics in a muṣannaf

The *ḥadīth* collections did not contain only material relevant to the law, although such topics often tended to dominate (contrary to their place in the Koran). An illustration of this can be found by looking at the chapter headings and subheadings of the *Ṣaḥīḥ* of Bukhārī, in four volumes of equal size:[30]

I – Faith. Knowledge
— Ritual purity (4 chapters). Prayer (15: Call to prayer, Friday prayer, prayer under dangerous conditions, shortening it, prayer at night, distractions from it, i.a.). Burials
— Taxes. Pilgrimage (4: Homage to Medina). Fasting.

II – Sales (3). Wage labour. Debts (2). Contracts etc. (9: surety, conflict settlement, witnessing). Freeing slaves (2). Donations (2). Testaments.
— Jihād (2). Khums (taxes)
— *The creation, the prophets. Homage to the companions of the Prophet.*

III – *The military expeditions of the Prophet (maghāzī).*
— Interpretations of the Koran / reasons for the Revelation. *Homage to the Koran.*
— Marriage, divorce (3). *Everyday life.*

IV– Slaughter. Sacrifice (during the *ᶜīd* festival). Drinking. Illness (3). Clothes etc. (2). Education. Private matters.
— Oaths. Criminal matters:[31] Blood money. Apostates. *Interpreting dreams / temptations*. Giving judgements.
— Aḥād ḥadīth. Basing oneself on God's Book and the sunna.
— *God's indivisibility.*

30 The topics not related to law (a minority, as one can see), are here put in *italics*, and groups of themes have been given separate lines. The figures in parentheses are the number of chapters under each topic, if any. The division into four equally large volumes follows the French translation; Bukhārī, *Traditions islamiques*.

31 Takes up just under one third of Volume IV.

Interpretations of the contents of ḥadīth

The *ḥadīth* are subject to the same kind of interpretative techniques as the Koran, using concepts as *ᶜāmm* and *khāṣṣ*, *muqayyad* and *muṭlaq*, and so on. But in this case, the basis for these interpretations are to be found in the *ḥadīth* material itself. As this literature is so much larger and contains much more detail than the Koranic text, the evaluation of it must also range more widely.

An example that has been used to explain this is: A rule based on *ḥadīth* says that everything that is watered from the sky (that is, of agricultural produce) is subject to the 'one tenth' tax, *ᶜushr*. This is a general, *ᶜāmm*, rule. Another rule says that anything weighing less than 50 kg is exempt from another type of tax, *ṣidqa*.[32] This is a specifying, *khāṣṣ*, rule, because it only concerns a subset of goods; those less than a certain weight. The question then would be, whether and how these two rules should be read together. Is the rule for 'less than 50 kg' also to be seen as applying to the *ᶜushr* rule, so that smaller amounts should also be exempt from this tax? Or should the rule about 'watered from the sky' also apply to the *ṣidqa* tax, so that produce that is grown on irrigated land (watered by the farmer, not from rain) is also exempt from that tax?

The accepted answer is that the two rules should be connected, and in such a way that the specifying rule qualifies the general, not the other way around. As the weight rule was specifying (it excluded a category of goods) and the irrigation rule was general (it said 'everything that is ...'), it is the former that qualifies the latter. A farmer who produces less than 50 kg of a particular kind of product a year, does not need to pay *ᶜushr* tax on it, but the *ṣidqa* tax applies irrespective of how the land is watered.[33]

32 Kamali, *Principles,* 112-3: 'what is watered from the skies has *ᶜushr*' (Bukhārī, 'Zakāt' 55); 'there is no *ṣidqa* on what is less than five *wasaq*' (*ibid.,* 'Buyūᶜ' 83 etc.). A *wasaq* is about 10 kg. On *ᶜushr*, see Chapter 16.

33 The Ḥanafī tradition is different in this, and will not accept this type of argument. They say that there are here two texts of Revelation that make contradictory statements, and that one must therefore use the rules of 'abrogation' (*naskh*, see below) to discover what is the most recent text (here the one on 'what is watered from the skies'). This then abrogates the earlier text, so that all agricultural products have to pay *ᶜushr*, whatever the amount produced; Kamali, *Principles,* 108 & 110.

Contradictions between Koran and ḥadīth

Both the Koran and *ḥadīth* contain rules that do or seem to contradict other rules in the same or the other text. There are several Koranic verses that can clearly be read as commands facing similarly clear commands saying the opposite. One verse says, 'Dispute not with the People of the Book [the Jews and Christians] save in the fairer manner' (29:46); another says, 'Fight those who believe not in God and the last day … [such as] those who have been given the Book, until they pay tribute out of hand and have been humbled' (9:29).[34] In one place it says that wine is a 'delight' to be enjoyed, in another that it is a sin but also has 'uses for man', and in a third that it is 'Satan's work'.[35]

This can partly be explained in the manner discussed above, by saying for example that one verse is 'specified' or 'dependent' on another and is only valid in a particular context which may be spelled out in the verse itself or was known at the moment of revelation (the scholars called this context the *asbāb al-nuzūl*, 'the background to the revelation'). *Ḥadīth* is the most important source for this knowledge and thus gives authority to certain explanations of the Koranic verses.

But such explanations do not cover all such cases, and Koran specialists accepted that there are real contradictions in the Koran. One cause for this could be that the Islamic revelation was given gradually. God knew that a sudden change from the pre-Islamic practices would cause hardship to the believers, so he first permitted it partly to continue; then, when the time was ripe, the final and eternal truth was revealed. They say that the first verse was 'abrogated' (*mansūkh*, from *nasakha*) or replaced by the later. This is not said explicitly in the Koran, but appears from the order of revelation: a later verse replaces an earlier if they are contradictory. Thus, the chronology of the revelation is important for the scholars. The Koran itself is not organized chronologically, but the scholars established a chronology for when each

34 Respectively 29:46 and 9:29.—These are just two of many contradictory verses about how to relate to the people of the Book and the infidel. On the *jizya* tax, see Chapter 16.

35 Respectively the verses 47:15, 2:219, and 5:90-1; see also the next chapter, and Kamali, *Principles*, 16-17.

chapter and verse was revealed.[36]

However, what then about the other form of Revelation, the *sunna*. Both Koran and *sunna* were given to the Prophet throughout his lifetime, in parallel. A *sunna* can also be abrogated in the same way and for the same reason as a Koranic verse. But can they abrogate each other? Does a sound *ḥadīth* telling of a statement by Muḥammad which contradicts a Koranic verse that was revealed earlier, make the verse invalid?[37] Or can a later verse abrogate an earlier *sunna* of the Prophet? Shāfiʿī was much concerned with this issue in his theoretization. His main aim was, as we have discussed, to give the law the strongest possible anchor in the Revelation, the Koran and *sunna*. Thus not only the content, but also the internal ranking of the two types of Revelation was important.

Logically, a Koranic verse, being the undisputed word of God, should weigh heavier than a *ḥadīth* that must go through a process of verification. So a verse in the Koran should be more important that the *sunna*. But Shāfiʿī is totally clear and solid on this point, and argues strongly: The Koran and *sunna* are quite separate and equal sources, and only the Koran can abrogate the Koran and only a *sunna* can abrogate a *sunna*.

This view of the equality of the two may be surprising, but was necessary in order to establish the *sunna* as an independent basis for the law.[38] In addition to the *raʾy* people and the *ḥadīth* people we mentioned in the last chapter, there was also a third, smaller grouping who accepted only the Koran and nothing else as a source for God's will; or at least would only accept *ḥadīth* that discussed topics already mentioned in the Koran, which

36 The scholars were not able to agree on the precise placement of each chapter, or even on whether each *sūra* was revealed at once, or were later combinations of separate revelation; *Encyclopaedia of Islam*, new edition, Leiden 1960– [*EI* (2)], V, 415-6. However, they did in each case of assumed contradiction between two or more verses suggest which of them was revealed after the other.

37 Assuming of course that the *ḥadīth* has reached the level of certainty through *tawātur*, in the same way as all of the Koran is true because it is *mutawātir*.

38 This argumentation is proposed by John Burton, *The Sources of Islamic Law: Islamic Theories of Abrogation*, Edinburgh 1990 and *The Collection of the Qurʾān*, Cambridge 1977. See also Hallaq, *History of Islamic Legal Theories*, 68-72.

would limit the value of *ḥadīth* considerably. To accept this would be to open the way for *raʾy*. Either, the scholar could say that if a matter was not expressly discussed in the Koran—and most matters were not—the scholar would then have no other recourse than his own opinions. Or, if *ḥadīth* were not accepted as interpreters of the Koran, the scholar could always say that 'this *ḥadīth* has no value, because I have here a Koranic verse which I believe (with my *raʾy*) to mean the opposite, and a *ḥadīth* can never replace the Koran'.

This was something Shāfiʿī had to avoid, thus his insistence on the equality of the two sources. The Koran and the *sunna*, both expressions of God's will, cannot contradict each other. To accept this would be to accept that the *sunna* was weighed against the Koran, and this could make the Koran, with its slim amount of legal material, stand in the way of the establishment of the *ḥadīth* as a secure source for Revelation. And if the law was to be based on Revelation, then *ḥadīth* had to be the cornerstone because of its much larger size and greater detail of legally relevant material. This was the reason Shāfiʿī insisted that the Koran and *sunna* were separate sources where one could not replace or abrogate the other; and in particular that the Koran could not abrogate the *sunna*.

However, the statement that the *sunna* and the Koran cannot abrogate each other quickly runs into problems when they appear to be in clear contradiction. Shāfiʿī solved this by elaborating three types of *naskh*, abrogation: The first was 'replacing the rule but not the text' (*al-ḥukm bidūn al-tilāwa*). That is the most common event: God first revealed an intermediate rule through a verse, this rule was later replaced by a later verse with a different content, but the text of the first verse, no longer valid as a rule, is still part of the Koranic text.

The second is replacing 'both the rule and the text' (*al-ḥukm wa'l-tilāwa*). In this case both the text of the original verse and the rule it contained have disappeared from the Koran. In other words, a theoretical construct that was only introduced because 'only Koran can replace Koran'. When a verse says that the believers 'should no longer do as you did before, but do this', the previous behaviour could not have been only what the Prophet had told them, because that would be *sunna*, and thus a case of a Koranic verse replacing a *sunna*, unacceptable to Shāfiʿī. The earlier practice must therefore have been based on a Koranic verse that we no longer have. An example of this is the verse (2:136-9) that the Muslims should no longer turn to Jerusalem, but to Mecca in prayer.[39] This must mean, according the theory, that there had existed an earlier verse telling the Muslims to turn to Jerusalem, but since no such verse exists in the Koran as we have it, God must have effaced it from our memory (as He says in the Koran that He has the power to do, K 2:106). A story illustrating this is of when ᶜĀᵓisha, the Prophet's youngest wife, came into their house and discovered a goat eating a piece of papyrus. It contained a Koranic verse which thus was lost and is not part of the Koran we have.

The third category is the most complex one. It is 'replacing the text, but not the rule' (*al-tilāwa bidūn al-ḥukm*). That is, there was a Koranic verse that presented a rule, this verse is gone, effaced from the memory of the Muslims, but the rule it expressed is still there because it was never replaced by a later rule. This sounds very peculiar, and was probably a way to justify a rule that was based in *sunna* when something else and contradictory is actually stated in the Koran. Shāfiᶜī's theory cannot allow this, as a *sunna* cannot abrogate the Koran. When the scholars still needed to do that, they postulated that there was in fact a verse that stated the desired rule and had been revealed after the verse we actually have and so replaces it. But then, subsequently, this second verse had been lost. So, we now only have the *text* of the original verse, which is abrogated as 'rule, but not text', and the *rule* of the second, which is abrogated as 'text, but not rule'.[40]

39 'What has turned them from the direction they were facing in their prayer aforetime? … We did not appoint the direction thou wast facing, except that We might know who followed the Messenger from him who turned on his heels … We will surely turn thee to a direction that shall satisfy thee, Turn thy face towards the Holy Mosque'.

40 Thus Burton. The idea of *naskh al-tilāwa bidūn al-ḥukm* is thus based on Shāfiᶜī's political need to strengthen the role of the *sunna* as equal to and independent of the Koran. Burton also believes that it is this need, which thus required verses to have been 'lost' after the time of Revelation was over with the death of Muḥammad, which led to the varying and partly contradictory stories that the Koran was collected either at the initiative of the caliph ᶜUmar or his successor ᶜUthmān, instead of the more logical solution that Muḥammad himself was in charge of the collection. Burton's

An example of this is the so-called 'stoning verse' concerning *zinā*, adultery or fornication.[41] It is one of the five punishments that are linked to the Revelation, but the Koran does not in fact contain a clear rule for this matter. Adultery is mentioned twice in the Koran, with quite different punishments. In 4:15-16 it says that if 'indecency' is proven, 'detain them [the women] in their houses until death takes them or God appoints for them a way. And when two of you commit indecency, punish them both; but if they repent and make amends, then suffer them to be'. In another verse, 24:2, it says, 'the fornicatress and the fornicator, scourge each of them with a hundred stripes'.

Both verses are unclear as to what acts they refer to, as different terms are used,[42] nor is 'God appoints for them a way' explained. But it is generally assumed that both verses refer to adultery, and that the distinction between the first and last line of the first verse, 4:15 and 16, is that the first, the 'women', concern those that are married or 'non-virgins', while the milder reaction in verse 16 refers to unmarried youths. Further, it is assumed that 24:2, the latter verse with the harsher sentence, is later than 4:16, which is thus abrogated and no longer a valid rule.

The problem was that neither verse refers to what was the desired practice. As for unmarried people, the scholars accepted the revised rule in 24:2 as valid, 100 lashes. But married people, both men and women, faced a much harsher sentence, death by stoning. There are several *ḥadīth* that support this sentence on the authority of the Prophet's practice. But *ḥadīth* cannot replace Koran, and it is impossible in this case to say that the *sunna* 'explains' the Koran since the practice was in evident conflict

---

theory is, like all revisionism, based on the premise that the Muslims' own historical sources for the period do not prove anything. Christopher Melchert has pointed out that Shāfiʿī does in fact not mention *naskh al-tilāwa* in his *Risāla*, it was other jurists like Muḥāsibī (d. 858) who made this conclusion to the argument; Melchert, 'Qurʾānic abrogation across the ninth century: Shāfiʿī, Abū ʿUbayd, Muḥāsibī, and Ibn Qutayba', in Weiss, *Studies in Islamic Legal Theory*, 75-98.

41 That is, all forms of sexual relations outside the legal bounds of marriage (or, in earlier times, between a man and his female slave). See further in Chapters 12, 13 and 15.

42 4:15 uses the word *fāḥish*, 'obscenity', 24:2 *zinā,* 'fornication', none of these words were unequivocal in the language of that period. The requirement of four witnesses is mentioned in the former verse, 4:15.

with a clear, albeit complicated Koranic text.

One solution was to link the stoning to the earlier divine revelation of the Torah. There are *ḥadīth* that tell of how the Jews in Medina asked Muḥammad to mediate in a dispute concerning adultery. Some of the Jews tried to cover up what their Torah said about the issue, but by a miracle Muḥammad was made aware that the Torah did in fact stipulate such a death penalty, and judged accordingly. However, the presence of such a rule in the Jewish scriptures was not a strong argument for overlooking the text of the Koran.

Instead, the assumption gained ground that there had been such a verse in the Koran, too, requiring the stoning of both married men and women (*al-shaykh wa'l-shaykha*), revealed after 4:15, but that this verse had disappeared. Some *ḥadīth* confirmed this story, and it even gained a fixed form, because some people had seen it and remembered it before it was lost: This was in fact the sheet of papyrus that the famous goat had gobbled down. This was not the only case where a disappeared but still valid Koranic text could justify abrogating an existing earlier verse.

However, one consequence of this line of argumentation is that the Koranic text as we have it now cannot fully explain the law that is based on the Koran. God is the one who has caused this, as 2:106 says, 'We abrogate or cast into oblivion'. Still, that makes for a discrepancy between the Koran as it exists with God and the Koran we have in front of us (the *muṣḥaf*).[43] Even if the Koran is still perfect because that is how God made it, and even if true *ḥadīth* gives us a complete expression of what the Prophet transmitted of divine intention, they must still be subject to human elaboration before mankind can transform this divine will into a pattern for their society and their way of life. Thus, the doubt that always accompanies human activity is also brought into the divine message and law, and methods have to be devised to accommodate that doubt.

43 Not all scholars accept the theory of an incomplete Koran, so this is an internal contradiction to theology.

4

ELABORATING THE SOURCES: *QIYĀS* AND *IJTIHĀD*

Through *ḥadīth* studies, *tafsīr*, and other methods of reading, one could develop an authoritative revelatory Text (*naṣṣ*) and understand the direct import of this text in Arabic language. But there was still some way to go before this could become a structured and consistent legal framework, a law. Some of these texts express unequivocal commands, others only give general indications, or may refer to particular circumstances that are specified in the Text or elsewhere. What is to be done in different circumstances, or where the Text does not specify directly the course of action? For this, further elaboration is necessary in order to discover what is God's will in a more general way.

Ijtihād

In order to derive and systematize the legal implications of the Text, we have to use human thought processes, ratio, on it. This, to develop legal rules, is what is called *ijtihād*.

This is probably the most misused concept in the discussion of Islamic law; virtually anything can be called and is called *ijtihād*. The term is thus not easy to translate; 'interpretation' is a common translation, but is only one of several possible meanings of its technical sense. The Arabic word refers to 'effort', and it always implies expending some form of human and intellectual effort in the legal process. But some say that *ijtihād* is the same as *raʾy*, they talk of *ijtihād al-raʾy*, that is to make legal rules based only on the jurists' personal opinions, independently of the Revelation. Others say it means the opposite, *ijtihād* for them means to limit the influence of human independent reasoning by building the rules directly on the Revelation sources; that is, by each scholar expending his own efforts in searching the Revelation rather than just accepting what previous (human) authorities have said. Shāfiʿī uses the term in yet another meaning, for him it is synonymous with the specific process of *qiyās*, his methods for analogical derivation.[1] Nor does it help that modern Muslims as well as Western scholars use the term for basically any sort of legal development, mostly as a sort of magical key for adapting the Sharīᶜa to modern society in whichever manner, although some older meanings of the term refer to exactly the opposite.

Thus, we have to go beyond the word *ijtihād* itself and look more closely at the methods the jurists developed for the formulation of legal rules, *ḥukm*s, based on the Revelation; that is, the various methods that fall under the general concept of *ijtihād*.

Qiyās

The most important of these methods is *qiyās*, which is most often translated as analogy or analogical deduction. This is not incorrect, but may indicate a more limited sort of activity that *qiyās* actually is. Rather than say that *qiyās* means only to 'compare new cases with established ones in order to see if they are similar', you may equally well say that *qiyās* is the main instrument used to formulate legal rules from the Revelation.[2]

The fact that *qiyās* links the rule to the texts of the Revelation is central. We are not talking of wild searches for 'things that remind us of something we know'. That would invite the danger of making quite haphazard conclusions, since anything can look like anything else if one only sets one's mind to it. What is at issue here is instead to expand the impact of the Text from what is specifically mentioned to a general category of cases, of which that mentioned in the Text is only a prime example.

The reason why this process of expansion is at all considered acceptable is because it is itself mentioned in the Koran, and that

1 *Risāla*, Khadduri's edn., 288; Schacht, *Origins*, 127, and Ahmad Hasan, 'The definition of qiyās in Islamic jurisprudence', *Islamic Studies*, 19, 1980, 4-5.

2 Ahmad Hasan, 'Methods of finding the cause of a legal injunction in Islamic jurisprudence', *Islamic Studies* (Karachi), XXV, 1, 1986, 11-44, 'Definition of qiyās', 1-28 and 'Subject matter of qiyās', *ibid*, XXI, 4, 1982, 97-129; see also his 'Early modes of ijtihād: rāʾy, qiyās and istihsān', *ibid*, VI, 1967, 47-79, all collected in his *Analogical Reasoning in Islamic Jurisprudence: A Study of the Juridical Principle of Qiyas*, Delhi 1994; further Alhaji A.M. Nour, 'Qias as a source of Islamic Law', *Journal of Islamic and Comparative Law*, V, 1969-76, 18-50.

the early companions used it. More rational justifications are also proffered. Legal rules are either presented as general and everlasting or refer to a moment in time (*ḥawādith*). Although the latter cannot be eternal in the form the Text cites them, they may include a meaning that goes beyond the moment mentioned in the Text. To bring out this lasting import, one has to study the Text with the methods of *qiyās*.

The process of qiyās

The way this works can be presented as a flow chart:

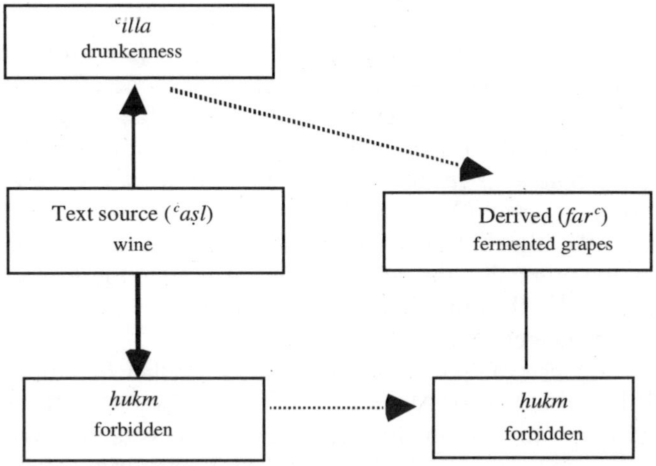

This is the classical case for explaining *qiyās*, and is fairly clear. The basis is a Koranic verse which says the Muslim should not drink wine (wine is the 'work of Satan'). This means that drinking wine is grouped in the category 'forbidden', *ḥarām*, in the structuring of acts described above. However, a question quickly arose: The Koran only uses the word *khamr*, wine.[3] The Arabs also had a wider term for alcoholic drinks, *nabīdh*, many types of which were widely used. Were all of these also covered by the ban on wine?

3 K 5:90-1: 'O believers, wine and arrow-shuffling, idols and divining-arrows are an abomination, some of Satan's works; so avoid it; haply so you will prosper', similar in 2:219. K 47:15 however mentions *khamr* as one of the delights of Paradise, but that is thus no longer legally relevant, see the last chapter.

The answer was found by asking; 'what is it about wine that makes it forbidden'? That is, not what God had *meant* by the ban, as not all of God's motives need be understood by us, but what actually led to the ban, the 'effective cause'. This was not quite evident; wine has several aspects that may or may not be harmful. Perhaps it was its cost, or that it was derived from a particular kind of harmful grape, or its colour, or the time of year it was produced. However, the jurists did not hesitate too long in deciding that the reason wine is banned is that it makes people drunk, it induced intoxication. This 'effective cause' behind a rule is called its *ᶜilla*.

When it is thus established that God has banned a substance that induces intoxication, it follows that this ban must refer to all substances that have the same effect. That is therefore the basis for the evaluation of other instances: does it fall under the same *ᶜilla* cause as that mentioned in the Text? As for *nabīdh*, yes, it does; people also get drunk from imbibing it. In this case, when the original case, *khamr*, and the second case, *nabīdh*, share the same *ᶜilla*, it must also share the same *ḥukm*: it can be transferred from the original to the derived case.[4] (The term for the 'original', that mentioned in the Text, is *aṣl*, 'the root', and the 'derived' is *farᶜ*, 'the branching off').

Another example from our times is whether betting on football is forbidden for Muslims.[5] The basis would be the ban on gambling which is mentioned in the same verse as wine, and which is connected to the ban on *ribā*.[6] To bet on football results isn't actually gambling, since it involves knowledge of the teams and the players, it has a limited and small stake, and is in several ways different from the kind of ruinous gambling of the pre-Islamic Arabs that the Koran bans. But many scholars have stated that the *ᶜilla* of the ban is the element of risk; the ban must be against any kind of games that through chance incur the danger of creating economic loss. This is as true for betting on football as it is on poker, and both must therefore be subject to the ban on gambling.

4 The Ḥanafī school does not accept this example of *qiyās*, and considers it permitted to drink *nabīdh*.

5 Nour, 'Qias as a source', 28.

6 This is based on the opposition to 'risk', see Chapter 16 and verse cited above on 'wine, gambling and idols'.

The unifying factor

The element that is common in the original and derived case is called the 'unifying factor' (*jāmi*ᶜ). They may share *legal*, or *internal* characteristics.

An example of the former is that that it is forbidden to sell a dog (*far*ᶜ) because it is forbidden to sell a pig (*aṣl*).[7] There is nothing in and of itself about a dog that makes it more like a pig than a donkey or other animals that may be sold. The similarity is legal: The dog is ritually unclean, and so is the pig. Thus, they are in the same legal category, and the ᶜ*illa* for the ban of selling pigs is that they are unclean. Hence, also the dog.

The example above, on *khamr* and *nabīdh* wine is an example of internal characteristics; it is the nature of these beverages, both cause intoxication, that is the reason the ban on one is transferred to the other.

Categories of qiyās

The relation between the original and derived case can be categorized into several degrees.[8] A *superior* (*awlā*) analogy occurs when the ᶜ*illa* is stronger in the derived than in the original case. For example, there is a ban on using 'harsh words' against parents (*aṣl*). As for using violence against them (*far*ᶜ) there is no particular rule, but the ᶜ*illa* for 'harsh words' must clearly be even more present against anybody using violence.

The wine example is one of *equal* (*musāwī*) analogy, the ᶜ*illa* intoxication is equally present in one and the other substance. However, when there is a question of *inferior* (*adnā*) analogy, where the ᶜ*illa* is less present in the derived than in the original case, there is more room for doubt. This is the case in a rule against exchanging grain. This is only permitted when the goods are delivered and received at the same time, and equal weight against equal weight (*aṣl*). That is, one cannot receive grain for sowing in the spring and pay it back after the harvest. This is linked to the principle of predictability, an exchange shall not be based on guessing what a future result may be; a danger of usury.[9] But only the grain of wheat is actually mentioned. What

7 Hasan, 'Definition of qiyās', 10.
8 Nour, 'Qias as a source', 24-6.
9 See more on this in Chapter 16.

about other produce, such as apples? This is unclear, because apples clearly have different properties than wheat; wheat is sowed annually (requires a material input) while apples are not, so the concept of 'surplus over input' is not relevant to the same degree.[10] However, the most used answer is to say that the *ᶜilla* for the ban is that the product is edible, so that apples are also covered. Still, it is less certain that the *ᶜilla* for the ban can be transferred in this case.

The Ḥanafī tradition differs from the other schools in their view of these categories. They consider only the latter, the inferior type of analogy, as actual *qiyās*. The two others aren't really *qiyās*, they say, merely direct readings of the Text.[11] Not hitting parents and not drinking other kinds of wine are self-evidently covered by what the Koran says directly; there is no need to go into all the technical formalities of constructing *ᶜilla*s and other *qiyās* methods to understand that. We will later go into why it is logical that the Ḥanafīs differ from the others in this particular view.

ᶜIlla

The central element of *qiyās* is thus the formulation of an *ᶜilla* behind a legal Revelation text. There are other expressions for what lies behind a rule, thus *maᶜnā* (meaning), *bāᶜith* (motive), *sabab* (reason),[12] while *ᶜilla* has the more restricted meaning of what 'sets the rule in motion'. Still, the difference between these terms is minor, and we will here focus only on *ᶜilla*, which is the most important of these concepts. How does one go about finding out what is God's *ᶜilla* behind a rule mentioned in the Koran or the *sunna*?

10 As we shall see in Chapter 16, this division between sown and perennial products have importance also in other contexts.

11 More detail on this discussion among the Ḥanafīs and other schools can be found in Zysow, 'Economy of Certainty', 157-76. The principles are often called '*a fortiori* / *a contrario*'.

12 Ahmad Hasan, 'Definition of sabab and its kinds in Islamic jurisprudence', *Islamic Studies*, XXI, 3, 1982, 48-60 and 'The legal cause in Islamic jurisprudence: an analysis of 'illat al-ḥukm', *ibid.*, XIX, 4, 1980, 262-7 (both also in *Analogical Reasoning*); Hallaq, *History of Islamic Legal Theories*, 83-107, and Kamali, *Principles*, 197-229.

Categories of ᶜilla

There are three basic methods of finding the *ᶜilla*. The first is textual, when the *ᶜilla* is mentioned directly in the Text that is the basis for the rule.[13] The motive may be stated explicitly using specific conjunctions ('so that', 'for indeed'); 'We have done this so that…', such as the rule that war booty is to be shared with kinsmen, orphans, the needy and travellers, 'so that it be not a thing taken in turns among the rich among you' [K 59:7].

Or it may be inferred from the text, as when a context is mentioned, as is the case in many *ḥadīth*: The Text relates a certain event which produced a problem, this was presented to the Prophet who gives an answer phrased generally, but still clearly referring to the context at hand. Thus in a *ḥadīth* on exchanging dried dates against ripe (a problem similar to the grain vs. apples exchange above: can an agricultural product in one form be exchanged for the same product in another form?). The Prophet asked the parties, 'Did the weight change?'. As they affirmed this to be the case, dates lose weight as they dry, he gave the answer: 'Then do not exchange them for each other'.[14] The statement only says that the dates should not be exchanged, but the context of the story clearly shows that the *ᶜilla* is because drying made the goods lighter; so the rule can be transferred to any other foodstuff where the intermediary process leads to a change in weight.

There are many other types of specifications based on implied conditions. A *ḥadīth* says that the Prophet was once lost in thought as he was praying and fell out of the ritual.[15] As he caught himself, he repeated that part of the prayer twice. Nothing more is said, but the implication for the *ᶜilla* is clear: It was his lapse of mind that caused that part of the prayer to become invalid, and the penalty was repetition of that part of the ritual only, but twice over.

It is evident that this contextualization will have an effect on *ḥadīth* studies. Most *ḥadīth* exist in several variants, where some tell of a full event, as we have done in these examples, while others only say, for example 'The Prophet said: "Do not exchange fresh and dried dates"', or 'The Prophet, when interrupting such-

13 Hasan, 'Methods', 13-15.
14 Hasan, 'Methods', 15.
15 Hasan, 'Methods', 19.

and-such a prayer, repeated that part twice'. These variants cannot explain if and how these statements can be expanded to new cases. Thus a scholar cannot base his legal work on only one variant of a *ḥadīth*, he must know all versions of the story to see if there is more to it than just the Prophet's statement alone.

A revisionist historian may thus also suspect that the cause and effect may have been reversed: One group working for a particular rule presents a *ḥadīth* where the Prophet affirms that rule. The opposition, who do not wish this rule, has a problem attacking the veracity of the *ḥadīth* itself by established means. Instead, they put forward another *ḥadīth*, which includes the same statement, but in a context which shows that the intention of the Prophet was quite different, for example only in a specific context specified by that variant. Then, the two groups of scholars can fight over which variant of the *ḥadīth* is most trustworthy instead of attacking the logic or desirability of the Prophet's purported statement directly.

Consensus

The other main method of discovering the *ᶜilla* is through consensus; what the scholars all agree must be the reason.[16] The issue of consensus is covered in greater depth below, but here the issue is fairly straightforward: if all scholars agree, then there is no debate, so there is no reason to look further. The problems and discussions only arise when there are disagreements about what has caused a rule. So, we can provisionally explain consensus as 'what is so obvious that no-one can be bothered to explain it'.

An example of such a rule is the Koranic penalty for drunkenness, which is 80 lashes with a whip. This is in fact not specified in the Koran; it only says that the Muslim should keep away from wine. However, it does specify the punishment of 80 lashes for wrongful accusation (*qadhf*).[17] By consensus, this penalty is extended to drinking wine because they are covered by the same *ᶜilla*, when a person gets drunk, he loses control of himself, talks wildly and often accuses others without cause. Thus, they must be grouped together and have the same penalty.

16 Hasan, 'Methods', 12-13.

17 K 24:4: 'And those who cast it up on women in wedlock, and then bring not four witnesses, scourge them with eighty stripes, and do not accept any testimony of theirs ever'. The Koran does not use the expression '*qadhf*'.

Derivation

The third category of methods, derivation (*istinbāṭ*), covers cases not found in the Text itself, but which one can discover by other methods. The ways of doing so are virtually innumerable, and we can here only briefly mention a few of the most important.[18]

One method is to classify the various cases mentioned in the Text. Having done so, one can suggest a hypothetical *ᶜilla* for a particular rule, and then go through the Text, all of the Koran and the *sunna*, to see if one can find other events that would be covered by the same *ᶜilla*. If these other cases all have the same *ḥukm*, then the *ᶜilla* is confirmed; if not, this cannot be the true *ᶜilla* for the first case either. For example, in the rule against selling dogs, mentioned above, we could have proposed an *ᶜilla* that it was just because it was a domestic animal that it could not be sold. We would then have to look through the *sunna* to see if we could find other cases where domestic animals were sold, and if this was allowed by the Prophet. We would easily find that this was the case: donkeys, camels and other domestic animals were reportedly sold without problem. So, the hypothetical *ᶜilla* 'domestic animal cannot be sold' is wrong.

Or, one could instead make a list of all possible *ᶜilla*s imaginable, and then cross them off, one after another, if they are unreasonable, improbable, or as above contradicted by other sources. Of those that remain the most probable is then selected. Clearly this is a recipe for problems: What is unreasonable, and what does 'most probable' mean? This method can give an answer, but it cannot be a truly *authoritative* answer, because it is based on logical and rational categories that other scholars can, and most often do, dispute.

There is a bewildering number of sub-methods for how one can exclude such potential *ᶜilla*s and reach the most plausible. If it is discovered that a case should be covered by the *ᶜilla* because it derives from a case that does, and this case does not share the *ḥukm*, then the *ᶜilla* is disproved. Or one can 'extend' the case, for example in the case of setting slaves free as a penance. We know there are cases in the Sharīᶜa where gender is important, as in testimonies at court or the distribution of inheritance, where women 'count as half'. Is the same true for freeing female slaves,

18 Hasan, 'Methods', 19-42.

so that twice as many must be freed? However, there are also many rules for slaves where no distinction is made between male and female slaves. By 'extending' the case concerning freeing female slaves to consider what is true for slaves generally, it can be found that gender can be excluded as an issue when the number of slaves to be freed as penance is concerned.

This exclusion method can only be used when there is general agreement that the *ᶜilla* is not a combination of different factors. If it is possible that there are several *ᶜilla*s at work, then it is logical that the exclusion method does not work.

The third main method for *istinbāṭ* is even more haphazard: One chooses the *ᶜilla* that seems most appropriate for the rule. It is up to the scholar what he thinks is 'appropriate', and there is much disagreement on whether this method is at all acceptable. What should the criteria for this be? One may be *maṣlaḥa*, the common good for the society, a concept which we shall address presently. Another may be the obvious connection between the proposed *ᶜilla* and the original case: Drunkenness is obviously connected to the consumption of wine. Or one may consider what is the divine motive that must be behind the rule, what is known as *maqāṣid* (which according to some is precisely the common good, the *maṣlaḥa*).[19]

Even more extreme is the possibility of simply looking at the different cases and considering what seems most similar. Again an example concerning slaves: There is no textual basis for what reaction is appropriate against someone who kills someone else's slave. However, there are two aspects of such a case that can apply: One is that the slave is an item of property which is alive; and can thus be compared to other living items of property, such as a horse; for which there is a textual basis. But a slave is not just an item of property, he is also a man, and focusing on that may make it more correct to base the punishment for killing a slave on the rules for killing a free man, which are well known. Since a simple comparison shows that a slave in his nature and status is more similar to a free man than to a horse, it is the latter option that is chosen: the general rules concerning manslaughter are the basis for the rules on killing slaves. This implies, of course, that

19 On *maqāṣid* and the 'intent' of the law (*maqṣūd*, *murād*), see Weiss, *Spirit of Islamic Law*, 54-58 & 80

one skips the process of locating the *ᶜilla* causative reason, it is a simple comparison of cases to find which is most similar. For many scholars this type of argument is therefore unacceptable. Others do accept it, provided that one can find some justification for the type of comparison used in a textual reference.

Many scholars reject several of these principles suggested to exclude potential *ᶜilla*s, such as the 'uncommon' being excluded from the 'common'. For example, what kind of liquids can be used for ritual ablutions if pure water is not at hand? Can vinegar be used, or broth? In some definitions, both of these must be grouped with water, they are liquid, and some rules that apply for water also apply for them. But there are also criteria for 'water' that do not apply to them: that it can be used for washing, that it is generally available in nature, that one can build a bridge over it. So, one cannot include vinegar or broths into the general category 'water'. We can thus exclude them as 'uncommon' from the 'common' definition of water, so they cannot be used for ablutions. This type of argumentation is based too much on logic for some scholars, who reject it as a basis for finding the *ᶜilla*—not so that they authorize the use of vinegar for ablution, but they believe other types of argument must be found, this type of logical conclusion cannot be put under the umbrella of *ᶜilla*.

Limitations in qiyās

Qiyās is also subject to other limitations.[20] It can only be used when other sources, the Koran, *sunna* or full consensus do not provide the rule. The *ᶜilla* must be based on an original text in the Revelation, a *qiyās* cannot be based on another *qiyās* (i.e., that a new, secondary, *ᶜilla* is constructed on the *farᶜ*, to justify extending the rule beyond the original *ᶜilla*).

The *ᶜilla* must be clearly apparent *(jālī)*, direct and reasonable. Criteria that cannot be observed, such as the actors' motives, cannot be used, because they are not apparent to the observer, and thus cannot be measured objectively.

'Direct' means that an *ᶜilla* must cover all instances of a case, not just one or some of them. One rule says that a traveller may interrupt the fast, because of the hardship fasting may cause when

20 Ahmad Hasan, 'The conditions of legal cause in Islamic jurisprudence', *Islamic Studies*, XX, 4, 1981, 303-10.

on travel. But the *ᶜilla* cannot be based only on the hardship. It is the act of travelling itself that is the 'effective cause' of the rule, so the rule allowing interruption of the fast must cover all cases of travel (beyond a certain length), whether or not it actually causes hardship in each case.

That the *ᶜilla* must be 'reasonable' means, to return to our example of the wine, that the issue of what kind of grapes have been used, or what district the wine was grown in, how strong it is or similar cannot have any influence. Those would all be 'unreasonable' attempts at explaining the rule, compared to the much more reasonable link with drunkenness. However, when other rules are under debate, it is quite possible that such more detailed criteria may turn out to be the 'effective cause'. It is thus not the criteria themselves, but the relevance for the rule that decides what is 'reasonable' or not.

Further, a suggested cause must not contradict 'stronger' reasons, and it must follow a principle that positive rules must have a positive *ᶜilla*, and negative rules a negative *ᶜilla*. By 'positive' and 'negative' are meant if the rule produces an effect or the absence of an effect. The 'absence of a sound mind' (madness) can be an *ᶜilla* for an 'absence of obligation' to honour contracts, for example. But it cannot be *ᶜilla* for a positive demand for a madman to perform some particular action.

How did the qiyās methodology arise?

So much for the technicalities; even if what we have described may make the head spin, we have only scratched the surface of the increasingly complex and detailed discussions of *ᶜilla*s and derivations in the legal literature. But, seen from the point of history, why did all this come about? What was the point?

Again, we return to Shāfiᶜī and his attempt to create an apparent compromise between the *ḥadīth* people and the practical jurists, based on revelation. His aim was to control the *raʾy*-based rules by creating links to the texts of the Revelation. *Qiyās* was the way to achieve this; it allowed bringing in legislation beyond what the Text actually directly said, while assuring that all such legislation was in fact based in a Text.

Thus the history of this relationship between *ḥadīth* and *raʾy* is a kind of endless serve and return. First, we had a law not particularly based in the Revelation texts. Then the reaction wanted to build the law on *ḥadīth* and Revelation. But this was so sparse that it left ample room for *raʾy*-based rules when the texts were silent. To get rid of this *raʾy*, or rather: to give these rules a basis in the Text, Shāfiʿī had to find a way to link rule (as practised) and Text. The answer was *qiyās*, the main point of which was that such a *qiyās* could only be done when the original case was found in the texts of the Revelation; the Koran or the *sunna*.

This allowed him to create new laws for new cases not established in a known Text, and having done this, to condemn all other practices as contradictory to the Islamic law. *Raʾy* was then redefined to no longer mean the *society*'s practice, as it was now inconceivable that the Muslim society could have any practice different from that of the Prophet. Instead, it came to mean private and personal opinions of ordinary individuals, opposed to these two rules which, however much they were formed through human intellectual endeavours, could still be linked to the Prophet and thus to Islam. In this manner, and making *qiyās* the method for producing new rules of law, Shāfiʿī had tamed *raʾy*.

Istiḥsān: to ignore a qiyās rule

However, this did not mean the end of the *raʾy* people. They accepted, willingly or not, the *qiyās* method, but still worked to expand the room for traditional *raʾy* without its name. One way was to reduce what *qiyās* actually meant; as we saw above, the Ḥanafī school, inheritors of the *raʾy* tradition, say that only the 'inferior' type of *qiyās* actually is *qiyās*. If the derived case is equal to (or 'stronger than') the original one mentioned in the Text, there was no need to bring in this whole machinery. It is perfectly evident that when wine is forbidden, then fermented grape-juice must be so as well, you don't need to write a thesis to see that. Thus, by reducing the space for *qiyās*, they could expand the room for directly 'rational' or jurist-based efforts, so it is no surprise that it is the Ḥanafīs who promote this way.

A more direct attack was developing the concept of *istiḥsān*, to 'seek the best'.[21] That means to ignore what *qiyās* would say if

21 Hallaq, *History of Islamic Legal Theories*, 107-11; Kamali, *Principles*,

that leads to results that are evidently unreasonable or have unforeseen negative consequences.[22] For instance, the rule that a thief should have his hand cut off. The text does not specify any exemptions from this, but it would be quite unreasonable to implement it in extreme cases, as when someone is dying from hunger.[23] Therefore, the rule is set aside in such cases. Similarly in the case of selling slaves. It is unreasonable that the general rule that slaves can be sold individually can be used to separate a mother from her child. Thus, the propagators of *istiḥsān* say, the rule concerning selling slaves cannot apply to a slave mother and child.

Also, it is of course forbidden for a Muslim to kill another innocent Muslim, in war as in peace. But what if the enemy drives captured Muslims in front of their army as shields? There is no *qiyās* to answer this, but one can by *istiḥsān* argue that if surrender would lead to greater hardship (casualties) for the Muslims, the rule text must cede. Less dramatically: No *qiyās* rule allows a man to see the naked body of a woman he is not related to. But it would cause greater harm for a woman if this were to prevent a doctor from curing her of an illness. So, *istiḥsān* says that the woman's welfare must override the rule text here.

A third example shows the adaptation rather than the waiving of a rule: When a man causes damage to someone else's cattle, he has to refund the value of the body part he damages. If he cuts the tail of a horse, he only has to reimburse the owner for the value of the tail, which is of course minimal. But there is an exception, established through *istiḥsān*. A mule is part of the 'uniform' of a working judge; he has to travel on a mule, no other animal. But he would be ridiculed if he went about on a mule with no tail. Such a mule would be without value for him, he would have to get a new one. So, if someone cuts off the tail of a judge's mule, he would have to reimburse the full animal, because the tail for him, but for no-one else, equals the full animal.

245-66, and Mohammad Fadel, '"*Istiḥsān* is nine-tenth of the law": The puzzling relationship of *uṣūl* to *furū*ᶜ in the Mālikī *madhhab*', in Weiss, *Studies in Islamic Legal Theory*, 161-76.

22 Hasan, 'Early modes', and Émile Tyan, 'Méthodologie et sources du droit en Islam (Istiḥsān, Istiṣlāḥ, Siyāsa šarᶜiyya)', *Studia Islamica*, X, 1959, 79-109.

23 See more in Chapter 14.

Istiḥsān can also be used to produce a new rule, but it is most commonly applied for adapting or restricting existing ones that are based on *qiyās*. It is only to be used on inter-human affairs, *muᶜāmalāt*, not on *ᶜibādāt* rituals.[24]

Istiḥsān can also be found inside an *ᶜilla*. The Text says that water from which a predatory animal has drunk is impure and cannot be used for ablutions. The same is true for predatory birds, by *qiyās*. But it has been established by *istiḥsān* that what causes the water to be impure is not that the animal drinks from it, but that the saliva on its tongue can become mixed with the water. This is not the case for a bird using its beak to drink, so water does not become impure through being touched by predatory birds. This sounds like an *ᶜilla* issue, but the techniques used in the argument are those of *istiḥsān*, not *qiyās*.

The basis for *istiḥsān* should be 'common practice', that is, what is considered fair. The 'common good', *maṣlaḥa*, can also justify *istiḥsān*, and we will discuss below what is actually a parallel method for circumventing *qiyās* rules. In theory, *istiḥsān* only refers to rules that are derived through *qiyās*, but in reality it is also used to make an exemption from rules based directly on the Text (as in the case of amputation, above).

This is thus a retort from the *raʾy* people against those who wish to base everything on *qiyās*, and it is accordingly controversial among the various traditions of law. It is particularly the Ḥanafīs who apply it, but the Ḥanbalīs also—surprisingly as they supposedly have their roots in strict *ḥadith* observance—accept and apply *istiḥsān*. However, those who identify with Shāfiᶜī are strongly opposed to the method. They can accept some of the amendments the Ḥanafīs have introduced, but they must then find other ways of justifying them, such as a more complex use of *qiyās* methodology, or accepting a *ḥadīth* text others find untrustworthy but which in some way links the amended rule to the Text.

The common good: istiṣlāḥ, maṣlaḥa and siyāsa sharᶜīya

Thus, the *istiḥsān* principle is particularly linked to the Ḥanafīs.

24 It is true in general for *qiyās*, some types of it should not be used for *ᶜibādāt*, but we have used here an example, taken from the books of theory, which clearly refers to *ᶜibādāt*, such as that concerning ritual ablutions.

The other tradition that is considered to grow out of locally practised law, the Mālikī school, has an almost identical principle, *istiṣlāḥ*.[25] This word comes from *maṣlaḥa*, which we have mentioned a couple of times as 'the common good' for the society, and *istiṣlāḥ* means to seek this social good.

We have seen it as a support for other types of legal argumentation. But it can also be considered as the carrying principle under the complete edifice of Islamic law. This was particularly elaborated by the Spanish scholar al-Shāṭibī, who died in Granada in 1388.[26] He is considered one of the most prominent medieval theorists of the law, and his works are still influential in modern legal debates. He tried to locate the divine *maqāṣid*, motives, behind the law. In this, he makes a strict demarcation between *muᶜāmalāt* and *ᶜibādāt*. As for man's relation to God, the Revelation is its own reason. These are eternal principles that God has laid down for the sole purpose of worship and need no further explanation, nor can they change with the times. But this is not the case for inter-human and social affairs. These rules were instigated by God for the good of humanity and the Muslim society. And since this society changes over time, then the rules must change with it, they cannot be eternal in their form.

That such ideas were formulated by a dominant legal scholar during those centuries that were supposedly frozen in immobile orthodoxy is significant in itself, and in fact shows how the legal scholars and the law were open to change. However, this more philosophical meaning of *maṣlaḥa* is not what is meant in the technical legal debate of the Mālikīs. They also use this concept more directly as a way to modify *qiyās*-based rules. This latter method is most often called *maṣlaḥa mursala*, 'free *maṣlaḥa*',

25 Ihsan A. Bagby, 'The issue of *maṣlaḥah* in classical Islamic legal theory', *International Journal of Islamic and Arabic Studies*, II, 2, 1985, 1-11; see also Yushau Sodiq, 'Malik's concept of *maslahah* (the consideration of the common good): a critical study of this method as a means of achieving the goals and purposes of Islamic Law', Ph.D., Temple University 1991, 1-161. The Mālikī tradition uses the concept of *istiḥsān*, but to a lesser degree; Delfina Serrano, 'Legal practice in an Andalusī-Maghribī source from the twelfth century CE: The *Madhāhib al-ḥukkām fī nawāzil al-aḥkām*', *Islamic Law and Society*, VII, 2, 2000, 205.

26 Muhammad Khalid Masud, *Shāṭibī's Philosophy of Islamic Law*, Islamabad 1995.

that is, independent from the Text.[27] The justification for introducing such rules are 'necessity', *ḥāja* or *ḍarūra*. An illustration is the mere act of collecting the Koran. The Koran itself does not say that it should be collected, nor is there any *qiyās* basis for its form, but it was necessary for the preservation and dissemination of the text that it be collected, and that was the justification for it. On this basis, the scholars developed more stringent legal principles for when and how this 'common good' should be introduced into the formulation of particular rules in conflict with or outside the rules that are based on the Texts. It is thus somewhat stricter in its form than *istiḥsān*, requiring 'need', but in the main these two principles cover much the same type of exemptions.

Siyāsa sharᶜīya

A third similar concept which is used often and in many different contexts, and which we shall discuss at length in the historical development, is *siyāsa sharᶜīya*. This translates as 'Sharīᶜa politics', to rule in agreement with the Sharīᶜa. It is thus linked to the political power and its relationship with the Sharīᶜa.[28]

But it also has a more technical meaning inside the legal methodology. It again has much the same meaning as *istiḥsān* and *istiṣlāḥ*, a way to make exemptions from *qiyās* rules. However, *siyāsa* is less specific than those two, and is not much used as a sole justification for a rule. Nevertheless, the concept has become central to modern reformers of Islamic law,[29] while the two other terms were more important in the classical period. It may have been influenced by the more general meaning of the concept that we shall meet later, applying the Sharīᶜa's 'spirit' without being bound by its text, which could then have been brought into the actual formulation of exemption rules in the Sharīᶜa itself.

Of the four schools, both the Shāfiᶜīs and the Ḥanafīs dislike using *siyāsa* as an independent principle in the formulation of

27 Hallaq is of the opinion that this concept was not much supported or used by other jurists, and that it was more of a philosophical justification than a way to create new rules; *History of Islamic Legal Theories*, 113.

28 Hasan, 'Early modes', and Tyan, 'Méthodologie et sources'. *Sharᶜī* is the adjectival form of Sharīᶜa, 'Sharīᶜa-ian', or 'what is related to the Revealed Law'.

29 See part 2 of this book and in particular Chapter 13 for more on this.

laws. The Mālikīs use it most frequently, but also some Ḥanbalīs accept it in this meaning.

Istidlāl, istiṣḥāb

In the books on legal theory, all these 'minor' or secondary principles, *istiḥsān*, *istiṣlāḥ*, and *siyāsa* are often grouped in a chapter on *istidlal*, 'to seek proof' or indications for a legal rule.[30] This term is thus normally used for all methods of *itjihād* outside of the major one, *qiyās*.

Another concept that does not concern the actual derivation of rules, as these do, but is a basic principle for both the formulation and the application of the rules in the courts, is *istiṣḥāb*, continuity.[31] This means that matters should continue as they are or in 'their natural state' unless there is a reason to change them. This is the justification for, for example, putting the burden of proof on the plaintiff in a case. If none of the parties in a dispute can present convincing proof, the court will rule in favour of what it considers to be the factual situation at the moment (the party which actually has control over a property will be considered the legal owner unless his opponent can prove otherwise), or what the judge considers to be the natural or expected state (that a good is in fact delivered according to the sales contract is 'the normal situation'; if the plaintiff claims that this did not happen, he must prove or justify this claim). The concept is particularly used by the Shāfiᶜīs, but is in principle applied by all schools, and is also the carrying principle behind many of the laws and legal rules they formulate.

The ᶜilla and ḥukm become the rule

When we look at this process from the text of the Revelation to the legal rule, we discover a surprising result. In its basic theory, what *qiyās* should mean is: First the scholar establishes what is actually the text of the Koran or the *ḥadīth*. Then, the matter

30 Hallaq, *History of Islamic Legal Theories,* 112.

31 Kamali, *Principles*, 297-309. For an example of this in a court case, see Anne K. Bang and Knut S. Vikør, 'A tale of three *shambas*: Shāfiᶜī-Ibāḍī legal cooperation in the Zanzibar Protectorate', *Sudanic Africa*, 10, 1999, 1-26 & 11, 2000, 1-24.

described in the verse or *ḥadīth* is categorized to belong to one of the three types of *ḥukm*, compulsory, forbidden, or neither (legally neutral). The rules go into details about how, when and under what conditions, but the central aspect is to carry out this categorization: A verse saying that a Muslim carrying out such-and-such an act will face eternal damnation means that the act belongs in the category 'forbidden'.

Next, when this raw material has been sorted out, the scholars expand the validity of each text by *qiyās*. This, as we saw, was a way to link practised law to the Revelation. It took the form of an analytical apparatus for extracting the 'causative reason', the *ᶜilla*, behind each rule in order to expand it to new, 'analogical' cases.

This was not only done when new problems occurred and the scholar wanted to find the answer in the Koran or *sunna*. Instead, *ᶜilla*s were produced for *all* legal rules that could be found in the Revelation. It became a generalized process, a part of the formulation of legal rules.[32]

But the nature of the process changed, in a way probably not foreseen or desired by Shāfiᶜī, and which the historians of the law seem not to have noticed. When we, in this model, start with a Text, then place it in the groups 'forbidden' or 'compulsory', and finally extract the *ᶜilla* which covers a larger category of cases, the *ᶜilla* becomes the rule. In our case, the Text was, '*khamr* is the work of Satan'. We placed it as 'forbidden', found the penalty (80 lashes), and extracted that what caused the rule was intoxication, and everything that leads to this has the same penalty.

So the rule then becomes: 'To consume any substance that causes intoxication is forbidden and is punished by 80 lashes'. This then is the *ᶜilla* (consume any substance…) and the *ḥukm* (forbidden). The original Text has disappeared, it is only relevant as a final justification and authority, but it does not express the rule: the *ᶜilla* and *ḥukm* are the rule.

Thus, it would seem that the aim of this whole process has become, if not circumvented, then at least hidden. The point was after all to make sure that the law was based on divine ordinances,

32 Scholars in *uṣūl al-fiqh* did not, however, conceive of this as a process of generalization; the extension of the *ḥukm* through the *ᶜilla* should be done only case by case, by looking at each potential new case and seeing if it fits the *ᶜilla*; Weiss, *Spirit of Islamic Law*, 68. The generalization of the rule is rather the effect of this practice of extension.

not human and insecure formulations of *ra'y*. The link to the Revelation is still there, in the final resort, but the rules themselves, as they are formulated in this system, are the result of purely human activity, based on a rational process of intellectual thought where the guideline is system and consequence, and where the space open for disagreement and divergence is just as great as in the *ra'y* that the system was designed to abolish.

5

GETTING SOCIAL SANCTION: *IJMĀ*ᶜ AND AUTHORIZATION

The various methods of *qiyās* and *istidlāl* allow the scholars to formulate legal rules on the basis of the Revelation. But there are so many different methods of *ijithād*, and so many ways to use them that they may produce any number of conflicting rules. They are all based on human effort, and allow doubt, discussion and disagreement. One jurist's rule can be rejected by another, who uses the methods in a different way, or finds opposing *ḥadīth* more trustworthy. Can this be what God meant for mankind?

Some scholars probably meant that it could not, and saw these disputes as the result of the corruption of this world and deviation from God's will. But most came to believe that this disagreement among the scholars was in fact a bounty, a gift from God. A variety of views among the scholars (*ikhtilāf*) was positive, not negative. This led to an expression (based on a *ḥadīth*) that '*kull mujtahid muṣīb*', 'anyone who performs *ijthād* is right'.[1] This means that when scholars, having used proper methods, arrive at different views, then there is no absolute right and no absolute wrong, only gradations, such that the scholars' activities to find the best answer among these views is praiseworthy whether the end result is one or the other.[2]

Commendable as such tolerance may be, it is difficult to

1 Many jurists disagreed with this statement, such as the well-known theoretician Shāṭibī. Disagreement is, he felt, a sign of human weakness, not divine bounty; Masud, *Shatibi's Philosophy of Law*, 245.

2 This is expressed in a famous *ḥadīth* that 'whoever does *ijtihād* may get a single or a double reward in Heaven. If he performs *ijtihād* to the best of his ability and makes a mistake, he will get a reward because of his effort. If he performs *ijtihād* and is right, he gets a double reward, once because of his *ijtihād* and once because he was right' (Burkhārī, 'Iᶜtisām' 20-1). (Thus, it is to be precise, not *ikthilāf* itself, but the acceptance of the results of *ijtihād* that is supported by this statement.) But there were also counter-*ḥadīth* of the type, 'my [the Prophet's] scholars will fall into 72 different groups, 71 of them will go to Hell [because they propose erroneous views] and only one will go to Heaven' (Tirmidhī, 'Imān' 18, alternatives in Abū Dāwūd, 'Sunna' 1 etc.).

practice law if all possible variant rules are potentially correct.[3] The religious scholars had already at an early stage defeated any attempt by the caliph to establish himself as a religious authority or 'pope'.[4] It may be that some early caliphs had envisaged themselves in such a role, and the proposal made by the poet Ibn al-Muqaffaᶜ (d. 756) that the caliph should establish a 'standardized' law for the empire may be seen in this light. But the proposal was not followed through and had no consequence.[5] Islam, at least in its Sunnī form, never acquired a unified religious authority, and was never made theologically subject to any state authority.

So how then could the legal rules elaborated through *ijtihād* be authorized and a choice be made between opposing variants? The answer was that it is the community of believers that determines which rule and which variant of it should be the guideline. This is the third stage on the way from revelation to law: consensus or *ijmāᶜ*: what 'some'—society in one form or another—agree is the right choice among the alternatives.

Ijmāᶜ

In many textbooks that present 'four sources of the law', *ijmāᶜ* is listed as the third of the four, before *qiyās*, because *ijmāᶜ* can be a source for irrefutably divine revelation, unlike *qiyās*, which is clearly a purely human activity and thus always open to error. The reason we discuss it here as the last element in the process for law formation is that *ijmāᶜ* as divine revelation is largely a symbolic, or at least not very productive element in the law. It is another, more mundane, but far more important meaning of

3 This was the main argument used against the the concept of *kull mujtahid muṣīb*: If every scholar is right, how can we say that what he arrived at is wrong? Such 'infallibilism' would undermine the reality of the law; Zysow, 'Economy of Certainty'; 459-83 and 'Muᶜtazilism and Māturīdism in Ḥanafī legal theory', in Weiss, *Studies in Islamic Legal Theory*, 235-65.

4 On the attempts at this, cf. Patricia Crone and Martin Hinds, *God's Caliph: Religious Authority in the First Centuries of Islam*, Cambridge 1986; also Christopher Melchert, 'Religious policies of the caliphs from al-Mutwakkil to al-Muqtadir, A.H. 232-295/A.D. 847-908', *Islamic Law and Society*, III, 3, 1996, 316-42. There is some disagreement as to what degree the caliphs really aimed for authority over religion.

5 The 'common' law was probably still too embryonic for this to have been possible in any case.

'consensus', that really is the key element in the process and thus gives a better understanding of what role the agreement of the community really played.

Thus we must be aware that the concept *ijmāᶜ* covers several fairly different meanings related to the production of law.[6] To simplify this, we may distinguish clearly between 'creative', or *ijtihādī* consensus, and 'confirming' or *naqlī* consensus.[7] The first is what can express divine revelation: the idea that when a total agreement—a full consensus—is reached among the Muslims on a rule, then that is in itself a proof of God's intention and is therefore, through the agreement, a sufficient proof that the rule must be correct. That is, that the consensus itself has created the rule.

The other type is much more limited, and only confers authority onto a rule that has been established through *ijtihād* in the manner described above, and ultimately based on a Text of the revelation. Such consensus is established when the scholars at some point agreed that this variant of the rule is the best one and the one that the Muslims must follow. This is what we will call confirmatory or *authorizing* consensus: That the community has united around this rule for the problem at hand and given authorization to this answer alone. This interpretation has thus become a 'positive' and the basis for a practised rule of law.

It is thus only the former type, the creative consensus, that is an expression of divine will and a 'source' for the law. But it is doubtful whether such a consensus has ever been established; it is certainly not a very active or practical principle. The confirmatory consensus is on the other hand not only active, but the culminating phase of any rule's way from revelation to law. We will therefore focus more on this process and how it affected the development of the law.[8] But, first, we will in this chapter discuss the principles behind the more exalted 'creative' consensus and the problems this idea of the community as an expression of divine will entailed when the scholars tried to show how it worked.

6 Ahmad Hasan, *The Doctrine of ijmāᶜ in Islam: A Study of the Juridical Principle of Consensus*, Islamabad 1984, and Devin J. Stewart, *Islamic Legal Orthodoxy: Twelver Shiite Responses to the Sunni Legal System*, Salt Lake City 1998, 37-45.

7 Abdel-Magid Turki, 'L'ijmâ' ummat al-mu'minîn entre la doctrine et l'histoire', *Studia Islamica*, LIX, 1984, 56-7.

8 Chapters 6 and 7.

The creative consensus

Consensus then means that 'society' in some form—all Muslims, or the scholars, or a selection of them—through their agreement establish that specific legal rules are part of God's law, the Sharīᶜa. Society confirms the law that God gave society.

That might not sound very paradoxical to a Western mind, as we are used to considering society in some form as the final legitimacy for the law. We saw in Chapter One that Islamic law in many ways resembles the Anglo-American common-law system, only that in the latter it is society through the judges, not God, that is the authority for the law. Now we see that in the practical elaboration of the law the difference is even smaller, as God here legitimates the law *through* society. (Or society through God, perhaps.)

But this is more problematical from an Islamic point of view, and particularly that of Shāfiᶜī and his followers who claimed that everything in the law should be based on God's revelation.[9] Particularly dubious was the idea that *ijmāᶜ* could be a source of law on its own, without any link to the established Revelation of the Koran and *sunna*. Consensus thus had to be integrated into the Revelation in some form, as a third expression of it beside the two Textual ones. But this was not logically evident: Why should mere agreement among humans express divine intention? Sunnī Islam very clearly states the distinction between man and the divine, and that revelation ended with Muḥammad; man is on his own after this. The Prophet was the last to communicate with the divine; so how can God continue to reveal laws through *ijmāᶜ*? The idea that God's community, the *umma*, incarnates His will goes far towards saying that the *umma* has taken over the Prophet's role as messenger, and this was a very problematic idea.

Nor are there are clear texts in the Koran or *sunna* that mention this concept that consensus equals revelation. There is, it is true, a well known *ḥadīth* saying that 'my community cannot agree on error', but that is an uncertain, *aḥād*, *ḥadīth*.[10] Shāfiᶜī

9 Hasan, *Doctrine of ijmāᶜ*, 36-71; Georges F. Hourani, 'The basis of authority of consensus in Sunnite Islam', *Studia Islamica*, XXI, 1964, 13-60, and Wael B. Hallaq, 'On the authoritativeness of Sunni consensus', *International Journal of Middle East Studies*, XVIII, 4, 1986, 427-54.

10 The legal historian Wael Hallaq on the other hand considers this a sound

did not refer to it,[11] so if he knew it, he could not have considered it relevant to the issue. It was often used by later theorists,[12] but was not considered sufficient evidence for all scholars.

The logically minded saw the problem. Some tried to explain the idea through *tawātur*, the idea that consensus expresses God's will is so widespread that it cannot be a lie. But that sounds like a fairly circular sort of argument since *tawātur* is itself a form of consensus.[13] A better idea was the suggestion that the general acceptance of the idea in the period shortly after the Prophet must mean that there had been a Text stating this, but which later had been lost. Without such a Text, the idea would never have been so accepted by the pious first generations. Still, this was not a very strong argument.

Most scholars therefore settled on a formulation that stresses 'practice'; or as Shāṭibī expressed it, that 'unity gives strength'. Even if individual practices do not confer great strength, we know that twigs break if you bend them one at a time, but bundled together they become unbreakable. The technical term for 'practice' was here formulated in a way that escaped becoming a circular argument, but it still sounded very much like 'it is this way because it is this way'; there is a consensus that consensus must be a source of law. However, these logical problems may

---

ḥadīth; *History of Islamic Legal Theories,* 75. It appears in the most common form in the collection of Ibn Māja ('Fitan', 8), and in another form in al-Tirmidhī ('Fitan', 7) and Ibn Ḥanbal (V, 145), but the context is then the union of the *umma* to one community, not the legal implication.

11 He did however use a similar formulation; 'we know that people cannot agree on something that contradicts the *sunna* or on a falsity'. This is thus just a logical conclusion on the idea of *tawātur*, the more people have knowledge about something, the less likely it is that they are all wrong; Hasan, *Doctrine of ijmāᶜ*, 39. Shaybānī (d. 804) used a similar *ḥadīth*, 'What the Muslims see as good is good in the eyes of God, and what the Muslims see as wrong is wrong in the eyes of God'. This is of course a much more vague formulation.

12 First used in a legal context by Aḥmad b. ᶜAlī Jaṣṣāṣ (d. 981); Hasan, *Doctrine of ijmāᶜ*, 50.

13 Another explanation that was often used was the assumption that since God could not have left the community in ignorance of His rule, there must be at least one scholar somewhere who had the right answer. If every scholar agreed, then that one scholar must be among them, and what they agreed on must represent God's intention; Zysow, 'Economy of Certainty', 202-10. The similarity to the Shīᶜī argument for *ijmāᶜ* (below, Chapter 7) is striking.

have been emphasized because of the resistance among many scholars to defining *ijmāᶜ* in such a way that it could actually function as an independent principle for the formulation of rules, as we shall see.

The growth of the idea

The concept of *ijmāᶜ* was thus controversial, and as such it of course entered into the general to-and-fro of the *raʾy-ḥadīth* debate. *Ijmāᶜ* is yet another of those *raʾy* concepts that Shāfiᶜī redefined to fit his own Revelation-based model. It originally meant 'what our society [where we live] agrees on', *ijmāᶜ ummatinā* was much the same as *sunnatinā*, 'our practice', what was common in our region, synonymous with *raʾy*. It was used partly to support *raʾ*y views by showing that it was not just the individual judge or scholar who held the opinion, but something the community in that place were united on.

Thus the early *ḥadīth* people did not favour the consensus idea much. Shāfiᶜī agreed with them to some extent, but the concept was so well established by his time that it was inconceivable to reject it outright. Instead he changed what it meant, and in such a way that it became virtually meaningless, or at least purely theoretical, so that it should not block his efforts of basing the law on the Koran and *sunna* alone.

However, this was one point where Shāfiᶜī did not win the day. His methodology eventually became the foundation for the methodology of all schools of law in most matters, as we have seen. Those who used to favour *raʾy* also accepted Shāfiᶜī's understanding of *qiyās* and his other concepts, with their own minor variations and elaboration. But on the issue of *ijmāᶜ* the 'orthodox' view has become less strict than that proposed by Shāfiᶜī. Thus, in this chapter we will have to make a distinction between Shāfiᶜī's ideas, which we will discuss at the end, and those of that became generally accepted by most of the scholars in classical Islam. However, this 'standard' view also contained many problems and engendered basic discussions.

How is ijmāᶜ established?

Among the issues that had to be clarified, was what 'consensus' actually meant. It has of course to do with 'agreement', but who are those who should agree? How many and what kind of people have to agree before we can call it a consensus, and how many may disagree before this consensus is broken? Clearly, widening the category that must agree and lowering the number of those who can disagree before the consensus disappears, makes it more difficult for a consensus to be reached and makes the concept less practical.

A basic issue was whether we are talking of *all* Muslims, lay and learned, or just those trained in the religious sciences, the scholars. In most cases 'all' would mean 'those who have knowledge about a matter', thus limited to the *ᶜulamā*ᵓ. But in this issue of divine sanction for a consensus, many felt that every believer, including those without learning, had to be involved. We shall see that Shāfiᶜī, whose conception was more complex, also included such ideas in his theories. However, the majority view came to be that only the scholars' views need be considered, those of the unlearned are not relevant.

What kind of scholars?

So, the criteria for inclusion in a consensus was knowledge and competence, but to what degree?[14] Are only those who have sufficient knowledge to perform *ijtihād*, who could formulate legal rules, to be included in a consensus? If so, it would be a fairly small group, and few scholars would argue this. However, what about piety? Should only the most god-fearing be included, or could a *mubtadi*ᶜ—someone who acts contrary to the Sharīᶜa—be included? That is, if a scholar, whose views are already suspect and is considered unorthodox, says that he alone disagrees with what everyone else agrees on, is that enough to block a consensus being formed?

The generally accepted view, which tends to lean far in widening the scope among the scholars, would say yes to this. One must count the view of a *mubtadi*ᶜ, assuming of course that he does not veer so far off-course that he is no longer considered a Muslim and a scholar; if he does, then his views are evidently irrelevant in any case.

14 Hasan, *Doctrine of ijmā*ᶜ, 83-7.

Local or global?

An issue arising from the historical development of the community, was whether a consensus can be regional or whether the whole Muslim world must be in on it. As we saw, the early views focused on the regional; in particular the Medinan people considered that the views they agreed on was the true measure of any consensus, as this was the original community of the Prophet; but the Kufans talked of a consensus among themselves. Some suggested this as a principle: Any Muslim society, as long as it is isolated from the others and cannot search the rest of the world, must be able to establish its own *ijmāᶜ* and the scholars there may use that as a basis for law.

Other later scholars differentiate in time as well as space, and talk of a consensus among the first four 'rightly-guided' caliphs. This view can of course only have been established later in the Abbasid period, when the concept of *al-khulafāᵓ al-rāshidūn* developed.

The general view rejected all these limitations, and agreed that an *ijmāᶜ* must unite the complete *umma*, all of the Muslim world, not just one single region.

How many must agree?

So then, how many of these people? What is the limit before we can say that the group 'agrees'? There are three or four possible answers to this, each supported by some scholars.

One view was fairly marginal, but still had some supporters: that 'consensus' meant 'majority'. If more scholars agreed than disagreed, then a consensus was formed. Today this has become a very popular view, as the idea of *ijmāᶜ* can then be used for democratically elected assemblies that operate on the majority principle; one could just replace 'the competent [scholars]' with 'the competent [delegates]' and say *ijmāᶜ* instead of 'majority vote', and hey presto, the parliament becomes an Islamic institution.[15] However, this was less considered in the classical period, for fairly obvious reasons. The scholars the world over never met at any assembly point where a show of hands could determine who had the majority. It would always be difficult or

15 Cf. Aharon Layish, 'The contribution of the modernists to the secularization of Islamic law', *Middle Eastern Studies*, XIV, 1978, 265-6.

impossible to establish which view had more in favour than against.

This is also why *ijmāᶜ* has no relation to the other modern meaning of 'consensus': to sit down and find a compromise that everyone can accept but where no-one gets exactly what he wants. The development of practicable laws inevitably does imply some trend towards conformity, but when the exalted state of *ijmāᶜ* as expression of the divine will is at stake, a rule must either have or not have this status; it cannot be the result of bickering and compromise.

A milder version of the majority view is what we can call the 'overwhelming plurality', or *tawātur*. This is a term we have met already as 'what is so widely known and accepted by so many pious and righteous people that they cannot all be wrong'. Thus, it is a matter of majority, and a view may be considered to have *tawātur* even if a small minority does not subscribe to it. Such an overwhelming majority view is easier to locate than a purely mathematical one. Thus, many equate the two and say that *ijmāᶜ* is the same as *tawātur*.

The opposite position is to say that everyone in the designated category, without a single exception, must agree before a view can be considered *ijmāᶜ*—a tall order. But among those who favour this there are also those who try to make it a bit more applicable, by saying that a tiny group of dissidents cannot be enough to block a consensus, it must be seen to exist if only two or three people disagree.

However, the most generally accepted view is also here the strictest one: Even if a single individual in the consensus group (that is, all scholars throughout the world) disagrees, then there is no *ijmāᶜ*. Clearly, that makes it very difficult indeed to apply this principle in new cases if there is any controversy or debate about it at all. The person who brings up the controversy then becomes the individual who blocks the consensus. This means that the principle is most useful as a kind of formal authorization of a view that is already established and is so obvious to all that it is not subject to legal discussion.

A positive or negative agreement?

How, then, are the scholars to make their views known? Must the agreement be stated in so many words by each scholar, they each say 'I agree'; or is a 'silent' (*sukūt*) agreement acceptable, that is that an *ijmā*ᶜ is established if no-one has expressly said they disagree?[16]

Only the latter viewpoint is of course practicable. If one has to get all Muslim scholars all over the world to state explicitly that they agree to a viewpoint that is so uncontroversial that not one of them will dissent, then it will occur very rarely if ever. However, this was in fact precisely what Shāfiᶜī, for one, claimed. A silent *ijmā*ᶜ has no value, he said, only positive and expressed support can give certain knowledge of what the community supports. This is, from his side, another nail in the coffin of the whole idea of *ijmā*ᶜ as an independent principle.

The standard view has been to accept silent assent. But the question leads to another, which turned out to be the most controversial and debated issue, that of time: *when* can you say that an *ijmā*ᶜ has been established among the scholars?

Waiting time

It is fairly obvious that *ijmā*ᶜ could not be confirmed by getting all scholars of the world together in one place and having them all agree simultaneously on the point in question, at least if the process was to have any meaning after the passing of the first generation in Medina. How, then, could it be known that all scholars had agreed, openly or tacitly, on a point of view?[17]

This was not a problem for those who demanded a positively stated acceptance from each scholar. But as we have noted, this fairly impracticable idea was not shared by the majority. However, even those who accept the absence of disagreement (silent approval) had to acknowledge that the scholars to be included in the consensus must at least know that the issue was under discussion, otherwise, how could they agree or disagree on it?

Thus, it was stated that there had to be a 'waiting time' from the moment someone formulated a statement 'I believe there is a consensus on so-and-so', until that consensus could be said to be established. The most commonly accepted period was one generation, that is to say, the existence of such a consensus could

16 Hasan, *Doctrine of ijmā*ᶜ, 111-18.
17 Hasan, *Doctrine of ijmā*ᶜ, 93-101, 135-46, and Turki, 'L'Ijmâ'', 63.

only be accepted when the generation of scholars who were alive at the time the statement was made had all passed away. As long as any one of that generation was alive, there was the possibility that he would say that he disagreed with the statement, and thus broke the consensus. Ibn Ḥanbal is one of the most famous scholars who demanded such a waiting time of a generation.

However, the normal view was the opposite, there is no waiting time. The consensus exists the moment it is established that there is no active disagreement in a particular issue.

The problem with the waiting time was, why should this particular generation be so special? What about the scholars who were educated and formed their opinions during this generation of waiting? They were of course free to express their own point of view on the issue as long as the *ijmā*ᶜ had not been established, and their viewpoints could then be different from this 'consensus in waiting'. So, the consensus could be broken in this waiting period. Why should then the first generation, those who happened to live at the particular moment the statement was made, have the privilege of say-so on whether an *ijmā*ᶜ existed at that time? On the other hand, if one did accept the viewpoints of the new scholars of the second generation, then one had, under the same principle, to wait until that second generation was dead to see if any of them in fact would express a disagreement, during which time a third generation would join the ranks, and so on indefinitely.

It could be answered to this that what one was waiting for was to see if there existed an *ijmā*ᶜ at the particular moment the statement was made. Since an *ijmā*ᶜ was eternal and unchanging, it is enough to establish that it exists however momentarily for it to be an expression of divine revelation, and if it did, then any later scholars who disagreed with it had to be wrong and opposing the Revelation. The waiting period is only there for us to make sure that the consensus was actually there at that first moment. However, this line of reasoning for a waiting period did not succeed.

*Can there be an ijmā*ᶜ *when there was disagreement earlier?*

Another issue was whether the views of earlier scholars who had passed away mattered. When we say ' all scholars', do we mean 'all scholars alive today' or 'all who live and have lived'? Many jurists believed the latter had to be right, and that one could thus not make an *ijmāᶜ* on an issue which had been a topic of discussion before: Any debate must necessarily end when it has been established either that everyone agrees on a viewpoint, or that not everyone agrees on it. If everyone does agree, then the issue is closed, there was *ijmāᶜ* at that point and it cannot be discussed further. If everyone did not agree, then there can be no *ijmāᶜ* because not all scholars we know of (including those of the earlier times) agree; and dead people cannot change their minds.

Again, the problem was whether one particular generation, the current one, should have any special rights over others, here over earlier generations of scholars. The community of Muslims had to mean all those who had embraced Islam, past and present, you cannot say 'all Muslims' and then disregard those who were Muslims in previous generations.

Other scholars, however, said that each epoch had its own answers, and it was fully conceivable that a later generation could acquire greater knowledge of an issue and on the basis of that reach a consensus on an issue that had been unclear before; a relevant *ḥadīth* that had not been known could appear and be generally acknowledged, or some other development might clarify the issue. If so, and everyone agreed this to be the case, then the earlier lack of knowledge could not block the establishment of a consensus around this improved understanding of the issue.

There were also those who did not accept the premise of the problem; an issue could in fact have been debated without any clear conclusion being drawn, thus neither 'agreement' or 'disagreement' was apparent. This was particularly the case when you considered the issue of 'silent approval'; the period may have passed without it being certain whether a consensus had been reached or not. However, these agreed that if it was positively accepted that there was *disagreement*, then the case was closed and blocked later consensus.

Clearly, these were not just theoretical issues, they concerned to what degree a continuous development of the law was permitted. Many theoreticians would accept that a later generation could revoke an earlier disagreement and thus use *ijmāᶜ* as a way to justify later development of the law. However, the majority did not accept this. They stuck to the view that once a disagreement becomes visible, it is eternal and cannot be replaced by a later consensus. This is again a viewpoint that limits the practical use of *ijmāᶜ* as an active and independent principle for the formulation of new legal rules.

Ijmāᶜ and the revealed Texts

These debates all revolved around what kind of agreement must be reached before it can acquire the status of *ijmāᶜ*. The other main issue was, what can an *ijmāᶜ* be about?[18] Can a properly established *ijmāᶜ* create law in any type of issue, disregarding any other source? Or must *ijmāᶜ*, as *qiyās*, have some basis in the revealed Texts, the Koran and *sunna*? This is a crucial issue, because if the *ijmāᶜ* can only treat issues already discussed in the Texts, then it is no longer an independent source of law, only a way to elaborate the Texts, just as *qiyās*.

This is Shāfiᶜī's main point, naturally enough given his interest that everything in the Sharīᶜa must be based on the Text in one or another. Here the majority of scholars largely agreed with his views. They say that an *ijmāᶜ* must have 'indubitable indication' (*dalāla*) in the Texts. This does not mean that it can only discuss matters expressly stated, *ijmāᶜ* is not just a commentary. The 'indication' does not need to be more than that a verse or a *ḥadīth* gives a general authorization for what the consensus establishes (thus the verse 'We want ease for you, not hardship' can be an 'indication' for any sort of easing of the Muslims' duties established by *ijmāᶜ*). Still, it does mean a limitation of the issues that can be treated, and goes a part of the way in seeing *ijmāᶜ* as a confirmatory rather than an independent legal principle.

One variant of this question, brought up by some scholars, is the matter of whether an *ijmāᶜ* can be based directly on a Text, or whether a consensus must refer to a *qiyās* rule and confirm this as correct and valid. This distinction between a consensus based on the Text or based on *qiyās* is not mentioned by Shāfiᶜī, and is probably of a later date, perhaps as a way to accommodate Shāfiᶜī's more restrictive view. This is actually a way to justify what we have called 'confirmatory consensus' theoretically, as *ijmāᶜ* in this view is not an independent source of law at all, only

18 Hasan, *Doctrine of ijmāᶜ*, 120-33.

a method to raise the status of a *qiyās* conclusion by saying that there is an *ijmāᶜ* around it.

Can an ijmāᶜ be abrogated?

As *ijmāᶜ*, however it is conceived, is seen is a source of Revelation in the same way as the Koran and *sunna*, it must be clarified whether it can be abrogated, like those two sources. The answer is an emphatic no.[19] No *ijmāᶜ* can be set aside or reversed by a later *ijmāᶜ*. In fact, nor can an *ijmāᶜ* be abrogated by a verse in the Koran or by the *sunna*. Unlike those two sources, an *ijmāᶜ* is eternal the moment it is established, it cannot be recalled by a later revelation.

This is logical, if an *ijmāᶜ* is actually grounded in some way in a Text of the Koran and *sunna*. The concept of *ijmāᶜ* is only conceivable after the death of the Prophet. He was himself the source and expression of God's revelation as long as he was alive. It is only after his passing that it is meaningful to talk of the consensus of his community not including him.

But the process of abrogation of the Koran and *sunna* did of course also end at the moment of his death, as these came about through revelations to him. Thus, a verse or a *sunna* cannot replace a consensus: The Koran was complete and all *sunna*s of the Prophet already existed before the first *ijmāᶜ* could have occurred. If an *ijmāᶜ* could conflict with an already established *ḥadīth*, that would mean that the *ijmāᶜ* is wrong, which is impossible. Further, a (later) *ijmāᶜ* cannot abrogate a *ḥadīth*, because the *ijmāᶜ* is itself based on Text. Thus, it is in that case the Text behind the *ijmāᶜ* that abrogates the *ḥadīth*, not the *ijmāᶜ* itself.

Clearly then, these conclusions, which are based on the 'creative' *ijmāᶜ*'s double status as both true Revelation and something that must be grounded in another Revelation, makes consensus appear to be more rigid and frozen than the Koran itself. This is of course an exercise in logic, not law, as it is normally fairly easy to find someone who actually opposed whichever *ijmāᶜ* one does not like, and thus to claim it never reached the status of divine revelation.

19 Hasan, *Doctrine of ijmāᶜ*, 148-61.

Shāfiᶜī's model

Here and there, we have referred to Shāfiᶜī's viewpoints. As mentioned, he had his own and more complex model which differs from the views that came to be generally accepted, and which reduces the role of the creative *ijmāᶜ* to virtually nothing. He does this by placing it in a wider argumentation.[20]

All knowledge is, he says, of two kinds: either general (*ᶜāmm*) or particular (*khāṣṣ*). By general he means 'what no adult and sane person does not know', obvious things that a Muslim does not need any special training or education to learn. That could be because it is mentioned in a Text everybody knows, or because 'everyone has told everyone'. Such knowledge can refer to the basics of Islam: that Muslims must pray, that the Koran is the word of God, that Muḥammad is his messenger; or things of nature; that rain is made of water and that apples fall downwards. *Ijmāᶜ* is possible in such issues.

The particular refers to more specialized knowledge on *how* Muslims should pray, for example on horseback, or what to do with the apples in an exchange between two kinds of them, or the rights and duties of Muḥammad's successor, the caliph. These are matters that normal people need not concern themselves with, it is the scholars' job to discuss and find solutions to them and inform the rest of the Muslims. This is a duty that is laid upon the scholars and a responsibility they cannot shirk. *Ijmāᶜ* is not possible in such matters, because all such issues are open to uncertainty and error, and *ijmāᶜ* does not allow for the possibility of error.

In other words, in Shāfiᶜī's concept of *ijmāᶜ* the divine element of revelation is virtually absent. He only accepts it as a way to confirm a Text or a practice that is so widespread that it cannot be subject to debate. In no other issue can *ijmāᶜ* come to bear, and thus it cannot be a productive source of law. Thus, Shāfiᶜī is in favour of *ijmāᶜ* in such a way that he is in fact opposed to it.[21]

20 Norman Calder, 'Ikhtilâf and ijmâᶜ in Shâfiᶜî's Risâla', *Studia Islamica*, lviii, 1983, 55-81.

21 Even if he actually uses *ijmāᶜ* in some of the examples in his book of theory, the *Risāla*. But he does not make an issue of the fact that this contradicts the theory he has set up.

Of these two categories of knowledge, the general is, as we say, based either on a Text or not. It is only knowledge based on a Text and confirmed by *ijmāᶜ ᶜāmm* that is evident and infallible. General knowledge not based on a Text is the basis for particular, *khāṣṣ*, knowledge where error can be possible; it is the scholars' duty to evaluate and reach a conclusion on that.

That is necessary, because such knowledge that is not based on a Text has a lower status than knowledge based on the divine Revelation. But it is the scholars who have the duty to take care of the Text; so they must also have the duty to take care of other general knowledge, as the latter cannot be above (be considered more certain than) the Revelation. On the other hand, being a human affair of the scholars, it cannot be infallible, because the scholars are fallible. So, as it is in the final analysis the scholars who are also responsible for this general knowledge, *ijmāᶜ*—which in its nature must give infallible and certain knowledge—cannot in fact refer to such general knowledge unless it is based on a Text.

The end result of Shāfiᶜī's model is that *ijmāᶜ ijtihādī,* the creative consensus as expression of God's revelation and a source of law, mostly disappears. What is left is confirmatory consensus, which is a way to establish how the scholars agree that a Text should be interpreted and what legal rules, formulated on the Revelation through *ijtihād*, are the best ones and the ones that Muslims should abide by.

PART II: THE APPLICATION OF THE LAW

6

THE FOUR SCHOOLS OF LAW

So the creative consensus was of little practical use. The other kind, however, the confirmatory or *naqlī* variant, was all the more fundamental as a way to make rules into law. If the scholars could not reach total agreement on new principles of law as real divine Revelation, they could at least agree on which among the rules that had been formulated through some form of *ijtihād* were those that the society should apply as law.

However, even this more limited agreement turned out to be ephemeral. Instead of reaching complete agreement across the empire for such rules, the scholars split, as we have seen earlier, into several—mainly four—parallel legal traditions that we call 'schools of law' or *madhhab*s. The four, named after the four early juridical authorities, Abū Ḥanīfa, Mālik, Shāfiᶜī and Ibn Ḥanbal, agree on the basic guidelines, but differ in many issues of detail.[1] They are tolerant towards each other, and are mostly separated geographically. We indicated their regions in Chapter One: the Mālikīs in the west, the Ḥanafīs in the north and east, and the Shāfiᶜīs in the south-east. That, however, is how they are distributed today. All schools originated in the central areas of the caliphate, in Iraq with Kufa and Baghdad, in Medina or in Egypt and North Africa; and all the founders came from those regions.

Putting the law in writing

The early period of the law was marked, as we remember, by the debate between the *ahl al-raʾy* and the *ahl al-ḥadīth*; those who gave advice based on what was commonly used and logical against those who related what the Prophet and the early generations had done. Having said that, we must emphasize that these

1 See the introduction in Chapter 1.

are simplified categories to aid our understanding, not fixed groupings that rejected the other's viewpoints totally. Those known as *raʾy* people also related *ḥadīth*, some even to a large extent, and many *ḥadīth* people must surely have accepted that 'what Muslims do now' must often be the correct way. The difference between the two categories of scholars was rather in what emphasis they put on one or the other principle.

There were also some differences in how they transmitted their knowledge, which to some extent made the two appear as different branches of science. Those whose main interest was the legal issues in contemporary society met for scholarly debates. Such an 'exchange of opinions', *munāẓara*, could be polemical and confrontational, the aim was to prove that one's own views were correct and the opponent wrong.[2] The method would be to point out illogical elements of the opposing argument or provide authorities that supported one's own viewpoints, as such authorities became generally accepted. Thus those who participated in these debates were specialized and trained lawyers.

Those who favoured *ḥadīth* disapproved of these confrontational debates. They met instead at something they called *mudhākara*, 'gathering of memories', where they exchanged *ḥadīth*. Rather than discussing whether a *ḥadīth* was 'better' or 'more correct', they used these meetings to accumulate *ḥadīth* or variants adding to those they already knew. Eventually they almost became competitions in knowing as many *ḥadīth* and *d*s as possible, as such became known. If two scholars disagreed about whether a *ḥadīth* was sufficiently trustworthy to 'count' and be related, the participants would put the issue to a third scholar who decided.[3] Thus it was not so much a competition in who was right, as in who knew the most Traditions, and these *mudhākara* gatherings worked in effect as a machine to spread as many *ḥadīth* as possible. Hundreds of thousands of Traditions were eventually tabled and could be used by these specialized *ḥadīth* relaters.

As time went on, the relaters started to put greater emphasis on quality in addition to quantity, and in particular as some started to put the *ḥadīth* together in edited collections. The oldest

2 George Makdisi, *The Rise of Colleges: Institutions of Learning in Islam and the West*, Edinburgh 1981, 128-52.

3 Melchert, *Formation*, 1-31.

of these works were not pure *ḥadīth* collections, but included such alongside stories of what other early and later Muslims have done, down to and including the collector's time and perhaps even his own legal evaluations. There are several such 'mixed' *ḥadīth* collections linked to the early jurists, such as the *Muwaṭṭāʾ* of Mālik b. Anas (d. 795), and the *Āthār* of the Ḥanafī Abū Yūsuf (d. 798), but also later collections sharing the title *Muṣannaf*, as those of ᶜAbd al-Razzāq al-Ṣanᶜānī (d. 827) and Ibn Abī Shayba (d. 849) were of this type.[4] About half a century later this genre had become more specialized into pure *ḥadīth* collections, such as those in the classical or 'orthodox' collections from Bukhārī (d. 870) to Nasāʾī (d. 915).[5]

The legal *munāẓara* debates were also put into writing, works which discussed legal problems and gave authoritative answers to them began to appear, with or without polemical attacks on opposing views. It is not clear how 'stable' the contents of these works were in the first period and whether it is correct to call them 'books'. This is probably because the religious sciences, among them law, went through a slow metamorphosis from an oral to a written form during these two first centuries of Islam.

At the first stage, from the late seventh into the eighth century, all transmission of knowledge was oral. Many of the early scholars disapproved of writing down what they knew; they considered this demeaning of the message, only what was stored in memory was truly known.[6] This is probably a continuation of the classical Arabic tradition of oral transmission. It was only in the mid-eighth century that the first teachers started to write down

4 Motzki, *Origins*, 51-2. All the four 'founders' of the schools have *ḥadīth* collections ascribed to them, but those purported to be by Abū Ḥanīfa and Shāfiᶜī, both called *Musnad*, are clearly from a much later period; Ṣiddīqī, *Ḥadīth Literature*, 73. Aḥmad b. Ḥanbal's *Musnad* is far better known and is a 'pure' *ḥadīth* collection, but was actually compiled by his son ᶜAbd Allāh (d. 903), about the same time as the works of Bukhārī and Muslim; Ṣiddīqī, *Ḥadīth Literature*, 83-4, and Melchert, *Formation*, 138-9.

5 On these, see above, Chapter 3.

6 An expression of this is a *ḥadīth* on the caliph ᶜUmar, who supposedly said 'If I could burn all books of law, I would have done so'. This is often taken to mean a defence of pure divine *ḥadīth* against human *fiqh*, but is—apart from the fact that there were hardly any books of *fiqh* during ᶜUmar's lifetime—more probably formulated as an attack on equating knowledge with writing.

the *ḥadīth*, or other types of knowledge they taught, into private 'notebooks' of whatever material they used at the time.[7] They still taught them orally, and the students were not allowed to see what the teacher had written—perhaps the teacher did not even let on that he had recourse to writing and only used his notes to refresh his memory before going to his lecture of the day. However, we can now see that there was greater consistency in their teaching; the early students of a teacher and those who studied with him late in life received and transmitted the same stories with little or no variation, indicating that the stories were no longer only related from memory. Perhaps the first teacher to exhibit such consistency was Ibn Shihāb al-Zuhrī (d. 742), one of the teachers of Mālik.[8] However, we do not know if his contemporaries accepted the soundness of this idea of putting knowledge in writing.

It must have been late in the same century, slightly before 800, that some teachers appeared not just to use these notebooks on a day-to-day basis, but started to collect them and organize their notes systematically by topic or in some other way, using this as the basis for their teaching schedule. Thus, we get what we may call the first structured 'books', although these were still only actually seen by the teacher himself, and were perhaps no more than an organized pile of papyrus sheets.

The students for their part wrote down what the teachers related onto tables of various material for memorization, and perhaps also on more enduring materials so they could refer to them later. These, then, became sources for their own notebooks to be taught to their own students. Thus, minor variations could appear between what one student wrote down and later taught and what his colleagues had written down from the same teacher. The basic story would be the same, but the order and wordings may

7 Gregor Schoeler, 'Die Frage der schriftlichen oder mündlichen Überlieferung der Wissenschaften im frühen Islam', *Der Islam*, LXII, 2, 1985, 201-30, 'Weiteres zur Frage der schriftlichen oder mündlichen Überlieferung der Wissenschaften im Islam', *ibid*, LXVI, 1, 1989, 38-67, 'Mündliche Thora und Ḥadīṯ: Überlieferung, Schreibverbot, Redaktion', *ibid*, LXVI, 2, 1989, 213-51 and 'Schreiben und Veröffentlichen. Zu Verwendung und Funktion der Schrift in den ersten islamischen Jahrhunderten', *ibid*, LXIX, 1, 1992, 1-43.

8 Harald Motzki, 'Der Fiqh des -Zuhrī: die Quellenproblematik', *Der Islam*, LXVIII, 1, 1991, 1-44.

have differed. Thus, what is recognizable as the 'same book' from the original teacher could have many variants or 'receptions' (*riwāyāt*) from different students, or from their students again, until the moment the written version became fixed.

Exactly how long this transitional period of half oral, half written transmission lasted is not known, but it is probable that sometime between 850 and 900 direct written transmission started to become acceptable, such that students were allowed to copy directly from their teachers' written notes, with the oral transmission only supporting this. It was then that the books became 'frozen in time' and acquired a fairly fixed and stable form, bar later copying errors or conscious editing. As long as the texts were still fairly fluid and mainly oral in form, and were of course still part of the on-going polemics between different viewpoints and currents, it was of course conceivable that 'supporting arguments' could be added, in particular by including *ḥadīth* that proved the chosen viewpoint. Modern historians are not agreed on how far such manipulation actually took place, but it is at least evident that the students edited these 'books' differently in spite of them sharing the same title and having the same 'author', the original teacher. The material is organized differently, and some *riwayāt* were probably more condensed and others more complete versions of what had actually been taught by the original scholar.[9]

This process of editing seems to have stopped at the end of the ninth century. This development of more stable versions of the text is also connected to a development of perceived authority, where the 'master's words' gained greater emphasis and the precise wording of what he, not those before and after, had said, became more and more important.

9 It is probably possible to advance knowledge of this process by comparing different *riwāyāt* of the same book as more fragments or complete mss of such are being discovered. We are, however, not yet in a position to give definitive answers. Important works in this directions are those of Miklos Muranyi, *Materialien zur malikitischen Rechtsliteratur*, Wiesbaden 1984, *Ein altes Fragment medinensischer Jurizprudenz aus Qairawān: Aus dem Kitāb al-Ḥağğ des ᶜAbd al-ᶜAzīz b. ᶜAbd Allāh b. Abī Salama al-Māğišūn (st. 164/780-81)*, Stuttgart 1985 and *Beiträge zur Geschichte der Ḥadīṯ- und Rechtsgelehrsamkeit der Mālikiyya in Nordafrika bis zum 5. Jh. d.H.: Bio-bibliographische Notizen aus der Moscheebibliotheek von Qairawān*, Wiesbaden 1997.

The schools

The development of these groups from different and complementary forms of knowledge and teaching to rival opinions of how the law was to be found is described in Chapter Two. We saw there that some views were linked to certain names of prominent scholars in Kufa, the intellectual centre in Iraq before Baghdad's domination, and others to Medina, the city of the Prophet.

Ḥanafīya

The first period was thus mostly marked by open 'currents' of scholars who shared some, but not necessarily all viewpoints in various cases, but with no particular authority structure beyond a general respect for the more learned. These were thus not yet 'schools'. The internal cohesion and loyalty of these currents became stronger as time went on, but it is only when we reach the tenth century that we can really call them 'schools of law' as fully formed legal systems with a recognized common structure and authority, and only a century later does the idea appear that every jurist must belong to one and only one school of law; that these have become mutually exclusive identities.[10]

However, when we read the biographical literature, we will often find that earlier scholars have been placed in this or that group; he was a 'Ḥanafī scholar', we read, or 'a Shāfiᶜī'. This is the result of post-dating by the biographers, who always wish to 'structure' their objects more than the people themselves would have recognized; this is seen clearly when different biographers put the same scholar in different and competing currents.[11]

Thus it is impossible to establish any clear boundaries of who was and was not, at any time in the ninth century, part of what

10 Wael B. Hallaq has found the idea that a judge must stick to only one school from c. 1050, but it was then not yet dominant; *Authority, Continuity, and Change in Islamic Law*, Cambridge 2001, 79. *Muftīs* and theoretical jurists had extensive liberty to refer to other schools far later than this.

11 Heinz Halm, *Die Ausbreitung der šāfiᶜitischen Rechtsschule von den Anfängen bis zum 8./14. Jahrhundert*, Wiesbaden 1974, 49-50. The same goes for theological currents, where later biographers tend to overly structure the early scholars into groups and currents they perhaps had never heard of.

later became known as the Ḥanafī school.[12] However, there were some jurists in Kufa, Baghdad and elsewhere who shared views on a number of issues and thus often supported each other in the debates, although they also disagreed on many occasions. This loose grouping, which we discussed in Chapter Two, included Abū Ḥanīfa and his younger colleagues Abū Yūsuf and Shaybānī. One of the things that seems to characterize them was that they put greater emphasis on rational systems, human logic, as an independent basis for legal discussion. This can even be seen after the 'Traditionalizing' of the methodology that took place when Shāfiᶜī's views became generally accepted, in that logical but also formalistic and formulaic reasoning is a typical feature of the Ḥanafī school today.

'Rationality' in early Islam is often linked to the Muᶜtazila, a theological current that emphasized that God is just in a way that humans can comprehend, opposed to those who said God could not be bound by anything but his own principles. This opposition was used by an Abbasid caliph, Maᵓmūn (d. 833) in an attempt to control the independent scholars. He demanded that they express agreement with one of the more esoteric views that the Muᶜtazila proposed. This was called the *miḥna*, and lasted from 833 until 851-2, when the then caliph gave up the effort.[13]

The most prominent of the scholars considered to be of Abū Ḥanīfa's group followed a strict neutrality in this conflict, which was partly between scholars, partly between the scholars and the caliph. Some of them, however, came out as strong supporters of the *miḥna*. Nevertheless, the Ḥanafī name is mostly linked to an opposing theological current, the Murjiᶜa, which favoured neutrality and tolerance in these religio-political disputes. Of course, as these legal positions were no more than vague currents of thought, there was no particular reason they should share a theological stance.[14]

12 Melchert, *Formation*, 48-67.

13 That is, a new caliph less keen on the idea, came to power; Melchert, 'Religious policies', 316-42. The issue that was tested was whether the Koran was 'created in time' by God rather than 'uncreated'.

14 It is also possible that a person may be considered a 'Ḥanafī' purely out of personal bonds of loyalty that need not be linked to agreement in issues of law; several of them were thus closer to the conception of e.g. Sufyān al-Thawrī (cf. Chapter 7), whose views were shared by many Kufans. Such 'semi-Ḥanafīs' may then later have been uncritically considered to be part

Still, it appears that the 'Kufa people' were slightly better represented among the jurists that were close to the caliph in this period. The Murjiᶜī viewpoints were also viewed favourably at court, as were of course those who supported the *miḥna*. However, the Mālikī current is also often described as close to the caliph or supported by him. Thus, there were no fixed links, and it would probably vary as to which scholars as well as which ideas and currents the caliphs or the court would favour at any particular time. But it is no surprise that these two currents, which in the early period were the two most closely attached to following 'established practice', were the ones most often mentioned as being close to the people in power.[15]

The 'Kufa people' were not restricted to Kufa, they can be found in Basra, in Egypt and in Khurasan in the east. It was, however, in Baghdad that the polemics between the *ḥadīth* and *raʾy* people were sharpest. This was a matter for the empire's centre.

The open and unstructured form of this Kufa current was thus maintained throughout the ninth century. Clearer structures started to appear after 900. At that time, books commenting on the classical Ḥanafī works, those of Shaybānī and Abū Yūsuf, began to appear. Abū Ḥanīfa himself is not said to have written anything (in his day, this was not yet done), but his viewpoints were passed on by his students. It is a particular feature of the Ḥanafī school that all these three have the status of 'founder' of the school, although it is named after only Abū Ḥanīfa. However, the three did not necessarily agree, there are in fact very few rules where all three have voiced the same opinion. Thus, Abū Ḥanīfa is not really the final authority in his school. The general view is that if he agrees with one of the two others, that is the authority,

---

of the Ḥanafī school; Nurit Tsafrir, 'The beginnings of the Ḥanafī school in Isfahan', *Islamic Law and Society* V, 1, 1998, 1-21.

15 It might perhaps be imagined that Shāfiᶜī's project, which we earlier (Chapter 2) said was well adapted to the centralizing policies of the Abbasids, being based on the wish for a unified, *ḥadīth*-based law for all Muslims, would have been closer to the court. But the Shāfiᶜīs did not formulate their current until later when the actual schools of law arose, and they were probably not themselves conscious of the political consequences that we in retrospect can see from their views. This was an issue of historical processes, not of conspiracies or funded research.

but there are cases where the school follows the view of one of the others against that of Abū Ḥanīfa.[16]

There also grew, alongside the development of a literature of commentaries, a need to fix these writings into a more coherent structure with a specific identity. We see that each scholar's identity and loyalty becomes stronger and clearer, the biographers do not waver any longer between who is or is not a Ḥanafī. Some people become known as the 'leaders' of the current, dominant judges or jurists who are considered the 'heads' of the schools in each town, a status that can be passed on. The first scholar that can clearly be seen as a leader amongst those who have thus been transformed from a vague current to an actual 'school of law', the Ḥanafī school, is Abū 'l-Ḥasan al-Karkhī, who died in Baghdad in 952.[17] We can also see nascent Ḥanafī groupings in Egypt and Tunisia, but the central areas for the current are Iraq with Baghdad as well as Khurasan.

The Ḥanafī current had at this time adapted itself to the post-Shāfiᶜī compromise: the process of 'Traditionalization' was at an end and it was generally accepted that rules that had earlier been based on practice must be grounded, as far as possible, in *ḥadīth* and Koran. The school had also been 'centred' in other ways: Sunnism had become the common theological framework for the community, so belonging to currents such as Murjiᶜa or Muᶜtazila became deviations. The honoured founders could not be associated with such, so it became increasingly clear that Abū Ḥanīfa had never had any contact with either of these currents.

Mālikīya

Another group that developed some views in common grew up in Medina and Egypt, probably around 800. They were later linked to Mālik b. Anas of Medina (d. 795). He was without doubt the most prominent figure in this group, but did not have the total authority in the first generation after his death as he was to acquire later.[18]

16 Hallaq, 'From regional to personal schools', 8-9 and *Authority*, 112. The Ḥanafīs have formulated the idea that Abū Ḥanīfa is primarily to be followed in issues of *ᶜibādāt* (ritual), the other two in various areas of *muᶜāmalāt*.

17 Melchert, *Formation*, 116-36.

18 Brockopp, *Early Mālikī Law*, and 'Comparing theories'.

However, this group took the name of its founder before the other currents in the legal debate started using personal names.[19] They were probably already known as the 'followers of Mālik' in the first half of the ninth century, although they were still only a loose grouping of scholars at this time. This use of Mālik's name appears first in Egypt, not in his own town Medina.[20] Why in particular they came to name their group after one scholar rather than a region or the content of their views, has been discussed by later historians. Some speculate that it may be because the Muslims were still a fairly small minority in Egypt; the Christians dominated for another century or more. This may have led the various Muslim groups to become more focused and search for a common, personified identity. Other reasons may be the greater geographic spread of this group; there were probably more of the 'Medina people' outside Hijaz than in that region. This may have led them to move more quickly to a personified identity that the Kufa/Ḥanafī group.

The hagiographical literature relates that Mālik was supposed to have been close to both the caliph Hārūn al-Rashīd and his son Maʾmūn, who supposedly made the Mālikīya the caliphate's school of law. However, he is said to have been in conflict with the local governor who ordered him to be whipped for disobedience so that he lost the strength of one or both arms for the rest of his life.[21] All of this is probably anecdotal, no current of law was sufficiently focused at this time to have been authorized as a 'school of the state'. This is of course the same Maʾmūn who introduced the detested *miḥna*, a fact that these anecdotes tend to skip over. It is only a century later that the Mālikīs of that time start finding favour at the court.

That this current started to use the name 'Mālikī' fairly early on did not mean that they had a much clearer internal authority structure than the Ḥanafīs of the same period. It is said in Shāfiʿī's biography that he was killed by 'furious Mālikī supporters' in 820 in old Cairo, where this current was in majority, because Shāfiʿī had complained to the governor over one of their

19 And not the Shāfiʿīya, as Schacht says; Schacht, *Introduction*, 58.

20 Melchert, *Formation*, 156-77.

21 Mansour, *Maliki School of Law*, 13-14; cf. also various biographies of Mālik.

fellows.[22] However, this is also anecdotal, and it is hard to know if the 'Mālikīs' of that early period yet knew that this was what they were. Again, later biographers may have added loyalties that did not yet have this form.

In any case, this grouping or current died out in Egypt, as does the one in Medina; we find no-one that we can identify as part of a 'Mālikī' trend in Medina after 850. It is further west that the current reforms and grows, in Tunisia and in particular in Spain; but also in the east in Iraq. Both of these clearly use the name of Mālik as a banner and certainly share a common basis, but over time the western and eastern branches tend to move apart somewhat, so that late in the ninth century we may talk of two different Mālikī branches, one in Iraq, and one in Spain and North Africa.[23]

The eastern branch died out in the early eleventh century, as the structuring and the geographical distribution of the schools was reaching a final stage. Thus the Mālikīs that we later find in Egypt, Iraq and elsewhere descend from the western branch, not from the early eastern branch. It was in Spain and the Maghreb that the Mālikīya grew from a loose current to a coherent school.

These two regions were linked across Gibraltar, but there were some differences that may have had an effect on the school. In Spain, the Mālikīs were supported by the local rulers and did to some degree gain the status of 'official' legal viewpoint there.[24] This was then a fairly coherent and politically independent region separated by a great distance from the centre, while the other schools grew in a more divisive and polemical surrounding, shaped by the continuous *munāẓara* confrontations. This may have caused some differences in how the Mālikīs and Ḥanafīs tend to legitimize their viewpoints in their legal works: The Ḥanafīs tend to argue their case through logic and polemic, while the Mālikīs tend to be more direct and authoritative: this is the answer, period. The mature Mālikī school also tends to give their founder, Mālik, greater final authority than the eponymous founders have in the other schools.

North Africa was marked by religio-political conflict throughout the period of the school's formation, from the Ibāḍī/

22 Melchert, 'Formation' (Ph.D. version, Univ. of Pennsylvania 1992), 137.
23 Melchert, *Formation*, 177.
24 Melchert, *Formation*, 159-62.

Khārijī states of the eighth and ninth centuries and in particular the Shīᶜī Fatimids who took control of Tunisia from 909. This must have been the period when much of the detail of the law was being worked out, and it is probable that opposition to the Shīᶜī views influenced this, at least in forming a closer identity among the Sunnī scholars. This may also have caused the school to argue from a point of collective authority.

Thus, the Mālikī development shows a slightly different pattern from the polemics that we can see behind the other, Baghdad-based schools. But communications were still working, and even distant Spain was aware of the great debates of the day. *Ḥadīth* supporters came there, and the Mālikīs went through the same process of 'Traditionaliziation' as the Ḥanafīs in the east, linking each legal rule to a *ḥadīth* or Koran whenever that could be done.[25]

Shāfiᶜīya

These were the two schools of law that grew out of the *raʾy* tendencies. The other two major schools are slightly younger in origin. Shāfiᶜī was himself most concerned with the theoretical aspects of law, not in the collection and discussion of specific rules of law as we find in other law-books from that time, so the 'Shāfiᶜī' school grew later.

Shāfiᶜī worked initially in Iraq, the Hijaz and Yemen, but then left for Egypt. It is generally said that he changed his views on many matters from the 'old' view of his time in the East, to the 'new' one in Egypt, where he was influenced by the group that came to be known as the Mālikīs. His death, however, was as mentioned said to have been at the hands of a group of Mālikī adherents. He does not seem to have had any specific group of followers himself, so there was no collective current of law dating from him.[26]

Biographical data show that a more or less coherent and structured group of scholars who referred to Shāfiᶜī grew up about a century after his death. Their centre was in Iraq and the first clear leader of the group was Abū 'l-ᶜAbbās Ibn Surayj, who

25 Maribel Fierro, 'The introduction of ḥadīth in al-Andalus (2nd/8th–3rd/9th centuries)', *Der Islam*, LXVI, 1, 1989, 68-93.

26 Melchert, *Formation*, 68-86. This is in contrast to Schacht's view, he says that Shāfiᶜī did found a school in Egypt.

died in 918.[27] From this period we start to see clear transmission of leadership from teacher to student in this group. Ibn Surayj is also the first scholar to write an abbreviated collection of rules of law practised by his school, a *mukhtaṣar*. Such commentaries or compendia are the hallmarks of the reality of what we may call a 'school' of law.

These Shāfiᶜīs based much of their legal material on Egyptian jurists who had studied with Shāfiᶜī, in particular Ismāᶜīl al-Muzanī (d. 878), but this was not developed into a coherent system before the Iraqis went to work in the early tenth century. They did of course use the methodological principles laid down by Shāfiᶜī himself, and those rules that Shāfiᶜī had included in his *Risāla* and other works (two or three other books of law are ascribed to him).

This Ibn Surayj, the actual founder of the Shāfiᶜī school, was, incidentally, a student of a judge who belonged to the older, 'eastern' Mālikī school in Iraq. It is not inconceivable that there was some connection between these eastern Mālikīs and the Shāfiᶜīs in their applied rules of law, or at least that the latter were closer to these Mālikī than to the Ḥanafīs in many matters. However, the methodology and the actual rules are still so distinct that we cannot draw more than a possible vague line of ancestry between the eastern Mālikīs and the new Shāfiᶜī school.

Ḥanbalīya

Aḥmad b. Ḥanbal (d. 855) was the youngest of the four 'founders' of the schools, as is the school that took his name. This school appears to have developed about a century after the other three. In fact, it is ironic that there should be a 'Ḥanbalī' school at all, since Ibn Ḥanbal was against *fiqh* in general.[28] He is said to have expressed legal opinions, but primarily by referring to *ḥadīth* only. There are no law-books ascribed to him, only his famous collection of *ḥadīth*, the *Musnad*, which was most probably compiled by his son, ᶜAbd Allāh. Ibn Ḥanbal was highly respected

27 Melchert, *Formation*, 185-221.

28 Melchert, *Formation*, 87-115; Susan A. Spectorsky, 'Aḥmad ibn Ḥanbal's fiqh', *Journal of the American Oriental Society*, CII, 3, 1982, 461-5; Ziauddin Ahmad, 'Al-Musnad min masāᵓil Aḥmad b. Ḥanbal—An important Ḥanbali work', *Islamic Studies*, XX, 2, 1981, 97-110, and Hurvitz, 'Schools of law'.

because of his opposition to the *miḥna*, and is said to be one of those most severely persecuted by it. He was a rallying figure for the Traditionists, those who wanted to build only on *ḥadīth* and who had become a religio-political party supported by the majority of the people of Baghdad and normally in opposition to the caliph. They were so strong that on a number of occasions they could force the caliph to back down.

It is possible that it is this renown that caused Ibn Ḥanbal's name to be given to a school of law. As the other currents in law were solidifying in the course of the tenth century, the Traditionists had to follow suit, and were transformed from pure *ḥadīth* transmitters to jurists. This transition is linked to the name of Abū Bakr al-Khallāl who died in 923; about the same time as the other 'real' founders of the schools such as Ibn Surayj and al-Karkhī. He was the first who started to collect legal opinions, and not just *ḥadīth*, that were ascribed to Ibn Ḥanbal.

Khallāl was also an innovator in that he wrote a biographical encyclopedia of those who transmitted *ḥadīth* and views from Ibn Ḥanbal, that is, defined the 'members' of the nascent school. None of the other schools had done so at that time. This was of course influenced by the *rijāl* lists of *ḥadīth* scholars, where critical biographies were a growth sector at this time.

Many of the scholars in the Traditionist current disapproved of these innovations of Khallāl.[29] Many stuck to the sole transmission of sound *ḥadīth* as an acceptable activity, with no legal conclusions outside the text being expressed authoritatively. But Khallāl and those close to them started to apply the methodological principles formulated by the Shāfiᶜīs, which became the school the Ḥanbalīs felt closest to, and from then the Ḥanbalī school began to develop parallel to the other three. They might express a stronger opposition to *ra'y* in methodology, but many such disputes show the Ḥanbalīs join the other two schools in opposing the Shāfiᶜīs.

The Ḥanbalī view may in some matters be more 'strict' than those of the other schools, closer to the Text of the Koran and *sunna*, but this is far from always the case, there is no systematic division between the schools in this. The four schools do not line

29 Melchert, *Formation*, 149-52. The leader of this group was Abū Muḥammad al-Barbahārī (d. 941).

up on a continuum from 'liberal' to 'strict': any one or more of them may agree with or differ from any of the others, varying from matter to matter. A systematic comparison may reveal some logic in how the schools' viewpoints are distributed, for example in their origin in the *raʾy-ḥadīth* debate. But this can seldom be seen in their stance on each individual rule, and never without careful scrutiny. Thus, none of the schools are either 'harsher' or 'less dogmatic' than any of the others.

Khallāl himself did not actually leave a coherent school behind, in spite of his innovations in that direction. It took some time before the group coalesced into a current with a clear identity, judges regularly linked to them and structured teacher/student transmission. This process was probably complete only towards the end of the eleventh century. Thus it is only around 1000 that we can really say that we have four cohesive schools of law, almost two centuries after the death of Shāfiʿī.

The geographical distribution of the schools

The process had not then yet made these schools into four *exclusive* groups that each scholar had to belong to. It was still possible for a while to belong to schools beyond the four, as we shall see in the next chapter, or not belong to any particular school at all.

In this period, the schools spread out in different directions. The Mālikī school already had a region of its own in the West, while matters were less settled in the East. The Ḥanafī and Shāfiʿī schools were both strong, and we also occasionally find judges who were known as Ḥanbalīs or of one of the smaller schools. We can get a picture of how these identities spread and became more cohesive by looking at who was made chief judges in the central towns and cities over this period.[30]

We cannot see a clear structure before the mid-tenth century, but from then a pattern starts to emerge. Iran had an early dominance of Ḥanafī judges in towns like Nisabur and Isfahan, but they were soon replaced by Shāfiʿīs who came to dominate this area. In the capital, Baghdad, roughly every other judge was Ḥanafī and Shāfiʿī, but the Ḥanafīs took over more and more

30 Halm, *Ausbreitung*, 23 and *passim*. Cf. also Tsafrir, 'Beginnings of the Ḥanafī school', 1-21.

from around 1120, at a time when Turkic dynasties mostly had control of Baghdad. However, Basra, the port city in the south, went the other way. Here the Shāfiᶜīs came to dominate, and the same happened in Mosul in the north. Still, Ḥanafīs were the dominant school in Iraq as a whole throughout the Middle Ages. Jerusalem, then under Damascus, was straight Shāfiᶜī. Egypt was divided, as it is today; the Mālikīs were already in dominance in the south, however the north was mostly Ḥanafī before the Fatimids took power in 969. There were also Shāfiᶜīs there, and as we shall see, they strengthened their position under the Fatimids and came out as the dominant school once the Sunnīs were back in power.

These identities were mainly those of the scholars. However, we can see that *maddhab* identity also had a wider social reality. Several towns of Iraq and Iran were hit by riots between 'Shāfiᶜīs' and 'Ḥanafīs', or at least groups that are described as such in the chronicles; thus Rayy in Iraq in the 1140s (where Shīᶜīs were a third party to the conflict) and Isfahan in 1160 and 1180.[31] These groups were based in different sections of their towns, and it is probable that the fighting was based on other and more socially pressing conflicts. But the identity of the schools of law was apparently now so clear that it was possible to use them to describe the parties in these urban rebellions.

Four consensuses

Thus, we have four schools which differ in methodology and positive rules of law. Why did this happen? And why exactly four schools, why not two or ten? This cannot be answered positively. There were more than four in the eleventh century, and later we may perhaps better speak of 'three and a half', as the Ḥanbalīya was always smaller in number than the other three; nevertheless, it was considered one of the major schools, the 'four', throughout its history.

We may perhaps see the growth of four schools as a result of a balance between *fusionary* and *fissionary* tendencies in the history of the law.

31 Halm, *Ausbreitung*, 135 & 148.

That which divides

The most obvious thing that drove scholars apart was the early struggle over *raʾy* and *ḥadīth*. This was just one of the many philosophical and theological debates that scholars participated in and which influenced law, and which could cause dissension.

Another factor is geography. There were in a sense two types of arena for the debates between the legal scholars in this early period. One was the new Abbasid capital in Baghdad and its surroundings in Iraq. These were places where scholars with different views met and discussed face to face, as it were, and formed groups and loyalties with those who shared opinions, on *raʾy* versus *ḥadīth* or other controversial topics.

Another arena was the provinces, which each had their own tradition and background. Spain, for instance, was an enormous distance from the centre of the Empire. The caliph and the court had little chance to control the details of what went on there, even before Spain pulled free in the late eighth century. And even if the rulers in Córdoba considered themselves part of a unified *umma* it was from that time politically independent.[32]

These two arenas differ in importance over time. The early debates were mostly focused in the centre, in Baghdad and the other major cities nearby. Later the geographical factor became more important, as we move into the period when the schools were consolidated. As each school came to dominate in different parts of the world, they moved apart. This was probably a continuous process, not only between the schools but also within them. We consider for example the 'Ḥanafīs' as one unified school, but there are probably many both minor and major differences in how the Ḥanafīs of Sarajevo and those of Karachi or Calcutta view any particular rule.[33]

32 It has also been suggested that social geography has had an impact on the content of the various schools' views, e.g. that the liberal Ḥanafī views on *dhimmīs* and on a woman's right to choose a partner were coloured by the social background of Persian clients and recently settled rural immigrants in Kufa, where this school grew, as opposed to the views of the Maliki school that was formed further west; Aharon Layish, personal communication.

33 Cf. e.g. Baber Johansen, 'Coutumes locales et coutumes universelles aux sources des règles juridiques en droit musulman hanéfite', *Annales islamologiques,* XXVII, 1993, 29-35 (and in *Contingency,* 163-71). Aron Zysow's major study of Ḥanafī *uṣūl al-fiqh*, 'Economy of Certainty',

However, this does not contradict the basic reciprocal tolerance of this system. It was not heresy to belong to another school of law, nor were the relations between the *madhhab*s sectarian in the way they can be between Sunnīs and Shīᶜīs. The view was not, as in the latter case, that the other side is *wrong*, but rather that 'we do things this way, and you do them that way', and it was always praiseworthy to stay informed of other schools' law, even if it was not allowed to draw their viewpoints into one's one school.[34]

Thus, these various *madhhab*s had the sense that they did belong to one community, the Sunnīs, whichever school they belonged to. This was then formulated as an acceptance of *ikhtilāf*, differences of view that were equal before God. What the jurists are doing is *ijtihād*, human and fallible activity; the eternal knowledge of right and wrong belongs to God alone. The jurist does as much as humanly possible, and he—and those who follow his authority—may believe that his views are better than the alternatives, but he cannot claim a stamp of approval from God. Thus all legal opinions end with the words *wa-Allāh aᶜlam*, 'but God knows best'. All we can do is within the realm of supposition.

That which unites

The most important cohesive factor is the need to make law workable. If all legal discussion consisted of only two levels—on the one the absolutely indisputable words of the Revelation that need no explanation and on the other each individual scholar's fallible *ijtihād*—then the law could never have worked. Any case in court could then have degenerated into a dispute between scholars and lawyers of equal status and with equal claim to the correct answer.

So if the law was to be practicable it would have to give

---

focuses on the differences of opinion between the Ḥanafīs in Central Asia (Samarqand) and those of Baghdad throughout the classical period, and shows that differences within the schools could be as great or greater than those between them.

34 There were, as we have earlier said in this chapter, exceptions from this when struggles between adherents of different schools did lead to riots, but this seems to be limited mostly to the early period, and it may have reflected deeper social contradiction.

society some norms that were commonly accepted, something the members of the society knew in advance would be applicable beyond the individual opinions of any particular scholar. But the scholars had successfully blocked attempts from the caliphs and any secular authority to decide what the communal norms should be. This was clearly placed in the hands of the *ᶜulamāᵓ*, the 'heirs of the Prophet'. But as long as these too did not have any internal authority structures that could settle disputes, no pope or council of superior scholars to literally lay down the law, that did not help much.

Therefore, the scholars had to develop something that could fill this function. The need for this must have grown apparent in step with the increased sophistication of the legal works. By the ninth century it was clear that the *umma* needed a common law, not regional practices, and this was developed through *qiyās* and the other methods we have discussed. Then the answer to the authorization of the particular rules was found in the concept of *ijmāᶜ*, the consensus among the scholars.

These were all unifying tendencies, in particular legitimation through *ijmāᶜ*. But consensus was still not terribly practical as long as one single scholar was enough to break the required consensus, and perhaps one should wait a generation anyway. *Ijmāᶜ* was of little use in this technical and 'pure' form. So, another existing and well known method appeared as a better option: to point at an existing, but dead, authority who had greater knowledge than we do now in these dismal days and who everyone should recognize as their superior. If he said that this rule is better than the alternative, then that is it and we should follow him.

This idea had already been in force in the early period of the ninth century, when Mālik, Abū Ḥanīfa and the others were used by individual scholars or local groups to support their views in polemics against opponents, in particular between *raᵓy* and *ḥadīth*. Now, as the jurists all came to accept a Shāfiᶜī-inspired 'Traditionalized' methodology, they focused less on the early scholars' *raᵓy*-based statements than on their choice among the rules established by analogy and selection of *ḥadīth*. Ideally, that choice should have been made by the consensus of all Muslim scholars, but the opponents of *raᵓy* had set the margins for *ijmāᶜ* so narrowly that this was impractical or impossible. Thus all scholars paradoxically had to accept the method of referring to dead individuals—actually a defence mechanism to promote the *raʾy* of particular groups—to make the *ḥadīth* and *qiyās*-based law a living reality.

This was one of the reasons why the schools of law grew in the name of these purported 'founders'. The need for a more stable legitimacy grew from a need to support one's own opinions on the basis of a recognized scholar, into a situation where these persons became the ultimate source of authority. What had been loose teacher/student relationships became institutionalized and acquired stable internal structures of leadership and an increasingly clear boundary to the 'outside'. And in pace with the solidification of the currents into 'schools of law', the names and status of founders became more central.

In a sense, what happened was that 'authority grew backwards'. The 'four great lawyers' were originally not just four, nor were they so much greater than their contemporaries. But as time went on, their superiority loomed larger and larger. They were increasingly viewed as not only being vastly more learned than any other in their own time and later, but even in comparison to those who came before them. While the 'real' Mālik and Abū Ḥanīfa clearly saw themselves as students and transmitters from eminent scholars among their predecessors, later perceptions tended to play down or ignore any such history. They were 'liberated' from those that had gone before them and stood alone as starting points for the legal development, owing nothing to earlier scholarship.[35]

This had two types of effect. It was evidently useful in promoting one's own eponymous founder, and thus one's own school, over the competitors. Raising the independent status of Mālik made it all the more clear that his view must be better than those of Shāfiʿī, his 'student' (according to Mālikī views), while inversely, Shāfiʿī's outstanding command of the Arabic language clearly shows that the interpretations that originate with him must be better (according to his school).

But more important is perhaps the effect it had *within* the school. As the status and authority of the early founders goes up, that of those who follow, and thus the current generation, falls in

35 Hallaq, *Authority*, 25. Cf. also Chapter 8.

equal measure. If Mālik had been only a good jurist who based himself on *ḥadīth*, then an ᶜAlī from the fifteenth century could probably sit himself down and make an equally good law based on the same or more *ḥadīth*. But if Mālik was an almost supernatural genius who uniquely established what was right and wrong, with or without recourse to *ḥadīth*, then it would be all the more difficult for latter-day scholars to oppose this and suggest their own interpretation in contrast to what Mālik had said.

Thus the inflation of the founder's authority and personal status had the effect of stabilizing the law into what was recognized as 'Mālik's view'.[36] In essence, the higher the status of the founder, the more practicable the law that the school was to unite around.

Ijmāᶜ within the school

With this point reached, confirmatory *ijmāᶜ* had thus been limited to mean a consensus *within* the school. A rule of law is considered operational and binding within a group, a school of law, if there is *ijmāᶜ* among the scholars in this school around that rule. The views of scholars in the other schools or groups are no longer considered; the law is defined strictly within the confines of the school. Instead of the polemics between the schools, the jurists started a more practical work on how to refine and delimit the actual system of rules of the school, in order to seek *ijmāᶜ* around them.

Thus this concept has changed its meaning. An *ijmāᶜ* within a school, a limited body of scholars, can of course no longer be an expression of divine revelation; everyone would agree that the scholars of the other schools were also part of the Prophet's community. Thus the debate about 'one single dissenting voice' and so on became irrelevant, the object was no longer to define strict criteria for revelation, but to find a workable solution for the society and the school. So the concept came to mean quite simply what a clear majority of scholars in the school agreed on. When such a pragmatic *ijmāᶜ* is achieved around a rule it becomes a practicable rule of law, and those who are to judge on the basis of

36 It is not by chance that we use Mālik as an example, this process is much clearer in the Mālikī school than in the others, but the same process took place in all four schools.

the school are bound to follow it. Thus a workable solution was achieved, which also gave some leeway for variation in so far as there were real divergences of opinion within the school on some minor points.

We thus got four different systems of law, parallel and fairly similar in their actual rules, but still separate and each a total and unitary system of law with its own methodology: As we have seen, the Shāfiᶜīs do not accept *istiḥsān*, while the Ḥanafīs do and the Mālikīs develop their own, parallel conception. Each school has its own detailed formulation of the law, and its own defining authority, *ijmāᶜ*, within the school. Thus we can talk of a Ḥanafī law, a Mālikī law and so on as separate law systems. Logically, this led to the establishment of parallel legal institutions, separate judges and courts for Ḥanafī law and Shāfiᶜī law and so on. So the Islamic law has become four different laws—or more, as we shall see, but certainly not less than four. Not all schools are practised everywhere, but as Muslims travelled to foreign lands, their *madhhab*s travelled with them, and eventually there were followers of different *madhhab*s in most larger towns of the Muslim world. Perhaps only Morocco and the margins of the world (south of the Sahara, east of India, north of the Caspian) remained as 'pure' regions where only one school was present.

What the dates mean

The chronology we have described here varies from that found in older history books, by placing the schools as 'actually founded' about one or two centuries later than was earlier believed. So what? Does it matter whether this happened in 800 or 950? Either way it is more than a millennium ago. However, this is of major importance when we are trying to look at the *reasons* why this happened, attempting to make an historical analysis that places this development in the context of wider changes in the Islamic world.

The development of Abbasid rule had led to a centralization of the empire focused on the person of the caliph, which required that there was a common law for all regions. However, the resistance of the scholars had kept the political institutions—the state and caliph—outside the process of the development of the law itself. The formulation of the law had been liberated from the state and was uniquely the task of the independent scholars, in spite of the problems this caused for finding an authority to establish one particular set of rules as those the society had to follow.[37]

These problems would have been avoided if the scholars had allowed the caliph, who after all was the leader of the community of Muslims, the *amīr* of the believers, to be not only the *executor* of the law but also the final *arbiter* of its content. Instead, the scholars had to build up the cumbersome system of consensus among the scholars, which is so imprecise that the end result is not one, but four different laws, in glaring contrast to the idea of one God, one community, one law. Why ever create such trouble for oneself?

One answer may point to the ideas behind the law. This was God's law, and haphazard rulers, iniquitous as they may be, cannot have any precedence in deciding what God meant. Only knowledge, not political power, can determine that. The process can also be seen as the result of a power struggle in Muslim society, where the scholars can win over the caliph in this area. If we follow the traditional historiography that the formulation of the law and division into four schools was basically over by 800, when Abbasid power was at its peak, then both of these are reasonable answers, although each would lead to new questions.

However, if we postpone this development and say that these processes of forming four separate schools only took place two centuries later, then we get a different and much more logical view. Because in those two centuries came the end of the caliphate. The Abbasids' power and cohesion had already started to decline in the late ninth century, and by 935 they had even lost control of Baghdad to local governors.[38] The empire was from that time only a collection of independent governorates and Shīᶜī sectarian dynasties, later replaced by a rapid succession of local sultans that ruled over smaller or larger parts of the world, in

37 One could already then discern the problems that the separation of the law from the state could mean for the *implementation* of it in a judicial system, as we shall see later.

38 The caliphate existed as a formality until 1258, but after 935 independent sultans ignored the caliph and built their own petty states in the various provinces, including Baghdad. The caliph had neither political or religious authority, so we cannot consider the caliphate as a historical reality after 935. Thus disappeared any hope for a political unity of the Islamic world.

periods seldom exceeding more than a couple of generations.

Thus this period is far from characterized by any stable, common state power that the law could rely on. So it became even more important to keep the legal development away from these local political rulers. To allow one of these sultans—even a Sunnī sultan—any determining role in the development of the law that was now being formulated would mean that the law was only valid within the area that this particular sultan controlled. That would mean splitting the law up along the borders of petty states that were ever changing and short-lived.

Thus the process of establishing an authority to legitimize the actual detailed law of Islam fell to the class of scholars, as a natural result of the political state of affairs in what we may call the Islamic Middle Ages, the 'sultanic period' from the fall of the caliphate in the mid-tenth century to the rise of the Ottomans in the early sixteenth. It becomes part of what may be called an 'ideological homogenization in the face of political heterogenization'. As political unity disappeared, ideological unity became paramount.

Thus the free-roaming debate of the *munāẓara*s of the early period had to be reined in or come to a close, and hence the law-books acquired the final and fixed form they have today. The jurists form stable groups with clear lines of authority that are drawn back to the ninth and eighth centuries, and start writing commentaries to what then becomes written authorities within each tradition, and they write biographical dictionaries over those who confer this authority to the current generation.

This happens concurrently with the restriction of theological and philosophical debates after Ashᶜarī's 'compromise' of what may now be called a clearly Sunnī theology, and an orthodox piety based on al-Ghazālī's works. The establishment of the schools of law, and thus the formulation of the law into clearly practicable rule systems, does not belong to the formative phase of Islam, but is, like the solidification of Sunnism itself, a sign that the formative period is over.

Unlike Ashᶜarī's theology, the law could not be merged into one single whole. Instead one had to settle for four schools, but that was better than no conformity at all.[39]

39 The difference is probably due to the fact that the law, more than

A reflexion of this relation between state power and law can be seen in which schools did and did not survive in each region. The late ninth century was a period when many judges who were linked to the 'eastern Mālikīs' were close to court, while the Ḥanafīs at this period seem to have kept apart from the caliph. The latter survived, the former did not. This in contrast to Egypt, and partly Tunisia, where there were many Ḥanafī scholars who were favoured by the new Shīᶜī rulers, the Fatimids. That did not work out well for the Ḥanafīs; when the Fatimids disappeared two centuries later, so did the Ḥanafīs, to be replaced by Shāfiᶜīs in Egypt and complete Mālikī domination in Tunisia.

If this is a pattern, that those *madhhab*s that were too close to the sultans lost out in this period of establishment, it is broken by Spain, where the Mālikīs did not seem to suffer from their closeness to the state authorities. However, Spain may have been somewhat of a case apart because of its geographic distance from the centre, and that there never really were any serious contenders to compete with the Mālikīs here, at least not after the end of the ninth century. So the law had to stand on its own feet, independent of the state authorities, because sultans came and went, dynasties fell at a regular pace, while the scholars remained. This seems to be the recurring situation in the Middle Ages, which was when Islamic law had its 'classical' age of influence and practice.

---

speculative theology, is confronted with a social practice. The weight of this established practice must therefore have limited the possibility of reaching full conformity in this field of thought.

7

LAW BEYOND THE FOUR SCHOOLS

The four Sunnī schools are not the only ones that have put their mark on the history of the law. There were many other, smaller 'schools'. Some sources talk of several hundred 'personal schools of law', by which is probably only meant that prominent scholars gave judgement in their own name without referring to one of the major traditions. But a few of these 'minor' schools in the first two or three centuries won enough support that they belong in a history of Islamic law. We will thus look briefly at some of the most important of these schools that did not make it; we may call them 'proto-Sunnī' as they died out before the great divide between Sunnīs and Shīᶜīs had been formed. In addition, we look at those non-Sunnī schools that did survive, the Ibāḍīs and in particular the various brands of Shīᶜism.

'Proto-Sunnī' currents

Awzāᶜī

In the histories of the regions we have largely talked about Iraq, Hijaz and Egypt, but little has been said about Syria. However, there was a current of jurists there as well, which later came to be known as the school after ᶜAbd al-Raḥmān al-Awzāᶜī (d. 774).[1] This is similiar in structure to the early Kufa and Medina currents, but represents the views common in Syria and Damascus, the capital of the caliphate until 750. Awzāᶜī was of the opinion that the practice of the Umayyads was the best indication of continuity from the early times of the Prophet until his own. However, this current did not go through any process of 'Traditionalizing' and adaptation to Shāfiᶜī's principles. Thus it fell behind what became the consensus of the jurists and disappeared, probably before the end of the tenth century.

The current also had some support in Spain before it was replaced there by the Mālikīs in the tenth century. The reason

1 Schacht, *Origins*, 119 & 288-9.

may be that there was an influx of Syrian exiles to Spain after the Umayyads fled there from the Abbasids of the east, bringing with them both scholars and legal practices.

Sufyān al-Thawrī

Another early jurist considered to be a focus for a small group or a current was Sufyān al-Thawrī (d. 778) of Kufa. He was, unlike his contemporaries Awzāᶜī and Abū Ḥanīfa, known as a Traditionist by inclination and a transmitter of *ḥadīth*. But he was also a rationalist jurist, unlike the early extreme Traditionists, such that he is often considered a *ḥadīth*-inclined member of the Kufa people, thus slightly distanced from the more famous Abū Ḥanīfa, and sometimes seen as a forerunner of Shāfiᶜī's unification of Traditionalism and rational law. Thawrī was particularly influential in Basra in southern Iraq, and had followers in several other towns in Iraq, Syria, but again particularly in Spain, before his views on law were overshadowed by the later and more developed schools in the tenth and eleventh centuries.[2]

Jarīrīya

The name of this current may not be well known, but the man it is named after is. Muḥammad b. Jarīr al-Tabarī was one of the most famous historians of Islam and wrote a Koran commentary that is today one of the most widely used *tafsīrs*.[3] Ṭabarī, who came from Iran, died in 930, so this is a much younger current than the two named above. It is often compared to the Shāfiᶜīya, and indeed grew out of Shāfiᶜī ideas. It is particularly known for its attempt at a rational structuring of the law.

Although the Jarīrī current held on for a while, it did eventually disappear, mainly by merging into the larger Shāfiᶜī school as this coalesced. Schacht claims the Jarīrīya was gone by the fourteenth century, but it was probably marginalized as a serious competitor to the four big schools long before that.

Ẓāhirīya

The three schools mentioned are mostly footnotes in the history of the Sharīᶜa. The fourth of these 'proto-Sunnī' currents is, how-

2 Melchert, *Formation*, 3-6, and *EI* (2), article 'Sufyān al-Thawrī'.
3 Schacht, *Introduction*, 60, and Melchert, *Formation*, 191-7.

ever, normally awarded more space. This is not because it had much greater support; we do not know if the Ẓāhirīya was ever practised as a school of law anywhere.[4] Still, all classical and modern works include it in their discussions, almost like a fifth school of law along with the four existing ones. The reason is that it is so neat to use as a logical counterpoint. These are the people of the pure line, the real extremists.[5]

The name of the current does not, like all others, stem from a personal name, although the purported founder was called Dāwūd al-Ẓāhirī (d. 884).[6] However, it is he who is named after the current. *Ẓāhir* means the 'external' or literal meaning of the words, and that is what these scholars say: The law must be based on the literal meaning of the Text in the Koran and true *sunna*, and nothing else. No compromise. There is no room for *qiyās*, or *tafsīr*, or any other human sorting, manipulation or evaluation of the divine message, beyond bringing out the actual text of the Revelation.[7] They do accept consensus, but only in the meaning of the Prophet's companions agreeing on the soundness of the *sunna*, nothing else.

Dāwūd was a Traditionist by inclination, and is as such considered more extreme than Ibn Ḥanbal, but not by profession; he did not himself collect or transmit *ḥadīth*. His interest was rather in the theories of the law, the formulation of legal principles on the basis of *ḥadīth*. He did apparently have some followers, but they did not establish themselves as a fixed grouping or school at his time. When the Ẓāhirīs are remembered, it is more

4 Some jurists of the early period are described as 'Ẓāhirīs' in the biographical literature, but lacking any comprehensive work of Ẓāhirī law (before that of Ibn Ḥazm of the eleventh century), we cannot know what kind of law they actually practised or if they themselves considered themselves as followers of Dāwūd. The term may simply refer to jurists who were known to put a greater emphasis on the literal expressions of *ḥadīth* in legal practices that might otherwise be formulated individually.

5 The most important study is that of Ignaz Goldziher, *The Ẓāhirīs: Their Doctrine and their History*, Leiden 1971 (trans. from *Die Ẓâhiriten*, 1884). Cf. also Zysow, 'Economy of Certainty'; Roger Arnaldez, 'La place du Coran dans les *uṣūl-al-fiqh* d'après la *Muḥallā* d'Ibn Ḥazm', *Studia Islamica*, XXXII, 1970, 21-30, and Fadel I. Abdallah, 'Notes on Ibn Ḥazm's rejection of analogy (qiyās) in matters of religious law', *American Journal of Islamic Social Sciences*, II, 2, 1985, 207-24.

6 Melchert, *Formation*, 178-90.

7 Nour, 'Qias', 311-12.

because of a much later scholar, who is known as one of the sharpest minds in the theory of law, the Spanish scholar ᶜAlī b. Aḥmad Ibn Ḥazm (d. 1065). His *Iḥkām fī uṣūl al-aḥkām* is still one of the foundational works of *uṣūl al-fiqh,* even if no-one believes in his theories any longer. His Ẓāhirī ideas gained support shortly after his death, when a Berber dynasty, the Alhomads, took power in Spain and North Africa. Their founder, Ibn Tūmart, who believed himself to be the *mahdī* sent by God, was strongly inspired by the writings of Ibn Ḥazm and made his views more or less the law of his state.

However, the judges were still Mālikī in great majority, and they continued in reality to practise a form of Mālikī law throughout this period although they may have modified their expressions in the direction of direct readings of the Koran and *ḥadīth*.[8] Mālikism was in any case still not fixed in all its detail at this time. However, the main importance of the sultan's pressure was that he demanded that every verdict in court should state expressly which verse of the Koran or what *ḥadīth* was used for the verdict, not just a *qiyās* formulation, although the actual rule might have been identical.[9] Thus, it was largely a cosmetic adaptation to the ruler's views, and we cannot really see this Almohad period as one of practised Ẓāhirism.

Later views on Ẓāhirism present it as a stern of even fanatical school. 'Literal interpretation', 'no room for *qiyās* or the evaluation of context and metaphorical language', normally lead one to think of extreme dogmatism, conservatism and intolerance. However, the result may be exactly the opposite. Ẓāhirism may lead to an extreme liberalism and in fact rationalism in the law—in theory to an extent that it could never have been applied in medieval society, and certainly never was.

The argumentation, as formulated by Ibn Ḥazm, runs like this:

(1) God is omniscient, He knows everything of past and future.

(2) God has made all his commands clear in the Revelation. This

8 Zysow also disputes that Ibn Tūmart was a Ẓāhirī himself, in that he accepted that *aḥād ḥadīth* could be *ẓannī* and yet form basis of the Law; in contradiction to Ẓāhirī theory; 'Economy of Certainty', 494-5.

9 Serrano, 'Legal practice', 228. Cf. also Maribel Fierro, 'The legal policies of the Almohad caliphs and Ibn Rushd's *Bidāyat al-mujtahid*', *Journal of Islamic Studies*, X, 3, 1999, 226-48.

must be read as it is; if God had meant it to be read allegorically or using analogy, He would have said so.

(3) All things belong to one of three categories, compulsory, forbidden or neutral. God has given a rule, a *ḥukm*, for everything, either by expressing it directly, or by being silent about it. (God knows everything, if He had had any views on modern developments, he would have said so in a manner that would become obvious when these occurred.)

(4) When nothing is said about a thing, or it does not clearly fall into one of the three categories in an evident Text, then God has given His *ḥukm* about it: That it is neither banned nor compulsory; it belongs to the third category, neutral. God has expressedly said so, by His words, 'we want ease for you, not hardship'.

(5) Thus, anything that is not expressly forbidden in evident and undisputable words in the Koran or *sunna* is permitted. Anything that is not clearly compulsory can be avoided.

This sounds pretty anarchic. Compared to standard Sunnī law, it would remove all those exception rules that other lawyers employ in order to dampen unreasonable consequences of the direct word, such as the cutting of hands for minor thefts or whipping for inconsequential breaches. However, beyond these few rules that are expressly stated, it would lead to a 'free-for-all' where very little could be banned or demanded. At least not in the name of God. The jurists would either have to use a non-sacred authority for such matters (which was to some extent already the case, but not acceptable as a principle), or accept any behaviour, which would make a lawless society.

Of course, it never came to that, and it was probably neither intended nor imagined. Although there was never any Ẓāhirī law that was put into practice anywhere, Ibn Ḥazm did in fact write a book on applied law, *al-Muḥalla*, where he sketches rules of law in many fields. These are far less dramatic than his principles would lead one to believe, they mainly fall well inside what was normal Sunnī *fiqh*. In fact he even accepts something very akin to *qiyās* as a method, but calls it *dalīl*, indications of God's will. These are conclusions drawn directly from the Text, but without the use of *ᶜilla*, God's 'causative effect' which man cannot know. He is on the other hand fairly uncritical in his use of *ḥadīth*, so that he can find a basis for the rules he favours in a *ḥadīth* that other jurists might not have accepted as sound.

A comparison of the rules of the *Muḥalla* to the dominant Sunnī schools shows discrepancies in only a few areas.[10] One example is a husband's duty to provide financial support for his family. This according to standard law is a duty that only falls on the husband, never on the wife, even when she has income and he has not.[11] However, Ibn Ḥazm says, Koran 2:233 states that 'It is for the father to provide them [wife and children] and clothe them honourably … The heir has a like duty.' Both men and women are heirs, and the verse says nothing about female heirs being exempt from taking over this duty. If God had meant they were not supposed to take this on, He would have said so. Thus it cannot be correct that only men have the duty to support the family; the duty must in the same way fall on whoever of the spouses has the economic means to fulfil it.

This is thus an example of conclusions drawn directly from the Koranic verse, and of course in its form a purely rational argumentation. The most important of the legal areas where Ibn Ḥazm differs from the other schools is that he does not accept any form of judicial divorce (*taṭlīq*), he accepts that slaves may own property, he limits the meaning of the *ribā* that is forbidden, he accepts that one can give donations while on one's deathbed, and makes certain changes to the rules of inheritance.[12] He also accepts some contracts of hire others consider illegal, and accepts that a man may marry his divorced wife's daughter, which the others do not allow. Thus fairly minor changes in the actual law; the most important of these are inheritance rules which become even stranger in Ibn Ḥazm's version. It is however impossible to say that these differences make the Sharīᶜa more 'liberal' or more 'strict' than in the practised schools. Some of his interpretations tend to a more 'open' practice, others to a more strict.

10 Y. Linant de Bellefonds, 'Ibn Hazm et le Zahirisme juridique', *Revue algérienne, tunisienne et marocaine de législation et de jurisprudence*, LXXVI, 1, 1960, 1-43.

11 See more on this in Chapter 15.

12 That the heirs who did not receive anything from the Koranic shares can demand inheritance based on a will; based on a Koranic verse others consider to be abrogated.

Ibāḍism

So much for the Sunnī, or 'proto-Sunnī' schools. However, we know that two theological currents escaped merger into the Sunnī compromise, one of them tiny, the Khārijīs or Ibāḍis as they are called today, and one large, the Shīᶜīs, who are divided into a number of different currents.

The Khawārij or Ibāḍīs

The Khārijīs early developed the concept of a charismatic society, but they still have no need for *ijmāᶜ*. They reject this idea, at least if it is to include anyone outside their own current. They do accept analogy as well as continuous *ijtihād*, more so than Sunnīs do.[13] Possibly this makes the need for consensus as an independent source less important, as it is among the Shīᶜīs, who also accept continuous *ijtihād*.

However, it is a problem for an historian to define precisely what is meant by 'Khārijīs' in the early period, when this term was used loosely to refer to many different, mostly rebellious, groups.[14] Those who gained permanence take their inspiration from early groups in eighth-century Iraq and later in Oman, but their main area of influence came to be North Africa, from the middle of the eighth century until 900. There different Khārijī groups established separate, mostly small, Berber-based states. The largest of these was the Rustamids with its centre in western Algeria, which was the basis for the Wahbī[15] branch of the Ibāḍī current among the Khārijīs, and it is this branch that is the origin for the Ibāḍī groups that remain today. This state fell to the Shīᶜī Fatimids in 911, and the Ibāḍīs withdrew into small desert oases or mountain areas, where they retained their independence until today.

However, since the tenth century, Ibāḍism's greatest impact has been in Oman. This sultanate has continuously been ruled by an Ibāḍī sultan, while the population of the modern state is about evenly divided between Ibāḍīs and Shāfiᶜī Sunnīs. Oman became a power in East Africa in the nineteenth century, with a centre in

13 Coulson, *History,* 103-6, and Hasan, *Doctrine of ijmāᶜ*, 166-8.

14 M.M. Shaban, *Islamic History*, Cambridge 1971-7.

15 Not Wahhābi! They turned up a millennium later in Arabia.

Zanzibar, and a number of Ibāḍī Omanis settled there. Some enclaves of Ibāḍism still exist in Tanzania and Kenya.[16]

Ibāḍī law has not really been studied in detail by Western scholars yet. However, it would appear that their law does not differ much from Sunnī law in most areas. They are probably closer to Sunnism that Shīᶜī law is. Many of the regions dominated by Ibāḍīs may have been too tiny to support a specialized class of scholars of law, thus hampering its legal development. In any case the major legal writings, comparable to those the Sunnīs developed in the thirteenth and fourteenth centuries, were mainly written in the late nineteenth century. The dominant author is the Algerian Muḥammad b. Yūsuf ᶜAṭfīyash (d. 1914).

It may once again be that the distinction from the Sunnī schools is greater in the theory than in the actual content of the law. We know that Ibāḍīs also emphasize *ḥadīth*, but put a limit at the death of the caliph ᶜUthmān. This was the moment when the Khārijīs left the majority community of Muslims, and they do not recognize any practice after this moment. The most famous Ibāḍī *ḥadīth* collector and early jurist was Jābir b. Zayd (d. 711 or 722), who lived in Baṣra in the period just before the Ibāḍīs emigrated to Oman, that is, before they got their own area to rule over, and perhaps before they actually constituted a separate group of scholars.

Shīᶜism

However, the major 'alternative current' in Islam is Shīᶜism, which is itself divided into several currents or branches. The dominant among them are the 'Imāmīs' of Iran, Iraq and Lebanon. The Shīᶜīs draw their history back to the story of the Prophet's son-in-law ᶜAlī b. Abī Ṭālib and the first conflicts after the Prophet's death. There were many Muslims in this period who believed that the Prophet's genealogical descendants through ᶜAlī's sons Ḥasan and Husayn should have led the community. These, however, were mostly to be seen as currents of thought (or minor rebellions) among the diverse multitude of religious positions that existed in this formative period. It was only at the

16 Although the 1963 revolution in Zanzibar led to most of the Omanis returning to Oman.

end of the ninth and into the tenth century that these currents started to form into two coherent and separate alternatives, Shīᶜīs with a unified theology on the one hand, Sunnīs on the other. This is also true in legal matters, we can find the first traces of a separate Shīᶜī legal theory in the tenth century, but Shīᶜī law developed slowly and gradually, and we can probably only see a fully fledged Shīᶜī law (of the Imāmī majority) in the eighteenth century.

The various currents of Shīᶜīsm developed independently from each other because of various historical events in the formative or early medieval period. Thus, they do not have a common 'original Shīᶜī legal theory' that each split away from, although there is evidence of mutual influences. They each spring independently out of what may be called a common source of Muslim legal thought, and they vary in how much they differ from the surrounding Sunnī law. What unites these Shīᶜī currents is the role of the *imām*,[17] the inspired leader of the community who must be a direct descendant from Muḥammad through his grandsons Ḥasan or Ḥusayn. They form the anchor for Shīᶜī law. However, the Shīᶜī currents differ in how the influence of the *imām* determines their law.

The Zaydīs

The most 'moderate' Shīᶜīs seem, like the Ibāḍīs, to be only marginally different from Sunnī law.[18] The Zaydīs had their main area in the Yemen from the Middle Ages, and were politically independent for much of this time. They believe like the other

17 The word *imām* may, as we know, have many meanings in Islam. We tend for practical purposes to distinguish some when we write English, so that straightforward 'imam' means the prayer leader that all Muslim mosques have, while *imām* with a transcribed long ā refers to the Shīᶜī understanding, the descendant of the Prophet who they believe is the leader of all Muslims, with divine inspiration.

18 That is, of course, in relative terms. From their own perspective, there were important differences between them both in theory and in many practical rules of law, as there are beween the Sunnī schools themselves. But from an outsider's viewpoint, there is always a danger to overemphasize these distinctions over what they have in common, as well as over differences within the schools. Thus a balanced and comparative view of the schools and currents must always focus on the particularities of how they differ and concur in theory and practice.

Shīᶜīs that the community should be led by an *imām* from the Prophet's house, a descendant from ᶜAlī, but unlike them do not grant him any specially inspired status.

Zaydī law developed from the ninth and tenth century in those areas where they then had political control, first on the Caspian area, and later in the Yemen. They came to see the first imām in Yemen, al-Hādī ilā 'l-Ḥaqq Yaḥyā (d. 911), as the most important authority for the legal system of the Zaydī state, known as the Hādawīya school.[19] He helped giving Zaydī law a more distinct Shīᶜī stamp.

Still, they remained closer to Sunnism than the other Shīᶜī currents, and there were in later centuries arguments among Zaydī scholars to reduce the distinction further.[20] It is typical that their most famous legal scholar, Muḥammad b. ᶜAlī al-Shawkānī (d. 1832) is often taken to be a Sunnī, although he was in fact a Zaydī judge in Ṣanᶜāᵓ and never left Zaydism.[21] However, he put very little emphasis on this identity, and is known as an ardent opponent on the restrictions of *ijmāᶜ* and for his support for the greater use of *ijtihād*.[22] He may have reached this position easier because

19 W. Madelung, 'Zaydiyya', *EI* (2), XI, 479 and 'al-Ḥādī ilā 'l-ḥaḳḳ', *EI* (2), Supplement, 334-5.

20 Ahmad Dallal, 'The origins and objectives of Islamic revivalist thought', *Journal of the American Oriental Society*, CXIII, 3, 1993, 341-59. This tendency can already be seen in the fifteenth century with the influential scholar Ibn al-Wazīr (d. 1436) who defended the positions of Sunnī law, but claimed, like the later Shawkānī, to be doing this on the basis of individual *ijtihād*; Madelung, 'Zaydiyya', 480.

21 There are different opinions on this. Bernard Haykel claims that Shawkānī broke with all basic elements of Zaydism, including the role of the *imām*, and thus must be said to have left Zaydism for a personal expression of law 'beyond the schools'. He was allowed to be a *qāḍī* because he was able to recruit the *imām* to his position; Bernard A. Haykel, *Revival and Reform in Islam: The legacy of Muhammad al-Shawkani*, Cambridge 2003 and 'Reforming Islam by dissolving the *madhhab*s: Shawkānī and his zaydī detractors in Yemen', in Weiss, *Studies in legal theory*, 337-64. However, as he thus received the acceptance of the *imām* in his rejection of the *imām*'s authority, it may be debatable how dramatic this rupture was. It does in any case show how close the Zaydī and Sunnī law must have been. Shawkānī is otherwise a central figure in the legal reformism of the nineteenth century, and the object of many studies. Cf. also Rudolph Peters, 'Idjtihad and taqlid in 18th and 19th century Islam', *Die Welt des Islams*, XX, 3-4, 1980, 132-45.

22 While the standard (Hādawī) Zaydī view was to accept the *ijmāᶜ* of their

of his Zaydī background, but his theories are part and parcel of a debate that dominated the Sunnī world at the time, and was being discussed without any of them caring that he belonged to another 'sect'.

Ismāᶜīlīs

The other two main groups of Shīᶜīs are commonly named after how many *imāms* they recognize, the minority 'seveners' or *Ismāᶜīlīs* and the majority, 'twelvers' or *Imāmīs*. Both have ruled over states, but in different periods. Thus one can, as far as Shīᶜī law is concerned, divide history in two: An early period when Ismāᶜīlīs governed states over much of the Middle East in the 'Shīᶜī century', around 950-1050, and then a modern period where it was the Imāmīs who got to build a state, and make the law there, in Iran after 1500.

Thus, it is natural to describe the Ismāᶜīlīs first. The best known of these were the Fatimids, an Ismāᶜīlī dynasty that ruled over most of North Africa focused on Tunisia, then Egypt and Syria, from 909 to around 1060 (maintaining formal supremacy for a period after that).[23]

We do not really known too much of Fatimid law. But we do know their leading legal scholar quite well; Qāḍī Nuᶜmān, who lived 909-73. This was in the 'North African' period, and Nuᶜmān just lived to see the conquest of Egypt in 969, where he was appointed chief judge. He was thus a practising judge, but also a theoretician, and we know him best through his books. In fact, his books are the major source for our knowledge of Ismāᶜīlī law in this period.

Since the central element in the Shīᶜī 'difference' is the role of the *imām*, it is not surprising that much of Shīᶜī law appears as adaptations of existing Sunnī theory to give the *imām* a more central role. Thus for example in *ḥadīth*: The Shīᶜīs have their own *ḥadīth*s with much the same content (*matn*) as the Sunnīs,

---

imāms and the Prophet's family. Hādawī law also accepts *qiyās*, unlike imāmī Shīᶜism, this as well was criticized by Shawkānī; Haykel, *Revival and Reform*, 93-6.

23 Bayard Dodge, 'The Fāṭimid legal code', *Muslim World*, L, 1960, 30-8; Asaf A.A. Fyzee, 'Aspects of Fatimid Law', *Studia Islamica*, XXXI, 1970, 81-91, and Amin Hajji, 'Institutions of justice in Fatimid Egypt', in Aziz al-Azmeh (ed.), *Islamic Law*, London 1988, 198-214.

but the *isnād* chains of transmitters may be different. An *isnād* should include an *imām* as transmitter, and it is he who gives authority to the *isnād*. Early Ismāᶜīlī *ḥadīth* sometimes went so far as to only include the name of the *imām*, the other links were so inconsequential that they could be omitted. This is thus a fairly primitive level of *ḥadīth*, as that excludes any way of controlling or evaluating the transmission of the *ḥadīth* from the *imām* to the collector who wrote it down; which is of course the main purpose of the *isnād*, to give later scholars an opportunity to declare a Tradition as false without having to evaluate the potentially divine content of the text.

The major difference between the Ismāᶜīlīs and the Imāmīs is that the former have a living *imām*. The Imāmīs never had that, in so far as this current only solidified somewhat after 900, that is, after their twelfth and last *imām* 'withdrew' from the world in 874. Some Ismāᶜīlī ideas also believe the *imām* to be hidden, but most, and in particular the Fatimids and their descendants consider the *imām* to be perfectly alive and present, thus the Fatimids was a dynasty of ruling *imām*-caliphs.

So they had no need for *qiyās*, *ijmāᶜ*, and all the other tools that the Sunnīs used to discover the divine will.[24] They could just ask the *imām* (the Fatimid caliph), who in himself had the authority to state that the answer was of God. Thus Nuᶜmān, their chief judge, is said to have consulted regularly with the *imām* over his decisions. But this was still a reference in the 'last instance'. The Fatimids established a court and justice system similar to that of their Sunnī predecessors, and the *imām* probably did not often intervene in the normal practice of law.

There are a number of similarities in the actual legal rules of the Ismāᶜīlīs and the later Imāmīs of Iran. The reason is probably that Qāḍī Nuᶜman's books were known and highly valued by the later Imāmīs, and thus inspired them, in spite of their theological differences and, in part, a different legal history. However, the Fatimids did not know some of the distinctions of later Shīᶜī law, such as *mutᶜa* marriage and the inheritance laws. They were in those matters closer to the Sunnī views of their time.

We do not have too much detailed knowledge of how

24 Nour, 'Qias', 34, and Ahmad Hasan, 'The Critique of Qiyas', *Islamic Studies*, XXII, 3, 1983, 45-69 & 4, 1983, 31-55, and *Doctrine of ijmāᶜ*, 174-8.

Ismāᶜīlī law was practised in Fatimid Egypt, except that they appointed a chief judge of their own, but otherwise left the Sunnī judges in their posts.[25] It is reasonable to assume that they continued in the main to practise their Sunnī law according to the current or school they might favour; the Fatimids seem on the whole to be satisfied with letting people under their rule remain within their religious convictions.

We do know that the caliph that took Egypt, Muᶜizz, insisted on some changes in the call to prayer, but we do not know what this meant for religious life in general. It is, however, reasonable to suspect that this mainly concerned the communal Friday prayers. The distinction between the denominations would be clearest at this common gathering, and the believers would probably go to different mosques, the Ismāᶜīlī masters to the new al-Azhar or al-Ḥākim mosques that they built, while the Sunnīs may have continued to use their existing mosques and prayed in the manner accustomed to them.[26] This would mirror the situation today, where the major cities will have different mosques for each *madhhab* present there, so that each Muslim can pray according the rituals of his school.

The Imāmīs

As for the Imāmīs, the vast majority of Shīᶜīs today, their history is clearly divided into two by the year 1501. Before that, in the Middle Ages, they mostly lived under Sunnī rule and had to adapt to a minority situation. After that, the modern or Iranian period, dating from when the Safavid ruler Ismāᶜīl declared Shīᶜism to be the state religion for the new state of Iran, they were thus given the possibility to develop as a majority and later state law.[27]

The Safavid state was not quite the first period that the Imāmīs had the favour of a ruler. The Buyids of Iraq and surrounding regions from 950 on also had sympathy for Imāmism; the 'Shīᶜī century' wasn't all Ismāᶜīlī. But the current

25 Chapter 6. See also further in Chapter 9.

26 The Azhar, which was originally built to disseminate Ismāᶜīlī propaganda, was after the fall of the Fatimids turned into a Sunni centre of learning. The Ḥākim mosque has been rebuilt in the modern period as an Ismāᶜīlī mosque.

27 Moojan Momen, *An Introduction to Sh'i Islam*, New Haven 1985 and Yann Richard, *Shiʾite Islam: Polity, Ideology and Creed*, Oxford 1995.

was still so young at this period that this benevolence did not have a major impact on the legal system of the area. Still, it was a time when a group of Imāmī scholars began to flourish and laid the basis for an intellectual development that continued after Sunnī sultans had taken control from the mid-eleventh century.[28]

Thus this first period is primarily a long formative period for Imāmī law. The early scholars had two main paths to choose from.[29] One was to attach themselves to existing schools and work within them, either openly as Shīᶜīs or covertly pretending to be Sunnīs (*taqīya*). Many scholars chose this option, and attached themselves in particular to the Shāfiᶜī school, which in many respects remains the Sunnī school that is closest to Shīᶜī points of view. Even ᶜAllāma al-Ḥillī (d. 1325), who is considered one of the greatest early Shīᶜī *ḥadīth* collectors and jurists, worked within the Shāfiᶜī current and was accepted by them as an open Shīᶜī. This was not uncommon, we can find Shīᶜī scholars working within Sunnī legal frameworks as late as the seventeenth century, that is as long as the Shīᶜīs had to work under Sunnī dominance.

The other option was to spilt away and form their own, 'fifth' school of law. The expression 'fifth school' was used early on among the Shīᶜīs, it is reported already in the fourteenth century, and was from the sixteenth century known as the 'Jaᶜfarī' school after the sixth and perhaps most scholarly of the twelve *imāms*, Jaᶜfar al-Ṣādiq.[30] The most prominent of the scholars of what was to become this Shīᶜī school were al-Shaykh al-Mufīd (d. 1022) and al-Sharīf al-Murtaḍā (d. 1044), who both worked under the Buyids. After the demise of this state the Imāmī school developed slowly, and primarily as a theory,[31] until the Safavid period in the sixteenth century.

It may perhaps be said that the Shīᶜīs went through the same stages as Sunnī law, but two centuries or more later. They started to gather *ḥadīth*, as had the Sunnīs, but a real science of *ḥadīth* criticism in the manner of Bukhārī and his fellows grew only in

28 Robert Brunschvig, 'Les *uṣûl al-fiqh* imâmites à leur stade ancien (Xe et XI siècles)', in *Études d'islamologie*, Paris 1976, II, 323-34.

29 Stewart, *Islamic Legal Orthodoxy*.

30 Stewart, *Islamic Legal Orthodoxy*, 112. Later Shīᶜī jurists have avoided this expression, as it places them in line with the Sunnī schools.

31 At least as far as *muᶜāmalāt*, the societal part of the law, is concerned.

the fourteenth century, that is four centuries after them. ᶜAllāma al-Ḥillī was the dominant name here. He placed great emphasis on *ᶜaql*, reason in the formulations. The Shīᶜīs were heavily influenced by Muᶜtazalī ideas in theology, and this influence can be seen in Ḥillīs works.

However, the great advance in methodology only came after the establishment of the Safavid state when there was a possibility to practise the law. The method developed alongside the application.

Here too there developed a parallel to the debate that had racked the Sunnī lawyers almost a millennium earlier, between *raʾy* and *ḥadīth*. The major difference was that 'established practice' was not a major issue, this practice was mostly Sunnī before 1500. The discussion was more about the use of *ijtihād* and how closely the rules of law had to be linked to *ḥadīth*. The *ḥadīth* are among Shīᶜīs often called *akhbār*, Reports, and those who only wanted to accept *ḥadīth* as a basis for law were called *Akhbārīs*, while those who supported the use of rationalist methodology were called 'Methodologists', with the Arabic word *uṣūl*, *Uṣūlīs*.[32]

The debate was an old one. The Akhbārīs had opposed the creation of a separate Shīᶜī school of law, which they considered unnecessary when the *akhbār* told the believers how to act. However, it is with the lawyer Astarābādī (d. 1627) that we can speak of them as a particular current.[33] The conflict became sharper in the eighteenth century, as the Akhbārīs gained considerable support, but the Uṣūlīs became the dominant view after Muḥammad Bāqir al-Bihbahānī (d. 1793)[34] formulated a coherent theoretical basis for it, and the Akhbārīs eventually died out as a separate current of thought.

32 Hossein Modarressi, 'Rationalism and traditionalism in Shî'î jurisprudence: A preliminary survey', *Studia Islamica*, LIX, 1984, 141-58, and Etan Kohlberg, 'The Akhbāriyya in seventeenth and eighteenth century Iran', in John Voll and Nehemia Levtzion (ed.), *Eighteenth Century Renewal and Reform in Islam*, New York 1987, 133-60.

33 Stewart, *Islamic Legal Orthodoxy*, 175-208 and Robert Gleave, *Inevitable Doubt: Two Theories of Shīᶜī Jurisprudence*, Leiden 2000, 5-8.

34 Known in Persian as Vaḥīd Bihbahānī. Sometimes confused with his son, Muḥammad ᶜAlī al-Bihbahānī (d. 1803), known as the 'Sufi killer' for his campaign against the Sufi brotherhoods; David Morgan, *Medieval Persia 1040-1797*, London 1988, 160, and Momen, *Shi'i Islam*, 127-8 & 137.

The main difference between their views was probably the issue of knowledge or doubt.[35] The Akhbārīs held that *ḥadīth* gave certain knowledge and was thus the absolute authority. If the answer to a question was not to be found in the *akhbār*, then the scholar had to use 'caution', *iḥtiyāṭ*, that is, he had to refrain from any act that might be wrong. Thus knowledge was clearly separated into two, that which is based in a clear Text, and that about which we can know nothing. So knowledge was knowledge about the *akhbār*.

The Uṣūlīs held, much like the Sunnīs, that all knowledge must pass through human reason and is thus subject to uncertainty and doubt. So there is only one kind of knowledge and no absolute certainty. The relative (*ẓannī*) certainty can only be reached through learning. Thus both currents believed that the ordinary Muslim had to follow the guidance of an accepted learned authority, but the basis for this authority was different: For the Akhbārīs it was the knowledge about *ḥadīth* only, for the Uṣūlīs it was the process of *ijtihād* and competence in it that gave the scholars authority.

The principles of Shīᶜī law

Much of practised law in Shīᶜism is so similar to that of the Sunnī schools that the term 'fifth school' is quite reasonable. The Shīᶜī view will, in most cases where there are differences of opinion between the schools, be somewhere in the middle, not alone in opposition to the others. But the theory behind the law shows some basic differences, mostly caused by the difference in theology between the two dominant currents. The most important of these is of course the role played by the *imām*, a role that is the foundation for Shīᶜī law while it is unknown to Sunnism.

The Imāmīs did not, unlike the Ismāᶜīlīs, have any living *imām* to refer to, so the *ḥadīth* (*akhbār*) of the *imām*s of the past were of necessity central to them, also to the Uṣūlīs. Traditions telling of the actions and statements of the twelve *imām*s had authority alongside those telling of the Prophet, in addition to, of course, the role of the *imām* as a trusted transmitter of Prophetic *ḥadīth*. Thus the concept that Revelation came to a sudden close

35 Gleave, *Inevitable Doubt*.

on the death of the Prophet becomes more diffuse, as the *imāms* inherit some of the Prophet's function as possible transmitters of divine intention (although the *imāms* are clearly not considered to be prophets). So the Shīᶜī view allows for a more dynamic development of the law; all sources to knowledge of God's will is not at an end with the death of the Prophet.

The Shīᶜī view of qiyās

The Shīᶜīs did not, having access to a continuous source for *imām* authority, really need the *qiyās* and *ijmāᶜ* methods in the way the Sunnīs did. The idea that only Koran can replace Koran and only *ḥadīth ḥadīth*, as we described for Shāfiᶜī, is unknown to the Shīᶜīs. They did not really need all the sinuous adaptations and compromises between existing views that he had to use, since they could start afresh building a new tradition for themselves. Thus, they could in many ways learn from Sunnī history, and establish more straightforward and 'logical' solutions. Revelation is for them Revelation, and any later Revelation, be it *ḥadīth* or Koranic verse, can replace an earlier Revelation of either type (assuming, of course, that the *ḥadīth* is considered true).

As for *qiyās*, al-Shaykh al-Mufīd formulated a logical criticism of it that runs somewhat as follows:[36]

If we look at the system where you take the original Text ('wine is forbidden'), then find an *ᶜilla* for it ('causing intoxication') and transfer the ruling to a new case ('fermented grape juice also causes intoxication and is thus forbidden'), then we must remember that God has divided all conceivable situations into *three* categories: the forbidden, the compulsory and the neutral. The first two are expressly stated in some way in the Revelation, but the third can either be expressed or not expressed. God does not specify everything that is neutral, but neutrality is also one of God's *ḥukms*. There are evidently many things that God positively intends to be neither compulsory nor banned.

The 'derived case', in our example the *nabīdh* juice, clearly has the property that it causes intoxication, hence falls under the *ᶜilla* of wine. But it may have *other* properties as well. Everything has different characteristics and different natures. These properties, which perhaps only God knows about, may be so important

36 Brunschvig, 'Les *uṣûl al-fiqh* imâmites', 328-9.

that they outweigh the property 'causes intoxication', and they may be of the type 'neutral'. Thus it may be that *nabīdh* actually falls in the category 'neutral', because God does not specify all things that are neutral. We cannot be sure about this. Thus we cannot use *qiyās* to transfer *ḥukm*s from one case to another, as long as we cannot exclude the possibility that the derived case falls under another, unstated *ᶜilla* that actual places it in the unspecified category, neutral. The reason for this is of course that the work of *qiyās*, determining *ᶜilla*s, only started after the death of the Prophet and the end of Revelation. So an error in *qiyās* cannot be corrected by a new revelation, 'no, *nabīdh* is neutral'. God has at this point said all He is going to say, and perhaps said it by being silent.

The Sunnī scholars responded to Mufīd: His mistake was that he confused levels of knowledge. *Qiyās* does not presume to provide absolute knowledge, as Mufīd seems to think. It is a result of *ijtihād*, human effort, and thus it may be right or it may be wrong. It is not the logic or argumentation that in the final instance decides if the *ijtihād* is right or wrong, it is the confirmation of the consensus of the community. In other words, the effort of *qiyās* is the best we can do, so we have to perform it even if there is always the danger of making a mistake.

However, this rejection of *qiyās* was probably stronger in the earlier phases of Shīᶜī law; their theories often started out as quite distanced from the Sunnī ideas, and then grew closer as time went on.[37] The Shīᶜī jurists did, from the time of ᶜAllāma al-Ḥillī on, find methods that were fairly similar to *qiyās*, although they were not called that (much like the Ẓāhirīs, the other principled opponents of *qiyās*). They now accepted that you can use a 'cause' behind a rule if it is unequivocally expressed in the revealed Text that this is the cause (what the Sunnīs call a 'textual *ᶜilla*', *manṣūṣ al-ᶜilla*). The rule can in that case be transferred to new cases in the same way as in Sunnī *qiyās*. But they do not use this name for it; they call it *taᶜdīyat al-ḥukm*, 'transfer of the rule'.[38]

37 Stewart, *Islamic Legal Orthodoxy*, 17.

38 Robert M. Gleave, 'Imāmī Shīᶜī refutations of *qiyās*', in Weiss, *Studies in Islamic Legal Theory*, 287-91.

Shīᶜī consensus in the absence of the imām

The Shīᶜīs also developed their own conception of *ijmāᶜ* for the period when the *imām* was hidden. The consensus can thus express the will of the *imām*. There is an idea that the hidden *imām* walks abroad among the scholars unseen and unknown. So a view that has reached full consensus among the scholars is thus also approved by the *imām*, since he is among the scholars who all agree on it.[39]

Thus genealogies and biographical information become very important. If there is a disagreement between two groups and we know the genealogy of all scholars in one group, but not of all in the other, then the latter must be correct. Because this means that the *imām* cannot be among the scholars in the first group, but he may then be hidden in the second group. Thus the latter has greater authority, even if there is a third group that has no stated opinion and which could also contain the hidden *imām*.[40]

However, consensus is no more an active creative principle here than in Sunnī law. It is mostly used to authorize a rule or refers to agreements in earlier history (much like the *ḥadīth* that say 'all Companions of the Prophet agreed that …' in Sunnī law).

The scholars have, during the time of withdrawal of the *imām*, inherited his authority and collectively constitute his 'general representative', *al-nāʾib al-ᶜāmm*.[41] This view does not follow logically from the concept of the hidden *imām*, and it did not develop right away. The first generations were rather of the opinion that the role of the *imām* was vacant when he was not present to communicate with us, and no other authority could fill his place.

39 Norman Calder, 'Khums in Imāmī Shīᶜī jurisprudence, from the tenth to the sixteenth century AD', *Bulletin of the School of Oriental and African Studies*, XLV, 1, 1982, 39-47.

40 Cf. Stewart, *Islamic Legal Orthodoxy*, 155. There is of course a gap in this argument: even if the *imām* is in fact a scholar, and evidently a Shīᶜī, he does not have to *appear* to be either to the outside world, as long as he is hidden. So it is quite possible that a consensus of all those who are known to be Shīᶜī scholars still does not include the *imām*. More sophisticated jurists such as Bihbahānī did thus not include this line of argumentation in their discussions on *ijmāᶜ*.

41 Norman Calder, 'Zakāt in Imāmī Shīᶜī jurisprudence, from the tenth to the sixteenth century AD', *Bulletin of the School of Oriental and African Studies*, XLIV, 3, 1981, 468-80.

But after a century or so, in the eleventh century, some scholars brought up the view that they could represent the *imām* in the practical purpose of distributing taxes, but nothing else. Then, with the continued development of Shīcī law, this right was in the fourteenth century extended so the scholars could also decide penalties and punishments. This was of course primarily a theoretical stance, as they then lived in Sunnī societies where the Sunnīs manned the courts.[42]

The full theory of *al-nāʾib al-cāmm* was only formulated in the sixteenth century, in the Safavid period when, for the first time, we really had an Imāmī Shīcī state. The scholars now had to try to find a balance in relation to a shah who demanded absolute power for himself. However, the issue was also part of the disputes between the Akhbārīs and the Uṣūlīs and was not finally settled before the victory of the Uṣūlīs around 1800.

The conclusion was that when *ijtihād* becomes an acceptable activity for a scholar on behalf of the *imām*, he becomes a *mujtahid*, someone who performs *ijtihād*. The object of this is to decide 'what the *imām* would have decided' if he had been apparent. But each scholar can evidently not have the same insight as the divinely inspired *imām*. Thus this conception puts strong limitations on the *mujtahid*. In the end his task is to decide matters so that he knows the *imām* could not *disagree*, in other words a quite prudent and conservative activity. 'Caution', *iḥtiyāṭ*, becomes the leading principle for the sholars. Thus their theoretical freedom to perform *ijtihād* does not in reality have the great effects one might have expected, nor does it lead to the anarchic dissolution of the law into personal and opposing systems as one might have feared.

Methods of ijtihād

Shīcī law differentiates the categories of knowledge through *ijtihād* slightly differently from the Sunnīs, dividing it into 'without doubt', 'probable', 'subject to doubt' and 'improbable'.

42 Except perhaps in small and peripheral sultanic states with Shīcī sympathies. The best known of these were the Qara-Qoyunlu, but it seems that their flirtation with Shīcism was little more than a vague sympathy. Thus it is improbable that they made any extensive attempt at formulating a separate Shīcī legal practice in their lands in the relatively short period they were in power; Morgan, *Medieval Persia*, 103.

The most controversial category is 'subject to doubt' and to what degree such may be brought into the law. The main concepts in this discussion are *ikthiyār*, the freedom to include the viewpoints of other currents, including Sunnī; *istiṣḥāb*, continuity, that matters should continue as they have been or in the 'natural state' unless there is any positive reason to change it (as we have seen, also a basic principle of Sunnī law) and then *ihtiyāṭ*, caution.

A hierarchy of scholars

The dispute between the Akhbārīs and Uṣūlīs showed that 'differenceness', *ikhtilāf*, is a controversial issue among Shīᶜī jurists. As long as there is only one *imām*, there must be only one law, not four or five. Many Shīᶜīs therefore reject being considered a 'fifth' school of law alongside the Sunnīs, although others use this expression. Thus the Akhbārī/Uṣūlī dispute was not between two 'schools of law' in Shīᶜism, as it is sometimes described, but a confrontation between two approaches that were different in their essence, where one had to win and the other lose; they could not co-exist as the schools do.

However, there are many *mujtahid* scholars, and consensus is here, as in the Sunnī world, an elusive commodity. How then, with the *imām* in hiding and without *ijmāᶜ*, can the scholars avoid each of them going off in a different direction?

The Uṣūlīs accept the principle of *ikhtilāf*, and Imāmī Shīᶜī law does in effect function as a *madhhab*, with 'consensus within the school' around the basic principles, as in the Sunnī schools. However, the Shīᶜīs have also, after the victory of the Uṣūlī viewpoint, developed something the Sunnīs never did, a hierarchy of scholars. This is only partially formalized, and there is disagreement of the proper structure of levels and the relation between them, but it can be fairly described as a semi-formal system with three or four levels. At the bottom are the *mullā*s, the local religious authority that the unlearned believers have to follow, then one or more middle levels (*hujjat al-islām, mujtahid*), and at the top the highest level, *āyat Allāh*, ayatollah. There are about a hundred of these today, among them the highest religious authority of the Shīᶜīs, the *marjaᶜ al-taqlīd* (or *āyat Allāh al-ᶜuẓmā*, grand ayatollah), whom all Shīᶜīs have to follow.[43]

43 In Persian *marjaᶜ-e taqlīd*, in Arabic *marjaᶜ* or *marjiᶜ*. Both Persian and

These ranks are not achieved by election in any formal manner. They are basically concepts of competence that are commonly accepted. A *mullā* must receive a paper from his teacher that he has the minimum of learning required to guide the believers (as Sunnī scholars also receive from their teachers), and an ayatollah must present a dissertation, a *risāla*, which proves his knowledge and competence.[44] But the higher levels are otherwise reached when those on the lower level accept a scholar as their religious counsellor. Any unlearned Shīᶜī must choose a *mullā* as his guide, and every scholar on a lower level must choose one from a higher as *his* guide, or *marjaᶜ*, whose advice he must follow.

These are personal and informal bonds, solidified primarily by whom one gives one's religious taxes to, and it is the accumulation of such bonds that propels a scholar to a higher level. The person on top, the *marjaᶜ al-taqlīd*, reaches this level through the recognition of some or all of the ayatollahs. There is no fixed number of such top figures, sometimes there are none, in others up to five such grand ayatollahs.

This is precisely the authority structure among the learned that the Sunnīs lacked. They had to develop their system of schools of law and how practised law was to be determined within them, something that gave both problems and flexibility. The Shīᶜīs had it easier, if a grand ayatollah or learned on a higher level has made a ruling (within the framework of 'what the *imām* cannot disagree with'), then those on the lower rungs are required to follow that. Thus it is only in the absence of such a higher statement that the *mujtahid*s may operate with 'tolerated disagreement'.

Arab (Iraqi) scholars have held this position. The expression is actually a general term for 'guide' ('source of religious authority'), so every scholar is a *marjaᶜ* for those on a lower level of knowledge, but the term is most often used for the highest *marjaᶜ*, the one who guides all others.

44 Probably introduced already in Bihbahānī's time, late eighteenth century; Stewart, *Islamic Legal Orthodoxy*, 224. Such dissertations are today prepared in the major centres of learning such as Najaf, Qum and Mashhad. Cf. Meir Litvak, *Shiᶜi Scholars of Nineteenth-Century Iraq: The ᶜulamaᵓ of Najaf and Karbalaᵓ*, Cambridge 1998, for the development of the religious authority in the nineteenth century.

Shīᶜī law under the Safavids and later

The history of Imāmī Shīᶜī law is thus fairly recent, and closely linked to the development of Iran as a Shīᶜī state after 1501.[45] Shah Ismāᶜīl's decision to make Shīᶜism the religion of the land did not automatically lead to the introduction of Shīᶜī law. Such a law did not really exist fully formed at the time. Nor did the import of Shīᶜī scholars from their established centres in Bahrain, Syria (Lebanon) or Iraq go without a hitch. There was considerable resistance from these scholars to go to Iran, where they were needed to spread the new faith, and there were also many conflicts between them and the Safavid state.

The early Safavid shahs were not pure Imāmī Shīᶜīs, their views show clear influence from Ismāᶜīlism, probably through their Sufi and Turkmen background, both milieux closer to the Ismāᶜīlīs. The first shah, Ismāᶜīl, first claimed that he was a divinely inspired *mahdī*, and thus probably also that he was the *imām* himself. He demanded personal power over religion, which the scholars strongly opposed. There were also sharp conflicts between the imported scholars and the Sufi order of the Safavids, that is to say the military troopers of the order who were the power basis of the shah, the *qizilbash*.[46]

Thus the scholars were not in command of the law. For a long time it was *ᶜurf*, custom, and not Sharīᶜa that was the law, and this was practised in the courts of the shah or the state where the scholars had little or no influence or presence.[47]

It took 150 years before the tug of war between the *qizilbash* and the scholars was over. The Sufis were weakened, and had by this time mostly become a military aristocracy. The scholars, who by then had settled into the population and become 'Iranized' came up with a theory that gave a shah a religious role under that of the *ᶜulamāʾ*, which he accepted. Then Sharīᶜa courts that

45 Charles Melville (ed.), *Safavid Persia: The History and Politics of an Islamic Society,* London 1996.

46 Cf. Roger Savory, *Iran under the Safavids*, Cambridge 1980, 1-76 and 'The principal offices of the Safawid state during the reign of Ismāᶜīl I', *Bulletin of the School of Oriental and African Studies,* XXIII, 1, 1960, 91-105, and N.R. Keddie, 'The roots of the ulama's power in modern Iran', in Keddie (ed.), *Scholars, Saints and Sufis,* Berkeley 1972, 211-29.

47 Katrhyn Babayan, 'Sufis, dervishes and mullas: The controversy over spiritual and temporal dominion in seventeenth-century Iran', in Melville, *Safavid Persia*, 117-38.

passed judgement on the basis of Shīcī law started to come into use.

This was a lengthy process, it was only in the eighteenth century and perhaps later that this was fully established. There seems to have been continuous shifts in the balance of power between the shah and the scholars. When the shah and his dynasty was strong, the Sharīca courts and the learned became less independent, when the dynasty was weak, the courts could work more on their own and for example pass judgement in criminal cases without involving the shah.

Differences between Shīcī and Sunnī law

There are, as mentioned, more differences in the theories of Sunnī and Shīcī law than in the actual rules. That is perhaps natural, given that Shīcī law was fixed so much later than the Sunnī and could use it as a basis; Iran was, as mentioned earlier, mainly Shāficī until 1500.

However there are some noticeable differences. These may be some of the more important ones:[48]

— *Mutcā*. The Imāmī Shīcīs accept something called 'marriage limited in time', or *mutca*. This is extremely controversial, and the Sunnīs call it, not without justification, legalized prostitution. Such a 'marriage' is established as a pure contract between two parties where the date when the marriage ends is written into the contract. As such, it is based on the same principles as any business agreement, and avoids all the particular duties that follow a normal marriage: there is no demands on financial support, no rights of inheritance, no waiting period before a new marriage or similar.

It is precisely this avoidance of restrictions on economic and other formalities, more than the actual time limit, that draws couples to the *mutca* form. Thus it is quite normal that the time limit is put at a century or longer, so that it is in fact a marriage for life. The difference is only that it allows for greater flexibility in arranging the economic relationship between the parties. However, it is evident that the arrangement is also used with less pious motives.

The reason the Shīcīs insist on the lawfulness of this is that

48 Coulson, *History*, 109-19.

the Prophet accepted *mutᶜa* for the soldiers who were going off to war in distant Syria, and he died before this campaign was over. The Sunnīs say this was a rule of exception that the Prophet had only intended to last for the duration of the campaign, while the Shīᶜīs insist that as long as he did not actually state such a retraction, then the later (Sunnī) caliphs had no authority to do so.

— *Ṭalāq*, divorce by the husband saying 'I divorce you' three times.[49] No scholar approves of this rule, which smacks of accepting immorality and is a threat to the family, but they must accept it as it is *sunna*. But each school puts some restrictions on this form of divorce. The Shīᶜīs are much more strict than any of the Sunnī schools in this respect, they do for example not allow the formula to be said three times at once to effectuate immediate divorce, as the others do. They say it must be uttered on three different occasions, and they also put other restrictions on *ṭalāq*. Contemporary Iran has also made a court appearance compulsory, and demanded that the man must always state the reason for the divorce.

— Inheritance: Sunnī rules of inheritance are extremely complex, and are based partly on rules of division found in the Koran, partly on rules for what is left over where the agnatic (father's) side of the family takes the lion's share.[50] Shīᶜīs have a simpler system. They first give out the Koranic shares in the same way as the Sunnīs. But the remainder is divided proportionally on the basis of genealogical distance from the deceased, closer kin gets a greater share. They do not make distinction between the agnatic and cognatic (women's) side.[51] Their system is clearly more straightforward than that of the Sunnīs, and must be considered more 'advanced' than the one the Sunnīs had developed some centuries earlier.

— A more particular issue concerns ritual ablution and the question of whether it is acceptable in some circumstance to perform the cleaning by wiping the feet on the outside of the shoes. This is accepted by the Shīᶜīs, on the basis of a *sunna*, while the Sunnīs do not accept it. In some ways this has become

49 Cf. Chapter 15 for details.
50 Chapter 15.
51 Another significant difference is that Shīᶜī law accepts that one who inherits according to the inheritance rules may also be a beneficiary in the deceased's will, while Sunnī law rejects such a double inheritance.

the main ritual distinction between the Sunnī and the Shīʿīs.

Thus it is mainly a question of minor points. The Shīʿī law, being younger than the Sunnī schools, could more easily adapt to changing circumstances in society. It could 'start afresh' to a greater degree than Sunnī law, which in spite of its adaptability still had a greater weight of tradition and established *ijmāʿ* to work under, an *ijmāʿ* the Shīʿīs could ignore if they wanted. This allowed them the opportunity to create a system that on some points was more flexible than that of the Sunnīs.

Some of the differences, like the *mutʿa* and the wiping of the feet, were clearly also ideologically motivated, to show that the Sunnīs had deviated from *sunna* and Revelation while the Shīʿīs maintained the original line. However, these distinctions concerned on the whole only a minor part of the body of law, and Shīʿī law is in the vast majority of cases similar or identical to what the Sunnīs had developed.

8

THE COURT AND THE LAW: THE *MUFTĪS* AND LEGAL DEVELOPMENT

So far we have only discussed the law as text, and mainly the theory behind the science of law, *uṣūl al-fiqh*. When we get to the history of the court system and how it developed, we get closer to the level of 'social reality', but not without facing the problem of sources. In a modern study of how a court system works, we can go to a court of law and observe the activities that take place there. This is actual social reality, what the anthropologists work with. But this can only show the situation today, and as we know, the Islamic court system either does not exist or is fundamentally changed in our time. We may to a certain extent study court records (*sijill*s), but there are not many of these left from the early centuries of Islam, and we must assume that these records may have gone through various stages or 'editing' to adapt reality to fit the norms, where at least whatever the writer or editor has considered irrelevant is excised.

Thus we have to begin at a fairly normative level, and describe how the various offices *should* function according to the classical theory. That puts us outside *uṣūl* proper, but into another genre called *adab al-qāḍī* and *adab al-muftī*.[1] These are a kind of 'manuals of good behaviour' for the judge and the jurist. But they may also, even if idealized, be a reflection of how practice was in the classical period here until the fourteenth or fifteenth century, even if there are many variations according to space, time or personal idiosyncrasies. Historical studies have been able to improve our knowledge of how it 'really was' to some degree, but we must still assume that what we believe we know from the earliest period is still a fairly abstracted picture.

1 Both are part of the legal literature, though, the *adab al-qāḍī* works normally under *furūᶜ* literature.

Fatwās

We mentioned in Chapter One that the institutions of the Sharīᶜa are clearly divided in two, on the one hand the court where the judge, the *qāḍī*, judges individual cases, on the other the jurist or scholar of law, *muftī*, who clarifies what the law is in general terms in legal opinions, *fatwās*, when asked to do so by the judge or a party in the case.[2]

Different types of fatwā

We can distinguish three types of *fatwā* according to their function, each formally similar but fulfilling different societal aims: judicial, political and private.

We may call 'private *fatwās*' those where an individual believer asks for clarification on a point of ritual or other religious issue, and the *muftī* thus functions as religious counsellor. These then mainly concern those parts of the Sharīᶜa that deal with Man's relation to God, the *ᶜibādāt*.[3]

They are part of the law, but seldom concern the court system, as the court always deals with conflicts between two (human) parties, a plaintiff and a defendant. God cannot be a party in the court, no-one can speak 'on behalf of God'.[4] So since the courts do not deal with such issues, they are left as the designated area of the *muftī*, where he is a direct authority for each individual Muslim. This role has become more important in a changing world where new problems not imagined before appear, such as how can a Muslim 'fast when the sun is in the sky' in polar regions where the sun is up all night? Recognized *muftīs* can give authoritative answers to such issues. Thus such issues are, in contrast with those in the court system, not adversial, while a judge always faces *two* parties, plaintiff and defendant, a *muftī* only faces *one*, the one who asks advice.

The legal literature has some discussions on how far into the

2 Muhammad Khalid Masud, Brinkley Messick and David S. Powers (eds), *Muftis, Fatwas and Islamic Legal Interpretation*, Cambridge, MA 1996.

3 Jakob Skovgaard-Petersen, *Defining Islam for the Egyptian State: Muftis and Fatwas of the Dār al-iftā*, Leiden 1997.

4 The judge does however in a sense 'represent God' in matters relating to *ḥuqūq Allāh*, 'God's rights', which includes the *ḥudūd* laws; see below, Chapter 10 (*ḥisba*) and Chapter 14.

field of theology a *muftī* may venture, whether he can for example decide issues of *tafsīr* commentary or general theological issues. Many writers of theory say that this is beyond the competence of a *muftī* in the *fatwā* format.

What we call 'political' *fatwā*s are in a sense no more than a variant of the private ones, where a sultan or other ruler or political entity asks for a statement, mostly in support of some action that he intends to take. A statement from a *muftī* that this is 'correct' will then justify the act. As time went on, some sultans started to refer to a certain class of 'high *muftī*s' who eventually might constitute a council around the sultan. But other parties could also ask for political *fatwā*s, such published opinions did for example play a role in the Iranian revolution of 1906-9.

The term *fatwā* has in recent years often been used for political statements, particularly those that condemn Muslims (or others) on a religious basis. The best known of these is of course Ayatollah Khomeini's *fatwā* of 1989 against the writer Salman Rushdie. There are some views that deny that this actually was a *fatwā*, as it did not follow the classical criteria of form or function for a *fatwā*. They would thus say that this type of general condemnation of religious opponents should not be seen as more than that, declarations based on whatever religious or political authority the author has.[5] However, it is probably fair to say that the term '*fatwā*' has always been so vague that such religio-political declarations can fairly be included if they are made by an authority that is considered to have the qualifications of a *muftī*, even if they, like the Rushdie *fatwā*, have no legal or judicial relevance or any relation to the courts.

But perhaps the most common type of *fatwā* over the centuries is the judicial one, a *fatwā* that is given on the basis of a case before the courts, and it is these that concern us here. Such a

5 E.g. Mehdi Mozaffari, *Fatwa: Violence and Discourtesy*, Aarhus 1998. Khomeini writes e.g. that Rushdie and those—unnamed—who help him are 'convicted to death', *maḥkūm be-iᶜdām mībāshand*, and that Muslims should execute them, while the Sharīᶜa position is of course that only a court may decide if an accused is guilty of the charges. This is thus not a *legal* document, but a 'charge' that is put by the guide and leader of the revolution on those who follow him. Khomeini did not himself use the term *fatwā* in this document, but when it became known as such (first in the French newspaper *Le Monde*, apparently), his supporters took up the term.

fatwā has a standard form: a 'questioner' (*mustaftī*) puts a problem that is before the court to the *muftī*.[6] The question must be put in an abstract form, 'if such and such is the case, what is the law on such a matter?' The *muftī* will then answer, 'in that case, the law is so-and-so'. The *fatwā* should be anonymized, and the *muftī* has no responsibility for, and need not know, the actual facts of the case. It is for the judge to establish those in the court-room. The *muftī* should only respond to what is stated in the question, *if* those are the facts, *then* the law is so. The judge will then, in the case, determine if these actually are the facts, and if they are not, then the *fatwā* is irrelevant and is discarded for that case even though it is a correct statement of law in itself.

Thus, the *muftī* still does not face an adversial situation; *futyā* (the process of asking for and giving *fatwā*s) is a one-to-one relation between the person who asks and the *muftī*. That person can often be one party in the case, who in this way seeks support for his view. But it may also be the judge who asks, either because he is uncertain about the correct rule, or because he seeks outside support for the verdict he is going to give. If he fears that the losing party will protest and not accept the ruling, then he can seek outside authority from a *muftī*, and preferably one with a higher status than himself, such as a recognized learned scholar in the capital or elsewhere.

The muftī, the state and the courts

The *muftī* is in theory fully independent of the state, that is the sultan, [7] and should not himself participate in the proceedings of the court. He is thus outside the court system proper, and we may see different types of relationship between the *muftī* and the (rest of the) legal system.

6 These normative rules for what a *fatwā* should look like developed over time, and were certainly not adhered to at all periods.

7 Many different titles have been used by Muslim rulers; *khalīfa* (caliph), *imām*, *sulṭān*, *walī* (governor), *amīr* (emir), *malik* (king), *shaykh*, etc. We will in this book use the general term 'sultan' (actually 'ruler') for whoever has political power, whatever title he may use in any particular instance.

Individual muftīs

A *muftī* may be fully personal; he declares himself to be a *muftī* and is recognized (or not) by the people of his community through his personal knowledge and competence, thus in an informal manner. That is the theory concerning the office, there is no 'exam' that an applicant has to pass to become a *muftī*; whoever considers himself knowledgeable starts to issue *fatwā*s, and these are then either accepted and he is in, or they are not, so he has to find some other line of work.

The theoretical literature emphasizes that it must be each *muftī*'s own decision when he is to start giving advice. Reality was of course different; *muftī*s received their education by studying with recognized scholars. A student would study law, *ḥadīth*, Arabic grammar and the other important religious sciences for several years, either with one particular teacher or at a larger centre of learning such as the great universities of Cairo, Fez, Qayrawan, Baghdad or elsewhere.

It would then normally be the teacher who decided when the student had enough knowledge to start practising, by giving him a certificate (*ijāza*). However, the *adab* books insist that if the student does not believe himself to be sufficiently competent, then he should refuse to give any *fatwā*s even if he is asked to do so. And if he does think he is, he does not have to wait for his teacher to agree. The point of this is of course that the *muftī* gives his *fatwā* on his own authority alone, not as a reflection of his teacher or others. Once he is established, it is in any case his own activity and the degree to which he is being sought for his opinions that decides his status and authority.

A *muftī* can function as an instance of 'appeal' in a case where one party disagrees with what the judge has decided. He can then go to a recognized *muftī* and ask if the judge applied the law correctly. The *muftī* may give an evaluation of this and thus in reality overrule the judge's authority. However, it varied to what degree the *muftī*s allowed themselves or could be used for such informal appeals, and how such a re-evaluation could be implemented.[8]

8 Cf. below and Chapter 9.

Advisors in court

A judge may in some cases attach a *muftī* to his court by making him a regular adviser at some level. The *muftī* may then be present in the court and take part in the proceedings, contrary to the norm described. This may in some cases make the *muftī* a subservient officer under the judge, and it may be a kind of 'lower-level' status for a *muftī* to fill such a position. We certainly see that judges that are in doubt will still ask for *fatwā*s from other *muftī*s in distant towns rather than from those attached to his court. However, the relation of authority may be inverse. The judge may be required to have his verdict in important cases confirmed by a *muftī*. That would in particular be normal in cases where the death penalty had been decreed (such cases would often also require the involvement of the political authority), but also in smaller matters.

In some cases, like Córdoba in Spain in the eleventh century onwards, this took the form of a '*muftī* council', *shūrā*, of the leading *muftī*s of the city. The judge had to have all his verdicts confirmed by a *fatwā* from it.[9] Here the distinction between a *fatwā* and a court verdict starts to become less distinct. However, it is clear that the *fatwā* should only confirm the use of the law, not the evaluation of the facts and thus the assignation of blame; in these matters the judge remained the final authority.

State appointments

As the state grows stronger it begins to appoint *muftī*s to particular courts. This points towards a different type of system, where the state dominates over the *muftī*s and the courts. This happened, but probably not on a general scale, in the pre-Ottoman period. We know that the Mamluks, who in many ways were intermediaries between the medieval and the Ottoman periods, did appoint *muftī*s at some of the major mosques, while the rest of the country still had 'self-appointed' *muftī*s. Morocco too saw the state taking more control over the *muftī*s from the fourteenth

9 Christian Müller, *Gerichtspraxis im Stadtstaat Córdoba. Zum Recht der Gesellschaft in einer mālikitisch-islamischen Rechtstradition des 5./11. Jahrhunderts*, Leiden 1999, 151-4 and 'Judging with God's law on Earth: Judicial powers of the *qāḍī al-jamāʿa* of Cordoba in the fifth/eleventh century', *Islamic Law and Society*, VII, 2, 2000, 163, and Serrano, 'Legal practice', 193 & 203.

century.[10]

The next step is when the sultan starts to draw some *muftī*s into his own circle as advisers. Their function would be to legitmize the sultan's rule, on a more permanent level than by simply issuing occasional *fatwā*s at his request.[11] It was again the Mamluks who innovated in this respect, they established a special council of *muftī*s called 'Iftāᵓ dār al-ᶜadl', a variant of the sultan's regular council Dār al-ᶜadl (Council of justice) that comprised the sultan himself and the chief judges. The Mamluks appointed *muftī*s from all four schools to the new council, following their practice of putting all schools on an equal footing.

The Mamluks also gave the chief *qāḍī* of Cairo the right to depose the *muftī*s in the same way as they could their own judges. This may have some logic in it, in that the judges could already ignore the *muftī*s and their *fatwā*s; they could say that 'this *muftī* does not have sufficient learning, so I need not listen to what he says'. The judge is not required to accept a *fatwā*, but he cannot on his own authority interpret the law in opposition to it, since judgeship does not give competence to issue *fatwā*s.[12] He must instead ignore the *muftī* and say he does not accept his general competence in the matter, so that there is no *fatwā* in the matter at all. This was, however, only possible as long as the *muftī*s were autonomous and self-declared. He could not in the same way ignore a *muftī* who had been appointed to his region by the same authority that ultimately had appointed the judge himself. Yet he still had the right to protest over the *muftī*'s competence, and there are cases where the judge did that. Thus if he is not satisfied with the answer from his 'local' *muftī* he can go to another for a second opinion. But a local *muftī* would most often be accepted as such by the population who would seek advice from him, and the judge would most often be under some contraint to accept the *fatwā* of a locally recognized *muftī*, otherwise his own authority might be impaired.

There were, in addition to these general *muftī*s, some who

10 David S. Powers, 'On judicial review in Islamic law', *Law & Society Review,* XXVI, 2, 1992, 328.

11 Tyan, *Histoire*, 224.

12 The roles of *qāḍī* and muftī are in theory incompatible and cannot be combined. It is still accepted that a judge who is qualified for it may give fatwās, but it is not the standard; Tyan, *Histoire*, 228.

specialized in certain areas of law, thus Fez had, in a period when there were many foreigners and other non-Muslims, a special *muftī* for Muslim-*dhimmī* matters, who only gave advice on such.[13] In later years, as the competence of the Sharīᶜa courts was on the wane, the non-judicial aspects of the *muftī*'s job became more important, and this latter dominates completely in modern times.[14]

The process of iftāʾ

It is the petitioner who takes the initiative to seek advice and who may freely choose his *muftī*. He should, according to the theory, not make this choice lightly, but should make enquiries to ensure the *muftī* is worthy and has the required knowledge, and may have to travel far to find the best qualified one (this, of course, was all formulated in the early period when there were no formally appointed local *muftī*s). The petitioner must be 'unlearned' in the matter at hand, that is, he should not have sufficient knowledge to perform his own *ijtihād* in the matter. If he has such knowledge, he must use it and cannot ask it from others (because it is the duty of the scholar to perform *ijtihād* to the extent of his competence). However, we often see *muftī*s asking other equally qualified *muftī*s for their views, or asking if they agreed with their assessment, and they may write in the *fatwā*, 'we have conferred with so-and-so and are agreed that …' The principle that *futyā* is a purely individual affair between he who asks and he who answers and fully the responsibility of the one *muftī*, may thus be attenuated in practice.

What is required of a muftī

A *muftī* must be a just man and not a sinner.[15] He must also be neutral in the case that he gives advice on. He should not investigate the facts of the case himself. He must give the petitioner the

13 David S. Powers, 'Legal consultation (*futyā*) in medieval Spain', in Chibli Mallat (ed.), *Islam and Public Law: Classical and Contemporary Studies*, London 1993, 89-90.

14 Skovgaard-Petersen, *Defining Islam for the Egyptian State*. Cf. also Chapter 12.

15 Tyan, *Histoire*, 224-8.

right answer if he knows it, but if not, then he must tell the petitioner that and refer to a *muftī* who may answer.

The books on theory accept that a woman can function as a *muftī*, while they do not allow this for judgeship. There were not many female *muftī*s at work, but it may certainly have occurred as we do know of a number of learned and respected women scholars in Islamic history. However, it is likely that any female *muftī*s there might have been would mostly give advice to female petitioners.[16]

The *muftī* also often worked as *mudarris*, teacher, so that one scholar would perform both functions in a local mosque. He could for example teach *fiqh* or other sciences during a part of the day, and then receive and answer questions later. This may also have provided an income for a *muftī* who was not appointed by anyone and thus did not receive any salary, as he should in theory not ask for a fee for giving *fatwā*s (although this may certainly have occurred). It is however perfectly acceptable to ask for a fee for teaching, paid by the students themselves, from their family or by a communal fund for the purpose.

Writing

A *fatwā* may theoretically be oral in form, but that is to be avoided, and a written form is the most common. This is of course more suitable for a document that should be presented to the judge in the absence of the *muftī* himself. There have also been other methods of publication in the modern period. The famous reformer Rashīd Riḍā had a *fatwā* column in his newspaper *al-Manār* in the early years of the twentieth century. It discussed the issues that had become troublesome for Muslims at the beginning of a new age, and was almost a religious 'Ask Abby' column. *Fatwā*s have in later years also been distributed on audio and videocassettes, and 'Sharīᶜa' programmes on satellite TV channels fulfil much the same function.[17] This has

16 It is also conceivable that the reason for this theoretical difference between *muftī* and judge is that a *muftī* need not meet the asker in person, they may communicate in writing, while the judge must of course be present in the courtroom and meet those who bring their cases; including men who would then be under the judge's authority. Such a situation may have been seen as unacceptable, but is not relevant in the case of a *muftī*.

17 Or on CD-ROM or the Internet. Here it is the personal authority of the

great impact, also on Muslims who would not normally be in contact with the more formal written religious literature. These mass *fatwās* are of course mostly of the social, political or ritual nature, not judicial ones that have decreased in importance as a result of the modern changes in the legal systems.

The form of the *fatwā* also varied in the classical period over time and space. A *fatwā* is composed of a question, *istiftāʾ*, and an answer. The *muftī* should answer on the same sheet of paper as the question, evidently to avoid later manipulation. The question must have a correct form, meaning that it should not mention the factual names of the persons involved. Instead, the document should refer to 'a person' and 'another person', or use standardized names like Zayd, ᶜAmr or Hind for the real names.[18] The question should also only contain what is relevant to it, irrelevant details should be removed.

These rules of how to frame the question were often only known in detail to the *muftī* himself and his associates. Thus it is quite common that a *muftī* and the petitioner talk the matter over first, and the *muftī* then formulates the precise question, or rewrites what the petitioner has brought with him, to fit the formulas. This may also, in larger towns, be done by a secretary or assistant to the *muftī*, who thus becomes the 'first line' of contact for the petitioner.

The *muftī* can, if he does not feel the question gives sufficient information, ask for more factual detail, or postpone the issue or refuse to answer. However, this information is only to clarify the legal basis for the question; the correctness of the fact is still the responsibility of the petitioner, not the *muftī*. The *muftī* must, when he is satisfied and has given an answer, explain this to the petitioner and ascertain that the latter has understood the answer. This means that there will be a certain amount of direct interaction between the *muftī* or his office and the petitioner, even though it is formally only a simple, written question, with an answer.

The *fatwās* present the law of Islam, and should therefore

---

scholar, the official or self-proclaimed *muftī*, and not any official appointment that determines whether these are accepted as authoritative answers.

18 'If Zayd buys a bushel of apples from ᶜAmr…' This rule is often disregarded in actual practices, thus if the *muftī* clearly knows about the case in advance or it is otherwise meaningless.

have an objective form, not the *muftī* saying, 'It is my opinion that...' He represents the Sharīᶜa and thus expresses himself unequivocally. But he should also know his limitations; in addition to his refusal to answer if he does not have sufficient knowledge or competence, he will also conclude the *fatwā* with the expression *wa-Allāh aᶜlam*, 'but God knows best'. This shows that the answer that the *muftī* gives is only the best that Man can determine for what God's will really is.

Fatwā and judgement

A *fatwā* is not a decision in the way a court judgement is. A *fatwā* only determines the rules that apply in the *type* of case in question, it does not decide any particular verdict in the case at hand. The theoreticians say that a verdict is creative or 'performative', it makes things happen, while a *fatwā* is communicative or informative, in the same way that a *ḥadīth* is. It relates the law in general, even if it is occasioned by a particular case, while the verdict is specific to the case.

The judge will probably not bother about *fatwā*s at all in minor cases, while more important cases would often involve a *fatwā*. However, there is nothing stopping the parties to a case from presenting several *fatwā*s with conflicting conclusions in the same case, evidently mostly in more complex cases.[19] Such contradictory *fatwā*s can lead to quarrels and conflicts between the different *muftī*s of a city or region. However, there may also be a source for conformity in this. Each *muftī* ultimately bases his authority on the general acceptance of the community around him.[20] If he starts issuing strange *fatwā*s contrasting with what most people expect, he might lose this authority as people start going to alternative *muftī*s for second opinions, and he might eventually not be considered a *muftī* at all.

We mentioned above that a *muftī* may in some cases function as a form of appeal body.[21] A court verdict is, in theory, final the moment it is issued; there are no formal forms of appeal nor

19 But of course within the system of the same school of law, that of the presiding judge.

20 At least in the classical period, before he becomes a state official. This is claimed by David Powers, who has worked extensively with this topic; 'Legal consultation', 98.

21 Powers, 'Legal consultation', 102-5.

hierarchical structure of courts in Islamic law. A dissatisfied party may use the plurality of schools of law, if there are several such in his town. The most normal situation is that if plaintiff and defendant belong to different *madhhabs*, then they should use that of the defendant. However, a losing party may try to bring his case up at the court of a different *madhhab*, if there is one in the town. But as this might lead to a conflict of competence between the courts of the schools, it would in most cases be difficult to get a judge from one school to accept a case that had already been decided by a colleague from another. That would depend partly on the relationship between the schools and the judges at that particular time and place.

Instead the losing party could go to a *muftī* and ask whether the verdict is correct. The *muftī* cannot then evaluate the evidence of the case—that authority belongs only to the judges—but he can give his view on the way the law was used, and declare this to be faulty.[22] That would not lead to any automatic reversal or reopening of the case, but it would be a good argument for the party to approach another judge for this purpose. Such a new evaluation should only occur when the first judge has died,[23] as his verdict does in a sense have final validity as long as he is the acting judge, but it may also occur that old cases are taken up again in new courts while the first judge is still in office. However, these would be exceptions, and there is no automatic way for a new trial, even with a *fatwā* in hand.

From ijtihād to fatwā

We discussed in Chapter Four various methods for formulating a law, under the general term *ijtihād*. To write a *fatwā* is also, in a sense, to formulate the law, and *iftā*ʾ, the *muftī*'s work in issuing *fatwās* is in principle the same process as *ijtihād*. Indeed both terms did originally refer to the formulation of law on the basis of Revelation through an accepted methodology. However, we may for simplicity consider the difference as one of level of ambition; while *ijtihād* represents the process of creating something that is

22 Although one may of course 'generalize' the use of evidence to a matter of procedure and ask if this procedure is according to the Sharīʿa.

23 Or deposed! See more on the procedures of appeal in Chapter 9.

new, be it a completely new rule or a change in an existing rule in a new context, *iftāʾ* should normally be a exposition of the rules that have already been formulated in the Sharīʿa, either in the Revelation or in the established consensus of the schools. It may not always be easy to see the difference between these two forms of legal work, and it is probably best to consider them stages on a continuum that runs from a full genesis of new rules at one end to the straight application of rules every scholar knows at the other. Somewhere in the middle *ijtihād* runs over into *iftāʾ*.[24]

The term *fatwā* is used from an early stage.[25] Shāfiʿī discusses *iftāʾ*, and it seems the function was established from the very first period. It was probably used in a more general way then, without the precise procedures that came later, but the idea that the law in a concrete case at court would be expressed by a separate *muftī* was probably already known at the time that the Islamic law was being formed.

However, everyone in this early period, including Shāfiʿī and later authors, assume automatically that a *muftī* is also a *mujtahid* in the full meaning of the word. The two terms are used interchangeably, or rather, a *muftī* is a *mujtahid* who answers individual queries in addition to his regular work of formulating rules and methodology, evaluating *ḥadīth* and so on. It is thus a function of the status of a *mujtahid*, and it is assumed that a *muftī* has full knowledge of the Text, about analogies and *ʿilla*s, about what is abrogated or not, and so on; there is in this period no particular hierarchy of scholarly status.

This seems to last until about 1200, into what we call the Islamic Middle Ages. Only then do theoreticians (such as al-Āmidī, d. 1234) start accepting that it may be possible that all *muftī*s do not have such a complete knowledge of the fundamentals of the law, 'as the situation is today', as the expression goes.[26] They start setting up a ranking of *muftī*s, so that in addition to *mujtahid-muftī*s who do have such total knowledge, there are also those with lower competence who only work within

24 Schacht also accepted this connection, he writes that the *muftī*s have taken over much of the functions of the *mujtahid*s, without openly recognizing that this is what they do; Schacht, *Introduction,* 73.

25 Tyan, *Histoire*, 219-30.

26 Wael B. Hallaq, 'Iftaʾ and ijtihad in sunni legal theory: a developmental account', in Masud *et al.*, *Islamic Legal Interpretation*, 35-6.

one school of law.

This began to lead to a division between the two terms *mujtahid* and *muftī*, where the latter referred to a more limited activity. Some Muslim scholars referred to this by saying that the 'gate to *ijtihād* (*bāb al-ijtihād*) is closed', as latter-day scholars did not have sufficient knowledge to formulate new rules.[27] The distance in time to the Prophet and the Revelation had become too wide, knowledge had been lost, and the scholars of the early times knew so much more about the Prophet's time than we possibly can, and no later scholar can change anything stated by these early scholars. Everything had in any case been said, the Sharīᶜa as they knew it covered all possible questions, and all that later *muftī*s and other scholars needed to do was to apply the established view in the school (*taqlīd*).

This view has been seen by modern critics as the proof that Islamic law was frozen in time and could not adapt to changing circumstances.[28] However, the view of the 'closing of the gate' was never universally accepted.[29] Contemporary authors would say that 'no epoch can be without a *mujtahid*', and that there would always be new situations and problems that required new answers. Many later scholars also considered themselves as *mujtahid*s or were considered as such by their fellows, or not. It is all fairly confusing.

Categories of muftīs and mujtahids

The picture becomes a bit clearer when one discovers that '*ijtihād*' may mean many different things. The term covers legal work on several levels, according to the competence of the scholar who performs it. The theoreticians describe it as a ranking of *mujtahid*s, mirrored by a similar ranking of *muftī*s. This shows that these are related activities, except that a *muftī* may also be a practitioner with so little knowledge that he may only repeat what other authorities have said before him, without knowing why they said it (a *muqallid*), which is clearly below the level of *ijtihād*.

27 Schacht, *Introduction*, 72-5.

28 Cf. Chapter 1.

29 Wael B. Hallaq, 'Was the gate of *Ijtihād* closed?', *International Journal of Middle East Studies*, XVI, 1, 1984, 3-34 and several other articles collected in *Law and Legal Theory in Classical and Medieval Islam*, Aldershot 1995.

While the earliest authors divide the *muftīs* or *mujtahids* into three levels according to their learning, others describe nine or more levels.[30] It is perhaps illustrative to use a schematic worked out by Ibn al-Ṣalāḥ al-Shahrazūrī, d. 1245.[31] He draws up four levels of *mujtahid*/*muftīs*:

(1) *M. mustaqill* (or *muṭlaq*), 'independent'. This is someone who does not need to concern himself with what earlier scholars said, as he has the same or higher competence to evaluate the sources of Revelation as any one before him. That means that he may establish his own school of law, if he wishes. However, this group is divided into two: On the one hand those scholars who actually did form their own schools. On the other, their students, who did have such competence, but refrained from forming separate schools because they agreed with what the founders had done and thus followed them in their views (for example Shaybānī and Abū Yūsuf of the Ḥanafī school).

(2) *M. fī 'l-madhhab*, 'in the school'. Scholars at this level could not make any changes in or form rules for the *methodology* of the law (*uṣūl*), they had to follow that of the school they belonged to. But they were otherwise free to develop new rules of law directly from the sources in cases where no consensus was established, using the methodology of the school.

(3) *M. muqayyad* (or *muntasib*), 'dependent', is someone who knows how the rules were formed, and can argue for them in a discussion. He thus does have the right to formulate subsidiary rules using *qiyās*, and could thus establish the reasoning behind those rules that already existed and how they should be generalized, but he could not make completely new rules.

(4) *Muftī-muṣannif*, a scholar-author, knows the rules of the school well, but not necessarily the reasoning behind them or why they have their particular formulation. Thus he can issue *fatwā*s as long as the rules are clear and the response is evident to him. He can also organize and refine them in books, but he must, when he is not certain about a matter, refer to a higher level or jurist. *Muftīs* below this level are pure *muqallids*.

This is a simplified list, and others may make a finer distinc-

30 Norman Calder, 'Al-Nawawi's typology of *muftīs* and its significance for a general theory of Islamic Law', *Islamic Law and Society*, III, 2, 1996, 137-64, and Hallaq, *Authority*, 2-17, show the development of these typologies.

31 Hallaq, 'Ifta' and ijtihad', 36-7.

tion of levels 2 and 3 as to what kind of rules these scholars may develop. But the basic component is the level of knowledge. It was clear to Ibn al-Ṣalāḥ that level 1 was no longer applicable at his time, no scholar at his age could claim such high level of knowledge. There was some uncertainty as to whether anyone could claim to belong to level 2. However, levels 3 and certainly 4 contained scholars active at his time.

The claim of independent *ijtihād*, the ability to create a completely new school of law, was probably dead by this time; no-one considered this possible any longer. The demands that were made for such a lofty level was far too high, it was even hard to imagine how anyone could ever have reached it.[32] *Those* gates were closed. Anyone who wanted to be taken seriously stayed within the four schools, and limited themselves to expanding them. But *ijtihād* continued within these, still fairly wide borders, and remained an important element of the legal activity. This could still be a very elevated level of learning, and there could be disagreement about how many active *mujtahid*s there were at each point. There are cases where a scholar who was considered an honoured *mujtahid* by his fellows, did—honestly or out of modesty—clearly say that the 'time for *mujtahid*s at this level has passed'.[33] Others, however, pressed their own claims more actively.

We may thus perhaps date such a differentiation between the roles of *muftī*s and *mujtahid*s to the twelfth or at the latest early thirteenth century, if we consider that these views took a century or so to work their way into the normative books of theory. This fits well with the dating of the schools of law as 'solidified entities'—frameworks in which the law not only may but must develop—to the eleventh century or so. As these more stable structures developed, the status of those on whom they were built, the 'Founders' including early students as Shaybānī, Abū Yūsuf, Muzanī and others, had to be raised to a level that could not be assailed in later days.

Saying that a *muftī* might now or in the future have the same level of competence as a founder or his first students would undermine the authority of the doctrine of the school. A *mujtahid*

32 Cf. Chapter 6, 'authority grows backwards'.
33 Hallaq, *Authority*, 85. His example is al-Mazārī (d. 1141).

muṭlaq cannot be subservient to the authority of a school, as he has the freedom to ignore it and even create his own; he works directly on the sources of Revelation. Allowing this would thus set the unity of the law, now finally reduced to four parallel schools, at risk. Thus the authority of these founders must be established so well that no-one present or future could endanger them. So in addition to the perceived status of the early founders being raised to an almost inhuman standard, the latter-day scholars moved in the opposite direction, downwards in perceived competence. It might not be directly a sin, but certainly unduly presumptuous to believe that one could on one's own evaluate or amend what consensus had established as being the founder's view. This decline in how the later *muftī*s were viewed was the price to pay for unity, and thus practicability, of the law that the schools had taken upon themselves to watch over.

Taqlīd and the rules of the school

Foundational works

None of the four founders of the schools had really left behind a coherent set of rules of law in their own name, with the exception of the *Muwaṭṭaʾ* of Mālik, which we have already mentioned. However, there are some books ascribed to their first generation students, such as the *Kitāb al-Aṣl* by Shaybānī for the Ḥanafīya, similarly by Muzanī for the Shāfiʿīya, as well as important later summations of views like the *Mudawwana* of Saḥnūn for the Mālikīya and the statements of Ibn Ḥanbal collected by Khallāl.[34] These books sum up the statements or views expressed by the founders, and are called the *Ummahāt* (mothers, or origins); we may call them 'foundational works' of the schools, as they were based on statements by the founders.[35] These are, apart from Khallāl's book, assumed to have been written down at the latest in the first generation after the founder. They may perhaps have

34 Wael B. Hallaq, 'From *fatwās* to *furūʿ*: growth and change in Islamic substantive law', *Islamic Law and Society*, I, 1, 1994, in particular 51-5.

35 The founders of the four most important schools of law are confusingly often called 'the four *imāms*'. This because the word *imām* simply means 'he who stands/is in front'; there is no connection between this usage here and e.g. the Shīʿī *imām*.

received their final form at the end of the ninth century. They were, as the school formation developed in the following century, supplemented by many commentaries that developed individual points they raised.

However, these foundational works were basically only collections of individual statements by the founder. We may, as described, see their final form as a result of a polemic between different currents and viewpoints, a debate that was frozen at some particular time, but where both 'early' and 'late' statements may be included more or less at random. And they were of course not exhaustive; although they may have been organized thematically, there were still many topics or issues they did not cover.

Ijtihād, tarjīḥ and taqlīd

Thus the law still needed to be developed and refined. There are one or two such foundational works for each school, some in several manuscript variants. The schools also had a body of views and opinions that were claimed to come from the founders, in commentaries, subsidiary collections or other sources, as well as other opinions that were common to the school. These gave room for divergent opinions in the school, all of which had some connection to its legitimizing authority.

Thus those who formulated the school law had to use *ijtihād*, their own rational faculties and specific methodologies to locate those statements that were to become the founder's authorized views. And, once again, when we say room for *ijtihād*, that means someone must decide what is the correct *ijtihād*, the one that is to be applied, and an *ijmā*ᶜ of the school must be established. It was also necessary to reduce the area of divergence in the school in order to reach an applicable, that is, predictable law; as an American judge said, the only thing that is important in a law is what the criminal expects the judge to rule.

This had partly been achieved by raising the founder's perceived authority and lowering that of the contemporary scholars, but that did not yet produce the goal of a unified law system within the school. Other methods had to be developed, both to make a selection from the many statements ascribed to the founder, and to understand them correctly. However, the very process of raising the level of the founders' authority undermined the possibility of developing their views. When the early great ones were elevated so high above our latter-day inadequacies, and we perhaps even do not know why they made the statements they made, how can we say which among their views was right or wrong?[36]

There were several possible answers to this problem of selection. One was to prefer the alternative that seemed strongest or best supported. That is called *tarjīḥ*, in general 'to prefer something above something else' by weighing the evidence and arguments for one or the other opinion. That then presumes that the scholar *does* know the evidence for the various opinions that are proffered; that is that he has a competence for *ijtihād* at least at some intermediate level. This might not always be the case, at least in so far as perceived competence is involved.

Another solution would be to select the opinion that was shared by the largest numbers of jurists at a high level. But Islam does not normally favour such voting, primarily because it is difficult to count; who to include and how to learn their views given the distances in space and time involved.

The third possible answer is to say that if there are different opinions to be found among the authorities, and no clear and evident consensus appears as to which is right, then all these opinions are equal in status. If one had been true and the other false, then a consensus would have formed around it. So the jurist can in this case choose freely among the views, which thus all become authorized views of the school. This is called *takhyīr*, free choice. This is a logical answer, and it was accepted by early Shāfiᶜī and Mālikī scholars. However, opinions turned, and both schools came to reject *takhyīr*.[37] This was not because the logic of it was flawed, but for purely practical reasons: it would lead to evident problems in court practice. To allow an open choice between alternative rules, even within this limited space, would mean that it would be impossible to predict what a judge would rule in advance, and thus make the law less useful.

Instead the result was thus that the scholars settled for the conclusion that the correct view was that which was *mashhūr* or

36 Wael B. Hallaq, 'Murder in Cordoba: Ijtihâd, iftâ᾿ and the evolution of substantive law in medieval Islam', *Acta Orientalia*, LV, 1994, 55-83 and *Authority*, 22-3 and *passim*.

37 Fadel, 'Social logic of *taqlīd*', 212-15.

ẓāhir al-riwāya,[38] that which is 'known' or the 'general view' of the school. The concept is not as strictly delimited as consensus, it simply means that it is the view that is commonly accepted as the authorized one in the school. This eventually came to mean the view that was expressed last, the *latest* view. As all these should in theory go back to the founder or be linked to him, and as one accepted that they all (if they were considered at all) were true stories, then they had to mean that the founder had changed his mind in his day. So the youngest opinion, the last, must be the one that he had settled with as final. Thus the principle of *naskh*, 'abrogation' was in reality also included in the schools of law.

The idea of the 'latest' was expanded beyond the views of the founders, and also came to include other early authorities. The labour of establishing the authorized, *mashhūr*, version thus became one of chronology of statements. A distinction was made between *qawl*, an opinion (among many) in the school, and *ḥukm*, which is the authorized rule of the school and which a jurist on a lower level has to apply, if he does not have a sufficient competence in *ijtihād*.

The scholars could also apply a more active form of *ijtihād* by using *takhrīj*, which means to construct new rules through the authority of the founders. It requires a fairly high level of *ijtihād* competence, but was widely and openly used.[39] One such method was to find a rule similar to the desired ones among those accepted from the founder. This was then 'transferred' (*naql*) to new cases not mentioned or intended by the founder. Or they could create new rules directly on the basis of the methodology and the principles enunciated by the founder. There are also cases, at least in the early period, where jurists openly borrowed rules from other schools through *takhrīj*.[40] This became more difficult as the barriers between the schools became more rigid. Such fairly creative *ijtihād* certainly lasted into the fourteenth century, long after the purported 'closing of the gates'.

38 *Mashhūr* is most used among the Mālikīs, *ẓāhir al-riwāya* ('the most probable reading') is the corresponding term among the Ḥanafīs; Hallaq, *Authority*, 26.

39 Wael B. Hallaq, '*Takhrīj* and the construction of juristic authority', in Weiss, *Studies in Islamic Legal Theory*, 317-35 and *Authority*, 43-56.

40 Thus the Shāfiʿī Ibn Surayj took from Abū Ḥanīfa; Hallaq, '*Takhrīj*', 324.

Taqlīd as counterfoil to ijtihād

This then is a form of 'lower level' *ijtihād*. But it is also a form of *taqlīd*. This term is normally the negation of *ijtihād*. When *ijtihād* is presented as a positive and flexible opening of the Sharīᶜa by adapting it to new conditions, then *taqlīd* is normally depicted as the opposite; ossified orthodoxy or 'blind imitation', as it is often translated. However, the two are in reality closely linked, parts of a dialectical unity in the development of the law.

This can be seen in the description of the levels of *mujtahid*s that we gave above. The *mujtahid* must at each level restrain his *ijtihād* activity to what he has the knowledge and competence to handle. He must beyond this use *taqlīd*; follow recognized knowledge. The same scholar is thus a *mujtahid* in those areas and topics where he has knowledge of the sources, but a *muqallid* (user of *taqlīd*) in all others.

Thus there are duties on both sides of the equation. Someone who has no legal training at all, an 'unlearned' Muslim, must follow the counsel of one who has knowledge. He cannot start reading the Koran and *ḥadīth* and apply their message in any way he wants. To properly understand God's intention with His message requires extensive knowledge, and only someone who has knowledge of the language, of the contexts of the Text and its relevance, of other sources of revelation that may affect our understanding and so on, can understand what the meaning of the Text 'actually' is. So the unlearned must accept the authority of the one who knows, and the term for this acceptance of authority is *taqlīd*. That is as true for the lower-level scholar in areas where he does not have required knowledge as it is for an unlearned Muslim; he must accept *taqlīd* of the scholar who has more knowledge of the issue in question.

However, if a scholar does have such knowledge, he not only has the right, but also the duty to apply it. It is forbidden for such a scholar to used *taqlīd* on this topic. That is part of the general duty of the *ᶜulamāʾ* to represent the sum of knowledge in society, a *farḍ kifāʾī* for the community.

Thus the history of Islamic law is not divided chronologically in two, one early period of 'independent thought' marked by *ijtihād* and no 'imitation', then a break (say in the tenth century) followed by a latter-day decline where only *taqlīd* was possible. The two are complementary concepts, *ijtihād* to the limit of the scholar's competence, *taqlīd* beyond. This principle goes back at least to Shāfiᶜī; he formulated it and emphasized that the unlearned must apply *taqlīd* to the words of the *muftī*.

Thus the central theme of *taqlīd* is not 'imitation' but authority. *Taqlīd* was a necessity if the free development of rules through *ijtihād* was to become a social reality in the practice of a school of law. Thus the method mentioned above, *takhrīj*, is a form of *ijtihād* through *taqlīd*, the creation of rules of law by attaching these to the authority of the founders, even if the content of these rules were quite new and adapted to the continuous changes of historical and social reality.[41]

It is impossible to conceive of *ijtihād* in any functioning system of law without *taqlīd*; it was precisely this acceptance of the authority of the school's rules by *taqlīd* that gives meaning to *ijtihād*. So *taqlīd* does not mean 'frozen orthodoxy' as much as loyalty to the school of law.

Manuals and supplementary works

Mukhtaṣarāt

The effort of collecting rules of law or legal points of view in a literary form is called *taṣnīf*, 'authoring' or organization. Perhaps the most important of these types of authorship are the attempts at formulating univocal rules for the school through a type of books that are called *mukhtaṣarāt*, 'abbreviations' or 'compendia'; they are sometimes called 'manuals of law'. They were primarily the product of the thirteenth and fourteenth centuries, and each school of law has one or more of them.[42]

41 Sherman Jackson calls it 'legal scaffolding', building a new construction around an established authority; '*Kramer versus Kramer* in a tenth/sixteenth century Egyptian court: Post-formative jurisprudence between exigency and law', *Islamic Law and Society*, VIII, 1, 2001, 47-51. Cf. also Baber Johansen, 'Legal literature and the problem of change: the case of land rent', in Mallat, *Islam and Public Law*, 29-47 (and in *Contingency*, 446-64). This is also, as we have seen, actually true for the founders themselves, they were also in a relation of *taqlīd* to their own teachers, a relationship that was later disregarded or 'forgotten' (Chapter 6).

42 Fadel, 'Social Logic', 215-33. The title *Mukhtaṣar* only means 'Abbreviated edition' and had been used for a long time; we have already mentioned it in relation to the literature of commentaries in the tenth century (Chapter 6). But it is as a technical *genre* of legal literature mostly

These books have two main characteristics. They systematize a technical vocabulary for the school, thus the legal terminology is mainly developed within each school and can differ between them. We have seen this in the use of the term *istiḥsān* by Ḥanafīya and *istiṣlāḥ* by the Mālikīs for processes which (although not identical) were close and served the same main purpose; this is because these terms for subsidiary methods were defined as concepts in the thirteenth century onwards, after the separation of *usūl* in the schools.

The second main object of these books is to give authority to one particular rule or variant to the exclusion of all other alternatives in the school. The most famous of these books in Mālikī law is the one written by the Egyptian Khalīl b. Isḥāq (d. 1350), named just the *Mukhtaṣar*. It differs from earlier works by only listing *mashhūr* rules, without mentioning any variants or discussing them. That does not mean Khalīl was unaware of them. He himself wrote commentaries on his work where he discussed each topic and explained why the stated rule is the *mashhūr* one. However, the point of the *Mukhtaṣar* was to be an aid to judges and lower-level jurists by establishing one clear rule for every situation, which they could then directly apply.[43]

It has been suggested that this is a step towards codification of the Islamic law.[44] The *mukhtaṣar* books may be seen as codes of law, because they postulate simple rules with no room for evaluation against alternatives, as the earlier *ijtihād*-based and discursive literature does. True, they do not contain any 'legislative' authority beyond the general acceptance that Khalīl contains the best summary of Mālikī law, but it is pointed out that there were no further *mukhtaṣarāt* published for the Mālikīs after Khalīl; only commentaries on him.[45] Thus it should place the

---

used for these 'epitomes' of the Middle Ages.

43 They of course also had, like all legal literature, an important didactic function. It was important in the *madrasa*, where law was taught, that the students who were going to become jurists or judges had short and concise texts that they could learn as easily as possible. The more extensive commentary literature could then be used for more advanced studies.

44 Fadel, 'Social Logic', 233.

45 The *Minhāj* of al-Nawawī (d. 1277) has a similar position in the Shāfiᶜīya, while it is the *Hidāya* of Marghīnānī (d. 1197; actually a commentary based on an earlier *Mukhtaṣar* by al-Qudūrī) that dominates among the Ḥanafīya.

Sharīᶜa in an intermediary position between common law and codified law.

This view may be overstated, because a *mukhtaṣar* is a tool, not a law. Khalīl did not actually perform *ijtihād*, he changed no rules, he only summed up what he considered the commonest opinions in his school. Later *mujtahid*s were free to disagree with him, within the limits of *ijtihād* that was at any time open. The *mukhtaṣar*s cannot be considered law codes as long as this process of *ijtihād* continued within the school, because any competent later jurist could overrule them without thus replacing them.

A survey of court practice in Granada in the fifteenth century shows this.[46] As many as a quarter to a third of all *fatwā*s issued in this period have conclusions that differ from Khalīl. This is a fairly large percentage when we consider that Khalīl based his work on what was already the majority opinions in his view, and it shows that the *muftī*s did not consider him as any final authority or code in their period.

However, it is evident that books such as Khalīl's, as well as the commentaries on them, became crucial for the practical application of the law, and are often as far as any judge or even *muftī*s will go in search of the correct rule. So it may be correct that the actual application of law rests largely on books such as these *mukhtaṣar*s, whether or not we accord them the status of a 'code' of law.

Fatwā collections

The *fatwā*s issued by *muftī*s for individual cases can also be used as sources for more permanent legal developments. The *fatwā*s could go through various stages of abstraction and systematization and be transformed from a statement made at an 'instance', one particular case, to a lasting formulation of how a law should be understood. The gathering of individual *fatwā*s into written collections had already started in the tenth century.[47] This became a standard practice, which still continues today. These collections were initially no more than copies of the *fatwā*s issued by well-known *muftī*s, grouped by subject. Of course only the *fatwā*s of the most prominent *muftī*s were gathered in this fashion, those

46 Fadel, 'Adjudication', 286-361.
47 Hallaq, 'From *fatwās* to *furūᶜ*'.

that in some way had an authority bestowed upon them by their *muftī* and/or were creative in solving new problems. Those *fatwā*s that were not preserved in this fashion would disappear; *fatwā*s are not everlasting. If the views in them are no longer practised, they become *gharīb*, 'strange' or 'unknown', and die out.

Some collections would then go a further step towards generalization. Some of the more central *fatwā*s would be rewritten to exclude whatever was specific for the case at hand, and any subsidiary problems that affected the case were deleted. The 'purified' *fatwā* became an example of the results of one particular issue or set of conditions and how they affect the interpretation of an existing rule of law. This abstracted *fatwā* is then collected with others of the same type, and is thus elevated in its normative status. If the scholars of a school then tend to agree on the understandings expressed by such a collection, it enters into the basic legal literature of the school, its *furū*ᶜ works, and will in turn be the subject of commentaries and used as a basis for later *fatwā*s. The *fatwā* may in this way be transformed from a personal view by one jurist to become the law of the school, or at least an authorized interpretation of a law; such a *fatwā* will of course in principle only deal with the understanding of a legal rule, not be the creation of one *ab initio*. This then is an example of the continuing dynamics of the law throughout the centuries.

Shurūṭ works

There are other specialized types of legal literature. One, which is also a standardization of practice, is what is called *shurūṭ*, 'conditions'.[48] These are collections of standard formulas for contracts and similar documents; that is for written agreements. They started out, like the *fatwā* collections, as documents that had been written in real-life cases. These had then been copied, cleared of whatever was irrelevant, and turned into generalized formulas for various types of contracts.

Such generalized formulas were then collected and issued as specific *shurūṭ* books, separate for each school of law, and each court would have specialized officials whose jobs were to keep

48 Wael B. Hallaq, 'Model shurût works and the dialectics of doctrine and practice', *Islamic Law and Society*, II, 2, 1995, 109-34, and Jeanette Wakin, *The Function of Documents in Islamic Law*, Albany 1972.

track of and refine these formula collections. There were also written commentary works on the most famous of these *shurūṭ* collections, explaining how they could be modified and used in particular circumstances. These are thus one source of knowledge of applied law in these types of cases.

Thus these works became more normative, not unlike the role of the *mukhtaṣar*s, but only within specific fields of law concerned with economic and contractual relations.

Qawāʿid

Another type of literature is the *qawāʿid*. This means 'general principles' that support the law. These were formulated in specific works, particularly in the thirteenth to the fifteenth century, that tried to abstract the rules of each school into small summaries that the students could easily memorize.[49] These could, in their extreme form, be so compact that a school was reduced to four or five pithy statements.[50] Thus this was a literary and theoretical activity somewhat akin to the attempts to define God's aims (*maqāṣid*) with the Sharīʿa, such as 'human welfare' and the like.

There were also different ways of formulating the legal rules to rhyming verse that the students could easily memorize.[51] These could aid the learning process, but could not replace more detailed knowledge of the law.

Other sources for legal practice

Ḥiyal

One judicial principle that was very controversial was what can be called 'legal fictions' or, more bluntly, tricks to get around the

49 Wolfhart P. Heinrichs, '*Qawāʿid* as a legal genre', in Weiss, *Studies in Islamic Legal Theory*, 365-84. See also Schacht, *Origins*, 180-9.

50 In the most famous formulation: 'Things are what they are through their intention—Harm shall be removed—Custom is the arbiter—Hardship leads to ease—Certainty is not erased by doubt'; Heinrichs, '*Qawāʿid*', 369.

51 Brinkley Messick, *The Calligraphic State: Textual Domination and History in a Muslim Society*, Berkeley 1993, 21. This anthropological study gives a good introduction to a traditional system of learning in modern Yemen.

meaning of a rule while remaining within its language. That is, should a judge accept something that clearly is contrary to the obvious intention of a rule, as long as it conforms to the strict letter of the rule, as formulated by his school; or should the judge look at the intention, as it can be ascertained, and ignore such tricks?[52]

An example of this is a rule which says that when a farmer sells a piece of land, his neighbour has first refusal to buy whatever plot is adjacent to is own. This is clearly intended to promote the unification of the many tiny plots that are often created by the divisions of the inheritance rules. However, this rule of first refusal only concerns the sale of land; it does not mention gifts. So a farmer who wants to can circumvent the rule by first giving away a narrow strip along the border of his land to someone for free. He can sell the rest later, as the neighbour is no longer adjacent to the land that is actually sold and can therefore make no demand on it. Another case of *ḥiyal*, which we will deal with later, is to circumvent the ban on interest by 'masking' a loan as first 'selling' a fictitious commodity, then later buying it back with a higher price, two legal sales.[53]

The Ḥanafī school accepts some such *ḥiyal* fictions. Their tolerance of it may be a result of their more argumentative and formalist methodology, however their old rivals the Shāfiᶜīs also largely followed them in this. The Mālikīs are those most opposed to these methods which they consider immoral, and in this matter they are supported by the Ḥanbalīs.

Customary law, ᶜurf

The terms 'custom' and 'customary law' interact with the Sharīᶜa in many different ways. Many of the rules of the law are probably based on ancient custom that has been enshrined into the Revelation because the Prophet accepted it, or expressly supported it in a *ḥadīth*; they have thus been 'Islamicized' and are no longer 'customary'. We can on the other hand see in later practised law, and in particular in the modern period, that 'custom' is used as a source for applied law alongside the Sharīᶜa,

52 Robert Brunschvig, 'De la fiction légale dans l'Islam médiéval', in *Études d'Islamologie*, II, 335-45 and in *Studia Islamica*, XXXII, 1970, 41-51.
53 See more on this in Chapter 16.

which the judge can base his decisions on without referring to the law books.

However, there may also be a third usage of custom, *ᶜurf* ('what is known'), as a subsidiary element in the creation or formulation of rules inside the Sharīᶜa without specific reference to the Revealed texts or the opinions of consensus or the early legal authorities.[54] Custom will in this sense work mainly as 'local variable', since custom is not uniform from place to place. Thus it cannot have a central or defining role in legal formulation or be a source for legal rules, but it can be accepted as a source for how to understand the rules in specific (local) contexts. It is particularly the Mālikīs that allow such a role for custom. They say that 'custom has the character of specification' (of how rules or statements should be understood). This is of course related to the idea of *istiṣḥāb*, that matters should continue in their 'natural or expected' condition unless there is any positive reason for the opposite. Custom then stipulates what this natural and expected condition, 'normality', is. The Mālikīs may also use the term *ᶜamal*, 'practice', for this function of custom.[55]

54 Kamali, *Principles*, 283-96.

55 This attempt to draw local practices and conditions into the realm of legal docrtine should not be confused with an acceptance of customary law as such, as its application is within and based on the methodology of the Sharīᶜa in its Mālikī version; cf. Scahcht, *Introduction*, 61-2.

9

THE COURT AND ITS JUDGE: THE ROLE OF THE *QĀḌĪ*

The office of *qāḍī* is probably the oldest element in the Islamic legal system.[1] The earliest legal disputes were mostly solved by go-betweens, *ḥakam*s who negotiated settlements between disputing parties. Christians could also fulfil this role as middle-men between Muslims.[2] The first actual *qāḍī*s were appointed in the first decades of the eighth century, when the Empire was in a process of rapid expansion. They were appointed by regional governors to help them settle whatever conflicts would appear among the settlers. Thus they were mostly there to take over a part of the workload of the governor, and had functions that would otherwise rest with him, that is the political and military authorities. They were in this way closely linked to the nascent state authority of the Muslim empire. The court based their decisions mainly on custom both among Muslim immigrants and among the existing population. Thus these early *qāḍī*s presided over a court that was more 'Arab and local' than 'Islamic'.

This changed after the Abbasids took power in 750. The most important new development then was that the caliph in Baghdad started appointing judges directly from the centre. Hārūn al-Rashīd is considered to be the first caliph to appoint a *qāḍī* in Baghdad in around 790. The capital had not until then had any particular *qāḍī*, as these functions were dealt with directly by the caliph himself. That this office was now introduced in the capital as well as the provinces led to changes in its prerogatives. The Baghdad *qāḍī* was given the title *qāḍī al-quḍāt*, high judge, and became superior to all the judges working in the various provinces.

The unification of the judiciary under a single chief judge could only work as long as the Empire was unified politically. The court apparatus was centralized and given a more autonomous authority and the high judge was one of the highest

1 A survey of the history of the office of *qāḍī* is in Tyan, *Histoire*, 100-429.
2 Tyan, *Histoire*, 73.

positions in the administration. However, this imposition of a high judge did not mean the court system itself became hierarchic; there was no appeal from the individual provincial courts to the high judge; or at least not formally so. The most important power of the high judge was that it was he who (in the name of the caliph) appointed and could depose the provincial *qāḍī*s.

The reality of this power can be used as a gauge to measure where the actual authority rested during the various periods of Abbasid power. The Tulunids, who were governors in Egypt in the ninth century, can be considered to have taken 'real' power in that province because they appointed the *qāḍī* there without asking the caliph for approval. However, when the central power regained its strength, they showed this by deposing the Tulunids' judge and appointing their own choice in his stead.

This system of caliphal appointment remained in place throughout the formative period, that is until the mid-tenth century. The decline and disappearance of the caliphate as a political reality also had effects on the judicial system. The Fatimids, the Shīᶜī dynasty that held power in Tunisia and Egypt in 909-69, opened the process of change by appointing their own high judge, as mentioned in a previous chapter. This Shīᶜī judge was ranked above the previously existing Sunnī judge of Cairo, but both were given the same title of *qāḍī al-quḍāt*.

The Fatimids based their counter-caliphate on a religious difference from the Baghdad caliph. The many small sultanic states that appeared after their disappearance did not, by and large, claim any such religious justification for their existence or for their difference from their neighbours. However, they followed the Fatimid model in appointing their own high *qāḍī*s. Each and every small sultan had his own.[3] Independent Spain had already had such a high judge of the own for centuries, but used a slightly different title, *qāḍī al-jamāᶜa*. Thus this office of chief judge was much closer to political power than scholars in general. Being able to appoint the head of the judicial administration was a symbol of a sultan's power and rule.

The Mamluks, from *c*. 1250, expanded the number of high *qāḍī*s. They appointed one high *qāḍī* for each school of law in

3 This process may have already started in the eleventh century further east; Halm, *Ausbreitung*, 30.

Cairo.[4] This was the first time a ruler had recognized the existence of multiple *madhhab*s by giving them separate and equal status. The reason for this change was probably that Cairo was then dominated by the Shāfiᶜī school, so the high judge was normally a Shāfiᶜī. The Mamluks had their origin in the northern fringes of the world, where the Ḥanafīya was the strongest influence, so they were all Ḥanafīs. Giving not only these two, but all four schools equal status made it possible to promote the status of their own school. However, the Ḥanafīs were not raised above the others, it was if anything the Shāfiᶜī judge who was to be the 'first among equals'.

This principle of appointing a high judge from each school was also introduced in Damascus, where scholars from all four *maddhab*s also worked, but it did not became a general practice; only those cities which had marked multi-school communities had more than one high judge. However, more and more of the smaller provinces were provided with local high judges, who worked as intermediary links in the system between the capital and the local level judges, as the number of courts and judges increased. Even Alexandria and smaller towns that did not have provincial status were given high judges of their own. Thus the exalted meaning of the term was deflated. The main figure remained the high judge of the capital, who retained the right to appoint and depose local judges, as long as the local governor in a smaller province had not arrogated enough power for himself to do this.

This remained the basic system throughout the Middle Ages until the changes brought about by the new Ottoman empire, which we shall deal with in a later chapter.

Competence and organization

A judge has both administrative and judicial tasks. He is formally a representative—*nāʾib*—of the ruler, be that the sultan or the governor. This may be the main task for a *qāḍī* who is a high

4 Joseph H. Escovitz, *The Office of* qâḍî al-quḍât *in Cairo under the Baḥrî Mamlûks*, Berlin 1984, and Yossef Rappaport, 'Legal diversity in the age of *taqlīd*: The four chief *qāḍīs* under the Mamluks', *Islamic Law and Society*, X, 2, 2003, 210-28. The late Fatimids had experimented with a system of four chief judges from the 1130s; one Ismāᶜīlī, one Imāmī, one Mālikī and one Shāfīᶜī.

judge, and who may spend more time in administration than in court. However, the high judge is of course also a leading scholar whose opinion is sought in important cases, and we shall later see that, in spite of the formal single-instance procedures of the Sharīᶜa, most of the serious cases will come before the high judge.

The judge does not administer the repressive apparatus of the court, that is the job of the sultan or his subordinate. Thus the repressive power of the judge does not stretch beyond the courtroom itself and the power that is transferred to him from the sultan.

The tasks of a judge can be divided into three types: to solve conflicts (*taḥkīm*), to judge right or wrong (*qaḍāʾ*), and to represent the community (*ḥisba*).[5] Even if the title *qāḍī* refers to the second type, most of the cases before him will normally concern conflict solving, perhaps with some form of negotiated settlement between the parties. The office of *qāḍī* was in the beginning restricted to larger towns, while the judicial functions in the countryside were still filled by lower-level 'justices of the peace', *ḥākims*, whose main function was always to be middle-men and conflict solvers. This term eventually disappeared as the more formalized judicial system spread into the countryside and all regions related to a *qāḍī*. The exception is the Maghreb, where the division between a *qāḍī* in the towns and a *ḥākim* in the villages was maintained.

There are a number of requirements for being a *qāḍī*. He cannot be deaf or blind. This is perhaps self-evident for someone who must listen to witnesses and see evidence in court, but it must be seen in the context that scholarship was often a career path for the blind in pre-modern society, a way to earn a living and gain status even when they could not produce material goods.[6] However, blind scholars could not go into the judiciary.

It is in theory an open question how much law the judge needs to know. The early theorists did not make a distinction between the *muftī*, *qāḍī* or other positions in the legal system;

5 Fadil, 'Adjudication', 66. The *qāḍī* has a special responsibility for those punishments that God has directly decreed, the *ḥudūd* punishments. More on these in Chapter 14; on *ḥisba* in Chapter 10.

6 Cf. Ṭāhā Ḥusayn's autobiography *al-Ayyām* from Egypt of the beginning of the twentieth century.

they assumed that everyone had to fill the scholarly requirements of a *mujtahid.*[7] However, as the understanding grew that these requirements were unrealistic, the view on *qāḍīs* and *muftīs* diverged. We remember that this led to a hierarchization of *muftīs*, where a *muftī* had to practise as high a degree of *ijtihād* as he had the competence to do. The result for the *qāḍīs*, on the other hand, was that the requirement of knowledge was dropped. Instead of demanding full competence for *ijtihād*, some theorists said that such knowledge of the law was really irrelevant, as the judge could rely on a *muftī* for this. The judge's job was factual, to weigh the evidence, evaluate and examine the witnesses, and to decide if the case at hand was in accordance with the stipulations that the *muftī* had set.

Thus the *qāḍī* could be seen as a man of the sultan, of power, while the *muftī* was the one who needed to know the law. But of course such a stark view did not reflect reality. Only someone who actually had a good command of the law would be appointed a judge, and it was quite common that prominent scholars were first appointed to be or were recognized as *muftīs* and then became *qāḍīs*, or the other way around, and there was no general ranking that stated which of the two positions was 'above' the other and thus represented a promotion (this rather depended on the size of the town or region that each appointment commanded). Thus in real life *qāḍīs* were always considered prominent members of the *ᶜulamāʾ*.

The judges did, as other scholars, have a distinctive clothing that reflected their rank.[8] We know from today the typical red cap (a fez without a tassel) with a white turban wound around it. This is a general sign of a scholar in the Arab world. The precise nature of this attire changed over time, however the significant part was most often the headgear. Reports from the ninth century tell of the same principle of a turban wound around a cap, this was however at that time tall and pointed and the turban black. The Fatimids used a simple turban, while judges in the the Mamluk period wore a cloth over the turban falling down the back.

These symbols of power followed the position, not the person. A deposed judge could no longer wear the distinctive

7 Tyan, *Histoire*, 168-70.
8 Tyan, *Histoire*, 195-211.

turban. Such symbols or special attire were also worn by other officers of the court, such as court servants, policemen (*shurṭa*), and others. The judge also had other status symbols, such as riding on a mule on his travels. These could be marks showing that he was to be respected as a judge.

Infrastructure

A court normally covered cases from a specific geographic region, a quarter in a city, a town or a region. The court should have only a single presiding judge, there is no collegium of judges in the theory of the Sharīᶜa court, since it is based on a principle of unicity. That does not mean such councils of judges did not exist; we do know of many instances and types of courts where judges conferred over cases or decided in unison (the Mamluks called this *mushāra*). Such have become increasingly common in the modern period, when Sharīᶜa courts are presided over by a group of judges; however these are all later adaptations of the court system.

There were no specific court buildings in the classical period, that is to say the formative and middle ages. Such only appeared with the Ottomans.[9] In the earlier period the court mostly met in the mosque or at the house of the judge. The court may in theory meet anywhere, but the most common system was that it had regular sessions in one part of the mosque complex, either inside beside the *miḥrab*, or (mostly in the Maghreb) in the courtyard of the mosque. However, the Shāfiᶜīs refused to have the court sit in the mosque, as the court was a 'profane' institution where people who were ritually impure (menstruating women and similar) should have access, while such should not enter a mosque. Thus the judge's home could serve as a courtroom instead.[10]

Standard procedure

The *adab al-qāḍī* books include descriptions of how a trial should be conducted in a fitting manner. The decorum described there may perhaps not quite match the sometimes rumbustious proceedings of a real-life courtroom, where everybody tries to

9 Tyan, *Histoire*, 275-9.
10 Powers, 'Judicial review', 320.

shout down everybody else, but the basic principles are probably the same.

A case always starts with a motion from one party, or from both, making a claim that is denied by the opponent. The first task of the judge is thus to decide which of the two parties is actually the plaintiff and which is the defendant, when both move in front of him with their claims. This is of crucial importance for the case, because the burden of proof rests solely on the plaintiff. He must show proof that what he claims is true. If he does not then the other party, the defendant, has won.

The judge decides which party fills which role according to what he deems to be the 'pre-existing or 'naturally expected' state of affairs, and which of them is asking for a change in this.[11] This may, in a conflict over a contract, be the person who claims that it is illegal. The party who has the contract is then the defendant, while the one who demands it to be nullified becomes the plaintiff, because the 'expected' state of affairs would be that a contract is valid. The burden of proof is thus on the one who claims it is not. Also for an heir that claims he has not received his due share, those who actually control the property in dispute are normally considered the defendants.

The parties to a case must be actual persons, not institutions, and they must be directly affected by the issue. It is possible to make a claim on behalf of the 'commonality', or the judge may represent it, this principle is called *ḥisba*. However, this is only true under certain circumstances, and is often treated separately in distinct courts outside the Sharīᶜa courts proper. We will deal with them in more detail in a later chapter. The Sharīᶜa does not know the concept of public prosecution, that the 'state' represents the community and takes initiatives to punish criminals. This is the prerogative of those who have suffered damage, not an outside third party, nor the *qāḍī* as representative of the community or the state. That is one of the fundamental principles of the Sharīᶜa, and has wide-ranging repercussions for how it functions as a law and what kinds of cases are brought before its courts.

Even though the parties should be directly affected by the case, they can appoint a representative, a *wakīl*, to meet for them

11 According to the principle of *istiṣḥāb*, cf. Chapter 4.

in court.[12] This is not a professional barrister or specialist in law, and a *wakīl* can be removed by the judge if it appears that he is only there because of his eloquence. He is only meant to stand in the stead of someone who cannot meet personally, because they are not of age, or women who do not wish to go before the court, or slaves or non-Muslims (neither of whom in theory has access to the Sharīᶜa court), or people who are travelling or have other legitimate reason not to appear. The *wakīl* had originally to be accepted by the opposing party, but this requirement later fell away. A judge could also either demand or deny the use of a *wakīl* for a party. This representative can then answer for the party not present in every way, except that he cannot admit guilt on his or her behalf.[13]

Both parties, thus also the defendant, must be present in court. A reluctant party can be made to appear by several means.[14] One that was in use for some time, but was later abolished, was to send a court clerk to the house of the defendant at three different times and read the summons. If the defendant did not appear at the third occasion, the clerk would order the house to be boarded up and all exits blocked.

The judge must be, and be considered to be, neutral in the case. This is of course crucial when he is to work as a middleman to negotiate a solution to a conflict. Then the 'losing' party must willingly accept the verdict of the judge, as it cannot normally be enforced against the will of the parties. This has been used in classical theory as an argument against accepting women as judges, because the losing party could then use her gender as an excuse for not accepting a verdict he did not like.[15]

12 Tyan, *Histoire*, 262-74 and 'La condition juridique de "l'absent" (mafḳūd) en droit musulman, particulièrement dans le maḏhab Ḥanafite', *Studia Islamica*, XXXI, 1970, 249-56. Cf. also Ronald C. Jennings, 'The office of vekil (wakil) in 17th century Ottoman Sharia courts', *Studia Islamica*, XLII, 1975, 147-69.

13 One might have thought that he should be able to do this too, since he represents a party that cannot meet and since admissions are an important part of the procedure. But this was rejected, probably due to a tendency not to accord complete trust in the disinterest of *wakīl*s.

14 Farhat J. Ziadeh, 'Compelling defendant's appearance at court in Islamic law', *Islamic Law and Society*, III, 3, 1996, 305-15.

15 Fadel, 'Adjudication', 130. It was the jurist Qarāfī who presented this argumentation.

Evidence

The court verdict is based on three and only three types of evidence.[16] They are, in order of importance, confession, testimony and oaths. Thus all evidence has the form of oral communications given in court in front of a judge. A confession must come voluntarily and be stated to the judge in court. A defendant may also at any time in the course of the trial retract his confession.

If there are no confessions, then the plaintiff and defendant present witnesses to substantiate their claims. An act is only proven if there are two independent witnesses to it; adultery is a special case where four witnesses are required. Witnesses can only attest to what they have actually observed; the fact that a witness has seen a person leaving a murder scene carrying a bloody knife is only proof that the person had a bloody knife in his hand, not that he killed the victim.[17] The judge does not have the freedom to draw conclusions from one to the other if there are no witnesses to the act itself. At least one of the two witnesses must be male, while the other can be replaced by two women who must all agree on what they saw. However, female witnesses are not accepted at all in cases that may lead to the death penalty (normally issues of adultery or in murder cases).

A witness must be a just person: someone who is considered immoral will not be accepted. This may, surprisingly enough, exclude the police, who are the servants of the sultan and thus morally suspect.[18] The court may reject their statements on this basis, and thus throw out a confession made at the police station if the policemen were the only witnesses, but accept it (as evidence) if there happened to be some outside parties, a doorman, someone bringing coffee or others who could verify the statement.

Written documents are not evidence as such, but can be used if the document is signed by witnesses, and these witnesses are known and can affirm what was signed. Thus it becomes paramount when old documents are presented to find out who those

16 Cf. e.g. Gerber, *State, Society and Law*. The judge may also use his own knowledge as a basis for a verdict; Müller, 'Judging with God's law', 165.

17 Rudolph Peters, 'Murder on the Nile: Homicide trials in 19th century Egyptian Shari'a courts', *Die Welt des Islams*, XXX, 1990, 113.

18 Peters, 'Murder on the Nile', 112-13. This is thus according to Ḥanafī court practice in the nineteenth century.

who signed it were and how reliable they are. The reason for this reluctance to accept documents is of course a fear of accepting forgeries: it is not the veracity of the document that can be evaluated, but that of the witnesses who signed it.

The judge can also ask for information that does not have the strength of proof, but which aids the judge in making up his mind.[19] These are called 'reports' (*khabar*s), and may be evaluations made by specialists in various fields. If there is a dispute over part of a building being broken before or after it was purchased, a builder may study it and present his view of the age of the damage. Such evaluations are made at the instigation of the judge, and he is not bound to follow their recommendations. Thus the normal restrictions of witness and evidence do not apply to these specialists, they do not need to number two, there is no evaluation of their morals (but the judge has of course evaluated their competence before appointing them), and they may certainly be women. In fact, in cases referring to female physiology, such as menstruation, pregnancy and similar, it is *only* women who can testify. The judge can, in addition to such expert witnesses use any personal knowledge of the case as he might have, but should not investigate 'matters that are hidden' in a case before him.[20]

*Fatwā*s can, as we have seen in a previous chapter, be presented by the parties in a trial. Although they are supposedly only general statements of law, they can of course often be formulated in such a way as to support the view of one party. However, it has varied to what degree such *fatwā*s have been used by parties to bolster their cases.[21]

Oaths and verdicts

The judge must evaluate the strength of conflicting evidence presented by the parties. He should in this use one out of three methods, in order of priority: First, he should try to 'unify' (*jam*ᶜ)

19 Fadel, 'Adjuduciation', 134.

20 Müller, 'Judging with God's law', 166.

21 Messick writes e.g. for Yemen that *fatwā*s are never brought into a trial (*Calligraphic State*, 137), while Gerber writes of Bursa two centuries earlier that it was quite common, but that judges do not appear to have given them much weight; *State, Society and Law*, 81. This thus in contrast to the judge's need for a confirming *fatwā* after the verdict has been passed in important cases, as mentioned in the previous chapter.

the evidence. That is, try to find an explanation that would make both statements true. If that is not possible, he should then decide which statement is most probably true, and disregard the other (*tarjīḥ*).[22] If he is not able to make such a decision, he should ignore both statements (*tasāquṭ*).[23]

If the plaintiff has presented sufficient and acceptable witnesses for his case, or the defendant has admitted the truth of his claim, then he has won. He is then asked by the judge to swear an oath that he is telling the truth. When he does so, the case is decided in his favour. If the plaintiff's evidence is not fully acceptable and the judge finds that the evidence of the defendant is stronger, then he will decide in favour of the defendant. The same applies if the plaintiff does not present any credible evidence at all; then the defendant does not have to present any evidence, since the burden of proof is on the plaintiff. The judge will again make his decision in the form of an offer of an oath. He will then ask the defendant to swear that his version of events is correct. When the defendant has so sworn, the case is again closed.

Thus an oath is under normal circumstances not 'evidence' at all, but rather the result of the judge's evaluation of the case on the basis of witnesses presented and other knowledge that he has.[24] He 'offers the oath' to the party he thinks is correct, and thus gives that party the opportunity to close the case in his favour. But the oath can also play a more important role in the proceedings. It may, in some cases, replace one of the two witnesses required for proofs. That is called 'a witness and an oath'; if one party only has one witness in addition to himself, and is willing to swear an oath that he is right, then the judge may accept this as sufficient evidence equal to the two witnesses normally required. However, not all jurists allow this replacement.

22 Cf. the different meaning of this term discussed above in Chapter 8.

23 Fadel, 'Adjuduciation', 174-7. This order is according to Mālikī and Shāfiʿī law, the Ḥanafīs say that the judge should first find what 'abrogates' the other (*naskh*), then evaluate them in the order *tarjīḥ, jamʿ, tasāquṭ,* that is to assess their relative strength before trying to unify them; Birgit Krawietz, 'The weighing of conflicting indicators in Islamic law', in U. Vermeulen and J.M.F. van Reeth (eds), *Law, Christianity and Modernism in Islamic Society,* Leuven 1998, 72.

24 Oath is strictly speaking not 'proof', but an indication of proof; Fadel, 'Adjudication', 160.

More surprisingly, it may also occur that one party is offered the oath and has thus won the case, but then refuses to swear that his version is right. If that happens, the offer is instead given to the other party, and if he so swears, then he will have won the case, in spite of the judge's initial view.

This sounds purely theoretical, that a party goes to court, pleads a case, in effect wins, and then spoils it by refusing to swear that he is right. However, this was not infrequent. Even those accused of serious crimes such as murder could refuse to swear their innocence, even if that meant a conviction and the death penalty. Why they should thus convict themselves is open to conjecture. It may be true religious fear of eternal punishment,[25] or it may be the result of social pressure: if the community knows the truth of the accusation it may—at least in less dire cases—be better to accept a loss in the courtroom than social exclusion afterwards. However, this can only be speculation, and the reality of it is that an oath can in this way actually be an independent and deciding factor for the result of a trial.

One party may also at any time break off the trial by asking the opponent to swear on the truth of his case. This may shorten the proceedings, but will of course not be very useful if the party that does so has more evidence to present: if the opponent accepts the challenge and swears he is right, then the trial ends and the first party has lost. Thus this can only really be productive when one party knows of his opponent's fear of perjury and swearing a false oath, and thus hopes or assumes that he will refuse the oath.

While the rules of evidence and procedure were defined very strictly, the same is not true for the penalties in criminal cases. The judge has a wide discretion in meting out punishment, except in the case of murder and bodily harm, which have separate rules. The law does not in most other cases specify any particular penalties, but leaves that to each judge to decide. The major exceptions to this are the five so-called *ḥudūd* rules. These are crimes where the punishments are specified in the Revealed texts, and are because of this considered to belong to *ᶜibādāt*, Man's duties towards God. The judge has, at least according to the books, no leeway, once it has been established a crime falls under these rules. However, all other crimes fall under the term *taᶜzīr*,

25 Gerber, *State, Society and Law*, 49.

discretionary punishment, where the schools may give indications as to what kind of penalties are involved, but where it is mainly up to the judge to decide in each case.[26]

After the trial has ended, the proceedings are written up in the court records (*sijill*). This is constructed in a formal manner: the plaintiff initiates the case by making his claim and presenting evidence, this is contested by the defendant with his evidence if required, and the judge makes his decision. This may in many cases be a re-arrangement of what actually took place, since it is the judge who decides in his evaluation who actually is the plaintiff and who the defendant. The parties are thus assigned their roles in the record according to this schema after the fact. The record may of course also leave out elements that the parties may have put forward, but which the court clerk or judge considers to be irrelevant for the case and the verdict.[27]

Practices of the court

Court witnesses

The process for accepting written documents through individual evaluations of the witnesses who signed it was cumbersome and could lead to unexpected results.[28] If a future judge or the local community does not know the names of the people who witnessed the document, perhaps when it is brought into a property dispute two or three generations later, the judge may throw it out as unsubstantiated. This was not an acceptable situation in economic issues where predictability was important. The parties must be able to assure themselves that a contract remains valid without vagaries of future memory or perhaps a re-evaluation by a vindictive judge.

A solution to this was found when some members of the

26 See more on this in Chapter 14. The five *ḥudūd* crimes are theft, highway robbery, drunkenness, fornication and false accusation of fornication.

27 Thus Gerber shows that there never was presented more than one *fatwā* in any of the cases he studied, and that the party that presented the *fatwā* won the case; *State, Society and Law*, 81. It may be suspected that this is the result of post-facto editing, any *fatwā* not accepted as relevant by the judge may also have been considered irrelevant for the records.

28 Tyan, *Histoire*, 236-51, and Claude Cahen, 'A propos des Shuhūd', *Studia Islamica*, XXXI, 1970, 71-9.

community were formally recognized by the court as 'just' and trustworthy and became appointed witnesses to the court, court witnesses (*shāhid*). This insured the parties against future disregard by the court, because a later judge could not question the veracity of such appointed court witnesses. Thus they acquire some of features of a public notary, someone who by his signature gives an official sanction to a document. A court would normally have between two and twenty such court witnesses at any time, and two such witnesses must be present at any trial to confirm the proceedings, one sitting on either side of the judge.

The system of court witnesses is old in the region; we can find similar functionaries far back as Babylonian times. However, these were primarily filling the last function mentioned, that of being present at trials and being witness to what took place there. They were supposed to be society's defence against capricious judges; they confirmed the proceedings and the verdict so that the judge could not later claim that something else had been decided. This function as society's witness to court proceedings and verdicts was thus also present in the Islamic court.

A court witness could also function as an assistant judge and issue verdicts in minor cases, or screen cases for the *qāḍī*. He could also be the one who in reality fulfilled some of the subsidiary tasks given to the judge, such as supervision of endowments (*waqf*s). Thus, this could be a career move for a young aspirant, he could start as a court witness, then later move up to be appointed a full judge. The court witnesses carried the same clothing and symbols as the judge, and increasingly became an integrated element into the court system rather than a representative of society outside.

There were also other assistants in the courtroom.[29] One important function was that of clerk, *kātib*, who wrote down the formal record of the proceedings. Another was the *muzakkī*, whose job was to screen court witnesses and investigate moral stature. There was an interpreter, *mutarjim* who always had to be present, as well as more menial assistants such as the doorman (*bawwāb*) who also gets a mention in the *adab* books.

Women could, as we mentioned, let themselves be represented by a *wakīl* in court. But they did have access to it and

29 Tyan, *Histoire*, 252-61 & 279-86.

would probably most often meet in person. This was regulated by a particular procedural rule saying that cases where a woman was a party should be heard before the others in the daily routine.

Appeals

The Sharīᶜa court is a single-instance court. All verdicts are immediately applicable and final, there is no form of hierarchical structure of appeal from a lower to a higher court in the classical system.[30] However, some rudiments of appeal did exist, whereby a case could be brought before a court at the same level as the first instance.[31]

This is most likely to happen when a judge is replaced by another. The new appointee may then reopen old cases and give a different verdict. This could, as mentioned in the last chapter, be occasioned by a *fatwā* stating that the first verdict was based on an incorrect understanding of the Sharīᶜa.

However, this was a restrictive form of appeal. The new judge was not free to re-evaluate the actual facts of the case; whatever verdict the first judge arrived at must be final. The only acceptable basis for a revision of a verdict was when the new judge decided there was a mistake in the use of law. If so, he may change the verdict. Some jurists would restrict the possibility for revision even further, and say that a verdict may only be reversed if it is contrary to an evident text of Revelation or rule of *qiyās*, but not if there is any disagreement about the matter. There are, however, cases, although not many, where new judges did in fact reverse verdicts by rejecting witnesses' statements that the first trial had considered trustworthy.[32]

The practice of law

This is how the *adab* books describe the process, where the judge of course is always a fair, pious and wise man. Other historical sources and more informal descriptions of court practice may present a different view, where corrupt judges take and demand

30 This has however become quite common in the modern period, including for Sharīᶜa-based courts, cf. the example from Nigeria in Chapter 15.

31 Powers, 'Judicial review', 315-41, and Serrano, 'Legal practice', 214-20. Cf. also Vogel, *Islamic Law and Legal Systems*, 83-117.

32 Müller, 'Judging with God's law', 171. A revocation may also occur if the judge did not have jurisdiction in the area or topic concerned.

bribes, and are in general more concerned with their own affluence than seeing justice done. That must certainly have been a part of the history of the judiciary, but such stories are always told with great indignation, and often linked to revolts against the judge and demands for his removal. That would indicate that such was not considered the normal and expected behaviour of a judge. On the other hand, hagiographic description of all-wise judges who almost appear as saints are probably a reflection of the adage that 'victors write the history' or the later need to emphasize the piety of these scholars in the face of possible criticism. The most probable situation is that we had a range of behaviour by judges from those who religiously followed the letter of the law to those who aimed mostly at personal gratification, within the limits of what their employer, the sultan, could accept.

One cause for corruption was that using the court should, according to the theory, be free for all parties.[33] The judge cannot claim a fee from the parties, and should, unless he has other means of income (from an endowment, teaching or in other ways), be paid by the sultan (the state). How far this worked must have varied from period to period, so we should be cautious in giving a general description except that lean times in this respect may have provided a motive for corrupt practices.

We mentioned at the beginning of this chapter that the judge had different types of tasks besides those of actually sitting in court. Among them was the administration of court, he was responsible for the court witnesses and its other staff. A third important task was to represent the community, such as being the legal guardian for a woman who did not have any close male relatives, when negotiating marriage contracts.[34] He was also responsible for the *waqf*s, the pious endowments, and oversaw the status of public roads, markets and other common concerns of the community. These latter tasks were normally siphoned off to a special judicial official, the *muḥtasib*. The judge was also in charge of a particular jail, mostly for taking defendants into custody for shorter periods—the long-term penal jails were handled by the police or separate prison officials. We will look further into some of these 'related services' in the next chapter.

33 Tyan, *Histoire*, 333-41.
34 Tyan, *Histoire*, 373, also 359-68.

Special courts

There were also, in addition to the geographically defined courts, some who took special types of cases. The army had its own judge, the *qāḍī ᶜaskar* (later turned into a Turkish title, *kazasker*).[35] This was in theory quite similar to the civilian court in status and function. It was separate only because it was not territorially limited, but attached to particular army units and followed it in its movements. It had competence to judge in cases involving military personnel. If an officer brought suit against a civilian, it should go to a civilian court, in the opposite case to the *qāḍī ᶜaskar*. That is, the defendant's status decided which court had jurisdiction.[36] The procedures of the military court were somewhat simplified to ensure a rapid decision, but otherwise similar to those of the regular Sharīᶜa court. It did not seem to have had any particularly disciplinary, that is repressive, function among the troops, it was not a military police. A *qāḍī ᶜaskar* always had a high position in the administration and society.

There were also more administrative special courts, such as the 'marriage court' (*qāḍī al-nikāḥ* or *al-ᶜaqīd*) whose function was only to register marriages; Muslim marriages being as we know conducted before a judge, not in a mosque. The job of 'marriage judge' could also be a career move before reaching the state of full *qāḍī*.[37]

35 Tyan, *Histoire*, 527-36.

36 However, that was arranged in a case where the identity of the defendant was determined post facto. These rules may have been more theoretical than real; the actual choice of court was often, as will be seen in the next chapter, decided *ad hoc* from convenience more than from formal rules.

37 Powers, 'Judicial review', 327.

PART III: THE HISTORY OF THE LAW

10

THE COURT AND THE STATE

The first section of this book focused mostly on how the theory behind Islamic law developed in the dynamics between *raʾy* and *ḥadīth*, between a basis for a unified authority for the Islamic world and local established practices. This was, as we said, a dynamic that followed the general historical development of the Empire, and which caused the authority for the law not to be vested in the state, the sultan or caliph, but put in the hands of an autonomous class of scholars. We mentioned that the sultan was responsible for putting the law into effect, but not for formulating it. There was thus a duality in the relationship between the sultan and the law. This reflects the main dynamic underlying the study of the Sharīʿa as a practised law: the relationship between the sultan and the independent class of *ʿulamāʾ*, between the state and the society beyond the state.

This is a particularly interesting issue when one considers that legal authority is normally considered an integral element of a 'state'. One definition of 'state power' is the monopoly of violence through a repressive apparatus enforcing social norms, that is, a system of law applied through courts. However, we see in the Islamic case that the law is drawn away from the state, personified by the sultan,[1] and so presents in many ways an anomaly compared to the theoretical model of state power as the embodiment of state law. This is a crucial element in the understanding of how Islamic law is and is not applied in social reality.

However, this distinction between what is 'state' and what is not, 'society' or 'civil society', is not always clear. And it is even more nebulous when we try to define such terms as 'civil society' (separate and self-conscious networks or institutions independent

1 By 'sultan' we mean here 'political ruler', whatever his title or formal competence. The state will often be represented by local governors, princes or other holders of power, but we will for simplicity consider all such de facto rulers as aspects of the generic concept 'sultan' in our discussion of the state in this book.

of or in opposition to the state) across barriers of culture and historical epoch. Even in our own time, in which these terms were coined, we may ask whether such institutions as schools and churches belong to one or the other. In Scandinavia both are integrated into the state and tightly run by government ministries, with 'free' private variants as marginal and irrelevant, while in the United States, the opposite is by and large true, and yet it is difficult to say that these institutions function fundamentally differently in the two countries (religion has probably more influence on state policy in the United States than in Scandinavia). Thus saying that church and school are 'ideological state apparatuses' in one country and not in the other is problematic.

These doubts are of course increased in manifold ways when we try to consider the huge diversity of political and legal structures that have existed in the Muslim world over the last millennium and a half. It is very hard to construct an 'ideal system' that sums up the Muslim political experience, except for the idealized one of the Prophet's own time, where both 'state' and 'society' were summed up in the Prophet's own person. All real history from that day on is a description of deviations from this ideal, since the distinction between 'ruler' (state) and 'subjects' (society) appeared immediately on his death.

However, even the descriptions of the deviations from the norm may themselves become normative, 'the best way we can and should do things in these deplorable days' after the Prophet's disappearance. Thus we may try to establish a 'descriptive norm' that partly reflects real practices in the classical period of Islam, say between 1000 and 1500, but is also an idealized abstraction of realities that must have even in this period varied widely from each other and from this 'descriptive norm'.

The law and the court, the muftī and the qāḍī

If we focus on the state rather than trying to find the 'civil society' outside, we may locate which social arenas the ruler controls; that is, what changes when one sultan replaces another or a town is conquered by a neighbouring sultan. From this we can see that the domain of the state appears to be fairly limited in classical Muslim society. Political changes have fairly little effect on trade or economy, nor do they greatly affect the community of the learned, the *ᶜulamāʾ*. Both tend to continue their activities within their own networks where towns, trade routes and centres of learning are crucial, but the identity of the ruler or the borders between the states matter relatively little.

Thus, the Sharīᶜa, being in the hands of the scholars, also remains unaffected by such political changes, and can reasonably be said to belong to a 'civil society' of scholars, within the limits of each of the four schools, but all crossing state boundaries.

However, while the *law* was independent from the state, the *courts* were not. As we saw, the first *qāḍīs* were appointed by provincial governors, later by the caliph or sultan or his appointee, the chief *qāḍī*. When the caliphate split into smaller sultanic units, the office of chief *qāḍī* was diversified in the same way, each small state got their own. So the judicial apparatus that the *qāḍī* headed was that of the sultan, and the *qāḍī* was the sultan's, the state's, man and aide. They might and did on occasion oppose the sultan of the day, but the normal situation was that the judge was loyal to the political powers that could depose him at will.[2]

This is in theory different in the case of the *muftī*. As we saw in the chapter discussing *muftīs*, in theory no-one appoints some-one to be a *muftī* and no-one can depose him except the public (by ignoring him). This theory was diluted over time when the *muftī* from the Middle Ages was as often a state appointee as he was an independent scholar, but the normative principle remained, and does so today. A *qāḍī* gets his authority by appointment from the state, while the *muftī* gets his authority through his own learning, his personal status and recognition by his peers and the public.

Thus we may say that in Muslim society the state/society line does not so much lie between the sultan and the scholars, as between the *qāḍī* and the *muftī*. The court belongs to the state, but the *muftī* stays (in principle) away from the courtroom and is only in indirect contact with it through the presence of his written opinions.

So the Sharīᶜa court is thus an apparatus of the state, but based on a law that is outside the state's domain. This leaves the *qāḍī* in a divided situation, partly the state's man, partly, as a scholar, a member of a 'civil society' network. The normative

2 For examples, see M. Isabel Calero Secall, 'Rulers and qāḍīs: their relationship during the Naṣrid Kingdom', *Islamic Law and Society*, VII, 2, 2000, 235-55.

muftī on the other hand only belongs to this civil society and not to the state, in so far as he is able to keep his role as 'explicator of the law' apart from the actual court proceedings. As the *muftī* starts to become integrated into the court practices, by appearing physically in the courtroom, or by all verdicts having to pass through an appointed council of *muftī*s, this distinction becomes increasingly unclear, but it never completely disperses. This may explain why while we have very few old-style *qāḍī*s left in the Muslim world,[3] the function of *muftī* is refreshed and growing, liberated from its legal functions.

Thus the relationship between *qāḍī* and *muftī* is dual. They are on the one hand both scholars, and are considered to be religious scholars, as the Sharīᶜa is an *ᶜilm al-dīn*, a science of the faith both in its theory and its application. But on the other, they are differently placed in their relation to the sultan and the state. This distinction is expressed in the saying that on the Day of Judgement, the *muftī* will go with the Prophet and the *qāḍī* will go with the sultan.[4]

This can also be seen in the large number of anecdotes about pious men, *muftī*s, who refused to be appointed *qāḍī*s, or were said to have refused money gifts from the sultan, out of fear that the money had been illegally gained.[5] Thus the two elements that the sultan, as a temporal ruler, must have associated with him elements of *ẓulm*, oppression, and that the *qāḍī* works for and takes money from the sultan, are anecdotally joined. This is

3 In the traditional meaning of the word. Modern judges may have the titles of *qāḍī* or *ḥākim*, but many of the traditional functions of the *qāḍī*, those that do not accord with the 'modern' conception of the competence of the court, have been taken over by *muftī*s; cf e.g. Skovgaard-Petersen, *Defining Islam*, 184 & 196-7; also Messick, *Calligraphic State*, 135-41.

4 However, this must be tempered with the realization that in most cases legal scholars moved from being a *qāḍī* to a *muftī* or vice versa at various points in their career, and could thus fill both roles in different contexts. It must therefore be emphasized that the distinction we make here between the two fuctions is primarily an analytical one, looking at the structure of the legal system, not a division that was necessarily felt by the practitioners themselves, or emphasized by the theorists of law.

5 Reinhart, 'Transcendence and social practice', 10-12; Richard C. Repp, *The Müfti of Istanbul: A Study in the Development of the Ottoman Learned Hierarchy*, London 1986, 118; Messick, *Calligraphic State*, 143, and Haim Gerber, *Islamic Law and Culture: 1600-1840*, Leiden 1999, 10. Cf. also e.g. an anecdote in my *Sources for Sanūsī Studies*, Bergen 1996, 17.

almost a *topos*, a standard element in the biography of a 'standard pious and holy man', the refusal to be appointed to the socially elevated position of judge, or at least going through serious anguish before accepting this post. However, real life was probably less traumatic. The two positions of *muftī* and *qāḍī* were career steps, and a scholar would freely move from one to the other according to merit or the sultan's (or superior's) whim, and he could divide his day between various scholarly and legal activities, as we saw described earlier.

Still the *qāḍī* can find himself drawn between the two poles. He is neither responsible for the formulation of the laws nor their legal interpretation, for which he has to rely on a *muftī*. He is also not responsible for the implementation of the verdicts that he passes in his court. In this, as in his authority in general, he has to rely on the sultan and his men, the police and other forces of order who answer directly to the sultan or state representative, but not to the *qāḍī*. Someone searching for a division of power within classical Muslim society may perhaps find its germ in this co-existence of independent elements of the legal and judicial system.[6]

Non-Sharīᶜa courts: Maẓālim and shurṭa

The Sharīᶜa itself is pulled between different poles, on the one hand to be an eternal law based on the word of God, on the other a practicable and practised law within societies that change and develop far beyond the simple ideal times of school founders of the ninth century, let alone those of the original community of the Prophet in the seventh. The schools did, as we have seen, change the content and the practice of this eternal law over time, but this was a fairly slow process, and the rules were still framed as applicable to the Islamic community in general, and not as adaptations to a changeable social situation.

The *muftī* could introduce such contextual adaptations of the law through his *fatwā*s, and the *qāḍī* had the discretion of evaluating the circumstances of each case. Still this was not enough.

6 Gerber calls the Islamic court for a 'public sphere' between state and society, autonomous from the state; *Islamic Law and Culture*, 16; cf. also p. 144.

The Sharīᶜa, as it was employed by the *qāḍīs*, could not cover all the needs of society in terms of legal practice. These needs had to be met elsewhere.

Thus the Sharīᶜa court was not, in spite of all we have said about it so far, the only court system in the Muslim countries; it was only one of several parallel courts. Nor is this is a recent or modern phenomenon; it has always been so.

We must, however, distinguish clearly between levels here. There is no doubt that all Muslim states before the nineteenth century considered the Sharīᶜa, as an ideal and as it was formulated in the *madhhabs*, as the only law of the land. There was no concept that 'the Sharīᶜa is not valid here'. But it functioned 'in different ways'. When we look at the actual practices we do however easily see the existence of two different types of courts: On the one hand, what we should call *Sharīᶜa courts*, where a judge, a *qāḍī*, alone or with colleagues employs the full range of rules and procedures of the Sharīᶜa, as it is defined in his school. On the other, one or more *non-sharᶜī courts*, where other types of judges deal with various types of cases without following the procedures laid out in the *madhhab*, nor the precise letter of the legal rules. They will not normally think of this as an opposition to the Sharīᶜa, but as practical efforts to put the 'spirit' or general principles of the Sharīᶜa into effect in situations where the Sharīᶜa itself does not provide a useable answer. They consider this a part of 'governing the society according to the Sharīᶜa', *siyāsa sharᶜīya*, and we may in general call these courts '*siyāsa* courts'.

The problem was often the very demanding procedural rules of the Sharīᶜa. It was frequently impossible to establish the evidence required by the very strict requirements of the Sharīᶜa court, even if the facts of the matter were fairly obvious. The *qāḍī* would still refuse to give a verdict if the evidence was not according to the book. Then the victim who had suffered damage could take the case to another, non-*sharᶜī* court, and receive a solution in accordance with the sense of justice of the parties and of society, but which could still be quite at odds with what the Sharīᶜa actually required.

Such *siyāsa* courts have existed from the earliest days of the caliphate, and have always been closer than the *qāḍī*-ruled Sharīᶜa courts to the sultan and the state. The precise format of these courts changed according to the needs of society, but we can group them into two main types recognized by the *adab* literature: *maẓālim*, or the sultan's court, and *shurṭa*, police courts.[7]

Maẓālim: the sultan's court

The first of these is the private court of the sultan (that is, whoever has the political power in the state or region). We already know of such courts where the sultan/caliph gave verdicts according to his own judgement from the Abbasid period, and they probably existed before that. The Abbasids took criminal cases away from the Sharīᶜa courts completely and kept them under their control in their own courts.

The *maẓālim* system has its roots in the Persian empire, in the shah's audience when he gave judgements. Much of the early structure of the *maẓālim* courts, which continued under sultans and other rulers until our day, is based on such Persian traditions.

Only a few of the theoreticians of Islam mention the *maẓālim* system at all, and then mainly as part of the theory of state and governance. Foremost among them is al-Māwardī, who goes through various convolutions to make it fit into the ideal system where the Sharīᶜa reigns supreme:

The aim of the *maẓālim* court is, according to theory, to right wrongs (*ẓulm*, from there *maẓālim*).[8] If the *qāḍī* is for some reason not able to put a verdict into effect, because it is beyond his power or he is compelled by greater strength, then a party may go to the *maẓālim* court to try his case there. He may also go there directly without passing through the *qāḍī*. The *maẓālim* court can also refer a case back to the Sharīᶜa court, or even pull a case back from it if it is not satisfied with the result.

The *maẓālim* court is free of most of the limitations that lie on the Sharīᶜa courts. The sultan makes his verdict freely; he is not bound by the Sharīᶜa rules in any way, he does not need to hear both parties—or even one of them—before passing his sentence. He is thus in a totally different position from the *qāḍī*, for whom the burden of evidence lies on the plaintiff, and the evaluation of the probity of the witnesses is often crucial to the decision made.

7 See the overview in Tyan, *Histoire*, 433-615.

8 Tyan, *Histoire*, 436-7. Shihāb al-Dīn al-Qalqashandī (d. 1418) discusses this in his book on secretaries, *Subḥ al-aᶜsha*.

The basic principle behind the *maẓālim* court is the 'common good' as defined by *siyāsa sharᶜīya*. We already know of this from the *uṣūl* theory as one form of *istidlāl*, one of the ways to develop individual rules of the Sharīᶜa. Here it is used more generally as the sultan's duty to rule and judge in accordance with the 'spirit' of the Sharīᶜa. Thus his decisions should be 'inspired' by and express the intent of the Sharīᶜa, even if it does not follow the letter of it. Thus it is here closer to the literal translation of the term, *sharᶜī* politics.

The format of these courts changed over time. The Fatimids, for example, did not let their *imām* waste his time on such tasks; he left that to his *wazīr*. The theory was that judicial powers were vested in the sultan's person—here in the literal meaning of the ruler of the state—or at most in his governor, *wālī*, of a [large] province, but not further down the hierarchy. However, the pangyrics of the Abbasid caliph Muhtadī say that he was so pious that he took charge of the *maẓālim* personally.[9] This probably means that the Abbasid caliphs did not normally spend their time in this court; it may also have been the *wazīr* who had this job on behalf of the caliph.

The *maẓālim* court may also have had a link to the Sharīᶜa court through a council of scholars that informed and counselled the caliph. Here the chief *qāḍī* could sit with other of the most prominent legal scholars of the land, court witnesses and others. Thus this court could work like a higher court or instance of appeal beyond the Sharīᶜa system proper. What the actual relation of power between the sultan and the chief *qāḍī* might be, how far he had to listen to any advice, would of course have varied from case to case. But this court is primarily, and perhaps also most often in practice, that of the sultan himself who had the final word.

The *maẓālim* courts may take up more or less the same type of cases as the Sharīᶜa court. A case here would as well most often be initiated by someone with a grievance, approaching the court with a complaint, with or without a prior appearance in the Sharīᶜa court. The principle that the highest political authority in the province or state should be present in the court clearly limited which and how many cases could be heard. But we know of

9 Melchert, 'Religious policies of the caliphs', 334.

instances where the Sharīᶜa court in a particular area met twice a week to hear cases, while the *maẓālim* court met once a week. Thus this was a regular and functioning court that could probably move through a considerable number of cases.

Shurṭa: the police

However, the other type of *siyāsa* court was probably more important for most people. The modern Arabic word for 'police' is *shurṭa*, and it was also in the classical period the name for what we call the repressive apparatus of the state; that which handles order in society and which physically effects the decisions made by the various courts.[10] But the *shurṭa* also had a type of court of its own, a kind of 'magistrate's court' where small cases could be heard. However, this was not a lower instance for cases that would proceed to other courts, but one that passed verdicts that were as final as those of the *qāḍī*'s court. We may call them 'police courts'.

We hear about the *shurṭa* from Umayyad times, sometimes under different names (as *maᶜāwun*, helpers). There was always at least one, sometimes two, *shurṭa* posts in any town. These were originally elite army divisions whose task was to protect the caliph or the sultan, before they were permanently placed in towns or quarters to maintain public order. The head of the *shurṭa*, *ṣāḥib al-shurṭa*, had a high social rank, just below the *wazīr*.

The *shurṭa* had various tasks: It was a police force, public prosecutor and prison service. It should preserve public order, protect the sultan, initiate and carry out investigations of possible crimes and effect the verdicts of the Sharīᶜa and *maẓālim* courts.

The Sharīᶜa courts had evident problems in prosecuting criminal cases. There was already a serious impediment in that the judge could not normally initiate a case, only react to a complaint from an injured party. No less important were the limitations that the procedural rules imposed on the court; the very strict demands for admissible evidence, that material evidence should not be given weight on their own, that direct eye witnesses could only be accepted if particular personal criteria were fulfilled, and so on. This all together made it very difficult to

10 Tyan, *Histoire*, 567-616.

achieve a conviction in a criminal case before the Sharīᶜa court, even when the guilt of the defendant appeared to be overwhelmingly evident.

The police were in a quite different situation, since they were not subject to the *qāḍī*, but the sultan, and thus could operate independently of these procedures. On the basis of suspicion or after notification from an uninvolved member of the public they could investigate cases at their own instigation (unlike the judge). They could base their verdicts on physical evidence that they had found on the scene of the crime, and they could prosecute on their own authority without the presence of a plaintiff. They could, in other words, operate much more like we imagine a criminal court does in our society.

The police court was in theory also not bound by the laws of the Sharīᶜa, or any other rules. They could, if they so decided, punish a delinquent on the spot without any deliberation. However, the police would normally establish themselves with a court apparatus, where the accused could appear, hear the accusation and defend himself before the 'magistrate', police judge, gave his verdict. The victim, if there was any, need not be present; while the Sharīᶜa court had three parties—plaintiff, defendant and judge—the police court only had two, accused and judge (like the *maẓālim* court, although this did not even require the accused to be present).

Only the *shurṭa* could compel an accused to confess, for example by whipping. Such confessions were only valid in the police court, the Sharīᶜa court would not, as mentioned, accept coerced confessions, unless the accused/defendant repeated the confession in front of the *qāḍī*. The police court could also hear testimony from non-Muslims and others who are (in theory, anyway) barred from the Sharīᶜa courts.

The police should, like their employer, the sultan, base their activity on *siyāsa sharᶜīya*: they should work for the 'spirit of the Sharīᶜa', even if they went outside the actual rules and procedures of it. However, the rules of both types of court were the same once the verdict has been passed and come to execution.

Thus the police court was a separate legal system, and one that mostly covered criminal law. This had the potential to come into conflict with the Sharīᶜa courts, which had competence in all types of cases, as the Sharīᶜa covers all aspects of society, including crime. However, the two also needed to work together: they were both part of society's legal apparatus, and both had in the final instance to answer to the higher authority of the sultan.

One example of how this relation worked in practice can be seen in murder cases. These could be handled by both Sharīᶜa and police courts, and the same case might come before both.[11] The difference is that the Sharīᶜa courts worked from rules where, on the one hand, the victim could choose between material remuneration or physical punishment,[12] but where it on the other hand was much harder to achieve conviction. In the police courts, securing conviction was easier, but the victims did not get any financial reparation: a convicted criminal was punished, but the victim's family received nothing, because the police courts took no notice of the Sharīᶜa rules for compensation.

Thus the normal process is that the victim's family, if they have evidence they consider sufficient, will first raise the case before the Sharīᶜa court to achieve conviction and possible compensation. If the court rejects the case because the evidence does not hold, then the family will take the case to the police court. The police will then make their own investigation and on that basis convict and punish the criminal, but only by throwing him in jail or dispensing some other punishment according to the gravity of the crime, which does not help the victims economically.

Ḥisba and the muḥtasib

Another court instance, which has some aspects of a municipal administration, is the *ḥisba* or *muḥtasib* system.[13] The word *ḥisba* means 'balance', and is thus linked to calculation. Here we can interpret this to mean maintaining a balanced society. In a legal context, the term is used in three different meanings, which may cause confusion:

11 Peters, 'Murder on the Nile'. This is from a later period (nineteenth century), but must certainly reflect a practice that was common in the classical period as well.

12 More on this in Chapter 14.

13 Tyan, *Histoire*, 617-50, and A.I. Omer, 'The institution of al-hisba in the Islamic Legal system', *Journal of Islamic and Comparative Law*, X, 1981, 63-76.

— In the court, it refers to the option for a third party that is not directly involved to, under particular circumstances, raise a case on behalf of an absent person or a collectivity of persons. This is a principle that mitigates the general rule that only someone directly affected by a situation may bring it to court, and it gives, exceptionally, a collectivity some of the legal rights of an individual.

— Beyond this, and more generally, *ḥisba* may refer to the religious duty to 'work for the good and counteract the illegal', *amr bi'l-ma^c^rūf wa-nahy ^c^an al-munkar*.[14] This duty is incumbent on all Muslims. When they see something that contravenes the law and morality, they should try to prevent this in various ways; from verbally counselling the transgressor, to intervening physically by destroying objects such as bottles of wine or instruments used for illegal gambling.

This, however, is a religious duty, and we have seen that such are of two kinds: those that lie on every individual, and those that are held collectively by society (*farḍ kifā^c^ī*).[15] Counteracting the unlawful, or performing *ḥisba*, is considered to be a collective duty, and is delegated to the ruler, the sultan. Thus it is illegal for private individuals to enforce laws on their own as long as there exists a legitimate ruler to do so (except for the mildest level of addressing a transgressor verbally). This follows logically from the existence of a law-based society; making the enforcement of laws an individual duty means letting everybody take the law into their own hands, leading to anarchy.

Thus, this meaning of *ḥisba* is not very important legally, it is more of a religious sanction for the sultan's power: He has legitimacy because he works for the good of the society and the law by enforcing *ḥisba* on its behalf. The concept is more important for extremists or over-zealous pietists, those who defend breaking into people's homes to smash musical instruments, caskets of wine, or other immoral objects. Such actions can also be a form of revolt, because those who do so arrogate powers to themselves that are vested in the sultan. Applying *ḥisba* in this sense on their own initiative, they show that the sultan is unable to do so, and thus does not have the legitimacy to govern. This has become

14 On the formulation of this principle, see Michael Cook, *Commanding Right and Forbidding Wrong in Islamic Thought*, Cambridge 2000.

15 Chapter 3.

particularly important in our day since some Islamist groups consider modern Muslim states to be infidel, non-Islamic. So, they say, the duty to impose *ḥisba* and the law falls on every individual Muslim, or in practical terms on themselves.

— The third meaning of the term is partly linked to the idea of *ḥisba* as public morality and following the prescriptions of religion. It takes the form of a particular office that was established at an early period, and existed in most Muslim cities, the *muḥtasib* (the person who carries out *ḥisba*). The tasks of this official may be somewhat vague, because the term is so general. In a way a *muḥtasib* stands in a position between the *qāḍī* and the police, and his main job is to see that religious and moral commands are being followed in the public arena.

It is thus a public position. A *muḥtasib* is a religious scholar and it is a high position, often given to a leading judge or a *muftī*. A *muḥtasib* can in theory take up almost every type of case within the Sharīᶜa, and he has himself the responsibility that his verdict is effected. Thus, he is not a conflict solver like a *qāḍī* in a Sharīᶜa court, but someone who oversees practical problems in the town, and he has his own corps of aides who help in this surveying and control. He can in this way come close to the duties of the police, but the *muḥtasib* has greater freedom to intervene in cases that approach the religious field, since his office is closer to the scholarly world and is formally linked to the Sharīᶜa.

However, in spite of these wide-ranging prerogatives, the *muḥtasib* works mostly on one very particular group of tasks: primarily those of the market and overseeing public roads and amenities. His main job was, in most societies, to guarantee the fairness of trade; that weights and measurements were true and correct, that a trader did not unfairly quote local prices, and similar tasks. The *muḥtasib* did not evaluate the quality of a trader's goods on the market and thus the fairness of his price, but he should intervene if the trader made false claims of what the standard prices of particular goods were at that market. He also was in charge of the mint; he could strike coins and was responsible for the metal value of coinage.

His main tasks outside the market was making sure that roads were kept open; he could force owners to repair or demolish houses that threatened to fall into the streets, and ensured the safety and quality of new buildings in the town, making sure they did not encroach on the streets, and so on. Thus the *muḥtasib* is perhaps as close as we get to a municipal administration in the classical Islamic period.

It was, in other words, an urban position: the *muḥtasib* worked only in towns. He was also responsible for public morality in general, but the extent to which he took this task must have varied widely. The police could also intervene in such cases, except for what went on inside the market area itself.

The *muḥtasib* had the legal authority to pass verdicts in his field of activity, but it was limited. A more serious case would most normally be passed to the regular Sharīʿa court. But the *muḥtasib* could operate in much the same way as a *qāḍī*, he could inflict corporal punishment up to a limit of 40 lashes and public humiliation, or send people to the debtor's prison. He could close down shops or expel people from the town for more serious offences.

Sharīʿa and siyāsa courts

To which courts then did the cases go to? The Sharīʿa courts could in principle take all types of case, since the Sharīʿa covers all aspects of life. But the sultan could also take all cases into his *maẓālim* court.

There is no general answer to this question that covers all periods of history. However, it would be a general tendency for 'private' cases where two equal parties sought to solve a disagreement to go the Sharīʿa court, although it could also go to *maẓālim* if one party disagreed with the result. However, few cases would go directly to a court where the sultan himself was in residence. This always involved a risk, since the sultan's decision could be capricious (depending, of course, on the independence of his power). As the *qāḍī* was the primary conflict solver, such cases with two parties would seldom end up in the police courts for arbitration.

Cases involving crime and criminal law would on the other hand most often go to a police court of some sort. If there was no direct (or indirect) plaintiff, the cases must go there; if there was a victim who claimed redress, the cases could go to either court, or, as we saw in the example of murder cases, to both in order.

Thus the solution would often be that if anyone wanted to

raise a complaint, he would go to the Sharīᶜa court. If no-one did but the police felt there was a case to be answered, they would take it to their court.

The theoreticians accepted such a division of labour to a certain degree; even if they really gave the *qāḍī* full competence in all cases, he could turn some cases over to the police. They drew the line between *ḥudūd* and *taᶜzīr* cases.[16] The *adab* books stated that the *qāḍī* had to maintain full control over the former, since they were crimes against God, and only the *qāḍī* as a religious scholar could preside over them. Thus only *taᶜzīr* could be handled by other types of courts.

However, this hardly fit the reality. The *ḥudūd* cases leaked at both ends. Less serious crimes of this category such as drunkenness were dealt with, often summarily, by the police. When they came upon a drunk in a ditch, they would most often give him a beating on the spot and perhaps lock him up for a couple of days, rather than bothering with a formal case before the Sharīᶜa court or for that matter the police court. On the other hand, serious cases, those that could lead to the death penalty, would always at some point come before the sultan or another political authority and be finalized there, even if they had passed by the Sharīᶜa court on the way and the sultan might have to bow to the religious establishment of scholars when they had been unanimous.

This is the 'descriptive norm' of classical Islam. We may see one example of how this worked from a study of the city of Córdoba in the latter half of the eleventh century.[17] It had three types of courts besides the Sharīᶜa court: the *ṣāḥib al-shurṭa*, which functioned as *muḥtasib*, the police answered to the *ṣāḥib al-madīna* ('responsible for the town), while the *ṣāḥib al-maẓālim* and *ṣāḥib al-radd* ('responsible for appeals') took complaints from these other courts. The *ḥudūd* cases at this period went only to the Sharīᶜa court, but the *qāḍī* had to confirm these by a separate council (*shūrā*) of legal scholars. Other criminal cases however mostly came before the other courts, and in the course of this period they also took more and more of the murder cases that had been the *qāḍī*'s prerogative.

16 See the previous Chapter, and with more detail in Chapter 14.
17 Müller, *Gerichtspraxis im Stadtstaat Córdoba*, 103-74.

Otherwise the *qāḍī* mostly handled cases involving property rights, endowments (*waqf*) and inheritance. The *muḥtasib* court did of course handle cases involving the market as well as public disorder. It also took disputes over the sale of property, divorce and economic conflicts. The town (*madīna*) court was mostly a criminal court, and was the one which took over cases of murder and bodily harm. It was common for this judge, unlike the *qāḍī*, to investigate the scene of the crime himself to search for material evidence, thus we can see here his wider basis for decision-making. The town court also took conflicts between private citizens and the authorities. The *maẓālim* court did not have many cases in the period that was studied. It could take some cases from the *muḥtasib* court, but most of its cases came directly.

The verdicts of the *muḥtasib* court could be appealed to the *qāḍī*, if one of the parties was dissatisfied. The *muḥtasib* thus stood below the *qāḍī*. Later, in the twelfth century, the *qāḍī* also started to intervene directly in the *muḥtasib*'s field of authority.[18] The head of the town court, the *ṣāḥib al-madīna*, on the other hand, answered directly to the sultan, and was not subservient to the *qāḍī*.

Looking at the actual treatment of the cases, it would thus appear in this example from Córdoba that the division did not follow strict lines but was decided pragmatically. It was more than anything else the social background of the parties that decided which court they would turn to. The *muḥtasib* seems to have been the preferred court of the 'little people'. Otherwise it seems that all courts saw the Sharīᶜa as an ideal and would try to follow it as far as practical, but went outside it when they considered it appropriate to reach a solution they felt to be just. They were in particular much less concerned with lengthy evaluation of the morality and probity of the witnesses than the *qāḍī* was.

There may at other times have been more rivalry between the various types of courts, but as described here it probably worked out pragmatically in most cases. The various parts of the legal system worked together and relied on each other in practice. The *qāḍī* was dependent on the state both for his appointment, and for effecting the verdicts he passed. It was the police that made this happen, whether it was a matter of execution or imprisonment.

18 Serrano, 'Legal practice', 189.

On the other hand, the Sharīᶜa was the only formulated legal framework of the society, at least before the Ottoman period. It must have had a great degree of legitimacy in society, if not in every rule then as a symbol for 'just rule'. The social conception of the Sharīᶜa set the limits for the sultan's personal authority and justice, he based the legitimacy of his government on his ability to protect and implement this general law of the society, *ḥisba* in the second of the meanings listed above, as focused in the Sharīᶜa.

So even if a strong sultan probably had considerable leeway in how he handled individual cases, he had to stay within the broad limits of what society accepted as 'the Sharīᶜa' (which might not be identical to what the law books actually said it was) if he was to survive politically. And these limits were set by the scholars. They thus had a strong weapon to raise against the sultan if they so decided, and he was consequently forced to keep good relations with them if he wanted to avoid public protest.

This laid the basis for a *modus vivendi* where both parties depended on the other, and the Sharīᶜa and the non-*sharᶜī* elements had to be balanced against each other in the judicial practice, if the political system was to survive. However, how wide the limits for non-*sharᶜī* practice was and how freely the sultan and the local police could dispense with the text of the Sharīᶜa must of course have varied greatly over time and space.

Secular or religious courts?

Is then the difference between the Sharīᶜa court and the non-*sharᶜī* court that the former is religious and the latter secular?

It may in a sense seem so. The Sharīᶜa court was presided over by a *qāḍī*, who was considered to be among the religious scholars, while at least some of the *ṣāḥib* heads of the other courts did not need to have such education. But some of them did, and the *qāḍī* co-operated with them. The *ṣāḥib*s might also approach a *muftī* for advice, even if they were not obliged to follow the rules of the Sharīᶜa. On the one hand one could have considered that the *ḥudūd* cases were put in the Sharīᶜa court precisely because they involve God, and thus belonged only in this religiously sanctioned courtroom. But we can on the other hand see that such cases were in fact treated by the other courts as well, and that the same cases could move from one system to another.[19]

The reality is probably that the Sharīᶜa is in itself as much a secular (or mundane) as a religious law. It is religious in the sense that its authority is based in God's revelation, which is fixed and is a part of the religious sphere, of faith. But the main types of problems dealt with in the Sharīᶜa court and decided by its rules concern secular issues: money, property, contracts, murder and damages. The law as practised has passed through human formulation and the legitimacy of its actual words is to be found in the affirmation of human scholars, *muftī*s and *qāḍī*s, who seek their authority in the human consideration of the early scholars of the school. Thus this perforation of the division between the courts bound by the Sharīᶜa and those more independent from it does not really cause a problem of legitimacy.

The difference between them is rather their respective relation to the political power. The Sharīᶜa court is also dependent on the sultan—the *qāḍī* may be deposed by him at any time—but is still far more autonomous, due to the *qāḍī*'s status as a scholar in the network of *ᶜulamāᵓ* that the sultan cannot directly control. This is evident from the fact that any verdict passed by a *siyāsa* court, those run by '*ṣāḥib*s' can be overturned by the sultan, while those passed by the *qāḍī* can only be reversed if the *qāḍī* himself is deposed.[20] This greater autonomy of the Sharīᶜa court thus also gives the parties that take their cases to it greater protection from haphazard whims on the part of the political power.

Law and justice

Does then this system fit our conception of a *Rechtsstaat*; would we today consider the legal system of classical Muslim society a just one? There are many aspects to this, but as far as the structure goes, a few points may be made:

— Predictability; that it is 'evident to the criminal what the judge is going to judge'; we may say that equal types of cases should get equal result.
— Consistency; that more serious crimes are punished more

19 Müller, 'Judging with God's law', 161.

20 And, at least in theory, only if the new judge can find a mistake in the use of the law, cf. the previous chapter; also Müller, 'Judging with God's law', 186.

severely.

— Flexibility; that the system should accommodate for actual mitigating circumstances by a varied reaction; that is, a counterweight to the first principle.

We will have to distinguish between the various legal areas before we try to answer these questions. As for the 'civil' cases, those solving conflicts between two equal parties, the answer is fairly straightforward: Most cases that were up before the court had an answer in the legal literature of the Sharīᶜa, and the answer could thus be predicted by those who knew the law. There was also room for flexibility through the adaptive work of the *muftī*s and the discretion given to the *qāḍī*s in evaluating the individual case. The only problem was the complexity of procedure, that witnesses were in most types of cases the only evidence admitted. This was partly mitigated by the existence of appointed court witnesses who *de facto* make documents evidence on their own merit, as we know from Western courts, where important documents also require witnesses or public registration. The judge would also have had a fairly wide range of methods to regulate the requirements of witnesses in a manner that he and the parties found just.

When it comes to criminal cases the answer is less clear. The Sharīᶜa makes a sharp distinction between *ḥudūd* and others types of cases, which may appear haphazard to society. The *ḥudūd* crimes should always be punished more severely than any other, although they include infractions that could hardly, even in a moral Muslim society, have been considered the most serious crimes thinkable. Further, the *ḥudūd* crimes were in principle completely inflexible—the punishments are either strictly applied or not at all—while the other punishments, *taᶜzīr*, were imprecise and mostly up to the individual judge. Islamic jurisprudence has tried to correct this imbalance by imposing restrictions on the application of *ḥudūd*, to add flexibility to them.[21] But that has only lead to these crimes being transferred to the more unpredictable *taᶜzīr*.

The Sharīᶜa thus seems partly to fulfil the criteria of predictability, but lacks consistence in severity, both by the division into

21 Chapter 14.

ḥudūd and *taᶜzīr* crimes and by the lack of precision in the punishment of *taᶜzīr*. This is compounded by the fact that such crimes may be dealt with, haphazardly, either by a Sharīᶜa or by a *siyāsa* court, where the latter is in principle not bound by any law text, only by the sultan's or his representative's decisions.

This may thus appear to be clear a deviation from the predictable justice of a *Rechtsstaat*. However, the situation may not have been so bleak in real life. The *siyāsa* courts based their conception of a just decision on the known texts of the Sharīᶜa, as formulated in the legal literature and *fatwās*. Their deviations were attempts at adaptating these rules to a reality in such a way as to promote precisely the consistency and flexibility that was found lacking in the strict letter of the Sharīᶜa. Thus the criminal can expect that he will be convicted of a crime even if the formal witness criteria of the Sharīᶜa are not fulfilled, making the system more predictable. Also the *siyāsa* courts have leverage in the strict division between *ḥudūd* and *taᶜzīr* cases so that they are treated more consistently with society's conception of the gravity of the crime. Thus they aid in making the courts more systematic.

We may also err if we try to amalgamate court practices from totally different societies and time periods over more than a millennium, and conclude that they are 'inconsistent', either with each other or with Sharīᶜa literature from another age, and also conclude that judicial practice was haphazard and unpredictable. Any comparison must be with court practices in the same time period and same type of society. Such will most likely show that the judicial practice was fairly consistent both with what society and the scholars of that period and society expected, and with their reading of the Sharīᶜa's text and formal jurisprudence. The Sharīᶜa courts represented the 'real existing Sharīᶜa', which was identified with and based on the legal literature. And the *siyāsa* courts, in as far as they deviated from this literary norm, were still seen to be inside the bounds of fair and expected law under the conception of *siyāsa sharᶜīya*, putting the spirit and aims of the Sharīᶜa into practice.

That does not necessarily mean that everyone agreed with this view; extremely pious judges or lay Muslims may have protested against practices they found deviant from the law of the school or the principles of Revelation. Conflict is part of flexibility, and change is always linked to conflict. We will have no problems in finding authoritarian sultans who break totally with what both society and they themselves meant was the Sharīᶜa, but did not care. However, only a system that is in conformity with the social norms, here society's conception of the Sharīᶜa, will in the long run be able to survive politically.

11

LAW AND COURTS IN THE OTTOMAN EMPIRE

We have so far seen the development of the law and the judiciary go through two different stages. In the first, formative period until *c.* 1000 the judicial practices of the Muslims developed from local arenas, with the emphasis varying, representing 'God's will' or becoming more centralized and unified for the Empire, and thus 'Islamized'. The law went through a parallel development as the individual rules were formulated, partly on the basis of practised law, partly on a common Islamic experience formulated in true *ḥadīth* and authorized interpretations of the Koran. The methodologies of jurisprudence developed in step with this, with the common Islamic factor as the final and absolute foundation of the Law.

By the time this unification of the Muslims' law into an Islamic law was finished, the unified Islamic state, the caliphate, had disappeared. It was, by the middle of the tenth century, replaced in the various regions of the *umma* by a number of small and ever-changing sultanates, first based on religious differentiation (mostly Shīʿī particularism), later simply founded on political and military prowess. It was during these Islamic Middle Ages that the four Sunnī schools of law were finally formed as parallel and eventually exclusive expressions of the Sharīʿa (in its Sunnī form). This could not, as we have seen, be anchored in a common political framework, a shared state for all Muslims, as there did not exist any such state at that time. Instead it became the task of the independent and inter-regional class of scholars to take care of the law. However, the judicial practices had to be linked to whoever had the repressive authority in each city or region, the various sultans, all of which lead to a changing and not always straightforward division of labour between the courts and the law, between the state and the independent *ʿulamāʾ*.

This general situation changed as we entered a new historical epoch, the modern period, which is symbolized by the establishment of the Ottoman empire as the major power in the central

Islamic lands. It could from the early 1500s claim to be the master of the Sunnī world, except for the peripheries.[1] It became a modern, strong and increasingly well developed state power that survived many centuries. The developments of this new power led to many fundamental changes for the law, which in many ways entered into a new type of relationship with society. The main feature was that the state, the sultan, increasingly took control and brought the legal sphere under his power. This had effects on most of the aspects of the legal system that we have discussed so far.

Kanun and Sharīᶜa

First, the laws. The sultans of the Middle Ages had not formulated any alternative laws to the Sharīᶜa, but some did pronounce individual edicts that only concerned the territory ruled over by that sultan, and in his own time. The Ottoman sultan also made such edicts, which he called *qānūn*, in Turkish *kanun* (from the Greek *kanôn*, Latin *canon*, rule of law). They were soon collected and formalized in separate books called *kanunname*. Such collections were initially only valid in particular regions, but were later made universally valid throughout the Ottoman lands.[2]

A *kanun* was in theory only valid in the lifetime of the sultan who had issued it, but new sultans tended increasingly to just sign the *kanunname* that was in force, with whatever revisions he deemed necessary. Thus, in the course of the sixteenth century, these *kanun*s developed into complete codes of law that were bound not to the Sharīᶜa but to the power of the sultan.

The *kanun*s primarily covered these three areas: the state and the administration, and the individual's relations with the state; taxes and property issues, and land that the sultan divided among his men; and criminal law. Criminal law is particularly important here, and was thus drawn away from the Sharīᶜa to be adjudicated

1 Actually quite large peripheries; there were probably more Muslims in Morocco, Muslim Africa, Central Asia and India than those living under Ottoman rule. But the Ottoman sultan still considered himself to be the heir of the caliphs and the supreme legitimate ruler of the Islamic world, and was mostly accepted as such in those regions he held power.

2 Richard Repp, 'Qānūn and sharīᶜa in the Ottoman context', in Azmeh, *Islamic Law*, 124-45, and Gerber, *State, Society and Law*, 57-78.

according to the sultan's *kanun*.

The *kanun* was in theory subservient to the Sharīᶜa, and should only have regulated areas were the Sharīᶜa was unclear, or have been practical specifications of the Sharīᶜa. However, the reality came to be the opposite. The *kanun* dominated over the Sharīᶜa, the latter only being valid in those topics where there was no *kanun*. This can be seen in typical formulations in legal works from the period of the type 'there is no *kanun* in this area, so the Sharīᶜa rules are to be followed'.[3]

However, the 'spirit of the Sharīᶜa' was still dominant, so the *kanun* often took the rules of the Sharīᶜa as their basis for further development. Thus *kanun* must not be seen as directly antagonistic to the Sharīᶜa, it is supposed to include for example the penal element of the Sharīᶜa. It develops this further and accepts alternative methods of punishment to those described in the Sharīᶜa. Thus *kanun* prescribe fines and prison as punishment for crimes that are already treated with different punishments in the Sharīᶜa.[4]

Issues of bodily harm show both elements. They are to be judged according to *kanun*, and are thus included in the regular criminal code, not treated as a separate category as in the Sharīᶜa.[5] But as this code is based on the Sharīᶜa it includes the provision that the victims can choose between punishment (revenge) or monetary damages, as in the Sharīᶜa.

There is in any case no particular reason why one should expect any rivalry or contradiction between these two systems. The *kanun* would largely be based on actual court practice, just as earlier sultanic rule had developed in the *siyāsa* courts. Thus just as these were based on the fundamental principles of the Sharīᶜa, but with greater freedom in setting the punishment and simplified rules for procedure and evidence, it is no great surprise that we find the same development in the *kanun*, as a form of further refinement and formalization of *siyāsa sharᶜīya* in the new state.

Thus when one considers the *kanun* criminal codes that were formulated in 1490 and 1540, they are—even though based on Sharīᶜa norms—closer to the 'common perception' of what the Sharīᶜa said, a 'public opinion' based on practice, than on the

3 Repp, 'Qānūn and sharīᶜa', 132.
4 Gerber, *State, Society and Law*, 61-3.
5 Chapter 14.

precise wording of what we find in *fiqh* literature.[6]

The difference between *kanun* and Sharīᶜa is thus not so much the content of the rules, but that *kanun* is based on the sultan's authority, and nothing else, and that it is a unitary and systematic system of law, more akin to a law code than the Sharīᶜa which is based on a diverse and contradictory legal literature and the *muftī*'s interpretation and adaptation of this.

The development of new *kanuns* continued until 1673, when the last revision of the *Kanunname-i cedit* was published; this edition remained in force until the changes of the nineteenth century put the system as such in jeopardy. There was in the eighteenth century a tendency to religious conservatism in the empire that emphasized the theory that it was the Sharīᶜa, not the *kanun*, which was the basis for society. But it is not clear to what degree this mood led to any changes in actual practice. The two systems had by then, as we shall see, already merged into one in the courtrooms.

The qāḍīs

The sultan of course also strengthened his position over those legal officials who were already state employees, the *qāḍīs* whom he could depose at will.[7] The Ottomans had, like most Turkish peoples, been versed in the Ḥanafī school, and the sultan decreed that this was the *madhhab* of the empire; all *qāḍīs* should judge according to Ḥanafī law. This could evidently not be put into effect immediately in all the conquered domains; Mālikī and Shāfiᶜī judges could not and did not switch over to a school they did not know. It was easier in those areas where the Ḥanafī school either already dominated or had an established base, as in Anatolia and probably also in Syria and Iraq, while in other Ottoman regions, in particular North Africa, it led to different adaptations.

The most important change for Ottoman *qāḍīs* was that they henceforth should judge not only according to the Sharīᶜa but also

6 Colin Imber, *Ebu's-Su'ud: The Islamic Legal Tradition*, Edinburgh 1997, 244-5.

7 Gerber, *State, Society and Law*, 58-78, and Ronald C. Jennings, 'Limitations of the judicial powers of the Kadi in 17th c. Ottoman kayseri', *Studia Islamica*, L, 1979, 151-84.

to *kanun*. Local custom, *rusum*, should also be taken into account and could be explicitly cited in the verdict, 'this case has been considered according to *rusum*', or according to *kanun*.

Thus the two legal systems—the Sharīʿa and the non-Sharīʿa *kanun*—were unified into a single court system under the *qāḍī*. The highest judge in the Empire was the military judge, *qāḍī ʿaskar*, in Turkish *kazasker*. He was a member of the sultan's council, his *divan*.

The sultan could issue an *emr* (*amr*), order, to the *qāḍī*. This had the same relation to *kanun* as a *fatwā* had to the Sharīʿa: it could explain and specify a *kanun*, or for that matter function as a new *kanun*. But the sultan could not force the *qāḍī* to adjudicate according to the *emr*. The *qāḍī* was still independent to make his own decision in individual cases, and it seems that the state authorities accepted the *qāḍī*'s decision even when it went counter to an *emr*. It would also appear that the *qāḍī* court was actually independent from the local administration, local officials could not instruct the *qāḍī*, only the sultan could do so, and he would normally not interfere other than by issuing an *emr*, or sending a letter saying 'such and such well-known robber is active in your district. Solve the matter.'

The procedures of the Ottoman *qāḍī*'s court appear to have followed the same principles as in the classical period; a case had to be initiated by a personal plaintiff, evidence was primarily in the form of testimony, and so on. Witnesses to the court were still important elements of court practice.

Our information of this practice is based on court records and only tell us what happened in the courtroom. Since most of the limitations in procedure—those that made the Sharīʿa court impractical as a court for criminal cases—were still in place, it was probably of little help that the court could now rely on *kanun* alongside the Sharīʿa itself. Thus the police courts continued to exist, but now explicitly based on *kanun*, not simply the magistrate's own authority as before. The institution that seems to have inherited the function of the *shurṭa* police most directly was the *subaşı*, but also other institutions as *ehl-i örf* are mentioned. Some officials also travelled the regions for 'inspection', *teftiş* (*taftīsh*), apparently with some limited legal powers.

However, the development clearly favoured that all cases should come before the Sharīʿa court. A comparison made between the court practices of the town of Bursa in the sixteenth and seventeenth centuries show that there are many more criminal cases before the court in the latter period, and that they were often referred to it by the *subaşı* police.[8] Thus the police were now starting to function as prosecutors for the *qāḍī*.

A peculiar aspect of the records is that they generally only relate the proceedings of the case, but do not register the verdict made. There is no apparent reason why this should not have been noted. The cause may have been that the conclusion was felt to be obvious from the case,[9] but it seems more likely that the Sharīᶜa court proceeding was only one stage for the case. If so, it may have returned to the *subaşı* police or state body who meted out the punishment on the basis of the findings of the court. That might fit a model where the Sharīᶜa and *kanun* grow together, where the Sharīᶜa lays the legal foundations, while it is the *kanun* and the state power, the sultan and his police, that decides the framework for how the law is to be applied.

The court system was probably less complex in smaller towns or rural areas than in the cities. There the Sharīᶜa court might hear cases between Christians or other non-Muslims, although such should not in theory be heard there.[10] Nor does religious difference seem to have led to any difference in how their cases were treated, such that the Sharīᶜa court must have been seen as a common court, perhaps the sultan's court, rather than as a specific Muslim court. In the bigger cities, however, these minorities would instead form their own *millet* communities that could regulate their own affairs, including legal matters, internally according to their own rules.

We can also find that *qāḍī*s in economic matters refer to the taking and giving of interest without any pangs of conscience or consideration that this is illegal in the Sharīᶜa. It does not appear that the *qāḍī*s saw it as a problem to disregard Sharīᶜa rules when they considered it necessary. Cases were normally handled

8 Gerber, *State, Society and Law*, 71. He sees this as the police taking on the role of public prosecutor, so that the judge does not have to wait for an individual plaintiff to raise a criminal case. Cf. also Gerber, *Economy and Society in an Ottoman City: Bursa, 1600-1700*, Jerusalem 1988, 203.

9 Gerber, *State, Society and Law*, 68. He suggest that about one fifth of all cases are without a recorded sentence.

10 Gerber, *State, Society and Law*, 56-7.

rapidly, often being decided in a single day,[11] in contrast to the long drawn-out cases we find described in other situations, where just the evaluation of the moral status of the witnesses, and thus their probity, could take weeks or months and require several hearings.

Thus we can see a clear change from the classical system where a Sharīᶜa court only operates within the restrictive framework of the Sharīᶜa and where separate sultan-dominated courts employ *siyāsa sharᶜīya*. As the Ottoman sultan 'unified' the law into a *kanun* that encompasses the Sharīᶜa, modified by the sultan's legislative work and local custom, he could also unify the judiciary into one unified court, administrated by a *qāḍī*, who could judge according to both Sharīᶜa and *kanun*, and thus take over the functions of the *siyāsa* courts of the earlier period.

The muftīs and the şeyhül-islam

The changes were more marked for the position of the *muftī*s. They lost their independent status and became state functionaries like the *qāḍī*s.[12] The Ottoman sultan or his representative could appoint and depose them in the same way, and create a system of public exams which the *muftī*s were required to take as offical recognition for their role.

These changes, however, only affected the higher echelon of *muftī*s. The function was made hierarchic, and we can distinguish three main categories:

— *The muftī*, in the definite singular, is used for the new position of chief *muftī* for the empire;

— *muftī*s in the major cities; and

— *muftī*s in smaller towns and villages.[13]

The latter were not normally appointed or paid by the state, nor did they necessarily have much specialized learning; they could often be school-teachers or others who fulfilled the required leadership function. Thus they can hardly be called state functio-

11 Gerber, *Bursa*, 205-6.

12 Uriel Heyd, 'Some aspects of the Ottoman fetvā', *Bulletin of the School of Oriental and African Studies*, XXXII, 1, 1969, 35-56; also Gerber, *State, Society and Law*, 79-112.

13 Repp, *Müfti*, 64 & 118.

naries. Those on a higher level were however ranked strictly according to their own status or that of the town or city they were appointed to, expressed in their salary from the state.

The highest scholarly position in the land was no longer held by the chief *qāḍī*, but by a new institution, the chief *muftī*. The sultan appointed one *muftī* in Istanbul who was superior to all others. He was given the title of *shaykh al-islām*, Turkish *şeyhül-islam*. This was a continuation of the way medieval sultans had sought support from 'their' *muftī*s for wars or other political initiatives. This often took the form of councils of 'friendly' or leading *muftī*s close to the court, which was thus formalized under the Ottomans into a position of chief *muftī* who was in charge of religious matters in the empire, and thus to some extent became the most elevated scholar in Sunnī Islam. And he was the sultan's appointee.

However, there was still some distance between the *muftī* and political power, which was shown by the fact that the *şeyhül-islam* was not a member of the sultan's *divan*, while the chief judge (*kazasker*) was, even though the latter's status (measured in salary) was clearly lower. Still, the chief *muftī* position was now in reality fully integrated into the sultan's administration.

This was a process that took some time to develop. The first scholar who is considered to have filled the position of *şeyhül-islam* was Mullā Fenārī, who died in 1431, before Constantinople had been conquered. But the position was not especially important at that time, and the sultan does not seem to have had much interest in it. This was still the case as late as 1516-17, when Sultan Selim invaded Syria and Egypt; he does not seem to have asked for the sanction of the chief *muftī*, in contrast to the importance such support was accorded later.

It was the most famous and influential of all chief *muftī*s who changed this. Muḥammad b. Muṣṭafā Abū al-Saᶜūd, known under the Turkish form Ebu's-Su'ud, took the position of *şeyhül-islam* in 1545 and kept it until 1574.[14] He strengthened the institution by making it a close partner of and support for the sultan. He gave thousands of *fatwā*s which helped lay the foundation for how the law was to be applied. The most central element of this was unifying the existing *kanun* with the Sharīᶜa rules. He thus gave

14 Imber, *Ebu's-Su'ud*.

kanun a legitimacy within the Sharīᶜa courts, as the sultan wanted, by integrating it into the Sharīᶜa-based *fatwā* format. Thus later editions of the *kanunname* show that they do include some *fatwā*s in addition to *kanun*. This is thus another example of mutual adaptation of the two, and the integration of the various elements of the judicial system into one unified structure.

The Ottoman fatwā

There was a difference in how *fatwā*s were issued in Istanbul and the provinces, mainly because the *şeyhül-islam* sat in the capital. This both in relation to other parts of Anatolia, and of course even more to the Arabic-speaking parts of the empire.

The format of the *fatwā* could differ from the model we have described above, where it mostly discussed a point of real uncertainty and where the *muftī* would set aside space for at least some discussion of the matter, from half a page to twenty, thirty or more. A productive *şeyhül-islam* like Ebu's-Su'ud could still write long discursive *fatwā*s, but the most typical Ottoman *fatwā* consisted of an *istiftā*ᵓ question that presented a case and asked, 'Is this right?', with an answer that was either 'Yes' or 'No'.[15] The *fatwā* had thus become a matter of form without any discussion of the problem.

This could be all that was said in a *fatwā* from the *şeyhül-islam*, who does not need to justify his answer beyond his personal authority. Those in the provinces could not be quite so brief. A local *muftī* attempting a mere 'Yes' or 'No' would be called to task by his superior: they should not pretend to be small *şeyhül-islam*s. They had to include a reference to a statement from the chief *muftī* or other authority to anchor their view. However, such local *fatwā*s were also normally as brief as possible.[16]

However short, Ottoman *fatwā*s were on the other hand very numerous. Ebu's-Su'ud is said to have written 1,400 *fatwā*s from the morning to the midday prayer, and 1,400 more from midday until the evening.[17] He could hardly have done so without help. The first *şeyhül-islam*s did all the work on their own. One of them had a basket hanging out of his window. Whoever had a question

15 Heyd, 'Ottoman fetvā', 37-44.
16 Heyd, 'Ottoman fetvā', 45.
17 Heyd, 'Ottoman fetvā', 46.

put it in the basket, the *muftī* hauled it up, wrote his answer, and sent it down in the same basket. Thus there was no need for physical contact between them, although they may have met face to face in some cases. However, this simple system did not work as the number of questions increased.

Then a bureaucracy (*fetvahane*) grew here as it had done in the classical period. The *muftī* had secretaries trained in law attached to him. These received the petitioners, looked through the cases, and wrote down the question in a formalized manner, such that the answer could always be a simple 'yes' or 'no'. This secretariat was soon structured in different levels and specialized functions, becoming far more complex than the early system where the *muftī* had perhaps only a single secretary. One late description shows how the chief secretary, *fetva emini*, evaluated and sorted all questions and put all those for which he recommended a 'yes' in a green bag and all 'no' in a red bag. The *muftī* proper did thus not even have to read the question, he only signed them accordingly. Eventually this *fetva emnini* bureaucrat started issuing the *fatwā*s himself, and only passed the most important to the chief *muftī*.[18] They sometimes also used pre-written *fatwā*s; the actual names of the parties were not supposed to be mentioned in any case. So in standard questions, the clerk could only give the appropriate *fatwā* to the petitioner on the spot.

The *fatwā*s thus became routinized, which is why there were so many of them. However, it does not appear that the use of *fatwā*s in the courtrooms increased dramatically. It is, on the contrary, more an exception if the records mention a *fatwā* being used in standard cases. It is possible that these standardized yes/no *fatwā*s were used instead of taking a case to court. Going to court cost time and money, so the parties may have agreed to present the issue to a *muftī* and abide with the result that he arrived at. In this way, the *muftī* would become an out-of-court judiciary, or at least a middle-man instance, parallel to the *qāḍī*'s courts.[19]

18 Heyd, 'Ottoman fetvā', 48-9.

19 There is some disagreement on this. Uriel Heyd, who has written the classical presentation of Ottoman law, writes that on the contrary every Ottoman trial must include a *fatwā*. Thus *fatwā*s were issued even in quite obvious cases. Haim Gerber, on the other hand, has not found this in his studies of court records, and thus assumes that the huge number of *fatwā*s

But when a *fatwā* is presented in court, it appears to have had considerable weight.[20] Whoever presented a *fatwā* won the case —or so the records tell us. This is surprising; if it was so easy to receive a *fatwā* and they were so influential, we would have expected many more and that both parties would present their own *fatwā*s, according to their version of events.[21] However, the records of Bursa studied for these centuries do not mention there having been more than one *fatwā* in any case.[22] One may suspect that some post-editing of the records has taken place here.

This may also be linked to the *fatwā* functioning in a slightly different way in the Ottoman system than we would expect. *Fatwā*s seem mainly to have been introduced when there were no acceptable witnesses.[23] So if the case could be settled through a witness, no *fatwā* would be considered (or recorded). If there were none, however, a *fatwā* or *emr* might be produced and the judge could deem it relevant. He could then use the *fatwā* or *emr* as evidentiary basis for his verdict. If he did not consider it relevant, he would of course ignore it.

The *fatwā* has in those cases changed its function. It is no longer a clarification of an unresolved matter of law or authoritative establishment of the relevant legal rule. Instead, it has become a sort of auxiliary evidence, a crutch that the *qāḍī* could use if he had no other acceptable proof such as witnesses or confession. He could still, by whatever transpired in court, have reached a decision regarding both what the true facts of the case were and what the correct verdict would be, but could not base his verdict only on his views. By referring to a *fatwā*—and perhaps choosing one out of several competing *fatwā*s presented—he would have an outside authority to support his view. Any other

---

must refer to a usage outside the courts; *State, Society and Law*, 86.

20 Gerber does, however, write that the judges do not seem to give much weight to the *fatwā* when they write out the verdict; but it does then appear that the party who has one will always win the case; *State, Society and Law*, 82. It would be surprising if this was just a coincidence.

21 Gerber and Jennings feel that the *muftī*s were conscientious and studied every case closely before reaching a verdict. But it is difficult to believe that no contradictory *fatwā*s were ever made in a case; at least in the major cities where the *muftī*s had to consider thousands of cases, or that the parties to a case would not try to find second opinions from different *muftī*s.

22 Gerber, *State, Society and Law*, 82.

23 Jennings, 'Limitations of the judicial powers', 176.

fatwā that had been presented would thus have to be ignored in order to give authority to the chosen one, and they would thus be excluded from the court records.

Ottoman law in the provinces: Tunisia

What we have presented so far is only a rough sketch of the changes that the Ottoman empire introduced. It was, as we have seen, a change in continuity; the Ottomans did in many ways continue a tendency that the sultans of the Middle Ages had started, but formalized the changes and went much further in drawing the law in under state authority. Thus the changes were still considerable. This was particularly so in the regions that had already had a long history of Islamic courts. How did these provinces handle the coming of new masters and a new system? We can see this by looking at one region that has been the object of a detailed study, the province of Tunisia.[24]

This was, as we have seen earlier, one of the cradles of the Mālikī school, and had a well developed legal scholarship around the Zaytūna university of Qayrawān. It was, until the Ottoman takeover in 1558, an autonomous sultanate where the legal system largely followed the classical model. The population was uniformly Mālikī. There was a strengthening of the role of the *muftīs* towards the end of the medieval period, and they had a higher scholarly ranking relative to the *qāḍīs* than in the classical system. The sultans kept a council of *muftīs* for his political purposes, as did their eastern neighbours, the Mamluks.

Then the Ottomans arrived. The first important change under their rule was the imposition of an external power centre, Istanbul. A governor was to rule the province in the name of the sultan; this led to rivalries between various Turkish military leaders (*deys* and *beys*) over the power in the province throughout the seventeenth century, but the structures they introduced were external, Ottoman.

The other major novelty was the introduction of the Ḥanafī school of law. The Ottomans had brought along their own Ḥanafī

24 This is primarily based on Robert Brunschvig's studies, in particular 'Justice religieuse et justice laïque dans la Tunisie des Deys et des Beys jusq'au milieu du XIXe siècle', in *Études d'Islamologie*, II, 219-69.

qāḍī, who was given the position of chief judge. The dominant Mālikī *qāḍī* in Tunis city was relegated to the position of *nā'ib*, assistant to the chief judge. Thus the two were integrated into a single system, rather than heading parallel courts for the different *madhhab*s as had been common in Mamluk Egypt. They were forced to co-operate, even if they still belonged to different schools and technically had no competence in each other's law.[25]

Later a Ḥanafī *muftī* was also imported, and was given the Turkish title of *bāsh-muftī*, great *muftī*. He worked alongside his Mālikī colleagues, who also had one recognized leading *muftī*. It was eventually accepted that the *muftī*s of the two schools should have some knowledge of their counterparts' *madhhab*, although it was still not accepted that they cite them in their legal opinions. Such direct cross-argumentation was a later innovation.

The government decreed in 1574 that the Ḥanafī school was to be used everywhere, but the Mālikī judges were still in place and maintained their own courts at the local level. They worked much as before, and a person who went to the Mālikī judge was judged according to Mālikī law. Only in the larger towns and cities were there Ḥanafī judges alongside the Mālikī ones.

Tunisia was drawn further from direct Ottoman rule in 1705, when a *bey* Ḥusayn took power in the province and achieved semi-autonomy. An effect of this was raising of the status of the Mālikī school. The foremost Mālikī judge regained the title of chief *qāḍī*, but used the Maghrebī form *qāḍī al-jamāʿa* rather than *qāḍī al-quḍāt*, which was used by his Ḥanafī counterpart. The appointment of chief *qāḍī*s from Istanbul came to an end in 1745, from then it was the *bey* who appointed them locally, and thus achieved judicial independence from the Ottoman centre.

Siyāsa courts: the majlis

The police, the *shurṭā*, was after the Ottoman takeover manned by Turkish officers, under a leader with the Turkish title *agha*. It had its own court, *dīwān*, which met every day. It judged according to the *qānūnīya*, the *kanun* declarations of the sultan. It was clearly a secular court.

As for what we have grouped as *maẓālim*, the sultan's court, it changed its character according to the political developments of

25 Chapter 12.

the province.[26] But it was always an important, and perhaps the most important court of the land. It was called the *majlis*, the governor's council, and included the chief *qāḍī* and his Mālikī assistant, the grand *muftī* and one or more of the leading *muftī*s of both *madhhab*s, as well as one other religious leader.[27]

The head of the country, and thus of the *majlis* was in the seventeenth century a military leader with the title *dey*. The sources seem to indicate that he had a fairly withdrawn role in the council and that it was the *ᶜulamāᵓ* who presided over the proceedings. But the weight of political authority became increasingly clear, and *bey* Ḥusayn took effective control over the council when he established his dynasty's power.

The council met once or twice a week. The *bey* also travelled around the country and held hearings where he gave verdicts without the help of his council. But all capital punishments were confirmed by the council; the acceptance of the *ᶜulamāᵓ* was essential in those serious cases.

The relations between the various court instances became increasingly hierarchic, and this was formulated explicitly in the 1770s. The first instance was the regular Sharīᶜa court, where the *qāḍī* dealt with straightforward cases on his own authority. But if he encountered a problematic case, he should take it to the *muftī* to seek aid and clarification of the issue. The *muftī* thus became a kind of second court instance above the *qāḍī*. All serious cases, whether they were straightforward or not, should be referred to the *majlis*, which thus became a superior court.

The relationship between the *madhhab*s was ranked accordingly. The *qāḍī* in the Sharīᶜa courts judged according to his own school, and would of course consult a *muftī* from his own school. If, however, the case was referred to the *majlis*, it came into a multi-school body. Both Ḥanafīs and Mālikīs were represented here, and in theory had to try to find a solution that was accept-

26 Gerber writes that all non-*sharᶜī* courts disappeared under the Ottomans, including the *maẓālim* and the *shurṭa* (*State, Society and Law*, 69), as mentioned above. This was thus only true of the central regions of the empire; there were, as we shall see in the following chapter, also clear distinctions between Sharīᶜa and non-Sharīᶜa courts in Egypt.

27 *Naqīb al-ashrāf*, an official who was responsible for the *sharīf*s, the descendants of the Prophet's family and regulated their social or economic privileges.

able to both schools through compromise or otherwise. If this was not possible, they went to the *bey* who had the final word. He was, of course, a Ḥanafī, although this does not necessarily seem to have been the decisive factor. One case from the early eighteenth century may show how this was played out. The *bey* had appointed a prayer leader, imam Yūsuf, to take part in the *majlis*.[28] He was not technically a *muftī*, but was known as a pious and learned person, and he was a Ḥanafī. He sat in on the meetings of the council, but did not normally speak. However, if there was a case of disagreement that could not be solved, he made a sign to the *bey* and was given the floor. He then presented his view and thus became the casting vote. But he always expressed his opinion so that the Mālikī *qāḍī* in Tunis—that is to say, the highest ranking Mālikī official—did not appear to have been in the wrong. Then the *bey* made his decision, and he always followed imam Yūsuf's opinion. This anecdote shows a culture of accommodation, and indicates that it was important for the *bey* not to offend the Mālikīs. But it may also show that it was the Ḥanafīs who actually had the final word if there was a conflict.

The two schools became fully equal only in 1840, then separate chief *qāḍī*s and grand *muftī*s were appointed, each to their own and separate court. The *majlis* was recast in 1856 and was then split into two sections, one Ḥanafī and one Mālikī, which met separately. Each were presided over by the respective chief *muftī*, the Ḥanafī with the Ottoman title of *shaykh al-islām*, the Mālikī now taking the title of *bāsh-muftī*. It was the defendant in each case who decided in which court the case should be heard.

However, in spite of this formal equality, it was still the Ḥanafī school that had predominance. It kept this into the colonial period, and perhaps beyond.

There were, in addition to these regular courts, separate courts (*kahia*) for economic conflicts between Muslims and Christians. These cases were thus not heard according to the Sharīᶜa. There was a particular need for such a court since the Mediterranean trade led a number of foreign Christian traders to come to Tunisia.

Some contemporary European sources describe the punishments meted out. They tend to say that these were decided by the

28 Brunschvig, 'Justice religieuse', 235.

bey personally, but it is probable that the Europeans were not familiar with the inner workings of the court system, or bothered to describe them if they did. The reports do in any case document some very drastic forms of punishment. The death penalty was used regularly. One case concerned an affair a Christian captain had had with Muslim lady in a house belonging to a Jew. All three were executed, the captain by decapitation, the woman was sown into a sack and drowned—the most common method of execution for women in Tunisia—and the Jew burned alive, a punishment apparently reserved for Jews.[29] It is hard to find justification for these types of punishments in the Sharīᶜa, in particular for the owner of the house, who had at best facilitated the crime. But the severity of the case was of course worsened by this being a relationship across religious boundaries, which was both a breach of sexual mores and considered a social danger. It was supposedly the *bey* who had used his discretionary authority, and this particular *bey* was known as a bloody ruler.

Other sources, from the rule of a later *bey*, do however present a picture more in line with what we know from other countries, where the death penalty was rare for both murder and adultery, and it was more common to sentence the miscreants to a whipping or prison.[30] It is likely that the severity of the punishments and the frequency of the death penalty varied with the governors, and perhaps even more with the political situation. If there was much opposition to the *bey*, he would be more inclined to show strength by imposing the more severe punishments.

It is also reported that summary judgements were common in the police court, the *dīwān*, and that the condemned would be beaten in public directly after the hearing; this being probably the most common form of punishment from the *dīwān*. There was however a clear distinction in status between the various groups and classes of inhabitants: Turks were beaten just in front of the judge, Tunisians (Arabs) near the exit, and *quloghli*, those from the class of mixed Turkish/Arab descent, in the middle of the room near a wall. Punishments were also quick in the *bey*'s court, the executioner stood waiting near the exit door.

29 Brunschvig, 'Justice religieuse', 247.
30 Brunschvig, 'Justice religieuse', 244 & 267.

12

ISLAMIC LAW IN THE MODERN PERIOD

The momentous changes that took place in the Muslim world after 1800 affected Islamic law in two main ways. One is a reduction of the role played by the Sharīᶜa, to the benefit of legal models taken from Europe. This has been the dominant tendency in practised law in most countries of the region. The other is a counter-tendency to strengthen the Sharīᶜa through modernization of the law and opening a wider space for *ijtihād*. This has been a factor in legal thinking from the late nineteenth century, and has become particularly marked in the last decades of the twentieth.

Changes after 1800

The political relations of power changed dramatically in the nineteenth and twentieth centuries, placing most Muslim countries under some form of Western control in the form of protectorates, mandates or other foreign rule. However, the changes in the legal regime can be seen as more of a slow evolution than a sudden transformation. As we have seen,[1] Islamic law was practised in the courts largely as any secular law, even if its final authority lay in religion, so there was no revolution from a 'religious' to a 'secular' law. The difference lay rather, as mentioned earlier, in who had the authority over the law and the courts, whether it was the state or independent scholars. The Ottoman period had definitely seen this power transferred in the direction of the state and the colonial powers need only continue this process.

The previous sultans or other masters were maintained in their positions under European supervision in many Muslim

1 Cf. Chapter 10. We are of course here talking of the law as it appears in the courts, the *muᶜāmalāt*. The ritual parts of the Sharīᶜa, *ibādāt*, which may more appropriately be called a 'religious law', are not touched by this. Even if the latter is fully a part of the Sharīᶜa with few or no distinctions as to sources and methodology, they had largely been irrelevant to the court practices, and became even more so now; but did, as we have mentioned, become more important tasks for the *muftī* and made this office survive after the classical Sharīᶜa courts and *qāḍī*s disappeared.

countries. Neither in these, nor in the countries where the Europeans took direct control, was there a sudden change in the laws. But there was in all countries a slower process of Westernization or 'modernization' which made Western models dominant in the legal field in most Muslim countries over the period.

Thus the early colonialists were mostly satisfied with making some minor adaptations to the laws already in place. The most important difference was of course that the new rulers saw no formal inspiration in the Sharīᶜa, only in the laws of their home countries, which all colonial rulers always considered the most just and correct legal system. The Sharīᶜa could only be justified as 'the existing practice' that was eventually to disappear when the 'natives' had developed sufficiently in culture and civilization. The various colonial powers differed in how much room they gave the Sharīᶜa, and in how fast they advanced the process of replacing it with Western norms, either by creating local laws that were based on those of the parent country, or by directly introducing European law in the colonies.

The new states of the post-colonial period have mostly just continued the practices and the legal systems of the colonial powers. Many have promulgated new constitutions and various detailed laws, but they have generally been cast in the same European mould as those of the colonial power, and often so that the Sharīᶜa was given even less space than in colonial times, as many new states were even less willing to give such 'uncontrolled' laws any authority. But many have compensated for this by stating that the Sharīᶜa is a formal 'inspiration' or 'source' for the laws of their country, even when it is very hard to discover what if any effect it may have had on the actual laws passed.

The difference between old and new

Although the transition from the Ottoman (and previous *siyāsa*) system to the colonial and post-colonial ones was gradual, there were of course major differences both in the principles and the legal rules as far as Sharīᶜa content was concerned. This necessarily led to conflicts, both in theory and in politics, when attempts were made to adapt the two systems to each other in the transition. Equally it leads to problems today with the attempts at 're-actualization' of the Sharīᶜa in a modern state based on Western legal models. We may thus attempt to draw up what in principle the most basic differences would entail.

Territoriality

The Western legal system, as we know it, assumes that law is one out of three kinds:

(1) a *national* law; which is valid within the territory of one state. This is the most normal and basic situation: the law is valid for all individuals who reside within a particular territory, the one under the control of the state. This is true whether there is equality before the law or not; if a person crosses a state border, he moves into the territory of the other country's law.
(2) an *international* law; treaties and agreements between states establishing that they will in future co-operation or conflict abide by certain principles, such as accepting the rulings of trans-national courts.
(3) *universal* rights; absolute and basic norms that transcend the jurisdiction of any individual state. It is the duty of the 'international community' to make sure these are complied with, even in the territory of states that have not recognized them. These may of course also take the form of international agreements signed by nations, but they can, as we know, also be implemented through military invasions of countries who refuse to recognize them.

The Sharīᶜa does not fit into any of these categories. It is not a national law, in that it is not restricted to any particular territory or state borders, nor does it apply for all individuals in the territory: not only is there a distinction between Muslims and non-Muslims, there is also one between different schools of law which is quite independent of state boundaries.

Nor is it an international law; it is not based on any agreement between states. It could perhaps resemble the basic norms of human rights in nature, but the Sharīᶜa is not universal, being valid only for Muslims. Nor is it simply a basal set of moral norms such as the human rights are, but a fully developed system of law which in theory is as equally detailed as (and thus alternative to) the national laws.

All of this creates theoretical problems when attempting to fit the Sharīᶜa into the modern state system that dominates the world, including the Muslim world, and into a legal system based on codified law in the Western fashion. Integration of the Sharīᶜa into a national state law system must, whether or not the actual rules of the Sharīᶜa need to be amended, necessarily lead to a change in the *way* the Sharīᶜa is practised.

Thus if one attempts to implement Sharīᶜa law into a national state system, one has to decide whether it still is to be considered a universal law for all Muslims, or a national law for all inhabitants of that country, or a law only for Muslims within the country, or only for those inhabitants who wish to be judged according to Sharīᶜa law. Also whether such a 'national Sharīᶜa' should follow the rules of a particular *madhhab*, or should be based on a unification of or compromise between the *maddhab*s, or whether one must accept that various Muslims in the country may follow the *madhhab* of their choice; that is, to accept parallel Sharīᶜa rules within the state, as in the classical period.

Further, how does the state or the courts arrive at the Sharīᶜa rules: Should one continue the classical method where the rules were either 'known' inherently by the judge or formulated by a *muftī* in a *fatwā*, based freely on existing *ijmāᶜ* and legal literature? Or can the *content* of the Sharīᶜa law be maintained while the *form* of the law and the courts is modernized? If so, who, if not the *muftī*s, can decide what is and is not God's law? And if any disagreement on this content of the law arises, will such a modernized law have the legitimacy that God and scholars gave it in the classical Sharīᶜa?

Codification

This need not be a problem from a purely theoretical viewpoint; nothing stops modern Muslim rulers from continuing or re-establishing the classical and pre-colonial system with *qāḍī*s and *muftī*s. However, this would mean the state abdicates its power over the law to an independent group over which the modern state would have no control. Few states would willingly accept this limitation to the authority.

Thus a change from the classical system is in reality necessary. So how then to adjust the two—the classical Sharīᶜa and the modern legal systems—to each other?

One way would be to split the legal field into two quite separate parts, where the Sharīᶜa is given control over one, and functions in a traditional manner with separate Sharīᶜa courts and judges, while the state retains full control over the other. The most obvious field that would be left to the Sharīᶜa courts is family and personal matters, which then would be defined as an area 'outside the law' from the point of view of the modern law codes. We may call this a 'containment' strategy: setting up a reservation for the Sharīᶜa and rescinding control over this area ensures that the Sharīᶜa does not impact or create problems for the rest of the legal sphere.

This strategy is functional in theory, and is in a sense a continuation of the pre-modern system of dual court systems, one Sharīᶜa court and one or more *siyāsa* courts closer to the state. However, it has turned out to be difficult for a modern state to accept that there is any area of social life outside the law that it controls.

An opposite strategy is to codify the Sharīᶜa itself: to construct a legal code with precise paragraphs where each rule is based on the consensus of classical *fiqh*, but in a modernized form. When this is done within a national state, all existential problems of 'who' is to do it, 'what' *madhhab*, and 'for whom', are solved: It is the national state that appoints commissions to formulate the code, they base their work on whatever *madhhab* they wish, or draw from several if they so decide, and the code is only valid within the borders of that state.

This is also a functional solution and several attempts have been made in various fields of law. But there is then a question of whether this code is 'the Sharīᶜa' or not.[2] Each code fomulated by one Muslim country is potentially, and often also in reality, different from the Sharīᶜa law code of the neighbouring Muslim state. There has since the dissolution of the Ottoman empire been

2 Some scholars would say that such a law would have nothing to do with the Sharīᶜa, precisely because it is codified; the Sharīᶜa being by definition uncodified. For contrasting views on this point, see Aharon Layish, 'The Transformation of the Sharīᶜa from Jurists' Law to Statutory Law in the Contemporary Muslim World', *Die Welt des Islams*, XLIV, 1, 2004, 85-113; and Rudolph Peters, 'From Jurists' Law to Statute Law or What Happens when the Shari'a is Codified', *Mediterranean Politics*, VII, 4, 2002, 82-95.

no serious attempt to create a Sharīᶜa code of law across national boundaries. Such a trans-national Sharīᶜa would also be difficult to accept for each nation state, as it would again lose control over one of the key aspects of state power, the law.

Thus this 'codified Sharīᶜa' would be a normal state-bound code of law, based in content on the classical Sharīᶜa rules, but not practised as the Sharīᶜa should be practised according to its own rules of procedure: no *muftīs*, no *fatwās*, only a single book of law that even then is different from country to country. That would also mean that the traditional scholars of law, those that for many are the guarantee of Islamic legitimacy, would lose control over the Sharīᶜa. Thus such a law would risk not having the legitimacy as 'the Sharīᶜa', and potentially even being seen as a 'fake' Sharīᶜa (if opposed by scholars with greater legitimacy), with the inherent dangers of such a view.

A third and more limited method is, rather than codifying 'the Sharīᶜa' as such, to let it influence a national law that does not otherwise claim to be identical to the Sharīᶜa. Thus a distinction is made between the Sharīᶜa and the national laws of the country, but it can still be said that the national law is in some way 'inspired by' or 'based on' the eternal principles of the Sharīᶜa.

That is a simple operation; all that is needed is to introduce a sentence to that effect in the constitution or preamble in any relevant law. The law itself and its procedures can continue to be based on the Western system, although the legislator—the parliament or the state—gives it the content that both the legislator and society feels is in conformity with the Sharīᶜa. A legislator will in any case usually base laws on the norms that are generally accepted in society, and there is a tendency in Islamic society to attach the label 'Sharīᶜa' to the norms that are generally accepted.

It is also common to establish different 'sources' that the judge is to use in his practice, generally in a prioritized order so that he should first look to one place (e.g. the law code), then if that does not give a sufficient answer, to another, and so on. The Sharīᶜa may also be mentioned as a source for the verdict in this hierarchy. But it is often not specified what is meant by 'Sharīᶜa' in these contexts. The lawyers and judges are often educated in modern law schools with scant knowledge of *fiqh* or ability to search in the legal literature. Thus these may be only vague references that meld together with 'custom' and 'public morality' in a way that judges may apply fairly freely.

All these various adaptations of the Sharīᶜa to a non-*sharᶜī* court system exist or have existed in real life, alone or in various combinations. But all are closer to the history of *siyāsa sharᶜīya* than to Sharīᶜa proper; the law is formulated by the state or by public convention, with a more or less explicit reference to the Sharīᶜa as an 'external authority'. The state may employ the sources of classical *fiqh* if it so decides, but it is the state that gives the law its authority.

From kanun to national laws

Thus the colonial power initially continued the tradition of the *kanun* laws, and shared the legal domain with the Sharīᶜa. The transition to new political powers did change the balance of power between the two systems, but this was felt differently in the various legal areas.

There was less impact in the field of criminal law, where in any case the Sharīᶜa had not been directly implemented, at least not in 'state courts', before the change. But the expanding introduction of new laws of European inspiration led to greater distance between the content of criminal law and the rules of the Sharīᶜa than had been the case in the *kanun* system.

Cases concerning property and economic affairs had been more directly regulated according to Sharīᶜa rules, and these matters were now increasingly transferred to non-*sharᶜī* courts. This was particularly notable in countries that had much international trade, or where foreigners took a marked part in economic life. These foreigners demanded to be treated according to European, not Islamic rules, and mostly had the power to be heard. Those countries and regions that had less direct contact with Europeans would normally allow greater space for Sharīᶜa-inspired rules in their economic matters, adapted to local custom.

Matters concerning personal law, such as marriage, children, inheritance and similar—what we normally group as 'family law'—was the legal area where the Sharīᶜa maintained the most real and direct importance. This became largely a protected and privileged area for Sharīᶜa law. But in some cases even this legal area came under the influence of non-*sharᶜī* principles or laws.

Changes in the court system

There seems to be two aspects of the classical Sharīʿa court system that Western legal administrators found particularly problematic. One was the lack of a hierarchy of courts and any formal road for appeal of a decision once made. That gave the individual judge far too much power for Western tastes. The other was the lack of legal specialists aiding the parties; the plaintiffs and defendants, who might not be aware of their legal rights, were alone in presenting their cases. These were the two aspects that most legal reforms attacked first.

As we have seen, it would seem that the Sharīʿa system had considered both of these issues to be problems even in earlier days, since various adaptations had been practised that can be seen as rudimentary forms of appeal systems. The acceptance of *wakīl*s can also been seen as a small step in the direction of legal advice for parties, although the general view was certainly that it is the responsibility of the judge to ensure that the parties realize their rights under the system.

Another problem that the colonial masters faced when they started to introduce European laws was, what kind of European law? The colonialists came partly from a background of British common law, partly from French and continental codified law. It was probably easier to import and modify a fixed law code to a new country than to adapt a system based on the common law of the colonizing country. Thus there is a clear tendency for 'Western law' to mean 'codified law', and there is a discrepancy in how British and French colonists related to the imported and 'native' law in their different colonies. This will become clear when we look more closely at the path of reforms in some of the central areas of the Muslim world.

Reforms in the Ottoman empire

The Ottoman empire went through a number of 'modernizing' reforms in the nineteenth century, many of which affected the legal system. The first major move was the *Nizam-ı cedit*, the 'New order' of 1793 which provided the name for all of these *tanẓīmāt* reforms. The first reform that had legal repercussions was, however, the *hatt-i şerif* by the minister Reşid Pasha in

1839.[3] This was an establishment of principles, among them that the law should be the same for Muslims and non-Muslims; that is, the integration of the various *millet* groups. Legislative assemblies such as the *Encümen-i âli* were also established.

A new criminal code was promulgated in 1840, which was mainly a continuation of the *kanun* laws. In 1856 a new reform programme, the *hatt-ı hümayun* was put into effect, and the criminal code was reformed again two years later, along with the laws on property. These new laws were based on a French model, but were Turkified. The existing *ḥudūd* laws were abolished, and a three-level hierarchy of appeal courts called the *nizamiye* courts was established.

This hierarchy was further developed in 1868 when the higher appellate court was divided into one legislative and one appeals instance. The latter changed its named from the older *meclis* (*majlis*) to the newer term *mehkeme* which is today the normal word for courts in the Arabic world as well (*maḥkama*).

A codified law: the Mecelle

The most decisive attempt at adapting the Sharīᶜa into this system was the development of a codified law based on Ḥanafī *fiqh*. A commission for this purpose was set up in 1869, consisting partly of *ᶜulamāᵓ* and partly of Western-trained lawyers. The chairman was Ahmed Cevdet Pasha who had worked both at the *şeyhül-islam*'s office and at the (modernized) university's faculty of law. Four years later in 1873 the commission presented its proposal, the *Mecelle-i ahkâm-ı adliye*, normally only known as the *Mecelle*, in Arabic countries the *Majalla*.[4]

This law covered only a small part of *sharᶜī* law, mainly contracts, hire, surety, obligations and trust, agencies as well as testimony and evidence; that is, mainly economic and procedural matters. It did not include family law, where traditional Sharīᶜa was dominant, nor criminal law, which was already codified on a European-inspired basis. The Mecelle laws were to be applied both in the Sharīᶜa and the new *nizamiye* courts.[5]

3 June Starr, *Law as Metaphor: From Islamic Courts to the Palace of Justice*, Albany 1992, 3-42, and Bernard Botiveau, *Loi islamique et droit dans les sociétés arabes,* Paris 1993, 103-8.

4 Starr, *Law as Metaphor*, 33-6.

5 C.V. Findley, 'Medjelle', *EI* (2), VI, 972.

However, it did not exclude classical *fiqh* nor was it an absolute authority. The *muftīs* and *qāḍīs* used the Mecelle as a basis for their verdicts, but could supplement it with other evidence from their understanding of classical Ḥanafī law whenever they found this necessary. From a modern legal viewpoint, based on Weber's understandings, the Mecelle is not necessarily to be seen as a fully codified law, because it does not establish basic principles and develop individual rules from these. Instead it enumerates a long list of separate rules without any internal connections between them. Thus the Mecelle may in many ways be seen as a continuation of the classical *mukhtaṣarāt genre* in new packaging, but now with the state behind it.

Still the Mecelle was put into practice. It was the valid law in Syria and Iraq well into the colonial period, and in those regions that were under Ottoman control we can still see the influence of the Mecelle in certain fields today.

Its history was shorter in the home regions of Anatolia. When Mustafa Kemal took power the Sharīᶜa was one of the first targets for his secularizing reforms. He abolished the Sharīᶜa courts in 1924, and the Mecelle and other classical and Ottoman laws were replaced in 1926 with a fully new, secular law based on Swiss and Belgian law.[6] Thus we can bring the history of Turkey to an end here, it is no longer relevant for the history of the Sharīᶜa.

Egypt

The path to reform in Egypt under Muḥammad ᶜAlī, its largely independent governor (later *khediv*), was partly parallel to, partly divergent from that of its Ottoman masters. Ideologically we can see two opposing trends in Egyptian thinking on law. One was an attempt to adjust to 'modernity' and Western inspiration by furthering the practice of *kanun* legislation and reducing the role of the Sharīᶜa.[7] The other was more concerned with the content of

6 Swiss because they had recently reformed their legal system, and was thus the most modern he could find.

7 The classical study by Albert Hourani, *Arabic Thought in the Liberal Age, 1798-1939* (Oxford 1962), presents this as fairly teleological development from the 'traditional' to the 'modern'. He withdraws somewhat from this model in his 'How should we write the history of the Middle East?', *International Journal of Middle East Studies*, XXIII, 2, 1991, 128-9.

the Sharīᶜa, that the challenge of the times must lead to a refocussing on the Sharīᶜa law, but through an internal change in the direction of the 'original' Sharīᶜa. Thus the inclination was a reversal towards the classical methods, but with the aim of adapting the Sharīᶜa rules through *ijtihād* in some form.

These two trends may seem similar in that both favoured reform and modernization of the law, but we can see today that they have led in completely opposite directions that have increasingly come into conflict.

Struggles over ideas

One of the most prominent early advocates of the first approach was Rifaᶜat al-Ṭaḥṭāwī (d. 1873).[8] He emphasized the need to adapt the Sharīᶜa to the new situation, based on the principle of *maṣlaḥa*, the common good. We have met this concept before as a minor avenue for development of laws within the Sharīᶜa, close to the concept of *istiḥsān*. We have also seen it as a more fundamental motive underlying God's intentions (*maqṣad*) with the law, and as an argument for adapting the law to changing social circumstances (as in the fourteenth-century thinker Shāṭibī).

The *maṣlaḥa* concept is in both cases used close to *siyāsa sharᶜīya*, social and legal efforts based on the general principles of the Sharīᶜa. This is what Ṭahṭāwī wanted to continue, by giving the sultan greater freedom to make laws in response to modern problems, within a general and more or less vague idea about the common good as seen from *sharᶜī* principles.

The most specific new principle that Ṭahṭāwī proposed for this process was *talfīq*.[9] This had become a topic for discussion in the eighteenth century with the meaning of 'borrowing between the schools of law'. The barriers between the schools had earlier been almost water tight. Even if a scholar could or should be informed about the views of the other schools, he could not in any way implement them in his own practice as a judge.[10] But at this

8 Malcolm Kerr, *Islamic Reform, The Political and Legal Theories of Muḥammad ᶜAbduh and Rashīd Riḍā*, Los Angeles 1966. Cf. also Gilbert Delanoue, *Moralistes et politiques musulmans dans l'Égypte du XIXe siècle (1798-1882)*, Cairo 1982, 435-51.

9 Kerr, *Islamic Reform*, and Syed Moinuddin Qadri, 'Traditions of taqlīd and talfīq', *Islamic Culture*, LVII, 2, 1983, 39-61 & 3, 1983, 123-45.

10 The concept may already have been used in other contexts in the thirteenth

point the idea was put forward that this must be allowed. This meant, in a mild version, that a scholar should be able to consider the works of other schools if he could not find adequate discussion of a particular problem within the literature of his own school. That is, he could look beyond his own school only if it was deficient; it was better to use views from another school than personal *raʾy*. It could, in a slightly wider meaning, also mean that a scholar could evaluate the views of other schools against one's own and prefer the other if it had a better basis, even while retaining the primary identification with one's original school. This was more or less Ṭahṭāwī's position.

The last and most radical version of *talfīq* was to disregard the divisions between the schools altogether and pick whichever rule one found to be best without bothering where the rule came from. This, which is the most modern form of *talfīq*, hence means a removal of the school boundaries altogether and makes *fiqh* one unified field of individual and alternative rules from which the legal scholar picks freely. Ṭahṭāwī, however, took an intermediary position. But this was mainly a point of theory, he did not construct any reformed law as such.[11]

The other tendency, which had the same concerns but was more interested in opening the Sharīᶜa for a more radical change than in widening the role of *siyāsa*, is that running roughly from al-Afghānī and Muḥammad ᶜAbduh to Rashīd Riḍā. These thinkers wanted to expand the role of *ijtihād* and limit that of *ijmāᶜ*, which they saw as a conservative principle. By reducing *ijmāᶜ*'s hold over the schools and lowering its status as a fundamental principle, they felt that it was possible to carry out the modification of the Sharīᶜa rules that was necessary to adapt it to the modern world.

---

century, but it was only in the seventeenth and eighteenth that it came into legal discussions. There were voices both for and against 'borrowing viewpoints' in the Mālikī and in particular Ḥanafī schools, while the Shāfiᶜīs were unanimously against. But there was probably not a majority for allowing the principle in any of the schools; Sherman A. Jackson, *Islamic Law and the State: The Constitutional Jurisprudence of Shihāb al-Dīn al-Qarāfī*, Leiden 1996, 111-12, and Birgit Krawietz, 'Cut and paste in legal rules: Designing Islamic norms with *talfīq*', *Die Welt des Islams*, XLII, 1, 2002, 3-40.

11 He aided the khedive in creating a quite different type of law later, but that is mostly at the latter's request and not much influenced by his own views.

Jamal al-Dīn al-Afghānī (d. 1897) emphasized that knowledge that came through *ijmāᶜ* was *ẓannī*, probable, not *qaṭᶜī*, certain, referring to Ibn Taymīya who had made this point. That may seem obvious; no serious scholar would claim that what we have called confirmatory *ijmāᶜ*—consensus within the school—constitutes certainty, and absolute consensus among all Muslims had become moot after the constitution of rival schools of law. However, Afghānī's point of view was clearly made to reduce the impact of *ijmāᶜ* within the schools.

Muḥammad ᶜAbduh (d. 1905), Afghānī's most important Egyptian follower, stressed the need to open up for free *ijtihād*. He seems by this to mean all the way up to unlimited *ijtihād*, working directly on the sources of Revelation. In his practical work as chief *muftī* and *shaykh* of the Azhar university he seems to have focused mostly on the modernization of the education system and adaptations within the existing system.[12] His ideas were continued by Rashīd Riḍā (d. 1935), whose period of activity fell in the time when Europeans had taken control over most of the Middle East. He is perhaps the one of the three who presents his legal views in greatest detail. Like Ṭahṭāwī, he brings up *maṣlaḥa* as the basic principle underlying the law, and cites al-Shāṭibī as his support.[13] As with Ṭahṭāwī, Riḍā makes a distinction between *ᶜibādāt* and *muᶜāmalāt*, and says that the former consists of absolute and unchanging rules, while *muᶜāmlāt* rules may vary with the times, the Revelation is not absolute in their formulation. He does not go as far as Shāṭibī in this; he divides the *muᶜāmlāt* rules in two, those that are relevant for moral norms, and those that are not. The former are like the *ᶜibādāt* rules, they are given by God (who has defined these moral norms), and those who break these rules sin against God. They must therefore be as final as the *ᶜibādāt* rules. This of course makes it important to distinguish which *muᶜāmalāt* issues refer to moral norms and which do not; Riḍā is not specific here.

Riḍā, who was a Ḥanafī, also brings in the Ḥanafī *istiḥsān* principle and makes it a central rather than subsidiary principle

12 Hourani writes that ᶜAbduh, when asked 'official' questions by the khedive, answered by referring to Ḥanafī law, while he in 'private' queries used radical *talfīq*, without regard for which *madhhab* the rule was taken from; *Arabic Thought in the Liberal Age*, 152.

13 Cf. also Masud, *Shāṭibī's Philosophy of Islamic Law*, 113, 133-4 & 162-4.

for defining the law. This makes adaptations more flexible, and in fact brings back the old rejected views of the *ahl al-ra'y*! But he also underlined how important *qiyās* was for the adaptation of the law, in that the Sharīᶜa had to be relevant for society. In light of the early discussions between the *ra'y* and *ḥadīth* positions, this sounds confusing. But this is a different epoch, a time when the Sharīᶜa was by many considered to be finally fixed (and *fatwā*s only as 'clarifications', not 'adaptations' of the law). Thus Riḍā argued for *re-opening* the process of *qiyās*, which indicates the level of *ijithād* he envisages: not a rejection of methodology, but a fairly high level of new formulation of laws, way beyond the *ijmāᶜ* stage.

Who should perform this new formulation of law and establish Sharīᶜa rules is a matter of constitutional law. Riḍā goes a long way towards accepting that an assembly elected by majority vote among the believers may have this authority alongside the scholars, but does not say so explicitly. However, he does say that the government must have great leeway in making those decisions that are required for society, and that the common good must weigh heavier than slavishly copying the example of the Prophet. This is an important point, but must be seen in the light of the division of *muᶜāmalāt* that we mentioned; Riḍā was in this presumably only thinking of the latter, non-moral part of the law.

This debate is important in view of the later tendencies we call Islamism or fundamentalism. Riḍā points in that direction by putting emphasis on changing the Sharīᶜa from within so that it can be enforced today, rather than reducing it to a more general inspiration for a modern legal system, which is how one may read Ṭahṭāwī's emphasis on *siyāsa*. But Riḍā's ideas are also opposed to what is at least the more vulgar interpretations of modern Islamists, by saying that slavish aping of the early period is wrong and that one must distinguish between those fields where the Revelation is relevant and those where the common social good is most important.

In any case, if we consider these two trends as being adapations of the *siyāsa* principle and development of *talfīq* on the one hand and a more radical opening of *ijtihād* to make a revised Sharīᶜa a complete social law on the other, it is the former line that won the day, although perhaps in a manner different and more 'Westernized' than Ṭahṭāwī ever imagined.

Changes in the legal and court systems

Muḥammad ᶜAlī followed his formal overlord in introducing a series of new law codes. A new criminal law for specific crimes, such as murder, theft and fraud, was introduced in 1821.[14] Another law dealing with issues of land property, based on *kanun*, followed in 1830. The Ottoman court system was partly introduced in 1851, and the laws were made universal across *millet* boundaries.

This was in 1875 followed by the proposal of a variant of the Ottoman Mecelle law called *Murshid*, covering contracts, economic obligations and civil procedure, but it was in the end not put into effect.[15] A new personal law (*shakhṣī*, a new term) was introduced. It covered issues of marriage, inheritance and bequests. Those parts of it that related to monetary issues were later siphoned off and transferred to the civil court.

A hierarchical court of appeals had already been introduced in 1842. Called the *maḥākim ahlīya*, it covered both civil and criminal cases. A court for civil, private, conflicts outside the Sharīᶜa system was new to Egypt, and the appeals structure of lower and higher levels was introduced here as well. A system of defence lawyers was also developed, using the old term *wakīl*. The defence lawyer systems was revised after 1880. Then in 1895 the khedive established the *Dār al-iftā'*, 'Office of the *Muftī* of Egypt', to aid Muslims adapt to the changes in society. One of the first and most influential of these state *muftī*s was Muḥammad ᶜAbduh, who filled the post from 1899 to 1905.[16]

The functions of the Sharīᶜa court changed as a result of this, and was reorganized in 1856. It was primarily given jurisdiction over personal law, and was bureaucratized and made hierarchic. *Qāḍī*s were now to be appointed by the khedive, not by the sultan in Istanbul, except for the chief *qāḍī* of Cairo, over which the sultan retained control. A case should first be heard before an

14 Rudolph Peters, 'The codification of criminal law in nineteenth century Egypt: Tradition or modernization?', in J.M. Abun-Nasr, U. Spellenberg and U. Wanitzek (eds), *Law, Society and National Identity*, Hamburg 1990, 211-25 and 'Islamic and secular criminal law in nineteenth century Egypt: The role and function of the qadi', *Islamic Law and Society*, iv, 1, 1997, 70-90, and Botiveau, *Loi islamique*, 108-66.

15 Botiveau, *Loi islamique*, 54, 143-4.

16 Skovgaard-Petersen, *Defining Islam*, 100-6.

assistant judge (*nāʾib al-qāḍī*), then by the *qāḍī*, and it could finally be appealed to a *majlis al-ᶜulamāʾ*. This last council of scholars was an innovation. It only heard appeals and consisted of one *qāḍī* and five other prominent *ᶜulamāʾ*.

The khedive also had his *maẓālim* court, called *dīwān khadīwī*, while minor cases were still dealt with in the police courts, the *shurṭa*. We must also consider the informal arbitration and conflict solution that was carried out by individuals in authority outside the formalized court system, an informal function that came increasingly to be at variance with the formalized, Western-inspired legal system.

The practising of criminal law seems until 1883 to have followed the same pattern as it had earlier in the *kanun* system. The new law codes implemented early in the century had mostly been revisions and modernizations of the *kanun* laws, which again were based on *sharᶜī* principles and earlier practice.

The same was true for the relations between the various courts in criminal cases. Cases that were taken to the Sharīᶜa court and on which the *qāḍī* had not passed a verdict because of procedure or lack of *sharᶜī* evidence, could be raised before a state court and adjudicated according to codified law, which under the khedives were based on *siyāsa* and *taᶜzīr*, that is, with some links to the Sharīᶜa.[17]

Court records from the period show that forced labour was often used instead of the *ḥudūd* punishments. To use prison for these offences was not new, but there had earlier been a reluctance to use forced labour, so this may reflect a changing practice.

Mixed courts

The major changes came when Egyptians faced Europeans in legal conflict. The foreigners had gained much influence and power in the country, and did not accept being judged according to the Sharīᶜa laws for Muslims, and certainly not those for *dhimmī*s.[18]

17 Cf. Chapter 14, many of the cases referred to there are from nineteenth-century Egypt.

18 B.A. Roberson, 'The emergence of the modern judiciary in the Middle East: Negotiating the mixed courts of Egypt', in Mallat, *Islam and Public Law*, 107-39.

They demanded, and were granted, particular rights or *capitulations* if they were to continue trading. The Europeans were to be judged only according to their own laws, administered by the consuls of their own country. This system was older than Muḥammad ᶜAlī and had been in force throughout the Ottoman empire. It became more important with the increased role of the Europeans in the nineteenth century. The capitulations gave much power to the European consuls, and they became more and more unrestrained. Nor did it help that each consul worked according to the law of his own particular country, so that a plethora of different European laws were practised in Egypt, and Egyptians who dealt with Europeans had to take them all into account (and the consuls could not, under the system, be questioned on his interpretation of what 'his' law said).

The khedive wanted to get some order into this system, so that Egyptians could at least know what laws were in use. The European powers reacted differently to this wish, following internal rivalries. The French had traditionally had a strong position in Egypt since the time of Napoleon's invasion, and Paris had close links with the educated middle classes in Egypt and the khedive himself. However, the British were strengthening their influence from the middle of the century. The French therefore felt that questioning the status quo could only weaken their position vis-à-vis Britain, so they resisted any changes. The British were for the same reason positive to the khedive's proposals. Istanbul voiced the opinion that Egypt could not, as part of the Empire, go ahead with any unilateral changes of the capitulation system, since it concerned foreign relations that the sultan insisted were under his authority only.

The khedive formulated his ideas in a proposal, written by his minister Nubar Pasha, in 1867. It proposed the establishment of 'mixed courts' that should cover all of Egypt and all relations between Egyptians and Europeans. It should be based on European civil and criminal law. To gain French support, the proposal said that this meant French civil law, that is Code Napoléon, a law that would be common for all citizens of the capitulation states. The courts should have an equal number of European and Egyptian judges; the consuls were to appoint the European judges, and the Egyptian government the Egyptians ones. A solution was also found to the French insistence that

France should dominate in the assembly of lawyers.

Discussions over the proposal lasted until 1876, when the system was finally introduced. However, the result was not as happy for the khedive as he had expected. His intention had not been that the Egyptian state itself should be taken to this court. But this was precisely what the European powers did, over the debts that Egypt owed to them. The courts were thus quickly given a political significance. The process eventually led to the British occupation of Egypt in 1882, which in effect transformed the country into a protectorate. This was the real turning point for the legal system in Egypt.

After the occupation: The Sharīᶜa in retreat

The first major impact was the introduction of French criminal law in place of the existing Ottoman-based one, and the formal removal of any competence of the Sharīᶜa courts in criminal cases. This was done in the following year, 1883. The content of the French law code was of course quite different from that of the Ottoman and Egyptian *kanun*, so this was a substantial change in practised law.

Some sources say that Khedive Ismāᶜīl first suggested that a criminal law should be codified on the basis of Sharīᶜa rules, but that the *ᶜulamāᵓ* rejected such an innovation and watering down of the Sharīᶜa. However, it is doubtful that the British would have accepted anything less than European law. Western-inspired courts were also introduced in place of the *maẓālim* and *shurṭa* courts, while the Sharīᶜa courts continued to function in those areas where they were given competence. But these areas became more and more constrained.[19]

The first impetus was thus a pure import of French law codes. These were then 'nationalized', adapted to Egyptian conditions (*tamṣīr*). This process took off particularly after Egypt gained formal independence in 1922. The early French-based system had employed lawyers mostly imported from Europe. However, there were soon established teaching institutions for Egyptian lawyers, and local lawyers had by 1920 mostly taken over the practice of law in the courts.

19 Botiveau, *Loi islamique*, 195-200, and Skovgaard-Petersen, *Defining Islam*, 202-3.

The personal law came up for revision in 1929, but was still based on Sharīᶜa rules. However, the state did attempt some modifications by employing the most radical interpretation of *talfīq*, picking some rules from one school of law and some from another, with a result that no Sharīᶜa scholar would perhaps have recognized it clearly as theirs. It was rather suited to what the government wanted to achieve.

This law was again reformed seven years later, in 1936–42. The task was given to one of the most important legal scholars of the Arab world in the twentieth century, ᶜAbd al-Razzāq al-Sanhūrī (d. 1971).[20] He was a theoretician and a teacher, and had a great influence on legislation in many of the central Arabic countries of this epoch.

His first attempt in the 1942 law was to unify all the various sources of law—French, Ottoman, Egyptianized, customary law and *fiqh*—into one single code. The Sharīᶜa was thus included as one of many sources. This was a drastic idea, and the final version of the law, which was passed in 1949, turned out to be in content primarily a continuation of the earlier limited personal codes, although 'Egyptianized' in Sanhūrī's expression.

The liberation hero and head of government, Saᶜd Zaghlūl, also attempted a codification of the Sharīᶜa—based on *takhayyur*, to take what is best from each school of law—but this did not have any practical result.

The Sharīᶜa court structure was modified to a clearer hierarchy in 1931. There were now three basic levels; a local Sharīᶜa court, the verdicts of which could be appealed to a regional court, and then to the national court in Cairo.

This process of adapting state-sponsored laws had made the need for a state *muftī* less pressing. This office thus fell further into oblivion, and some politicans suggested abolishing it. It only came into significance again in the 1980s, but now with a new task: to be a spokesman for general views on the role of Islam in society, and to give authoritative answers to issues of the day. The *muftī* is, however, most often seen by the public as the 'state's

20 Enid Hill, 'Islamic Law as a source for the development of a comparative jurisprudence: theory and practice in the life and work of Sanhūrī', in Azmeh, *Islamic Law*, 146-97; also Oussama Arabi, 'Intention and method in Sanhūrī's fiqh: Cause as ulterior motive', *Islamic Law and Society*, IV, 2, 1997, 200-23.

man', and faces competiton from other and unofficial *muftī*-like institutions of advice.[21]

The Sharīᶜa courts had by that time been abolished by Nasser, from 1 January 1956. They were replaced by justices of the peace, and merged with the other judicial system in Egypt.

The Sharīᶜa's place in Egypt today

We may thus say that after Sanhūrī's unification was rejected and the law codes found their final form, the Sharīᶜa did not have any formal place in Egypt's legal system. The *qāḍī*s disappeared with the 1956 reform,[22] while the *muftī*s were still there, now not so much with a judicial function but as a private or public 'counsellor' in questions relating to religion. The law codes have replaced the Sharīᶜa in all areas, including elements of family law.[23]

But while the structure is Western, there is still a struggle over the content of the rules of family law, between conceptions based on Western norms and others based on some sort of combination of Sharīᶜa and custom. This struggle became very visible in the debate over the so-called 'Jihān laws' under Sadat, when a new personal law with a more Western-inspired content was fiercely resisted by religious forces and a section of public opinion, and was finally declared 'unconstitutional' in 1985.[24]

Those advocating a stronger influence of Sharīᶜa norms within the existing family law were on the offensive in the last two decades of the twentieth century. Some also want to increase the influence of the Sharīᶜa in most other parts of the legal system. It must be said that their conception of 'Sharīᶜa' is probably closer to the classical concept of *siyāsa sharᶜīya*, the general spirit of the Sharīᶜa, than any particular school's rules. The classical concept of *ḥisba* has also become significant in this debate. A part of this debate has centred on a paragraph in Egypt's constitution, §2, which said that the Sharīᶜa is 'a principal source' for the laws of the country. This was in 1980 changed

21 Skovgaard-Jensen, *Defining Islam, passim.*

22 Those *qāḍī*s that were still active in 1956 were integrated into the state court system, but were not replaced when they retired.

23 Family law is however still partly practised according to the uncodified Sharīᶜa, cf. Peters, 'From jurists' law to statute law', 91. Egypt marks here an exception to the rule in the Arab world.

24 Botiveau, *Loi islamique*, 200-5.

to '*the* principal source'. However, it has not been given retroactive force on existing laws, and up until today has still not dramatically changed the legal system.

The trend is however that Egyptian judges now increasingly refer to 'the Sharīᶜa' and less to the code when they give their verdicts, partly in defiance of the government's opinions. The development thus seems to go in favour of a greater role for the Sharīᶜa in some form, but within a system of Western-based codes of law. The Sharīᶜa is mostly used to legitimize a view of norms and morality, as an addition to the existing code—and not always used quite correctly according to traditional *fiqh*, since the judges still mostly have a Western-based education, rather than a classical one in *fiqh*.

Algeria

A different case is the developments in Algeria, the first Arab country to come under direct European control in 1830, half a century before Egypt. The course of legal change there meandered back and forth over the century, because of both the recurrent revolutions in France and the changing relations of power and resistance in Algeria itself. However, the main factor for most of the century was the division between those areas where civilian French immigrants, *colons*, had the power and those that were 'Arab' lands, under military control as long as there was a danger of rebellion.[25]

The theory was established from the beginning that Algeria was to be a part of France, not a colony. This was formalized after the 1848 revolution, when some of the former revolutionaries were sent there to build villages. This lead to a long-lasting conflict between the civilians, who took the theory at its word and tried to create conditions as similar to those in metropolitan France as possible, and the military, who had more direct contacts with the Arabs. Thus it was in fact the military who most favoured the continuation of existing conditions, including giving

25 Charles-Robert Ageron, *Modern Algeria*, London 1991, 22-81, and Allan Christelow, *Muslim Law Courts and the French Colonial State in Algeria*, Princeton 1985 and 'The transformation of the Muslim court system in Colonial Algeria', in Azmeh, *Islamic Law*, 215-30.

the Sharīᶜa a place in the legal framework in the areas of Arabs population. But it was the civilians who eventually gained the upper hand, resulting in rising tensions that eventually lead to the war of liberation a century later.

The 1848 revolution also introduced the principle of assimilation and made French law and French courts effective for everyone, and hence the Sharīᶜa courts lost jurisdiction over criminal cases. But this was only valid for the civilian areas, while most of the Arabs lived in military-controlled territory.

A new court system was established for the Arab areas in 1854, based on *maḥkama*s, modernized Sharīᶜa courts. The major novelty was that these courts were hierarchical, with two levels: the basic unit was the old *qāḍī*-based court; the country was divided into about 300 court units (*circonscriptions*). Verdicts in these courts could be appealed to a higher instance, which here was called *majlis*. This court was based on the earlier Ottoman *majlis*, the *maẓālim* courts of Tunisia, which we described in the last chapter. These were now made into pure appeal courts. There were fifteen such *majlis* regions, each consisting of four *qāḍī*s. The French authorities did not intervene in the working of these courts leaving it to the Arabs. Lawyers (*wakīl*s), also Muslims, were, however, introduced in these courts.

The problem was that Algeria differed from East to West. Those who lived in the eastern part of the country quickly recognized this system, based on the Tunisian *majlis* that they knew; many of the legal scholars there had been trained at the Tunisian Zaytūna university. But the word *majlis* meant something else in Western Algeria. Here it was a council of four court officials (*shuhūd*s) that the *qāḍī* had used to confer with, that is, a part of the basic court unit. This council played an important part in the local communities by helping to negotiate the settlement of conflicts before they reached the formality of a court proceeding.

The French did not know, or care, about this distinction and abolished this form of local negotiation council. This not only estranged the system from the people—it was also in the West that armed resistance to the French had been strongest—but also made the court system less flexible, making it harder to solve conflicts outside the court.

The new state also abolished the *waqf* system and instead paid the wages of the *ᶜulamāʾ* through the colonial budget. But it felt that there were too many of these scholars and started reducing their number. Many mosques were closed down or transferred to new functions. This led to a reduction of this alternative power base in society, but also lowered the level and quality of learning among the traditional scholars of law.

The army's control of the Arab territories was abolished after the final defeat of armed resistance in 1858. The new civilian rule led to a marked restriction of the role of the Sharīᶜa in Algeria. The colonists felt that the system established only four years earlier, still founded on the Ottoman basis, did not work well. The judges were 'corrupt', they said, meaning that they were inefficient, although this was in part a result of their own attempt to undermine the classical system.

The attack was first directed at the higher levels of appeals. The Sharīᶜa instances of appeal were already abolished in 1859. From this date, all appeals should go directly to the French court with French judges, who should judge according to local law, in which they were evidently not well versed. The result was that the appeal system was not much used. Certain categories of cases should also go directly to the French court for their first treatment. There was otherwise no codification of what law should be used in the remaining Sharīᶜa court.

As the *majlis*, the appeals court for Sharīᶜa cases, thus largely became meaningless, it was abolished in 1866. But it was at the same time recognized that making appeals go to the French court did not work either, so appeals from the Sharīᶜa courts were now instead directed to a new mixed French/Muslim court.

Another interesting but short-lived experiment was the introduction of a *Haut-Conseil* for Muslim law. This was a 'council of *muftī*s' which was to interpret the laws, thus an attempt at institutionalizing the function of a *muftī* in a modern form; a fairly singular approach at this period. New institutions of learning for *qāḍī*s, *muftī*s and other scholars were also established. This still left some space for the Sharīᶜa in the Arab areas; the Muslims were to be tried according to Sharīᶜa law at all stages, even if it fell to French judges to apply it on appeal.

But a new war followed in France only a few years later, the French-German war of 1870-71, and the new republic instituted yet another new policy for Algeria. Now all of Algeria was to be integrated into France, and the civilian colonists were given the power to implement their wishes. Instead of maintaining the geographic distinction between Arab and *colon* territories, they introduced a system that was unified in space, but divided socially, where the 'natives', *indigènes*, became second-class citizens. The colonists set about reducing the scope of the Sharīᶜa through a number of efforts.

In 1881, a *Code de l'indigénat* was introduced. This was a series of special laws that should replace the previous exemptions of the military areas while restricting the social rights of the Arabs. At the same time a regular campaign was initiated against the position of the Sharīᶜa, particularly in the first twenty years 1870-90. The number of *qāḍī* courts, originally 300, was in this period reduced from 180 to 60. They were not abolished outright, but cut down bit by bit. They were fully abolished in the Kabyle area in 1874, since the Kabyle Berbers were 'weakly Islamicized' and were to be a preferred group among the natives. The colonists saw this as a defence of *kanun*, by which they apparently meant the 'customary law' against the 'foreign' Sharīᶜa.

The High *muftī* council was abolished in 1875, and the *qāḍī*s lost the right to treat cases concerning land property in 1886. This was transferred to French 'justices of peace'. This was evidently of concern in a period when the extension of colonists' land at the expense of the Arabs was a controversial issue.[26] Criminal cases were from now on only to be treated in jury courts, where only French colonists sat in the juries.

As Algerian nationalist currents started to grow in the twentieth century, the issue of the discriminatory special laws came under attack. There were two different currents in the opposition to these laws. One believed that the result should be only one, and thus French-based, law for everyone in the country. Others worked to defend the remains of the Sharīᶜa and traditional law and their right to exist. But it was the first tendency that came to dominate in the liberation movement FLN and was consequently put into practice in the new state after independence.

26 The French carried out an extensive expropriation of Arab land, not least through the *Loi Warnier* of 1875, which made in possible to expropriate communal land. The *qāḍī*s thus lost jurisdiction in this field ten years later; Tuomo Melasuo, 'The problems and contradictions of land conflicts in Algeria', in Bo Utas and Knut S. Vikør (eds), *The Middle East Viewed from the North*, Bergen 1992, 86.

Africa: Islamic law in British colonies

The British were less concerned with imposing their home country's laws in their colonies than the French were in Algeria. They worked instead from the concept of 'indirect rule', which means to restrict the colonial power's direct interference at the local level and instead rule through the intermediaries of existing chiefs and local leaders. This attitude may be influenced in the legal field from the tradition of British common law, which was closer to a conception of established custom as a basis for law, and which may have increased sensitivity for referring to local customs and laws in the colonies. However, the British colonies differed from each other in how this was interpreted, and how they saw the Sharīᶜa, which was, after all, not quite the same as local custom.[27]

In East Africa the Sharīᶜa was called an existing 'fundamental law' which was something different from custom. That is, it is a law basically foreign to the region. In West Africa the views on the Sharīᶜa were also fairly restrictive in the Gambia. In the largest Muslim territory under British control in Africa, North and Central Nigeria, it was, however, defined to *be* the 'native law and custom'. This was of course linked to how well established Islam was in the various parts of Africa. Northern Nigeria had been solidly Muslim for centuries, while Islam in East Africa had been a coastal and to some extent an immigrant phenomenon until the late nineteenth century.

British lawyers did to some extent transfer their common-law principles to the new lands, and felt that custom had to be decisive, even if it was not a custom the colonialists sympathized with: 'The court cannot itself transform a barbarous custom into a milder one'.[28] Thus they practised the law as it was in the area; that is to say, the law as the local authorities, the 'chiefs', said it was; the colonial authorities generally came with little local knowledge and would most often accept what was offered to them as 'our law'.

This meant that the Sharīᶜa in the British areas became identical to what local rulers had practised, not the letter of the

27 J.N.D. Anderson, *Islamic Law in Africa*, London 1970.
28 Anderson, *Islamic law in Africa*, 4.

Sharīᶜa literature. This turned out to be a flexible solution, which did, however, gave the local authorities acknowledged by the colonizers a fairly wide authority to determine what the Sharīᶜa 'was'. But this was of course tempered by the common view held by people in the region of what had been practised before.

As for the courts that should put this custom/Sharīᶜa law into effect, they also varied. The law was in some cases left in the hands of a particular Sharīᶜa court, perhaps with certain possibilities to appeal to a British court. In other cases the British court handled all cases. In yet others both types of court worked together (as was normal in British Somaliland).

The procedures and rules of evidence followed the system of each type of court; the Sharīᶜa courts continued traditional Sharīᶜa rules of procedure, while the British appeals courts used British rules, even in cases where the law they were to judge by was customary, that is, the Sharīᶜa.

There was initially no distinction between criminal and other fields of law, so that criminal cases were also handled by this localized Sharīᶜa system. The role of the Sharīᶜa in criminal cases was in any case different in Islamic African regions than in the Arab or Ottoman-ruled ones,[29] and there was no reason why the British should introduce the Ottoman *siyāsa* courts, the *majlis* or *maẓālim*, where they had no tradition. But binding the legitimacy of the local ruler's power over legal cases to the Sharīᶜa gave it a real authority over criminal law that it probably did not have in the Middle East in that period.

Islamic law in Nigeria

The Sharīᶜa court system was thus continued in Muslim Nigeria in principally the same way it had been before the British conquest. The existing Sharīᶜa courts were initially given free rein to take up criminal cases, as described, except in such cases that the colonial power found to be 'repugnant to natural justice and humanity'.[30] A death penalty also had to be confirmed by the

29 In Northern Nigeria the 'minister', *waziri*, who was often the actual political power holder, had the rights to supervise and revoke the sentences made by the *qāḍī*; Ahmed Beita Yusuf, *Nigerian Legal System: Pluralism and Conflict of Laws in the Northern States*, New Dehli 1982, 42.

30 Suleimanu Kumo, 'Shari'a under colonialism: Northern Nigeria', in N. Alkali *et al*, *Islam in Africa. Proceedings of the Islam in Africa*

British governor or his representative.

The Sharīᶜa courts were incorporated into the British court system in 1933. As Nigeria was of course divided between Muslim areas in the north and west, and non-Muslim ones in south and east, the court system was divided into three.[31] The purely colonial or British system with a hierarchy from provincial to supreme court was valid throughout the country, and had jurisdiction of particular cases. Alongside this was recognized a system of 'native courts' divided into two, one for the non-Muslim 'customary law' areas in the south, and one for the Sharīᶜa courts, or *alkali* (*al-qāḍī*) courts, in the north. The two were not identical in structure; the Sharīᶜa courts had more levels in their hierarchy, with the legal council of the local emir as the highest instance. Cases could then be appealed from either of these two native court systems to the British courts, up to its Supreme Court.[32]

The Sharīᶜa courts could still follow their own rules of procedure, and did not have to apply the general Nigerian Criminal Code.[33] This was changed in 1947, after which the *alkali* courts had to follow the national criminal law, if that had a rule that was relevant to the case. This meant that criminal cases should in reality no longer follow Sharīᶜa law, but state law. But this change was thus made as late as after World War II, a century or more after the Sharīᶜa had lost this authority in the central lands of the Middle East.

The colonial system was by and large continued after independence in 1960, only the names were changed. 'Native courts' became 'local courts', but were still split into one system for non-Muslims in the south and another for Muslims in the north. The national or state law continued to be based on British common law, with addition of such 'statutes' as were passed by legislative assemblies at federal or state level.[34] Family law under

---

Conference, Ibadan 1993, 7-21. This was formulated in 1900. The Sharīᶜa courts were from 1916 called 'alkali [Hausa for *al-qāḍī*] courts'.

31 Yusuf, *Nigerian Legal System*, 33-49.

32 Matters of family law could not be appealed over the alkali court; Kumo, 'Shari'a under colonialism', 11.

33 As opposed to the customary courts of the south, which had to follow this law from the beginning; Kumo, 'Shari'a under colonialism', 13.

34 And, lacking such, British statutory law as it was at the moment of colonization, 1 January 1900. After Nigeria became a federation, each

the Sharīᶜa system could still be appealed to a Sharīᶜa Court of Appeal, while criminal cases were now removed completely from the Sharīᶜa system and were judged according to a new federal criminal law with appeals fully within the national court system.

A reform was proposed in 1977, leading to heated debate.[35] The national courts had two stages of appeal on the federal level; a 'Federal Court of Appeal', which took cases from courts on the state (regional) level, and a 'Federal Supreme Court of Appeal'. But the Sharīᶜa cases only had one such level, they went directly from the highest Sharīᶜa court in each state to the Federal Supreme Court. In order to create a balance between the two systems, a commission proposed to establish a separate federal Sharīᶜa court of appeal, as a first appeals court for Sharīᶜa cases on the federal level.

This lead to rioting, in particular by Christian and other non-Muslim groups in the south. The change may appear marginal and technical, as it only involved cases that were already within the Sharīᶜa system as appeal cases. But it was seen as a symbolic matter. The protesters felt that establishing a federal Sharīᶜa court would confirm that Nigeria (which had been politically dominated by northern elites for most of its history) was considered a Muslim state, and that non-Muslims were relegated to minorities.[36] The result was that the reform was dropped and no such federal Sharīᶜa court was established.

New riots occurred twenty years later, in the late 1990s, as some northern states introduced criminal laws based on the Sharīᶜa. Family law had always been Sharīᶜa-based in those states, but it had not had any influence on criminal law since the 1947 verdict. The new laws were codified within the established statutory system, but were marked by the rhetoric of 're-introducing the Sharīᶜa', and gave emphasis to applying the *ḥudūd* laws, often with little regard for the restrictions on these

---

local state also has the right to pass laws.

35 Ghazali Basri, *Nigeria and Sharīᶜah: Aspirations and Apprehensions*, Markfield 1994, 41-9, and Ibrahim K.R. Sulaiman, 'The Sharīᶜah and the 1979 constitution', in S. Khalid Rashid (ed.), *Islamic Law in Nigeria: Application and Teaching*, Lagos 1986, 52-74. It was a part of the formulation of a new constitution for the country.

36 This conflict was simultaneous to the attempt by the government to make Nigeria join the 'Organization of Islamic States', which led to similar riots and on the same basis.

that traditional *fiqh* had imposed. This was met with resistance by the minority Christian groups in the north. The Sharīᶜa laws were still meant to be only a parallel road to the national laws, which still applied in all states, but the minorities feared that the sentiment of 'Islamization' in those states would make the Sharīᶜa laws applicable to all citizens, including non-Muslims.[37] The federal authorities were also opposed to these laws, and the struggle became an expression both of local and ethnic divisions, and of a power struggle between the federal and regional state levels.

Traditional states in a modern world

Some Arab countries only recently came into the 'modern' state form, and still appear as 'traditional' islands in a modern world. These include in particular the small states around the Arabian Gulf; Kuwait, Bahrain, Qatar and the United Arab Emirates (UAE).[38]

Even if they are 'traditional', they are in fact fairly recent as societies and states. Some of them (such as Kuwait) were formed in the eighteenth century or later in desert regions, and base their modern existence on the oil production that was developed into the twentieth century. Thus none them had any very elaborate Sharīᶜa court system before the colonial period.[39] The most important legal framework had been the private court of the ruler, where he gave verdicts based on custom; or tribal courts where local leaders did the same.[40] There were also some organs for arbitration of commercial disputes, and some towns also had Sharīᶜa judges who dealt with family and personal matters.

As these societies became more settled and came under

37 It was only in 1958 that the non-Muslim Africans were allowed to 'opt out' of the Sharīᶜa courts in the Muslim areas; Yusuf, *Nigerian Legal System*, 108.

38 And Saudi Arabia, which has its own history; cf. Chapter 13. Much of this is also true for Oman and Yemen, but they have their particularities through the existence of non-Sunnī, respectively Ibāḍī and Zaydī Shīᶜī, law.

39 Nathan J. Brown, *The Rule of Law in the Arab World: Courts in Egypt and the Gulf*, Cambridge 1997, and William M. Ballantyne, *Essays and Addresses on Arab Laws*, London 2000.

40 It is must be remembered that these were small and marginal societies, mostly populated by nomads.

British influence, they went almost directly from a predominantly 'pre-Islamic', or at least custom-based, court to a 'post-Islamic', Western system. There were conflicts between the local sultans and the British, where the sultans tried to argue on the basis of the Sharīᶜa's legitimacy. But the British built civil courts, and those Sharīᶜa courts that had existed lost importance or were abolished, as in Kuwait. There, the civil court was instead to base its verdicts on the Sharīᶜa.

It was however Egyptian law that came to dominate. Kuwait introduced the Ottoman Majalla law in the 1960s, but soon changed to Egyptian-based laws. Bahrain first implemented Anglo-Sudanese law, a British-based law with an impact from Sharīᶜa rules, but they also changed to Egyptian laws in the 1970s.

Qatar is in a slightly different situation, because of the influence of the Saudi Wahhābī movement there. They emphasize Ḥanbalī law, and Qatar is probably the only country beside Saudi Arabia where the Ḥanbalīya has a dominant role. They thus have a developed Sharīᶜa court system instead of customary courts, but they too introduced a codified law at independence.

Most of these countries mention the Sharīᶜa as a source of law alongside the codified law. How this is specified varies from country to country, and it may be useful to quickly summarize some of them to see how they place the Sharīᶜa in relation to codified law and to custom.[41]

— *The United Arab Emirates*

Groups the sources of law on four levels:

1. If there is a rule in codified law, that is applied without interpretation.
2. If there is no such rule, the verdict should be passed according to Mālikī and Ḥanbalī *fiqh*.
3. If the judge finds nothing in these sources, he should apply Shāfiᶜī and Ḥanafī *fiqh*.

41 William Ballantyne, 'A reassertion of the sharī'ah: The jurisprudence in Gulf states', in Nicholas Heer (ed.), *Islamic Law and Jurisprudence*, Seattle 1990, 149-60.

4. If these are not helpful either, he should use custom, which may vary from emirate to emirate in this unified state. Codified laws cannot, however, be contrary to the Sharīᶜa or public morality.

— *Qatar*
Also has four levels in the rules for economic matters. Here the first priority (1) is the contract; then (2) what is said in codified law; further, if that gives no answer, (3) custom, and finally, (4) the Sharīᶜa.

— *Bahrain*
Refers to three sources, first (1) codified law; then (2) the principles of the Sharīᶜa; and finally (3) custom.

— *Kuwait*
Here the judge should use first (1) codified law; then, if that is not satisfactory, (2) custom; and if this does not apply, (3) *fiqh*. Custom is thus ranked above the Sharīᶜa law, but it is also stated that 'it is not possible that anything that contravenes [the] established precepts of Islam should constitute custom'. The Sharīᶜa should be the 'most important source' for the law, and there was in 1991 set down a committee to study the laws and change those that might be in contradiction to the Sharīᶜa. But they had, by 1996, not made any proposals to make such changes.[42]

Thus the codified law is everywhere the first source of law, as expected. But the countries then use different formulations in how they rank custom versus Sharīᶜa, as formulated in *fiqh* literature. The assumption, in some cases made explicit, that Sharīᶜa and custom cannot be in opposition, is probably common, but that is on a more normative level where 'the Sharīᶜa' may as well refer to the divine and abstract precepts known only to God, as to the actual rules formulated through *fiqh*. However, those systems that do refer to *fiqh* and to schools of law are more precise, and the UAE here thus places *fiqh* over custom, while the three others all put custom over *fiqh*. The Emirates also give the Mālikī school

42 M.F. Mühlböck, 'Modernization and traditionalism in the legislation of Kuwait', in Vermeulen and van Reeth, *Law, Christianity and Modernism in Islamic Society*, 93-4.

precedence over the Ḥanafī and Shāfiᶜī schools, showing that Mālikism has a foothold in this region. Generally, however, the particular *madhhab*s are not specified at this general level of priorities.

13

'IMPLEMENTING THE SHARĪᶜA'

We have now arrived at a period where state power is paramount. The time has passed when the law was placed *between* state and civil society. Only in those countries where Sharīᶜa courts are allowed to regulate family conflicts outside the 'regular' legal framework does the Sharīᶜa have a role 'autonomous' from the state. It is in other cases mostly an inspiration, real or symbolic, for a legal system that is formulated as well as put into effect by the state.

When the legislator thus creates new laws, he can either base himself on and adapt to the norms that are prevalent in society (with the 'common man'), or he can try to use the laws to change norms in society in a direction desired by the state.

This is the case with Western as with Muslim society. But in Muslim countries there is a separate element in this equation: the existence of an alternative and parallel legal norm, the Sharīᶜa; either as a 'real' alternative, in that there actually is a rule in the Sharīᶜa literature that corresponds to the norm that public opinion adheres to, or a 'symbolic' alternative where people will refer to the Sharīᶜa as a defence against state-supported norms that they do not accept, whether or not the Sharīᶜa actually has any text on this issue (or is more ambiguous that most people assume).

The latter is not uncommon, not only in Muslim countries, but also among Muslim immigrants to Western countries, where conflicts over norms are often direct and brutal. Such immigrants will often refer to Islam or the Sharīᶜa (or 'the Koran') as support for a practice that is actually only the local custom in the home country—in particular in relation to family norms, honour and virtue—and which may have little or no basis in either religion or the Sharīᶜa. Thus the Sharīᶜa may, as Islam itself, become a cultural reference for an undifferentiated 'home world', often as much an expression of 'differentness', as a distancing from the surrounding Western society.

It is thus not the letter of the Sharīᶜa, but the norms prevalent in society that define many non-scholarly Muslims' view of what the Sharīᶜa 'is'.[1] If Muslims have the view that for example honour killing is based on the Sharīᶜa, while there is in fact no support for this in the legal literature, is it then part of the Sharīᶜa or not?

An answer would lie in differentiating the concept 'Muslims', and not seeing them as a unified totality. There are disagreements between Muslims in the same time period, and between views of what the Sharīᶜa 'is' from epoch to epoch. We must also be able to consider that there are levels of opinion of what the Sharīᶜa is.

Normatively it may be argued that it is fully the prerogative of the believers to define the content of their religion, and thus the Sharīᶜa. The Sharīᶜa is in that sense to be defined as a shared understanding between Muslims at any particular point in time, and outsiders may not dispute this shared understanding as being the 'true' expression of their religious beliefs.

But such shared understandings are seldom achieved, or at least seldom universal among those who say they share a religion. There will always be different opinions, different currents that argue over content; and this certainly occurs in a widespread religion such as Islam. These discussions will refer to authorities, written or otherwise, to support their claims of authenticity, and outsiders may also have access to these written authorities and study them descriptively. Thus we may establish that one particular conception or rule is 'in accordance with' or 'divergent from' the Sharīᶜa, not as a religious expression or as our belief in God's true will, but in the meaning 'in accordance with the authoritative sources' that are a part of the Sharīᶜa's history and are used as anchors in discussions between Muslims.

Thus we may, from independent criteria, separate those views that are within the broad spectre of variation that we find in classical *fiqh*—those we can say are 'in accordance with' the Sharīᶜā—from those views that were not accepted or not dealt with in classical *fiqh*. Some views, although claimed to be 'the Sharīᶜa', must be outside what we can reasonably say is the classical conception of *fiqh,* either explicitly rejected by the legal literature or opposed to the evident logic that the law is based on.[2]

1 And also some of the scholars! Or at least those who consider themselves as such and are considered as authorities. Hence this falls into the area of observable disagreement or variations among the class of scholars.

2 Thus one may, among the issues that often crop up in discussions on

These we may then fairly objectively say are views 'in contradiction to' the Sharīᶜa, not normatively, but descriptively from our understanding of *fiqh* as a logically coherent and observable system, even if Muslims today may argue that these views are 'what the Sharīᶜa commands us'.[3]

We may thus, in this descriptive analysis, distinguish between possible variations inside classical *fiqh*—as it was expressed by *muftīs* and other scholars on the basis of the methodology of law, including late *ijtihād*, *takhrīj*, *talfīq*, and other methods of adapting the law—and 'views in society' on 'what Islam says' that are outside this. But precisely the variable nature of the Sharīᶜa—and that our sources for this evaluation are works written by a self-generating class of scholars—does of course mean that this line between what is 'reasonably within' and 'outside' may be challenged and will change over time.

The decisive question thus becomes, who decides what the Sharīᶜa and its outside limits are? Is it the *ᶜulamāᵓ*? The state? The 'average' Muslims (and then how?), or perhaps independent groups of Muslims who arrogate themselves to be 'alternative *ᶜulamāᵓ*', as we see today in many radical Muslim groups? This is not a matter of logic, but of power. Who controls the symbols, and who controls the Sharīᶜa, is both a result of and a factor for

---

immigration, reasonably consider 'honour killings' as clearly against the Sharīᶜa, forced marriages to be clearly against Ḥanafī law (thus for Pakistani and Turkish immigrants) while it may be supported in Mālikī law (North and West Africans), and while female circumcision is hardly mentioned in the Sharīᶜa literature, those sources we have would mostly indicate that it is 'neutral' (neither banned nor required), but they can support both the view that it is required (in the 'milder', 'Sunnaic', form, thus some Shāfiᶜīs), and that it is banned (so claimed by many Muslim feminists). Cf. Chapter 15, also Baudouin Dupret, 'Sexual morality at the Egyptian bar: Female circumcision, sex change operations and motives for suing', *Islamic Law and Society*, IX, 1, 2002, 54-6.

3 This view is, as mentioned in Chapter 1, not uncontroversial, as one may define 'Sharīᶜa' to mean 'what Muslims today practice'. By this definition, honour killings would be part of the Sharīᶜa if all the actors in a local community considers it to be that, even though the Sharīᶜa scholars and literature say otherwise. If that were the case, 'the Sharīᶜa' would not exist as any common and describable entity, only as a name or reference point for whatever local practices there be. As it is our aim in this book to present the history of this entity 'the Sharīᶜa', this would make everything we have written so far meaningless and irrelevant for the study of law.

the relationships of power in society.

We are thus approaching the topical discussions of the day, when we see demands from many corners for 'application of the Sharīᶜa', primarily promoted by radical Islamists, or 'fundamentalists', as the media likes to call them.

Islamism

The situation today is that more countries refer to the Sharīᶜa as an 'inspiration' or otherwise than was the case a generation ago, and several attempts at changing family laws in a more libcral direction have been quashed. However, this 're-islamization' of the laws has mainly been symbolic and has had at most a marginal effect on the actual laws in force. By and large, it must be correct for most Muslim countries to say that the Sharīᶜa does not have any greater influence on the laws now than it did at the end of the colonial period.

However, many countries have seen the rise of 'Islamist' movements that work to change this. The concept of 'Islamism' is vague and covers many different currents and tendencies whose aims and methods vary. But many of them focus on the Sharīᶜa as a political programme and use it as a definition of 'Islamization'.[4] It holds, they believe, the key to the solution of the various social, political and economic problems that the Muslim world is facing. Thus it must be 're-introduced' or 'applied' as the law of the land, and for many as the only law of the land.

This point is quite generally voiced among those political movements that we call Islamist. However, what they mean by 'the Sharīᶜa' varies, in particular when one steps down from the level of principle and symbolic reference to the actual rules to be effected. Here the many currents that are often grouped together as 'fundamentalist' may go in different directions. For some, the Sharīᶜa is only a symbol that is not terribly precise as to content, more or less synonymous with 'the Koran', 'Islam', 'morality' and 'fight against corruption'. These Islamist movements—many of them small groups with little or no hope of actually getting to run a country, so with no need to specify their rhetoric—often

4 For a discussion of some concepts of legal development used by leading Islamists, see e.g. Hallaq, *History of Islamic Legal Theories*, 226-31.

consist of youths who have rejected the 'Western secularist' society, but do not have much actual training in theology or classical law. They mostly know the Sharīᶜa from propagandist leaflets and as a pattern for ritual acts and symbolic markers in clothing or otherwise, as spread by their grouplet. For these, the rules of *ᶜibādāt* and a general moral attitude in their personal life are the most concrete expressions of the Sharīᶜa.

Reintroduction in practical terms

However, some groups have been able to win a wider audience, so that they have had to consider how to put their ideas into effect. They thus have had to address, at least in some form, the problem of 'what it means'. Even if currents of Islamist ideology have only won power in a few countries (Iran and the Sudan, and to a point in Pakistan), several such groups have won wider support in other countries (Egypt, Algeria, Tunisia, Palestine and elsewhere), and a few theoreticians of these currents have given some indications of what they mean by the application of the Sharīᶜa.

The most important aspect is how they see the transition from the legal situation today, which in most of these countries is thus both influenced by Western codified law and the Sharīᶜa, but with the former in dominance. If a transition from this situation to Sharīᶜa dominance is seen as a slow reform process aiming to gradually extend the area controlled by the Sharīᶜa, it can be imagined in several ways.

Those countries that still have rudiments of Sharīᶜa courts in family matters (or a 'Sharīᶜa bench' of judges trained in *fiqh*), may give these courts wider competence to also address other areas of law, including criminal law, maintaining the traditional structure of the court system as it is. That would be the most 'traditionalist' method that would in some way re-create the pre-modern situation, perhaps in a more idealized form. That could thus be a solution favoured by the *ᶜulamāᵓ* trained at institutions of religious learning, as it would enhance their role in the field of law. The state itself would then not have to worry about the content of the Sharīᶜa, as that would be based on the established *fiqh* of the school of law that dominated in that region, as it does today in family law in these systems. However, if this extension was to include criminal law, it would also recreate the problem such cases faced in the Sharīᶜa courts in the pre-modern area, where the rules of evidence made conviction in those courts difficult to achieve. This strategy of 'regression' seems old-fashioned and probably has little support among the political Islamists.

A more commonly favoured solution is to use the Sharīᶜa as a reference for vetting existing laws. The laws of the country are then decided in a codified form in a legislative assembly as today. The laws are then passed on to an Islamic instance of examination or a supreme court of Islamic scholars who can reject the laws and send them back to the legislature if they consider them to be contrary to the Sharīᶜa. This is a process that has been introduced in one form or another in many countries, both 'Islamist' (such as Iran) and non-Islamist, as mentioned for Kuwait. Many scholars use this as the definition of *taṭbīq*, 'application' of Islamic law.[5] Thus the Sharīᶜa is here only used negatively, to stop laws that are not wanted, which makes it less urgent to give a positive definition to the content to the Sharīᶜa. It also clears the way for a form of division of power, where the Sharīᶜa scholars share legislative authority with the secular organs of political power.

In addition, or instead of this, the state may also codify a complete new set of laws that express the content of the Sharīᶜa. This has already been done in many countries as part of the process of modernization in the areas of family law and others; new law codes of personal laws wholly or partly codify what the legislature considered to be the rules of the Sharīᶜa. A strategy of 'application' could continue on this path, change those laws that are disapproved of and pass new codified laws based on their understanding of the Sharīᶜa rules on a much wider scale than was possible before, including *ḥudūd* laws, economic laws and so on.

5 This was also the way Zia al-Haqq 'Islamized' the laws in Pakistan in 1979; he appointed 'Sharīᶜa benches' both in the Supreme court and at lower levels, each with five judges, which would at the request of the public evaluate any laws passed by Parliament against the Sharīᶜa. The judges were not *ᶜulamāʾ*, but would seek the counsel of competent scholars (such *ᶜulamāʾ* were introduced into the courts from 1986); Mir Zohair Hussain, 'Islam in Pakistan under Bhutto and Zia-ul-Haqq', in Hussein Mutalib and Taj ul-Islam Hashmi (eds), *Islam, Muslims and the Modern State*, London 1994, 62. There were also laws ('ordinances') passed for the five *ḥudūḍ* crimes and murder. Cf. also Rubya Mehdi, *The Islamization of the Law in Pakistan*, London 1994.

This does not pose any structural problems as the new laws are codified laws passed by a legislature as in any modern system of law; only the content is different. Thus it is still the state, although a new, revolutionary and Islamist state, that defines the law. The state or legislature may thus make whatever decision it wants as to which school of law or tradition is to be used, which level of *talfīq* or *ijtihād* is to be applied, and so on. However, from the point of view of the 'application of the eternal Sharīᶜa', this will of course weaken the symbolic effect of divine intervention, and may in itself not appear as a sufficiently sharp break with the practices already applied by current secular states. Thus there is a tendency to 'over-compensate' in the content of the laws to emphasize that this really *is* a more 'pure' Sharīᶜa than the mixed laws that existed before the Islamist revolution; particularly by focussing expressly on the *ḥudūd* and similar strict rules.

There are of course other ways of expanding the area of the Sharīᶜa, such as when individual judges arrogate for themselves the power to ignore codified law and pass verdicts based on their own conception of what 'is said in the Sharīᶜa', either in opposition to the state's view (as in Egypt, e.g.) or as part of an accepted hierarchy of 'sources of law'. However, a revolutionary Islamist movement working towards a new state based fully on Sharīᶜa rules will most often favour the third of these alternatives, codifying a full new system of laws based on the Sharīᶜa.

Who should formulate the new Sharīᶜa laws?

The issue is thus who should have the right to formulate these laws. When we say codified law—and it seems that virtually all Islamists who have expressed themselves today favour a codification—we must also say who is to perform the codifying.

The most common concept used for this process in Islamist political and legal discourse is *shūrā*, council or consultation. This is because it is the term used in the classical sources for such forums of debate. However, the meaning and role of this term is presented in different ways.

The most traditionalist view among Islamists of today is to expect that the Islamic state elects or appoints a *khalīfa*, a new caliph who resurrects the classical powers of the first successors to the Prophet.[6] Some who propose this assume that the caliph would then enact laws on his own authority. The *shūrā* is then only an advisory council, giving suggestions he is free to follow or ignore. This conception is mostly linked to a utopian idea that all Muslims are joined in a Muslim *umma*-nation or caliphate that encompasses all Muslims of the world. Thus with only one Muslim world-state, there is only one law, defined by the caliph, not 'regional' laws for today's territorially limited states.

This is thus mostly a utopian vision. Those who have a more practical or time-limited approach to introducing Sharīᶜa law in one of the countries or states of today, which they aim to rule after a future Islamic revolution, all assume that it is the *shūrā* itself that holds legislative power. Some, such as one of the two leaders of the Algerian FIS, ᶜAlī Belhadj, say that this *shūrā* should only consist of competent *ᶜulamāʾ*.[7] The head of the Islamic state (the *ḥākim*) should not participate, nor should those who are not scholars. He says that *ikthilāf*, differences of opinion, among the scholars is a bounty from God, but this is not so among the unschooled.

A far more influential Islamist author, the Sudanese Ḥasan al-Turābī, sees the *shūrā* as something quite different. He rejects the notion that the scholars should have any authority or power. This fits with the common view among many Islamists that these scholars are part of the problem, they are responsibile for the Muslim world being in crisis and having 'fallen behind' (*takhalluf*).[8] To overcome this underdevelopment, *ijtihād* must be used, and all Muslims must participate in this, not just the

6 Thus Taqī 'l-Dīn al-Nabhānī (d. 1977); cf. Suha Taji-Farouki, 'Islamic state theories and contemporary realities', in Abdel Salam Sidahmed and Anoushiravan Ehteshami (eds), *Islamic Fundamentalism*, Boulder, CO 1996, 35-50. This is also the view of one the best known Islamist thinkers, Mawlānā al-Mawdūdī, cf. Abdelwahab El-Affendi, *Who Needs an Islamic State?*, London 1991, 50-1.

7 Mustafa al-Ahnaf, Bernard Botiveau and Franck Frégosi (eds), *L'Algérie par ses islamistes*, Paris 1991, 81-2 & 94. He also says that *ijtihād* may only be done on issues of *furūᶜ*, not *uṣūl*. This would limit the *ijtihād* to be 'within the school', the Mālikīya in his case, but it is not clear if he draws this conclusion or only believes that a text of Revelation must be the foundation of the *ijithād*.

8 Ḥasan al-Turābī, interviewed in Mohamed Elhachmi Hamdi, *The Making of an Islamic Political Leader: Conversations with Hasan al-Turabi*, Boulder, CO 1998, 89 & 118.

scholars. Even those who founded the schools of law were, says Turābī, only 'spokesmen' for views that the *umma* held in common at their time. Thus Turābī brings a conception of popular sovereignty into the *shūrā* and the development of a Sharīᶜa for our times. The state is thus the instance that, through elections, wields this authority, not the *ᶜulamāᵓ*.[9]

We can find similar principles expressed by the Tunisian Rashīd Ghanūshī, who is normally considered a more 'moderate', but highly respected Islamist.[10] He too thinks that it must be a *shūrā* elected in universal elections that should formulate the Sharīᶜa. He also says that political parties must play a role in these elections, and that the non-Muslim citizens of the state must play an equal role with Muslims.[11] Ghanūshī makes a distinction between the basis in Revelation, the Koran and *sunna*, and the *fiqh* that is based on it. The Revelation cannot of course be subject to democratic procedures, so it cannot be touched by the *shūrā*. But this still leaves 'wide areas, empty spaces' where *ijtihād* must be applied, he says.[12] And such an *ijtihād* is open to the democratic process of the *shūrā*. Thus Ghanūshī probably goes further than Turābī towards accepting political pluralism in the legislative process. He considers the Revelation more as the 'final authority' behind the laws than as a set of precise formulations ready to be applied.[13] But the two agree that the *shūrā* cannot be limited to only one school of law, at least not in principle, but must go beyond it and thus beyond classical *fiqh*.

There does, however, seem to be one point that all proponents of 'application' agree on: the five *ḥudūd* rules. These were not, as we have seen, much applied in the classical period, at least in their direct form, and traditional law has stated that they should not be applied if there is a way to avoid them. But since they have the authority of being 'God's rights towards men', a part of *ᶜibādāt*, they have so much symbolic power that they are often

9 Affendi, *Islamic State*, 52.

10 Mohamed Elhachmi Hamdi, *The Politicisation of Islam: A Case Study of Tunisia*, Boulder, CO 1998, 110.

11 This is a small concession to the principle of popular sovereignty for his country Tunisia, as the number of non-Muslims there is minimal. It would have far greater implications for the Sudan, with its large non-Muslim minority (about 30 per cent of the population).

12 Hamdi, *Politicisation of Islam*, 106.

13 Affendi, *Islamic State*, 53.

seen as identical to the Sharīᶜa; 'the Sharīᶜa is only five rules': the *ḥudūd* laws.[14] Thus Sharīᶜa-oriented Islamists often emphasize the application of these in particular, also because they are the parts of the Sharīᶜa that awaken most abhorrence in the West and thus underline the Islamic 'difference'. Even Ghanūshī accepts that these rules must be applied, but repeats and emphasizes the classical restrictions on the use of them.[15]

Thus the 'application' of the Sharīᶜa spans views from letting each individual judge oppose the laws of his country and base his verdict on his own opinion of what the 'Sharīᶜa' entails, to making a complete new set of laws through a democratic process where even non-Muslims may in theory participate in the formulation of Islamic laws. Neither of these views are without problems when seen from the viewpoint of classical methodology. The 'traditional' approach can soon face the same types of problems that made the Sharīᶜa less than practicable in certain areas of law (like criminal law) and led to the rise of separate *siyāsa* courts, as we have seen. The 'radical' current, on the other hand, may run into problems of legitimacy. A Sharīᶜa enacted by a state organ, democratic or otherwise, will only have legitimacy as long as the state has it, as in any other legal system. As long as people have faith in the *shūrā* or state that implements it, it may have authority as 'the' Sharīᶜa and may mobilize support on that basis. But if the state should lose credibility, it will be easy for any opposition to say that what has been codified is not the 'real' Sharīᶜa, and thus produce competing codes. The religious authority is thus largely subject to political authority.[16]

14 This is probably connected to the view that 'Sharīᶜa' does not refer to the result of human *fiqh* extraction, but to the divinely existing law known only by God. The only rules that God has revealed in detail (in criminal law) are thus the five *ḥudūd*, according to the classical understanding.

15 Hamdi, *Politicisation of Islam*, 125. The Tunisian Islamists have never been close to political power, so it may be that Ghanūshī plays down more 'unpopular' viewpoints. But that would in any case be in clear contrast to the triumphant emphasis on *ḥudūd* made by other Islamist groups.

16 This argumentation is further developed in Vikør, 'The Sharīᶜa and the nation state: Who can codify the divine law?', in Bjørn Olav Utvik and Knut S. Vikør (eds), *The Middle East in a Globalized World*, Bergen 2000, 241-50.

Sharīᶜa in practice today: Saudi Arabia

Some countries have, particularly in the last two decades of the twentieth century, started along the path of an 'Islamist' application of the Sharīᶜa, and it may be useful, from the theoretical problems outlined, to see how some of them have carried it out.

One country, however, which has since its inception had the Sharīᶜa as its only law, is Saudi Arabia. They say that the Sharīᶜa is the 'law of the country', and only enacted a constitution or 'basic order' (*Niẓām asāsī*) in 1992.[17] This establishes that the country is purely monarchical, the king in person holds all political power. He can thus pass 'rules and regulations', *niẓām*s, but these are kept quite isolated from the system of Sharīᶜa laws that the courts work from.

When Saudi Arabia was first established in 1926, it consisted of two parts: The west coast Hijaz with Mecca and Medina, which had earlier been a separate region under Ottoman supremacy, and Najd, the central and eastern provinces that had been ruled by nomadic tribes, among whom the Saᶜūdīs came to dominate. The Ottomans had established Ḥanafī law in the Hijaz, while most of the population were Shāfiᶜīs, as were its northern Syrian neighbours. The Ottomans had, as in their major cities, established a system of one chief *qāḍī* and three assistant judges, one from each school of law. Najd, on the other hand, maintained a traditional legal system in which the sultan (the king) was the highest legal power. It did, however, also have a chief *muftī*, who was supposed to be from the family of Muḥammad b. ᶜAbd al-Wahhāb (the Āl al-Shaykh, and thus a Ḥanbalī); he also functioned as an instance of appeals. By the time the state was established the Ḥanbalī school had probably come to predominate in this region, as the Wahhābī influence here dated back to the 1770s.

After the Saudis had unified the country into one kingdom (formally unitary since 1932), the two regions maintained their separate legal systems, except that the king introduced an appeals court in the Hijaz in 1927. But the king started the process of unifying the two legal systems, and based it on the more

17 Ann Elizabeth Mayer, 'The 1992 Saudi Arabian and Moroccan Constitutions: A Comparative Assessment', Josef Schacht Conference on Islamic Law, Leiden & Amsterdam, 6-10.10.94.

developed Hijaz model. This lead to opposition from the ᶜulamāʾ, and this has been the typical feature of the Saudi legal development: a tug-of-war between the royal power, which has at times pressed for reform, and the scholars, who have held back, and who have mostly won out. This was also the result when the king tried to introduce a broader access to appeals in 1962. After resistance from the scholars this was only made possible when the verdict was seen to be in contradiction to a text of Revelation, that is to say, following the classical doctrine for appeals.

The court system in Saudi Arabia is thus fairly independent from state power, and in fact seems to recreate the classical *qāḍī* ideal much more than in any other Muslim country. What separates it from the classical practices is, according to those studies we have available, that the *qāḍī*s appear to be even more autonomous in their rulings than in the classical period.[18] They are not, at least in theory, bound to any school of law, not even the Ḥanbalī school with which Saudi Arabia is normally identified. The Wahhābī ideology was not, as is often stated, based on the Ḥanbalī *madhhab*, but rejected in theory any bond to the schools of law and favoured free *ijtihād* based on the sources of Revelation.[19]

This autonomy is also a result of the internal differences in the new country. Allowing the judges to use whichever school they favoured, permitted the Hijaz judges to lean towards the Shāfiᶜī rules that had traditions there, while those in the east could base their rulings on Ḥanbalī rules. The judges appear to have adopted this ideology and claim that they can and do practice judicial *ijtihād* in the courtroom. However, here they seem mostly to be referring to their freedom to adapt the verdict to the specifics of each individual case. The court system has moved towards a unified approach and it is in fact the Ḥanbalī rules that dominate in the actual practices of law. The judges will

18 Vogel, *Islamic Law and Legal System* from 2000 is the only detailed study of Saudi law and court systems. It is based on field studies, but he was only give limited access to court records, so it is possible that this presentation is slightly 'normative', based on the self-representation of the jurists.

19 Esther Peskes, *Muḥammad b. ᶜAbdalwahhāb (1703-92) im Widerstreit. Untersuchungen zur Rekonstruktion der Frühgeschichte der Wahhābīya*, Beirut 1993, 41.

deviate from those only if there are strong arguments for it (as when they find disagreements between the early Ḥanbalī lawyers).[20]

The court system, based on the Hijazi model, is hierarchical with four levels: cases are first presented to a court of first instance which deals with both criminal and private matters.[21] There is a separate variant of this for nomads, who used to be tried by customary, not Sharīᶜa law. Above this is the level of the actual Sharīᶜa courts. Like the courts of first instance it has one single judge who passes verdicts independently, except in cases involving the death penalty, which require the agreement of three judges. Appeals go to a superior court, later named the Higher Sharīᶜa court. The fourth and highest authority is the office of the chief *qāḍī*. There is also a supreme court of 11 judges.[22] As in the classical systems, the courts do not accept circumstantial evidence or other modern procedure to any great degree.[23]

Saudi Arabia has a bad reputation in the world community for its strict application of criminal law, and in particular the wide usage of the death penalty. This reputation is deserved, but surprisingly not because it is based on classical Sharīᶜa. They do apply the *ḥudūd* rules, and are probably stricter than in the classical period.[24] But Saudi jurists have also accepted the classical principle that the *ḥudūd* penalties should be avoided if possible. Thus the many death penalties passed down are not given according to the *ḥudūd*, but almost exclusively under *taᶜzīr*, that is to say, the judge's liberty to establish the penalty from his own evaluation. The harsh penalties applied over the last decades are

20 The courts may according to the rules refer to other *madhhab*s if they cannot find an answer in the six basic works of the Ḥanbalī school.

21 Fouad Al-Farsy, *Saudi Arabia: A Case Study in Development*, London 1982, 66-9, 89-99 & 114, and James Buchan, 'Secular and religious opposition in Sauda Arabia', in Tim Niblock (ed.), *State, Society and Economy in Saudi Arabia*, London 1982, 106-24.

22 There is also a separate appeals court, 'court of cassation', which has different departments. It is not clear if this is part of the Sharīᶜa or *siyāsa* system.

23 Vogel, *Islamic Law and Legal System,* 238.

24 In the decade 1981-92 the death penalty was imposed in four cases of adultery, as well as 45 amputations for theft from a total of some 50,000 convictions of theft in the same period; Vogel, *Islamic Law and Legal System,* 246.

the result of an opinion, shared by the king and the courts, that a 'crime wave' has passed over the country since the early 1970s. Thus they have consciously, and in unison, stepped up the usage of such harsh penalties to discourage and stem the tide of violent crime. The Saudi use of the death penalty is thus more of a parallel to similar attitudes in China and the USA than the result of the Sharīᶜa laws.[25]

The *muftī*s do not play any direct role in courts. However, Saudi Arabia has, in addition to the office of chief *muftī*, a Council of Leading *ᶜulamāᵓ*, which issues *fatwā*s. These play a determining factor in judicial practice and judges will normally follow these *fatwā*s, irrespective of the their theoretical freedom to apply individual *ijtihād*.[26]

The king's *niẓām*s, on the other hand, play little or no role in courts.[27] The king has issued many such, in particular relating to trade and other economic matters and especially after the oil economy started to flourish in the 1930s. The scholars considered such *niẓām*s as being a part of *siyāsa*, thus outside the realm of the Sharīᶜa courts, and ignored them. A decision was made in 1962 that the Sharīᶜa courts had to follow the king's *niẓām*s, but judges have tended to see them as no more than advisory and subject to their own discretion in each individual case.

This strong conservatism, or rather independence, of the *ᶜulamāᵓ* has also led them to directly oppose the *niẓām*s that were issued, and the number of such edicts has decreased markedly since the 1960s. An early attempt to build a code of obligation modelled on the Ottoman Majalla failed,[28] as did several other reformist plans to codify the Sharīᶜa laws in the country.

A system of courts outside the Sharīᶜa courts was set up in 1955. These *siyāsa* courts called *dīwān al-maẓālim* should consider cases that 'fell outside the realm of the Sharīᶜa courts', that is, following the original ideology behind the *maẓālim* courts.

25 Vogel, *Islamic Law and Legal System,* 274. Not all schools will, as mentioned, accept that the death penalty may be passed under *taᶜzīr*, but the Saudi judges use their right to *ijtihād* in this matter. The Saudi view is also that apostasy is a *ḥudūd* crime, which is a minority view in classical *fiqh*, *ibid*, 241.

26 Vogel, *Islamic Law and Legal System,* 8 & 93.

27 Vogel, *Islamic Law and Legal System*, 285-94.

28 Vogel, *Islamic Law and Legal System,* 287.

These courts are directly subservient to the government. There are also a number of special courts, '*niẓām* courts', for separate types of cases, in particular relating to administration and trade. The *ᶜulamāʾ* have mostly looked unfavourably on these, and been able to neutralize their importance, except for the *maẓālim* court itself, which is of course in line with the classical system. As a part of the king's reforms, a judicial council was established in the 1970s with 20 members, as well as a ministry of law.

Saudi Arabia is also known for its 'public morality committees' (*muṭāwiᶜa*), popularly known as the 'religious police'.[29] Their task is to ensure that religious commandments are followed, including those that fall under *ᶜibādāt* and personal ritual practices. This may be justified by *ḥisba*, but has not traditionally been an important part of, or even linked to, the workings of the court. These committees were established as a concession to the *ᶜulamāʾ* after a civil war between the king and the more extreme *ikhwān* groups in the 1920s. Thus the committees do not answer to the state, but to the *ᶜulamāʾ*, in particular the dominant family of *ᶜulamāʾ*, the Āl al-Shaykh.[30]

Saudi Arabia has thus made a concerted effort to build a legal system based directly and only on the Sharīᶜa. This is partly based on the Ottoman model they found in Hijaz in 1926, but adapted to an ideology where the judges' right to practice *ijtihād* has made it possible for them to 'traditionalize' the court beyond the original. But the legal field is also marked by an underlying conflict between the scholars and the king, where mostly the scholars appear to win out. Thus it may paradoxically seem that Saudi Arabia, one of the most autocratic regimes in the Muslim world with an all-powerful monarchy, is also the country where

29 '*Hay'at al-amr bi'l-maᶜrūf wa-nahy ᶜan al-munkar*', we might call them '*ḥisba* committees', but the term 'religious police' is commonly used; Tim Niblock, 'The Saudi Arabian Political System', in *State, Society and Economy in Saudi Arabia*, 92.

30 Helen Lackner, *A House Built on Sand: A Political Economy of Saudi Arabia*, London 1978, 75. The term *muṭāwiᶜa* comes from partly uneducated Wahhābī enthusiasts who functioned as religious authorities in nomad communities in the middle of the nineteenth century, before the rise of the modern Saudi state; John S. Habib, *Ibn Sau'd's Warriors of Islam: The Ikhwan of Najd and their Role in the Creation of the Sa'udi Kingdom*, Leiden 1978, 119, and Charles M. Doughty, *Travels in Arabia Deserta*, London 1924, II, 369, 395 & 412.

the 'civil society' shows, with autonomous power in the legal field, most independence from the state. It is probably the only modern case of a Sharīᶜa system where 'civil society' dominates over the state in field of law—perhaps with the exception of revolutionary Iran, where, however, the basis of the development is completely different.

Iran

The only country to have gone through a successful Islamist revolution 'from below' in our time is Iran. We might therefore have expected an attempt to emulate the model set up by Saudi Arabia, making the classical Sharīᶜa the law of the country and giving the *ᶜulamāᵓ* power over the courts. This did not happen. The situation in post-revolutionary Iran may rather be described as one of 'dual power'. They have on the one hand maintained the established institutions from the Shah's regime; a parliament, a secular president to replace the shah, and a legal system based on a law code determined in parliament. Replacing the personnel in this system and amending the law codes to reflect the Islamist ideal was sufficient to adapt the old system to the new realities.[31]

On the other hand, the revolution led to the creation of separate 'revolutionary' institutions that were to defend the ideals of the upheaval and combat the enemies of the revolution. These were thrown up quickly, almost ad hoc and suited to the demands of the day, and often had few or any restrictions on their power. They normally have 'Islamic' as part of the rationale, but are in their form often quite parallel to similar instances of 'dual power' that followed other great revolutions such as the French and the Russian. The history of Iran since 1979 has been one of never-ending rivalry and conflict between the 'ordinary' institutions and these 'extra-ordinary' ones.

Two new elements were added to the political system to ensure the ideals of the revolution. One was the *Shūrā-ye negahbān*, the 'Council of Guardians', composed of religious scholars who has the power to vet the decisions of either parliament or the president and decide if they conformed to 'Islamic

31 Chibli Mallat, *The Renewal of Islamic Law: Muhammad Baqer as-Sadr, Najaf and the Shi'i International*, Cambridge 1993, 79-107.

principles'. The council has complete authority in this field; all acts of parliament should be passed to this council to get its stamp of approval before being put into effect.

The other was the 'jurist' (*faqīh*). This new institution, the core of Khomeini's state theory of *velāyat-e faqīh*, was established for him and adapted to his needs and his age; that is, a withdrawn post that only intervened when necessary. The Jurist, or 'Leader', is independent of the Council of Guardians, and has the power to intervene everywhere, but only at his own initiative.

The role of the Council was reduced as time passed, not least through an intervention from Khomeini in 1988. A conflict had arisen between Parliament and the Council, which had increasingly become a deadening bottle-neck as it did not have the capacity to treat the number of acts that parliament passed, thus leading to long delays in implementation.[32] Khomeini gave an edict that dramatically widened the scope of the state's power to make decisions. He said that the Islamic state must, when it considered it necessary, have full freedom to make whatever decisions it wanted, even if these contradicted the stated law of the Sharīᶜa; for example when he denied Muslims the right to go on *ḥājj*—this was an issue at the time, as Iran was in conflict with Saudi Arabia. Thus Khomeini supported pure *siyāsa*: when the revolution has taken place, the state, governed by the 'jurist' *faqīh*, can give whatever laws it decides, independent of the established rules of the Sharīᶜa.

This clearly undermined the power of the Council as its role was to test the state's decisions against the Sharīᶜa. To break the deadlocks that occurred between the parliament and its guardians a new conciliation council between them was established in the *Majmaᶜ-e tashkhīs-e maṣlaḥat-e niẓām,* which was to have the final word in any conflict. The majority of its members were appointed by the president of the republic.

Thus it is the institution of *faqīh* that remains the guarantor of the revolutionary gains. Being formed around Khomeini's personality, it should, when filled with a *marjaᶜ-e taqlīd*, have the full support of all Shīᶜa. Of course Khomeini's established position as *marjaᶜ* made this self-evident, but his appointed successor in the position, ᶜAlī Khameneᵓī, did not have anywhere near the

32 Mallat, *Renewal of Islamic Law*, 89-91.

authority of a *marjaᶜ* in religious terms.[33] Thus a new structure for appointment of the *faqīh* was elaborated, and he is now to be selected by the Majmaᶜ council, and thus in the final instance also integrated into the regular political system.[34]

Post-revolutionary Iran also established other 'extra-ordinary' organs, such as the *pasdarān*, the revolutionary guard that came to be a parallel army, and *komitehs* that, in the same way as the Saudi public morality committees, implement what they consider to be the Sharīᶜa in their neighbourhoods.[35] Revolutionary courts were established to defend the revolution against its enemies on a broad basis. These organs were mostly free from any outside authority, and often ignored any reference to actual laws or due process. They were in continuous conflict with parliament or other 'regular' institutions, and were repeatedly admonished by Khomeini himself, without necessarily taking much notice of that.

The theory of sources of law in Iran makes the Sharīᶜa a secondary source as we saw in the Gulf countries. The judge should first consult the law code, then 'trustworthy Islamic sources', and finally *fatwās*. There was some disagreement after the revolution over what to do with the old laws from the Shah's regime; should they be discarded *en masse*, or maintained until each of them had been tested against the Sharīᶜa?[36] The Supreme

33 He was not an ayatollah at all, but was quickly upgraded when he was to take over the role as the *faqīh*.

34 Khāmeneʾī did however desperately try to have himself appointed *marjaᶜ* when five *marjāᶜ*s had passed away over a brief span of time in 1992-4, but he was unsuccessful, not least because he wanted to have the Iranian parliament make the appointment. This was rejected both by the *ᶜulamāʾ* and in particular by Shīᶜīs outside Iran. Cf. also J. Esposito (ed.), *The Oxford Encyclopedia of the Modern Islamic World*, New York 1995, II, 231 & 423, and Momen, *Introduction to Shi'i Islam*, 195 & 249.

35 The two have a common ancestry in the revolutionary committees, but went in different directions during the war with Iraq; the *pasdarān*, *Sipāh-e pasdarān-e enqelāb-e islāmī*, became a fully developed parallel armed force, with an air force, navy and ground troops. Attempts were made after the war was over (in 1991) to integrate it into the regular armed forces, but the *pasdarān* were able to resist this. The *komitehs*, which had been spontaneously formed 'neighbourhood groups' during the days of revolution, were first used to suppress the opponents of the revolution, then decentralized into guardians of *ḥisba*. They were integrated into the regular police in 1990 and thus ceased to exist as a cohesive body; Esposito, *Encyclopedia*, II, 438-9 & III, 77-8.

36 Asghar Schirazi, *The Constitution of Iran. Politics and State in the Islamic*

Court, now filled with revolutionary judges, asked the Council of Guardians in 1981 to annul all laws. The Council refused to do so and insisted that each law must instead be tested individually against the Sharīᶜa, by them. This presumably would give the Council greater influence than if the parliament was given the authority to formulate a full new set of laws *ab initio*.

Khomeini here supported the more radical position, and in the following year declared that 'all the laws of evil' were now abolished. The Supreme Court declared on this basis that the judges were now to base their laws on 'accepted legal sources' in the Sharīᶜa and in *fatwā*s, until parliament had been given the time to formulate new codes. But the Council still opposed the implementation of this. The *ḥudūd* rules and laws of murder and bodily harm were fairly clear-cut from *fiqh*, and were accepted to be part of the criminal law, without further elaboration. But the Council rejected the Supreme Court's decision that the ministries should send 'all other laws' to the Council for evaluation; the Council was itself to be the only arbiter of what laws should and should not be vetted, and the old laws were to remain in force until any decision to the contrary came from them. This did not happen to any great degree. Only 24 laws were changed in the first decade of the revolution, most of them relating to the activity of the *ᶜulamāʾ*.

At the same time parliament continued to enact new laws which were of course in conformity with their interpretation of the Sharīᶜa. Thus a set of 'sharīᶜified' laws came into being. But laws were also passed that were clearly contrary to established *fiqh*.[37] This was mostly done because of pressing social needs, out of an argument of necessity. In these cases the Council and the *ᶜulamāʾ* functioned mostly as a conservative force, doing their best to stop such laws by emphasizing consistency with *fiqh* more than social necessity, while parliament appeared to be closer to social reality. However, most of these laws were still forced through, not least with the aid of Khomeini.

Thus we see again that the leader of the revolution did not necessarily take the side of the *ᶜulamāʾ* and the Sharīᶜa text. This was probably because he saw the new revolutionary state as an

---

Republic, London 1997, 162-5.

37 Schirazi, *Constitution of Iran,* 175-202.

essential element for the development for the Islamic society, while the conservatives mostly saw the state as an opponent or as irrelevant. In this way the state had a priority for Khomeini, even above the text of the Sharīᶜa. His view, when one looks behind the words, was thus the same as the *siyāsa* view of the traditional sultans; the state's power to carry out whatever was necessary to promote the 'spirit' of the Sharīᶜa without being hampered by its wording when that stood in the way.

Sudan

Another country that has gone through an Islamist transition is Sudan, but here in the form of a military coup in 1989. The Sharīᶜa has played an important part in the recent history of this country which has, unlike Saudi Arabia and Iran, gone through a period of colonial rule, making it useful to see how this affected its legal history.[38]

The Sudan has been under Islamic influence since the sixteenth century, but it was only much later that an actual Sharīᶜa-based judiciary with trained *qāḍīs* entered the region, and then only in the major cities or capitals of the various kingdoms of the land.[39] The dominant system in the countryside was customary law, and the concept that customary law may be used where the Sharīᶜa was silent was here transformed into allowing the Sharīᶜa to give the answer if there was no customary rule. This was for example the case for homicide cases, which were decided by a tribal court.

Even if the region had a clear and well established identity

38 Carolyn Fluehr-Lobban, *Islamic Law and Society in the Sudan*, London 1987; Anderson, *Islamic Law in Africa*, and Safiya Safwat, 'Islamic laws in the Sudan', in Azmeh, *Islamic Law*, 231-49. A detailed study of the legal reforms under Numayrī has recently been published in Aharon Layish and Gabriel R. Warburg, *The Reinstatement of Islamic Law in the Sudan under Numayrī: An Evaluation of a Legal Experiment in the Light of its Historical Context, Methodology and Repercussions*, Leiden 2002.

39 R.S. O'Fahey, 'The office of *qāḍī* in Dār Fūr: a preliminary inquiry' (*Bulletin of the School of Oriental and African Studies*, XL, 1, 1977, 110-24) shows that *qāḍīs* and Sharīᶜa courts started to develop in the Darfur sultanate in the western part of the country from the latter half of the eighteenth century.

with the Mālikīya,[40] there was thus no clear Mālikī court practice established before the Ottoman Egyptians occupied northern Sudan in 1821 bringing Ḥanafī law with them. In this 'Turkīya' period Ḥanafism remained the 'state law'. This was at a time when reforms of the *tanẓīmāt* period were already under way, and it was thus these reformed laws that the countryside first met under the heading of 'Islamic laws'. The criminal law of the Sharīᶜa was thus never really introduced beyond some urban areas, and as a whole the Sharīᶜa was mostly limited to personal and family law.

From 1885 to 1898 Sudan was governed by the revolutionary Mahdi movement. The Mahdi, who had died already in 1885, had a religious authority that was based only in his own person, standing above any other human. He thus abolished the schools of law and governed from his own convictions. The Mahdi thus introduced a full Sharīᶜa system in all the regions under his control; that is to say, the Sharīᶜa in his interpretation.[41]

British forces abolished the Mahdist state in 1898, and introduced a 'joint rule' (Condominium) with Egypt. The country was however in reality run as a British colony, and the legal system was based on what the British had done in other colonies. Criminal law was based on 'Anglo-Muslim' law; a code of law developed in India based on British law but adapted to Muslim norms. The Sharīᶜa courts were given only very limited tasks, they could deal with issues of marriage, divorce, responsibility for minors, donations and inheritance. The could also mediate in other types of conflicts if both parties agreed in advance to follow its verdict. Other types of cases were dealt with by British judges practising common law, that is, no specific code but 'common sense and justice', which was of course British.

The Sharīᶜa court system was hierarchized in basically the same fashion as the parent country, with a Primary Court, a Secondary Court, Province, Appeal and High Courts. The latter two were located in Khartoum. This system was established in the period 1902-15.

40 Except for the coastal region around Sawākin, which was dominated by the Shāfiᶜī school.

41 Cf. Aharon Layish, *The Mahdi's Legal Methodology and its Application in the Sudan: A Selection from the Mahdi's Documents (1881-1885)*, Jerusalem 1996, vii-x.

The judges in these courts were *qāḍīs*, and otherwise followed the Sharīᶜa as they knew it. The High Court consisted of a chief *qāḍī*, a *muftī*, and other *qāḍīs*, at least three people altogether. Thus the *muftī* was made a required element in the higher levels of appeals, again borrowing from the Ottoman *majlis*. The procedures were mostly as in the classical Sharīᶜa courts, except that the penalty for perjury was codified. There was also some formalization of evidence and witnesses, but again basically along the same lines as the classical Sharīᶜa courts.

There was later a tendency, as in the other countries studied here, towards merging the two types of law or regulating the relationship between them. Irrespective of which court system they were to enter, judges were to have passed exams at one of the two universities of Khartoum and Omdurman. Both types of legal systems were in reality taught to both types of candidates, those going into the 'civil' (British-based) and those going into the Sharīᶜa courts. A Court of Jurisdiction was established in 1959 to mediate between the Sharīᶜa and civil courts in case of any conflict of competence. Apparently such conflicts never arose, because the court in fact never met.

A common Supreme Court was also set up in 1956, with 30 judges in all, 21 from the civil system and 9 from the Sharīᶜa system. An innovation was made in 1970 when a female judge was appointed for the first time to the Sharīᶜa court. There were in 1980 782 judges in the Sudan, of whom 517 sat in the civil courts and 265 in the Sharīᶜa courts. The Sharīᶜa judges mostly received lower salaries and were considered socially inferior to the civil court judges.

After independence in 1956 the laws of the Sudan were formulated in codes that changed with some regularity, a new set of codes tending to be implemented every decade or so. A new civil law was established in 1971, but abolished in 1973.

This coincided with a marked shift in the ideology of the then military regime, putting the emphasis on Islamization and the Sharīᶜa. A new civil code was again formulated in 1974, and laws were now to be based on the Sharīᶜa as well as custom. Several commissions were set to Islamize Sudan's laws, and in 1983-4 a series of new laws were implemented to bring the Sharīᶜa into practical law.[42] This also led to the *ḥudūd* rules being introduced into criminal law and put into practice. They included rules that had no basis in the traditional or literary Sharīᶜa, but 'appeared to' mean a strict application of its norms. Thus it included 'attempts at fornication', which was taken to include an unmarried man and woman walking on a public street. It would be difficult to find any basis for such a ban in a Sharīᶜa legal text, but it gave the impression of combating fornication, which is of course a norm in the Sharīᶜa. Thus these rules were often not based on a legal logic, nor in any actual application of Sharīᶜa rules, but were political statements in judicial form.

The court system was also 'Islamized' in parallel with this development of the law texts. The divide into a Sharīᶜa and a civil court was abolished in 1980. The office of chief *qāḍī* disappeared, while the Supreme Court was changed into a unified High Court with seven judges, of whom two were Sharīᶜa *qāḍī*s. Some criticism was made of this change, because the courts were unified before the laws they were to work from had been coordinated. There was also the issue of what was to be done with the large Christian minority in southern Sudan. Not only was it a moral and political issue to ignore their rights, but it might also be a problem for the Islamization process. Non-Muslims had earlier only been judged in, and served as judges in, the non-Muslim civil courts. Now, as the courts were unified and all judges, Muslim and Christian, were to practise in these new courts, cases may come up where Muslims might be judged in Sharīᶜa-based cases by Christian judges. Of course this was nothing new; the same had happened when the British had taken on administering 'native law' in the colonial period, but it was an odd element in a process of Islamization.

Thus the Sudanese development does not directly implement the classical texts, but develops law codes based on Sharīᶜa rules as defined by the state and practised by a unified Sharīᶜa/civil court. A mixture of old and new, or perhaps rather an attempt to

42 For a study of the various techniques that were used to integrate the Sharīᶜa into the codified system of law, including combining rules from various schools through *talfīq*, judicial circulars from the Grand *qāīḍī* or Chief justice, referring directly to the Koran and *sunna* outside traditional *fiqh* and accepting principles in effect from British common law, see Layish and Warburg, *Reinstatement of Islamic Law*, 94-142.

appeal to existing values and norms without caring too much about the actual content of the Sharīᶜa as classically understood.

However, these changes were pervasive. This process thus goes as far back as to 1973, fifteen years before the Islamists came to power. It was another military regime, that of Jaᶜfar al-Numayrī (ruled 1969-85) that had carried out all of these changes.[43] After his fall a civilian regime, made up of many of the same politicians who had ruled the Sudan before 1969, came back to power. But in spite of the logical and other problems that Numayrī's legal reforms had brought—in relation both to a possible solution to the war in the south, and to the Western powers, the main backers of the civilian regime—the fall of the military regime did not lead to any legal changes.[44] The civilian regime announced that Nymayrī's laws were to be suspended and that new laws based on 'Sudanese traditions' should be implemented, or at least in the non-Muslim south, but nothing happened. When the Islamist military toppled the civilian regime in 1989, they thus found a system to their liking already in place. They confirmed (1991) a criminal law based on the Sharīᶜa, which was only a continuation of Numayrī's laws, but announced that this was not to be implemented in the three southern provinces.[45] Otherwise they could just prolong the system that Numyarī had introduced a decade earlier.

43 Numayrī was not originally an Islamist, rather a leftist secular ruler. But he broke with the strong leftist movements in the Sudan in 1971 and tried at the same time to neutralize a strong civilian opposition based on religious parties.

44 The *ḥudūd* penalties were however not applied in this period.

45 The law as such applies to all citizens of the country, but certain rules within it are applied differentially according to the religion of the actors. Thus, certain *ḥudūd* penalties are less grave for non-Muslims, or are to be 'according to the religion of the perpetrator', if this religion has a penalty for the offence, if not the Sharīᶜa rules apply. But as concerning e.g. murder and blood money, no distinction is made between the the religions of the victim; Layish and Warburg, *Reinstatement of Islamic Law*, 255-63. This issue was however very unclear. The regime has reiterated the non-application to non-Muslims several times in the course of various peace efforts, but one backer of the regime, the Islamist National Islamic Front party, has consistently opposed this view, although non-Muslims should not in any case be subject to the Sharīᶜa in the classical system.

Sharīᶜa through siyāsa

What we can thus see in these Islamist revolutions is that the Sharīᶜa has, in different ways, acquired a national form and been nationalized into a larger legal apparatus. Only Saudi Arabia, which entered the twentieth century with an established 'proto-Islamist' model, has been able to maintain a more classically formed Sharīᶜa system in which codification has little room. Thus the Sharīᶜa has also taken on different colours in those states that claim to build on the same fundamental basis of 'applied Sharīᶜa'.

By comparing, for example, the various forms of the *ḥudūd* rules such as the death penalty for fornication, one can see that the states that 'apply' the Sharīᶜa all share the *principle* of a death penalty, but under different circumstances.[46] Pakistan introduced the classical model, stoning for married offenders, lashing for unmarried ones. Sudan introduced hanging for married ones, and sent unmarried men (but not women) to jail, in addition to lashing. Iran has many categories of offenders, where some are condemned to both lashing and stoning, while others receive various other types of denigrating penalties of a milder form (e.g. shaving off the hair), which are not mentioned in the Sharīᶜa. Libya, which claimed to introduce the Sharīᶜa for a period, did not then have the death penalty at all, only lashing for all offenders. Thus a principle based in a fairly clear Sharīᶜa rule has been given many different national forms of application.

Of course this particular *ḥudūd* rule is not, as we recall, really based on a Koran verse at all, but is the result of a legal side-stepping of the actual text of the Koran through the aid of *ḥadīth*. This particular point of methodology was brought up when the military regime of Zia al-Haqq in Pakistan wanted to 'reintroduce' the Sharīᶜa and thus apply the *ḥudūd* rules.[47] A secularist citizen made a protest to the Supreme Court against this paragraph, claiming that it was not in conformity with what the Koran said, and that the *ḥadīth* it was based on was a dubious one.[48] This claim was accepted by the Supreme Court and the law

46 Ann E. Mayer, 'The Shari'ah: A methodology or a body of substantive rules?', in Heer, *Islamic Law and Jurisprudence*, 192-8.

47 Mayer, 'Shari'ah', 194-6, and Daniel W. Brown, *Rethinking Tradition in Modern Islamic Thought*, Cambridge 1996, 135-7.

48 Chapter 2.

was abrogated. However, to amend or abolish the *ḥudūd* was hardly what the policy makers had intended, so the government intervened and replaced some members of the Supreme Court. It then re-convened, studied the issue once more, and reneged its earlier decision, now accepting the law.[49]

It is thus of course possible to make national *laws* that conform with the content of the Sharīᶜa; in the absence of international sanctions any country is free to make whatever law it wants. But the introduction of the Sharīᶜa as a *court* system in a modern national state is rare. The Saudi exception is clearly due to their political history; they were never colonized and went almost directly from a nomadic form of rule with an autocratic shaykh to a 'national state' with a strongly autonomist ideology. All other states in the Middle East have either passed through some stage of foreign rule, with some element of enforced bureaucratization from outside, or a voluntary copying of Western models by 'modernizing' secularist leaders. In all cases, whatever the political hue of the regime, this has had the result that the country's law has been codified. Thus the Sharīᶜa is also conceived of as a codified law in these states. An 'application' or 're-introduction' then must also entail a codification, and hence a break with the way the Sharīᶜa was formed as a law and worked in Muslim societies. In the revolutionary Islamist as in the modernist secular countries, the state has taken control and decides what God's law is, or at least how and to what degree society should conform to God's will.

Thus, it is *siyāsa sharᶜīya*, Sharīᶜa politics, which is the framework for the Sharīᶜa in our day, in principle identical to the system inherited from *kanun* that the same forces attack with such fervour. Unfortunately, it appears that when they try to apply *siyāsa*, these 'Islamist' states pick out the rules that have greatest symbolic power, the *ḥudūd* rules, which are those that were *least* practised in actual Sharīᶜa-based systems before, and thus those that have been least refined and adapted to social reality throughout Muslim history.

49 Clearly this was a political and not a legal issue. Neither the former nor the latter set of judges were *ᶜulamāʾ*, and their competence to state one opinion or the other derived only from who had appointed them.

PART IV: SOME AREAS OF THE LAW

14

CRIMINAL LAW

We cannot in this short survey of the history and background of Islamic law examine in detail the actual content of the Sharīᶜa's rules in the various fields of law. That would require not just another book, but a large series of volumes. However, it may be useful to give just a few impressions of the Sharīᶜa rules that are the outcome of this history. The following three chapters must be read in the light of what has been said before regarding methodology and history. We cannot give any 'true' answers to what the Sharīᶜa 'says' or 'is'. Not only must all exceptions and reservations be omitted here, but also jurists past and present would question every one of the rules that we are going to present. However, it should still be possible to sum up some of the basic rules in selected fields of law. What we present below are thus views that are commonly held among scholars—in one school or common to all schools—and that we may find in the legal literature. They may constitute a 'shared view among jurists today' on the topics discussed.

The field of the law

Firstly, who are covered by the law? Islamic law is not, in its nature, linked to any particular territory or state, it is linked to man's nature as a believer, someone who must follow God's commandments. This means that it does not distinguish between the individual Muslim countries, but makes a distinction between these countries (*dār al-Islām*) and non-Muslim territories. In short, the Sharīᶜa is potentially valid for everyone in the Islamic lands and for all Muslims in non-Muslim countries.[1]

1 The *muᶜāmalāt* rules do not actually apply for Muslims in *dār al-ḥarb*, enemy territory; if a Muslim breaks a Sharīᶜa rule there he cannot be punished for it after having returned to the Muslim state; Rudolph Peters, 'Islamic law and human rights: a contribution to an ongoing debate', *Islam*

Non-Muslims in non-Muslim countries are of course not touched by it, and resident non-Muslims in the Islamic lands (who in principle all belong under the category of *dhimmī*, thus are 'of the book') are allowed to organize their own legal affairs internally according to their own rules.[2] But the Sharīᶜa comes into play when the *dhimmī*s relate to the external Muslim society. Thus the Sharīᶜa has rules, as we mentioned, for the conduct of non-Muslims in the Sharīᶜa courts: they cannot themselves attend, but may be represented by a *wakīl*. There is also a fairly extensive literature on what is allowed for non-Muslims although it is banned by the Sharīᶜa: Is it for example allowed for a Muslim to own wine for the purpose of selling it to a Christian (who is allowed by the Sharīᶜa to consume it)? May a Muslim make a profit on such a sale? Such problems had practical backgrounds and were solved as they came up.

There were also legal distinctions between categories of Muslims, such as between men and women and between free persons and slaves. Thus the Sharīᶜa does not see all humans as equals in a legal sense; but it varies from rule to rule how these distinctions are played out. It is for example an over-simplification to say that a slave has no responsibility or value, because he may in some cases be in a situation identical to that of a free man, while he may in others be without any rights at all.[3]

Similarly, women may, as is commonly known, be compared to half a man's value, such as in inheritance and partly as concerns testimony, but it is not correct to say that women in general are considered 'half of a man', because men and women may in other matters have equal rights (for example, in economic affairs, where a woman has complete and personal rights over her property). Women are in principle fully independent legal

---

and Christian-Muslim relations, X, 1, 1999, 8-9. The duties towards God, however, are of course still valid in these lands as well.

2 Christians and Jews who are on short visits to Muslim lands are not *dhimmī*s, they have different rights and duties according to the Sharīᶜa.

3 Slavery is only theory today. All Muslim thinkers, even the most conservative and fundamentalist, accept that slavery is history and that no rules pertaining to it are valid. This is partly a realization of current realities (whatever hidden slavery there may be in some countries is outside the law), partly because they claim the many moral statements against slavery in the Koran and *sunna* show that God meant slavery to disappear when the time for this was ripe.

individuals. Even if both the law and social custom has placed this legal individuality in a framework of social control by a male 'representative', husband or close relative,[4] she may in many cases come into legal conflict with such representatives in her own right.

Ḥudūd

The most important parts of the Sharīᶜa are what we may call 'private law'. That is to say conflicts between two independent parties where the judge is primarily an arbitrator. But there is also another side to the law, criminal or penal law (*ᶜuqūbāt*) where the court imposes sanctions on those who commit crimes. This may in fact often be what non-specialists think of as the primary aspect of a court system. It has, as we have seen in the historical survey, varied greatly how far or how directly the Sharīᶜa's criminal laws have been applied, but the letter of the law has generally been known and had a normative force even when the actual court practice has deviated from the precise rules and procedures.[5]

In a sense the Western concept of 'criminal law' does not correspond to any particular category of law in Islamic law since the basic presumption of the court is, as we have discussed earlier, not that it works as the state's agent to punish crimes, but that it settles disputes between two parties, one or both of whom claim to be wronged by the other. However, these disputes may concern issues we consider 'crimes', such as theft, murder, bodily harm and the like, and thus cover the areas we may call 'criminal law', even though they technically fall under 'private law' in the Sharīᶜa.

Islamic law divides such cases involving punishment or compensation for crimes into two main categories. One, which we have mentioned many times already, is the *ḥudūd* rules. These are the crimes that God has expressed a penalty for in the Koran or

4 Any woman must have a 'guardian', *walī*; her closest male relative if she is unmarried, her husband if she is not. Today this has the effect that e.g. some countries require the signature of a *walī* for any woman to receive a passport.

5 Tyan, *Histoire*, 566-71. A modern presentation of Islamic criminal legal norms (from a Mālikī viewpoint) is ᶜAbdur Raḥmān I. Doi, *Sharīᶜah: The Islamic Law*, London 1997, 218-69.

sunna, that is, where not only the *crime* has been mentioned, but also the *punishment*. These are 'God's limits', *ḥudūd*, for Man.

It is not a large group, there are only five such crimes:
(1) 'Fornication', *zinā*: the punishment is death by stoning for non-virgin free men and women,[6] 100 lashes for unmarried youths, and 50 lashes for slaves, married or unmarried.
(2) Theft: amputation of the right hand.[7]
(3) Highway robbery: death by crucifixion. This has a harsher penalty than theft, because it is assumed that it involves killing the victims. It is based on the social situation where the law only held in towns, while the highways outside were more or less lawless territory, where beduins or bands of robbers often stopped caravans, took all valuables and killed all their victims.[8] A highway robbery that did not lead to murder is treated as theft.
(4) False accusation of fornication: 80 lashes for free men and 40 for slaves.[9]

6 There is no distinction between men and women in this, and it naturally only concerns *voluntary* sex; in the case of rape the man shall be condemned for *zinā* while the woman is without guilt. But there is a problem of producing evidence for this, since the requirement is still four trustworthy male witnesses to the act if the *ḥudūd* are invoked. So it is more common for such cases to be tried under *taᶜzīr* with its milder punishment. A worst-case scenario would be if a hostile judge decided that without witnesses there is neither proof of violence nor that the accused man was involved, so there is no *zinā* for him, while the woman's accusation must be considered admission of sexual relations with an unspecified man, and as such punishable under *ḥudūd*. However, this will of course depend on social practice; the Sharīᶜa clearly holds that rape is *zinā* only for the man, not the victim; *EI* (2), 'Zinā'.—Homosexual activity is considered illegal in all schools, but only the Shāfiᶜīs, Ḥanabalīs and Shīᶜīs technically consider it *zinā*.

7 The Koran only says 'a hand'; it is the jurists who decided that the right hand is meant. Repetition is punished by amputating first the left foot, then the left hand, then the right foot. The Ḥanafīs and Zaydīs do not specify beyond the left foot, repetition beyond that being punished by imprisonment. The Imāmī Shīᶜīs use imprisonment for the third repetition and death for the fourth. However—as can be seen from the following—this is probably mainly meant to deter a theoretical escalation of the punishment.

8 Such robberies took place even on short and central roads such as that between Mecca and Medina as late as the nineteenth century, it was not just a medieval occurrence; Vikør, *Sufi and Scholar on the Desert Edge*, London 1995, 175-6 and *Sources for Sanūsī Studies*, 184-5.

9 The law also has rules for how the lash is to be handled, mainly to limit the force of each stroke.

(5) Drunkenness: 80 lashes.

There is some disagreement on this categorization. Some jurists, including many Ḥanbalīs, consider apostasy to be a *ḥudūd* crime, while others include rebellion against a legitimate ruler; and some even include regular murder.[10] These additions are probably made mostly for reasons of systematic neatness, as all these crimes can lead to the death penalty, as do some of the *ḥudūd* crimes. But the large majority of jurists restrict the actual *ḥudūd* to the five mentioned.

These appear of course to be a fairly haphazard set of crimes. Few would probably argue that inebriation or false accusation really is a worse crime than many of those not included (such as murder). But these were the ones God selected, so they must have a separate category.

Not only are the penalties very severe in our modern eyes, but they were clearly intended to be frightening even when they were formulated, as they were for transgressions against 'God's rights' over men. They were for the same reason untouchable; if a crime is deemed to fall under the *ḥudūd* category, then the judge has no recourse except to pass the verdict indicated. But they were already at an early date clearly considered to be excessively harsh. Thus there are *ḥadīth* that say, 'if you can, then avoid using the *ḥudūd* penalties'.[11] This is also implied in the fourth of the rules, against false accusation, which is clearly based in a Koranic verse. This verse follows immediately after the verse that deals with fornication, and says that whoever makes such an accusation must provide four witnesses to back him up; if he cannot do so, he is to be punished for his false accusation.[12]

This is thus a stronger demand for evidence than in regular conflicts, where two witnesses are sufficient to provide proof. The jurists followed up this perceived intention to limit such accusations, and added further restrictions. The witnesses must of course

10 Others disregard the rule on drunkenness, perhaps out of liberal concerns.

11 Imber, *Ebu's-Su'ud*, 210. The exception is the rule on false testimony, which is to be strictly enforced. But that is in itself a restriction on another of the *ḥudūd* rules. It is also considered more praiseworthy to cover up a *ḥudūd* crime than to bear witness of it.

12 The story on the circumstances say that this verse was revealed after some rumours had been told about the Prophet's youngest wife ᶜĀʾisha; more on this story and the *ḥadīth* on it in Schoeler, *Character und Autentie,* 119-70.

have an impeccable reputation and probity, and they must have witnessed the actual penetration. A general rule that women cannot be witnesses in cases involving the death penalty also applied here. 'Material' evidence, such as pregnancy, was not considered proof of fornication.[13]

Similar precision, or limitation, was made on what was meant by 'theft' in the *ḥudūd* sense. The goods taken must have a value of more than 10 dirham, and should be of 'durable' quality, that is, not perishable foodstuff,[14] and the thief should not have acted out of need or hunger. There must be no doubt that the possessor actually owned the food and that the thief could not make an arguable claim to it. What was stolen had to have been stored securely in the owner's house (thus not in a shop or in a place of public access), and the thief had to have broken in and brought the goods out of the house himself. That is, he could not be judged if he stretched his arm in a window and took something, nor if one thief was inside and threw the goods outside to a colleague, neither of them had then (individually) taken the goods out of the house. In general the theft had to be made secretly, but there must still be two eye witnesses that agreed on seeing the act.[15] All of these rules made it rare for a judge to establish that all the criteria of a *ḥudūd* theft had been filled, and this was clearly the intention: these punishments were made to deter, not to be regularly applied.[16] If a judge found that a crime did not

13 Except for the Mālikīya, which accept this as proof; *EI* (2), 'Zināʾ'. A not uncommon way to circumvent such situations was the idea of 'dormant pregnancy'. It is based on a fiction, partly supported by popular beliefs, that a foetus can lie 'dormant' for several years while the woman is menstruating normally, then spontaneously start to develop even up to ten years later. A child born long after a divorce can thus be considered to be legally conceived in wedlock, as long as the ex-husband does not challenge this. However, a husband may reject paternity of his existing wife's child and thus accuse her of adultery without the *ḥudūd* rules being invoked on this accusation alone (*liʿān*); see more on this in Chapter 15.

14 Nor books, as the assumption is that the thief is then only interested to know what was in them.—This, according to Ḥanafī law, the Shāfiʿīs and Mālikīs put the limit before the *ḥudūd* is applied to 3 dirham; Imber, *Ebu's-Su'ud*, 213-14.

15 Confession is also proof, but can be withdrawn, and it is 'recommended to plead not guilty if at all possible' according to the literature; *EI* (2), 'Sariḳa'.

16 There were also clear rules on *shubuhāt*, cases that technically fall under

meet the strict criteria of *ḥudūd*, but still had probably taken place (a thief had taken the goods, but the owner had not secured them as safely as required), he could still punish the criminal, but then using his own discretion give him a punishment of his own making.[17] Thus the limitations on the *ḥudūd* penalties were not made from a liberal concern for the criminal, but to give the judge greater flexibility in matching the punishment with the severity and circumstances of the actual case.[18]

Murder and bodily harm is a separate category discussed below. All other criminal cases, those not falling under either *ḥudūd* or bodily harm, belong to the 'remainder' category *taᶜzīr*, actually 'chastisement', which we may translate as 'regular criminal law'.[19] The law is fairly vague as to the level of punishment to be meted out in *taᶜzīr* cases. The principle is that the judge can use his discretion; the law books give little or no indication of what penalty each individual crime of this group should be lead to.[20]

ḥudūd, but which 'resemble' a legal situation so that the culprit may have been confused; the *ḥudūd* should not be applied in such cases.

17 A theft that does not fulfil the requirements of *ḥudūd* will most often fall under the category *ghasb*, illegitimate acquisition of someone's property. The principle here is that the object is to be replaced to the owner in the same condition as it was taken, if that is possible. If any damage has occurred, the culprit should pay the owner the value of the object. Thus, this does not fall under criminal law but is seen as a case of compensation.

18 As far as *zinā* is concerned, the possible *taᶜzīr* cases from the Ottoman period include e.g. castration of the man, but a fine or imprisonment was probably more common. Women found guilty of fornication under *taᶜzīr* were in Egypt normally sentenced to a period of forced labour; Ron Shaham, *Family and the Courts in Modern Egypt: A Study Based on Decisions by the Sharīᶜa Courts, 1900-1955*, Leiden 1997, 133 & 158. Judges could sentence the guilty parties to marry so that the actual penalty was for the man to pay a normal dower to the woman. If a child was born, it would in such a case be considered the man's child with normal rights. Thus the court could adapt to a social reality of pre-marital sex, but probably only when such relations were normal and accepted by the surrounding society. But it was only the 'guilty' man who could marry the girl, so the aim of the solution was to formalize the relation 'as if' the marriage contract had been established before the sexual relation, not the opposite; Judith E. Tucker, *In the House of the Law: Gender and Islamic Law in Ottoman Syria and Palestine,* Berkeley 1998, 160-1.

19 Peters, 'Codification of criminal law', 211-25, and 'Islamic and secular criminal law', 70-90.

20 Tyan, *Histoire*, 570.

However, there are a few restrictions on the judge's freedom in *taᶜzīr*. Some make a distinction between crimes that are related to a *ḥudūd* rule, such as being accessory to a *zinā* crime, and those that are not. The penalty in the former must be related to the *ḥudūd* rule. Others, like the Ḥanafīs, say that no *taᶜzīr* rule can be more severe than the mildest of the *ḥudūd*, because God would otherwise have included that crime in the *ḥudūd*. That makes for a maximum of 39 lashes, as the lowest *ḥudūd* penalty is 40 lashes.[21] However, Mālikīs and others give the judges a free rein to impose any penalty for *taᶜzīr*, including death.

Murder and blood money

Homicide and bodily harm belong in a separate category that is treated according to different principles. Those who wish to present the Sharīᶜa as a modern and progressive legal system will probably have most difficulty with this part of the law, because one definition of civilized law is the transition from private vendetta to social regulation where it is the community (society or the state) that sanctions infractions, not the victims or their relatives that exact revenge. The Islamic rules, however, are based on the principle of direct retaliation and 'an eye for an eye, a tooth for a tooth'. Still Islamic law must also be seen as an attempt to draw such conflicts away from the private circle of revenge and make it a public responsibility. It was just not considered possible (or right) to make a clean break with the traditional ideal of retribution.

Presentations of the Islamic law of murder and retaliation are sometimes a bit confusing in that sufficient attention is not made to distinguish between compensation (which is paid in the form of *diya*, 'blood money') and punishment.[22]

The distinction is based on intent. If there was no intent to

21 Noel J. Coulson, 'The state and the individual in Islamic Law', *International and Comparative Law Quarterly*, VI, 1957, 54. But the Ḥanafīs can also accept the death penalty for *taᶜzīr* if the 'public order' was under threat; *EI* (2), 'Taᶜzīr'.

22 Peters, 'Murder on the Nile', 102-5. Again it should be noted that these matters are not treated as a 'public' law separate from 'private law', as in Western law, but in the context of a conflict between two parties, the victim (or his or her heirs) and the perpetrator.

harm,[23] the perpetrator is not punished. But the victims, or heirs in the case of death, still have the right to compensation: they have suffered a loss, which may be economically significant in a society with no life insurance or public pensions. This compensation is called *diya*, blood money.

If there was an illegitimate intent to harm,[24] then the same harm that the perpetrator inflicted on the victim shall be inflicted on himself; a hand be cut off if he crippled the hand of the victim, and so on. Thus the death penalty for murder. But the victim (heirs in the case of murder) has the opportunity to request that the perpetrator instead pays him an economic compensation. The reason behind this is of course that the victim (or heirs) has also in these cases suffered a loss that has economic implications. It would be unreasonable if the victim of accidental damage received such compensation that was necessary for him, while the victim of an intentional crime did not. Thus they have the right to ask for 'settlement' (*ṣulḥ*). In doing so they forfeit the claim to physical retaliation. They cannot demand both money and revenge.

We can see a 'civilizational' intent behind this rule. The impact of nomadic ideals was still so strong that the early legislators did not aim to abolish the idea of *lex talionis* or blood revenge outright. But the intention behind making the victims choose between revenge and compensation that they made sure was real and considerable, was clearly to direct the victims towards the less severe punishments. And it was in either case society, the court and the judge, that decided if the accused really had committed the crime intentionally, and it was society that effected the punishment if the victim chose revenge. Thus there was never any acceptance of private vendetta in the Sharīᶜa. Still the strength of the tradition made sure that it was left to the victim or heirs to choose, it was not up to the judge or the condemned to make such an initiative to 'purchase his body'.

23 Ḥanafī law distinguishes between 'intent' and 'similarity to intent', defined by what weapon is used; a sharp weapon such as knife or sword proves intent to kill, while using a weapon that is not necessarily lethal (a club, for example) means that intent is not certain and proven. In that case the perpetrator pays *diyā*, but is not subject to retaliation. Mālikī law may order retaliation when such a weapon is used with a deadly consequence.

24 In case of self-defence there is neither payment of *diya* nor retaliation.

The size of the compensation was set so that it should be a significant sum. The killing of a free man led to a compensation of 1,000 dinars, which at the time this was established equalled 10,000 dirham or about 100 camels. That would normally correspond to between five and ten years' income at an average level. The law books have long discussions of the precise amounts that are awarded for each type of damage on various parts of the body.

The basic rates were the same for compensation for accidents, *diya*, and settlement of a crime, *ṣulḥ*. But there were some differences in procedure. The rates for compensation were fixed and could not be amended for each case. When it came to settlement for a crime, however, they were only advisory. It is here the victim who takes the initiative and makes a claim, which may be higher or lower than the established sums, as he so desires (and he can even forgo receiving payment completely). If the convicted criminal is not able or willing to pay the required sum, the *talionis* punishment is then put into effect.

There is also a difference in who pays. A convicted criminal is alone responsible for meeting the sum asked in settlement. But that would not be reasonable for one involved in an accident. In this case the burden is shared between him and those close to him, who form a 'solidarity group', *ᶜāqila*. It may consist of relatives up to a certain degree, members of his tribe or of those who live in his quarter in a town; his army unit for a soldier, in general a category he belongs to and which stand mutually responsible in such cases.[25]

How big this unit is depends on the sum that is to be paid; the principle is that no individual should be asked to pay more than four dirham, so if a death has ensued, 2,500 paying colleagues have to be found. If this is not possible the state may intervene or the person who made the accidental killing will have to take on the loss after all.

We do not know how far this idea of a 'solidarity group' actually survived the transition from the nomadic tribal to an urban environment. It is likely that such *ᶜāqila* groups were more theoretical than real both in the medieval period and later.[26]

25 It is of course the tribe that is considered, but the concept has been extended as the links to tribal society weakened.

26 Ruud Peters has found that the principle was reawakened in the nineteenth century in a new form; 'Murder on the Nile', 108.

There are also other important methods of compensation. One of them is *qasāma*. If a murder case is left unsolved, the compensation may fall upon the person who owns the land where the body was discovered. In this case he and a group of fifty other people must all swear they were *not* involved in the death, and will then take on a joint responsibility for the payment. This will in practical terms mean a collective charge taken on by the village where the body was found. However, this principle cannot be used if the heirs have taken any of the group to court and not been able to secure conviction. This is thus a damper on any desire to raise hopeless cases against suspected killers. By doing so the heirs lose the possibility of later asking for *qasāma* from the village where the suspect lives.

It can also be observed that the Sharīᶜa courts have, or have put on themselves, severe restrictions in how they may convict suspects in homicide cases.[27] They often strictly apply the rule that the murder must be intentional, and that there cannot be any doubt that the intent was to effectuate death. Thus any weapon used must have been sharp or pointed, as any other could possibly only lead to maiming. Murder by poison or strangulation cannot be held to be certainly intentional, as it may have been unclear to the perpetrator whether death would ensue or not.

The same restrictions apply to the testimony of witnesses, these must be evident and identical. A man raised a case against another for having been dragged out of the building, beaten up and kicked. He had one witness who saw him being dragged out, another that he was beaten and a third that he was kicked. The case was dismissed, because he did not have the required two witnesses of each of the three acts.[28]

So also for confessions. A case involved two robbers who admitted having taken the objects stipulated by the plaintiff. But they refused to say, 'we stole', only 'we took'. They were acquitted, as they had not admitted to stealing. Of course that did not mean they walked free; they were immediately arrested by the police, taken to their court and imprisoned on the basis of the police's *siyāsa*, which of course did not have to bother about the strict procedural restrictions of the Sharīᶜa court.

27 These examples are from nineteenth-century Egypt, that is, Ḥanafī practice.

28 Peters, 'Murder on the Nile', 113-14.

Apostasy

The third category of crimes that could lead to the death penalty, besides the *ḥudūd* and murder, was religious: apostasy, to leave Islam (*ridda* or *irtidād*). Exactly what is meant by apostasy varies, as does the way such religious deviance was sanctioned, from ostracism to application of the death penalty. These rules may, as those that relate to *ḥudūd*, be practised leniently or strictly, in some cases it would appear that an apostate, someone who wishes to convert from Islam to another religion, almost has to insist on the death penalty before it can be applied.

Thus the judge has first to establish that the statement of apostasy was expressed in earnest and that the accused was in his right mind. He must then, according to some schools, call the accused to the court and ask him to repeat his desire to leave Islam, after having made sure that the accused understood the serious implications of this wish, that it will lead to his death.[29] If the accused insists on his apostasy, and the judge is convinced that he is sane and responsible for his statements, he should put the accused in jail for a certain period—normally three days—during which he may be subject to 'physical encouragement' (beatings) to see the error of his ways. If he does not 'repent' and still, on being presented to the court, insists on his views, he is then taken away and executed.

These are the standard rules for 'straight' apostasy, where a Muslim gets up and states 'I am no longer a Muslim, but a Christian' or other religion. But there were of course many other forms of blameworthy deviance from the established religious views, for which there were different terms in the law.[30] One was

29 Thus with Shāfiᶜī and the Ḥanafī Abū Yūsuf. One variant is that the accused apostate is asked on five different occasions to perform the prayer; if he does so, then he is free. Shīᶜī law says, on the other hand, that an apostate born in Islam is to be executed at once. Or at least men are: Shīᶜī and Ḥanafī law do not accept that women can be sentenced to death for apostasy, while the other schools make no such distinction. Generally speaking the later jurists put greater limitations on the conditions for apostasy than earlier. A convicted apostate is to be beheaded, but other methods are also used, and there are cases from the Middle Ages where suspected apostates were tortured to death; *EI* (2), 'Murtadd'.

30 Maribel Fierro, *La heterodoxia en al-Andalus durante el periodo omeya*, Madrid 1987, 177-87. Cf. also her introduction to Muḥammad b. Waḍḍāḥ

bid^c^a, 'novelties', which could be 'good' and acceptable or 'bad' and illegal. This term covers all practices or ideas that deviated from that which was accepted (*sunna* or *ijmā^c^*), and could be used against individuals in one's own school of law or ideas from other schools or currents of thought that stepped beyond the limits of toleration. There was no particular sanction against such novelties, and a *mubtadi^c^* was neither an apostate nor unbeliever, but the expression may still have been used legally when religious disputes were brought to court. The normal sanction for conviction in such cases would be that the culprit was quarantined until he saw the error of his ways, or he could be subject to various *ta^c^zīr* punishments.

The issue was more serious for a *zindiq*, a heretic. This term was used for someone who said he was a Muslim, but in reality presented ideas that were in opposition to the foundations of Revelation, be it the nature of God or the status of the Prophet. Someone who claimed to be a Muslim and yet in this way rejected the basic tenets of the Islamic faith, was thus a liar, and his words could not be believed, even if he later 'recanted' and denounced his earlier views. Thus the law on him was clear: *zandaqa* qualified for death for apostasy from Islam.[31]

Kufr means unbelief, to be outside the Islamic faith.[32] This covers both the 'people of the Book'—the Christians and Jews—and the heathens. Thus there are no specific sanctions attached to the term, as the former had accepted rules of tolerance, while the pure heathens, the polytheists (*mushrikūn*)[33] cannot be tolerated. To claim someone is an unbeliever is called *takfīr*, and there are many *ḥadīth* that warn against making such accusations without foundation; 'if one Muslim calls another an unbeliever, then that is true for one of them'.[34] But if such a *takfīr*

---

al-Qurṭubī, *Kitāb al-bida^c^ (Tratado contra las innovaciones)*, Madrid 1988, 92-117.

31 The Koran also mentions *ilhād*, which is used more or less synonymously to the later term *zandaqa*, *Zindiq* originally referred to adherents of the Manichaean religion, but was later generalized to mean 'heretic'.

32 An unbeliever is a *kāfir*, pl. *kāfirūn*, from which came the derogatory term for blacks in apartheid South Africa, '*kaffir*', probably originally used on them by Muslim immigrants.

33 The noun 'heathendom' is *shirk* from *sharika*, 'to associate', that is, to 'associate God' with more deities.

34 Thus in Abū Dāwūd, 'Sunna' 15; similar *ḥadīth* in many other collections.

charge is proven, the accused is to be executed. Other forms of heresy are 'insults against the Prophet' (*sabb al-Rasūl*),[35] which is considered a sin (*fisq*) or apostasy, depending on the severity of the case.

There are some studies that show how this worked in the classical period. As an illustration we may look in more detail at apostasy cases from the first period of Mamlūk rule in Cairo, in the fourteenth century.[36]

One of these cases took place in 1320. It concerned a scholar who was called Ismāᶜīl al-Zindiq, 'the Heretic'. He had studied *fiqh* and grammar, but also the Torah and the Bible. He was known for his jokes about religion and discussions of free thought, as his name indicated. He was arrested for atheism and brought to a Mālikī judge. A large number of witnesses to what he had said and done were presented and heard, and the judge asked for any witnesses for the defence. The judge waited for three days, the stipulated period for reconsideration in apostasy cases, but no witnesses came forward. Thus, in lack of any witnesses for the defence, the judge condemned Ismāᶜīl to death. Then the case was brought to the Dār al-ᶜadl, the joint council of the chief judges of the four schools with the sultan. The sultan was rather dubious about the case, and asked if all these witnesses were really trustworthy, but all four chief judges confirmed that this was the case and supported the conviction. The sultan thus signed the order, in spite of his misgivings. It appears that it was only now that Ismāᶜīl was allowed to speak, and he answered 'in a confused manner', so the question of his sanity was brought forward. But since it was uncertain whether he was really insane, the conviction was upheld and carried out.

Another case had taken place twenty years earlier, and varied

35 Lutz Wiederhold, 'Blasphemy against the Prophet Muḥammad and his companions (*sabb al-rasūl, sabb al-ṣaḥābah*): The introduction of the topic into Shāfiᶜī legal literature and its relevance for legal practice under Mamluk rule', *Journal of Semitic Studies*, XLII, 1, 1997, 39-70. It may also be said that certain concepts can constitute an 'infidel discourse' (*kalimāt al-kufr*), which may be proof of apostasy; various jurists have given different definitions of this.

36 This is based on research by the German historian Joseph Escovitz in the court records. We cannot of course say that this is true of all pre-modern societies, but it covers such a long period that it cannot be quite untypical; Escovitz, *Office of* qâḍî al-quḍât, 134-47.

somewhat from Ismāᶜīl's. It concerned one Fatḥ al-Dīn al-Baqāqī, who was brought before the Mālikī chief judge Ibn Makhlūf. The plaintiff claimed that this Fatḥ al-Dīn had not performed the fast in Ramaḍān and had mocked those who did. He had used coarse language, and it was known that he had used the Koran as a footstool; he had in general made fun of religion and had prior convictions for this. However, it was also known that this Ibn Makhlūf was out to 'get' him, because he had written satirical verses about this judge, and it was Ibn Makhlūf's friends who were behind many of the accusations.

Fatḥ al-Dīn declared his belief in the unity of God and the prophecy of Muḥammad, but Ibn Makhlūf refused to accept his declaration of faith and condemned him to death on the basis of the witnesses' statements. But now the Shāfiᶜī chief judge Ibn Daqīq al-ᶜĪd voiced his opinion. He is a well-known scholar from this period, with several major works of law to his credit.[37] He was in his own time known as a particularly pious judge and was highly valued. He felt that it was incorrect to use the apostasy laws against someone who professed his belief in the unity of God (i.e., recanted from any apostasy he might have made). Some friends of Fatḥ al-Dīn therefore asked Ibn Daqīq to intervene, on the basis that Fatḥ al-Dīn should be declared incompetent through insanity; a formalist way to avoid the sentence. But Ibn Daqīq refused to do so, as he knew the man to be perfectly sane. The case was thus referred to the Dār al-ᶜadl, and Ibn Daqīq presented his reservations on the matter, but none of the other judges supported him. Ibn Makhlūf was supported by the Ḥanafī judge and the sultan went with their view. So in spite of Fatḥ al-Dīn's renewed professions of faith he was executed.

The interesting element in these cases, apart from showing how the various chief *qāḍī*s and the sultan interacted, is that the *ridda* rules were applied more strictly than the theory accounts for. Rather than it having to be positively proved that the accused was sane, he was in the first case executed because it could not be positively proved that he was not sane. The rule of a three-day waiting period was applied not for the accused to recant, but for any witnesses in his defence to turn up. His own declarations of

37 He died in 1302, Carl Brockelmann, *Geschichte der arabischen Literatur*, Leiden 1937-49, II, 63, *S* II, 66.

innocence of the charges were not taken into account. Thus these were treated as cases of *zandaqa*, not open apostasy, and the theoretical restrictions on condemnations were thus ineffective, at least in these cases.

It seems quite obvious from the court records of the latter case that what was at stake was a political or private quarrel between the Mālikī chief judge and an opponent; a personal revenge. Rivalry between the chief judges may also have played a role, although no such disagreement was mentioned in the first case. It is noteworthy that Fatḥ al-Dīn was described as a religious scholar who was accused of pure atheism, an incongruity that rather than raising doubts among the other judges rather strengthened their resolve. The other examples one sees of such apostasy cases very often involve scholars who are accused of various levels of heresy. It thus seems that apostasy is mainly used within the class of scholars as a weapon against perceived heterodoxy.

It was also said in the last case referred to that Ibn Daqīq, the opponent of the condemnation, at the end capitulated and joined the other judges in accepting it. This would indicate that it was either a formal requirement or an assumption that all four chief judges had to stand behind a death sentence, at least officially. The records also include some other cases where the accused are acquitted. This occurred in one case that was transferred from one *madhhab*'s court to another. So if Ibn Daqīq had taken Fatḥ al-Dīn's case to his own court, his life would probably have been saved.

A parallel case, the third conviction in this period, concerned a Christian man who attacked Islam and was taken to court. He continued his abuse of Islam and said it was a false religion and that he sought martyrdom. The judge sentenced him to beating and threw him in jail, but the Christian continued unabated with his attacks. Thus he was sentenced to death and executed. Although this case was rather more in line with the theoretical procedure of an apostasy case, it was thus not a case of actual apostasy, but of an attack on Islam and its Prophet (*sabb al-rasūl*) by one who had never been a Muslim.

The records show about twenty executions for heresy or related crimes through the fourteenth century in Egypt.[38] Thus

38 Rapoport, 'Legal diversity', 223-6. Of the twenty, four concerned

there were only a handful of such cases. Three or four others ended in acquittal. This shows that apostasy or heresy did actually lead to the death sentence being carried out and were not only theoretical laws of deterrence, in spite of the many restrictions that the law books put on them. But they were mostly applied in cases of 'heresy', *zandaqa*.

Methods of punishment

The methods of punishment were thus not fixed for most crimes, and must have varied greatly over time, so it may be wrong to even try to give any general description. Nevertheless, the most typical types of punishment we can find in the classical sources from the first centuries of Islam are, besides death, corporal punishments like beating with sticks, imprisonment, forced labour or public humiliation.[39] Typical penalties included the police leading the convicted criminal around the streets of the town facing backwards on a donkey, often with his face painted black and in prison clothes while the policeman shouted out the crimes he was convicted of. This was a simple and inexpensive form of punishment, damaging the honour of the convict more than his body. Fines could also be imposed, but were not the most common form of penalty.

There are few references to prisons in the sources, so it is difficult to draw a clear history of how they were used. However, it would appear that there were two types of prison; a *qāḍī*'s jail, which was mostly administrative; and the prison proper, or 'thief's prison' as it was called, which was entirely under the authority of the *shurṭa*. The judge's jail was used for keeping the prisoner locked up while awaiting trial, and for debtors. Imprisoning people for failing to pay their debts should only be done to force a convicted defendant to pay the plaintiff (or the court) what he owed. It should not be a substitute for unpaid debts (as the injured party gained little economic benefit from the defendant's staying in jail rather than paying). If the judge was certain the

---

Christians or converts.

39 Irene Schneider, 'Imprisonment in pre-classical and classical Islamic Law', *Islamic Law and Society*, II, 2, 1995, 157-73, and Peters, 'Islamic and secular criminal law'.

convicted man was insolvent and unable to pay, he should let him go. It was also considered forbidden to make the convicted man work as payment for his debts, although this did occur in some cases. The rule that an accused apostate should be kept in jail for three days to consider his views also referred to this jail.

The prison proper was much harsher than the judge's jail, and was a very real form of punishment. Prison could be used instead of other types of penalties, such as for cases of homicide that was unintentional, but still blameworthy, or when the heirs in an intentional murder case has asked for neither *talionis* nor compensation; such cases actually occurred. The accused may in both cases be sent to prison for one year. This may also be the case for highway robbery where no death occurred, rather than the *ḥudūd* rule for theft which should in theory then be imposed. It was also accepted that prison may be used in addition to corporal *ḥudūd* punishments.

The reality appears to be that prison was often (but not always!) used *instead* of the *ḥudūd* punishments, and in particular the physical ones like amputation of hands or lashing. The development seems clearly to have been continuously towards less severe punishments than those prescribed by the law books, with the increasing use of imprisonment, but also humiliation, for crimes that might in theory incur far more drastic penalties.

Taᶜzīr convictions mostly led to imprisonment, but we know little of how, since it was up to each judge to mete out the length, and we do not have sufficient records that detail how (not least since many such crimes were actually treated in the *siyāsa* courts, not the Sharīᶜa courts). The law books give little indication of the length of imprisonment, except for some discussion of the maximum that can be enforced. The Ḥanafīya have a rule saying that a debtor's jail sentence should not last more than four months, the Shāfiᶜīya says one year, while Mālikī law accepts imprisonment in perpetuity. These rules were probably mostly only applicable to the prisons the *qāḍī* actually controlled, in his own jail, whereas those who ran the thief's prison set their own limitations. Even if forced labour was not accepted in the early period, we do know from nineteenth-century Egyptian records that it was common then, so it was probably practised differently throughout the ages.

There is, at least for *taᶜzīr* cases, no equality before the court as to punishments. Only 'commoners' were to be imprisoned, not the *ashrāf*, the higher classes in society. However, there are innumerable cases where prominent people were jailed for political reasons, so they were not out of danger.[40] We know from thirteenth-century Cairo that there were three different prisons; one for political prisoners, one for those sentenced to death, and one for the rest. Conditions in the political prison were so bad that the sultan built a new one in the Citadel, but this was soon known to be even worse.[41]

There was thus a separate prison there for those sentenced to death. We know otherwise that corporal punishments were executed quickly and summarily; there was often an executioner waiting to do his work immediately after the final verdict had been given. These cases had then been to the governor, the sultan or his *maẓālim* court or council, but the existence of a separate prison would still indicate that a longer stay on 'death row' must have occurred, although we cannot generalize as to the extent or conditions for this.

Prisons were probably used less in the earlier period and became more common from the Middle Ages onwards, before fines and monetary penalties grew in prominence. This would mirror the situation in Europe, which in the same period went through a more or less parallel development; imprisonment was first used for the duration of a case or for debtors, then increasingly as the most common form of punishment replacing corporal or humiliating penalties, which had also been common forms of punishments there.

40 Schneider, 'Imprisonment', 163. This term also included other jurists, in addition to the *ashrāf* properly speaking, those of the Prophet's kin. Land owners and military leaders were also not imprisoned, but the 'middle classes' (*awṣāt*, Schneider says 'businessmen') could be imprisoned, but not flogged.

41 Schneider, 'Imprisonment', 170.

15

FAMILY LAW

In spite of the attention it has received, criminal law is not, as we have seen, the most widely used part of Islamic law, and in particular not in the modern period. The area of the Sharīᶜa that has had widest application, directly or through codifications based on the Sharīᶜa rules, is clearly family and personal law. It is also the most controversial area in relation to 'modern', Western norms, in particular on issues of the position of women and gender.

There are significant differences between the various schools of law in this area, but they do share some basic rules. All consider husband and wife as separate economic individuals. There is no concept of the family as a joint economy. The husband owns his property and has his income, the wife has hers, both during and after a marriage.[1] Evidently a family will normally function as an economic entity in daily life, merging the affairs of husband, wife and children, and involving the extended family, but the law does not recognize the principle of a 'community property' of the family. Thus much of the issues of family law revolve around sorting out such economic conflicts between family members.

This legal individuality does not mean that the positions of husband and wife in law are identical. Each is considered to have a separate role. Even if one may speak ideologically of a 'balance' between rights and duties for each of them, the legal rules are based on gender differences and are therefore different for husband and wife, son and daughter, almost all the way through. This is of course not surprising for a 'traditional' society. If we were to make a general assessment of 'the position of women' in the Sharīᶜa, we must thus decide what to compare it with. If we consider other cultures from the time the Sharīᶜa was first formed—such as pre-modern Europe—we would find that

1 Thus husband thus has no rights on the wife's property. However, this of course also means that the wife acquires no rights over the income that the man—normally the economically active partner—brings in during the course of the marriage, except for 'maintenance'.

the Sharīᶜa is clearly ahead in terms of the status of women, both in terms of economic independence and the fact that failing marriages may at all be dissolved, unlike for example in Christian Europe.

The same would be the case if we compare with the pre-Islamic Middle East. Women must have had a fairly precarious situation both socially and economically and the rules of the Sharīᶜa seem to a large degree to aim at bettering their status as far as was morally acceptable to the community, beyond what had been the case in the earlier society where men had a much freer rein.

However, when compared to modern conceptions, where women and men should stand on a basis of equality, it is evident that the Sharīᶜa and its classical rules represent a striking contrast. This is easily seen in the rules of marriage and divorce.

Marriage

The process of marriage will in all societies consist of a composite transition of civil status. It involves relocating one or both parties to a new household; it may have an official or legal aspect of registration of the new family unit which entails new economic responsibilities; it may also include a social demarcation of the changed status celebrated by the surrounding society (a wedding); and it may have a religious aspect, a sacrament before God. We know from our modern society that not all these aspects need be present, and that they need not be contemporaneous; a couple may celebrate their wedding years after they have actually moved in together and formed a family unit.

Marriages in Islam do not actually have a religious or ritual aspect; a couple goes to a *qāḍī*, not to a mosque, to get married. The central aspect of marriage in the Sharīᶜa is that it is a contract between two parties, which may be confirmed formally by a *qāḍī* and socially in a wedding, but strictly speaking is established directly when then two sides have signed the contract.[2] The bride

2 And made the statements 'I marry you' / 'I accept', in front of two witnesses (the Mālikīs do not require witnesses). The Ottomans already demanded that marriages had to be registered formally (Imber, *Ebu's-Su'ud*, 165), but it appears that unregistered marriages based only on a

and groom are here both represented by a guardian, *walī*, normally the closest male relative (father, grandfather, brother). Adult males may often be their own guardians, and the Ḥanafīs also accept that an adult female can be her own guardian and thus marry without seeking acceptance from her relatives.[3] This is not accepted by the other schools, and it is not much practised even in societies where Ḥanafī law dominates, as it mostly contravenes social customs.

A marriage contract may be established at any time, including when the parties are small children. If that is the case the 'bride' and 'groom' will live with their parents while they are growing up and only move together when both parties have reached marriageable age at puberty, in some cases formalized at 15 years of age. But the contract is legally binding from the time it was signed, so the legal marriage can be separated in time from the physical and social establishment of married life by many years.

It is up to the parties to determine the content of the marriage contract. It is, however, normally a formal requirement that it specifies a dower (*mahr*), a sum of money that is given from the groom to the bride. This is thus not the 'bridewealth' that one can find in other societies (such as some African ones), as it is not the *father* of the bride who receives the sum (as a 'sale' of her reproductive power); the dower remains her property and follows her into the marriage.[4] The size of the dower is established by the

---

contract have existed into the present; Shaham, *Family and the Courts*, 45, and Ziba Mir-Hoseini, *Marriage on Trial: A Study of Islamic Family Law: Iran and Morocco Compared*, London 1997, 171-4.— Other general overviews over family law are in Doi, *Sharīᶜah*, 114-216, and Bakhtiar, *Encyclopedia of Islamic Law*, 395-497.

3 The woman's guardian can, however, still demand dissolution of the marriage if he feels that the normal requirements for dower or social equality (see below) are not fulfilled. Shīᶜī law also accepts that a widow or divorcee can be her own *walī*; Mir-Hoseini, *Marriage on Trial*, 168. By 'male relative' here and below is normally meant 'male agnate', i.e. male relative on the father's side.

4 Annelies Moors, *Women, Property and Islam: Palestinian experiences, 1920-1990*, Cambridge 1995, 82-4. These are the legal rules. The practice may be different; there are cases where a wife demands that a dower that has been paid to her father or other relative is turned over to her; thus this may often have been the normal practice. The law would here support the wife. A dower paid by the husband to someone other than the wife is

parties and is often an important point of discussion between the two families; a high dower confirms that the bride's family has a high social status. We have in the modern epoch seen tendencies to a drastic inflation in the amounts given in dower; it may on occasion be equal to many years' wages.[5] The dower is often in such cases divided in two, a 'direct' dower that must be paid at the time of the marriage, while the rest—perhaps half or two thirds of the total—forms a 'deferred' dower that only falls due when the marriage is ended by divorce or death. It is only the total sum of the two which is made known publicly and thus has social significance; the direct dower is a private matter between the families. This division is not legally necessary, although it is the most common way of organizing the dower.[6] But it is legally required that the direct sum is paid before the marriage can become valid.[7]

Other economic transactions are based on custom more than law. The husband is required to provide the housing for the new family, which thus remains his individual property, not that of is wife. However, the wife will normally provide furnishings or utensils, mostly through a present from her father, a 'bridal gift'. It is socially expected that this gift should also include some gold in the form of jewellery or coins. These form part of the bride's social security and are outside the husband's concern.

---

legally non-existent and the husband would in this case owe the full amount to his wife.

5 Other couples may, on the other hand, reject the system completely by setting a nominal dower of e.g. one dinar. Thus they show that they follow modern norms, but also that their families are so rich that they can rise above such outward concern for money; Moors, *Women, Property and Islam*, 106-13. There was in the Ottoman period a minimum of 10 dirham set for dower; Imber, *Ebu's-Su'ud*, 175.

6 This system does have a long tradition, it is already known from the eleventh century that a deferred dower may reach the value of a house, and that it was justified by being an insurance for the wife against divorce. The deferral could then also be of limited duration, e.g. for one or five years, rather than open-ended until death or divorce dissolved the marriage; Yossef Rappaport, 'Matrimonial gifts in early Islamic Egypt', *Islamic Law and Society*, VII, 1, 2000, 9-15. It was also common in the Ottoman period that the deferred dower might be bigger than the direct part, and the system was used in almost all marriages; Imber, *Ebu's-Su'ud*, 175.

7 Thus in Mālikī law; Ḥanafī law considers the marriage then valid, but the wife may refuse to move to the husband's house until the dower is paid.

The Sharīᶜa defines certain mutual responsibilities for husband and wife. The woman should obey her husband. This is stated as a general adage, but it is normally taken primarily to mean that she must stay in the house that the husband has provided for her.[8] If she leaves his house and refuses to return, she may be considered obstinate or rebellious (*nāshiza*) and the judge may intervene and demand that she returns.

All economic responsibilities fall on the husband, who must provide for the wife and children according to specific rules. The wife has no economic obligation for the family's income, irrespective of which of the two actually has income and a fortune. Even if the woman has income and the husband has not, she may still keep it for her own purposes and demand that the man pays her the established maintenance, *nafaqa*.[9] This is not just an empty formality; many court cases between husband and wife (a wife is free to sue her husband and often does) concern the non-payment of *nafaqa*.[10] This is where a wife's 'obstinacy' comes in; if the man can claim that she has left the home and refuses to return, he is freed from the requirement to pay for her maintenance.[11]

8 With the exceptions defined in the law, such as the right to visit parents and her family within reasonable and defined delays. She must also be sexually available—this is a reciprocal right between husband and wife—and take care of the children and run the household. A breach of any of these four duties constitutes 'disobedience' and means the woman loses her right to maintenance from the husband; Shaham, *Family and the Courts*, 80-3; Layish, *Divorce in the Libyan Family: A Study Based on the* sijills *of the* sharīᶜa *Courts of Ajdābiyya and Kufra,* New York / Jerusalem, 1991, 20-1, and Mir-Hoseini, *Marriage on trial*, 47.

9 The wife thus has the right to be economically active and e.g. take employment, carry out trade or other work on her own. But the requirement that she must stay in the husband's house means that she must have his general acceptance to leave the home to carry out such work. The husband may also, with the court's approval, refuse her the right to carry out such work as is considered 'immoral' under the threat of losing *nafaqa*. What is 'immoral' is of course dependant on social mores; a Sharīᶜa court has e.g. in the modern period stated that education is an absolute good and that the husband is not allowed to deny the wife the right to work as a teacher; Shaham, *Family and the Courts*, 94.

10 Cf. Shaham, *Family and the Courts, passim*, on the practice in Egypt in the first half of the twentieth century.

11 The size of the *nafaqa* depends on social and economic status, primarily the status of the wife's family; what she has the right to expect, rather than

Evidently most marriages are harmonious in Muslim as in any other society. However, it is those cases that lead to conflict that interest a legal historian, and which we should examine more closely. Among the possible areas of conflict is the woman's influence on the choice of her partner.

The bride's right of refusal

All marriages under the Sharīᶜa are assumed to be arranged by the closest male relative, the father if he is alive, who acts as a 'legal guardian' (*walī*) for the bride.[12] This does not in most cases lead to any conflict, because the daughter will either implicitly accept her father's choice, or has had an actual influence on the choice, directly or through her mother or uncle as 'spokesman' to her father. However, what happens if the daughter does not actually agree with her *walī*'s choice is a matter of disagreement. There is an inherent contradiction between two principles in the Sharīᶜa: On the one hand, it is stated in all schools that bride and groom should both agree to the selection of a partner.[13] On the other, all assume that the daughter should accept her father's choice, However, this is formulated differently in the different schools.

Some of the problems lie in the age of marriage, and the possibility to contract a legally binding marriage while the parties are minors. No-one can expect a child to freely accept or reject a future partner. But the contract is valid from day one, and dower and other economic transactions are to be paid at once, even in child marriages. Thus the jurists make a distinction in the 'right of refusal' as to whether the bride and groom are children (under the age of puberty) or adults,[14] but they also distinguish between the

---

what the husband actually has the ability to provide. This is one of the reasons why judges put an emphasis on *kafāʾa*, equality in social and economic status between the spouses. The court may in case of conflict intervene and set a particular sum as the husbands *nafaqa* duties.

12 And bridegroom if he is a minor or otherwise his father's ward.

13 These rules are all valid both for bride and groom. But the legal discussion on them only deals with the possible protests by the bride, where the importance of the *walī*'s will is evidently much greater.

14 Some schools made a distinction between the age of puberty, when the couple would move in together, and the age of maturity, when the acceptance of the parties to the contract is required; the latter may be up to two years higher than the former. Any marriage contracted in the intervening period is in the modern period only considered legal if the court has

'first marriage', when the father has greater rights, and 'later marriages', that is the marriage of a widow or divorcee. The older the woman, the greater her influence, as may be expected.

All schools agree that a father has the right to give a minor away in marriage without her having any right to refuse, as she is not yet legally competent. The Mālikīs extend the father's right to make contracts of marriage without consulting his daughter (the *jabr* or *ijbār* right) to include adult daughters, up to their first marriage. But it is only the father who has this right.[15] No other relative has the right to marry off a minor if the father is dead. A more distant relative can marry her off when she has reached adult age, but she must then give her consent, at least in the form of 'silent acceptance'; that is, that she has not (openly) rejected the proposed marriage. Women have full right to be heard in later marriages (widows and divorcees), and must then give a positive, 'vocal' acceptance to the marriage, whether it is her father or any other relative that is the *walī*. Still this gives, as can be seen, the father very great powers over his daughter in the Mālikī school.[16]

The Shāfiᶜīs do not go so far. They consider, like the Mālikīs, that it is only the father (or father's father) that can give away minors in marriage. They restrict this power to include only marriages concluded before the child has reached puberty. For any marriage concluded later the *walī*, be he the father or other relative, must have either silent or vocal support from the bride: She has the right to refuse, if she does so openly.[17]

The Ḥanafī school is the one that gives women the widest

---

confirmed it; *EI* (2), 'Nikāḥ'.

15 The idea is that that these two relatives would put the greater emphasis on the daughter's welfare, while more remote relatives might marry off the girl just to be rid of the economic burden an unmarried relative constituted. —The Mālikīs restrict the right to marry off a minor to the father only; the Shāfiᶜīs and Ḥanbalīs include also the father's father.

16 This is, however, explained to be relevant when the girl is 'fickle' and has refused one suitor after another, thus some jurists consider this *jabr* rule to only apply in exceptional cases; cf. the modern example from Nigeria, below.

17 Some Ḥanbalīs seem to accept that a more remote *walī* may marry off underage girls, but counsel against it; while others follow the Mālikīs in this, they otherwise share the views of the Shāfiᶜīs. The Shīᶜīs follow the Shāfiᶜīs in restricting it to father and father's father; Susan Spectorsky, '*Sunnah* in the responses of Isḥāq b. Rāhwayh', 57, and Bakhtiar, *Encyclopedia of Islamic Law*, 424-5.

room for choice. They do not, however, recognize the distinction between father/grandfather and other *walīs*; any male relative may contract a marriage for a minor, under the *jabr* rule. But they give the bride the right to renege.[18] When a child bride has reached the age of consent and the couple is to set up a household, she can reject the marriage. This right is strictly formalized; she must use a specific formula and present it to a *qāḍī* within a short period after she has reached the age required. If she manages to do this, the marriage is cancelled as if the contract had never been made.[19] If the bride is adult at the time the contract is made, she must according to Ḥanafī law give a vocal acceptance, and technically she also has the right, as mentioned, to be 'her own *walī*' and marry in opposition to the wishes of her relatives.

Thus it may with some justification be said that there is no forced marriage in Ḥanafī law (or that such, if they occur, are against the law), while the same is not so evident in Mālikī law, although they also accept the basic principles that a marriage is the voluntary union of bride and groom.

There is thus an internal contradiction in the Mālikī rules, which can lead to varying results in a court of law. A modern example of this is a much cited case from Nigeria in the 1970s.[20] It involved one Alhaji Yakubu, who wanted to arrange a marriage for his daughter Karimatu. He presented her with two candidates, Alhaji Mahmoud and Alhaji Umaru, and asked her to choose between them. She chose Alhaji Umaru, and although her father had preferred Mahmoud, he accepted her choice and made the arrangements with Umaru's family. But Karimatu changed her mind in the period before the contract was signed, since Umaru had apparently not shown any great interest in the marriage. She thus rejected Umaru and asked for her father's first choice, Mahmoud, instead. But at this point the father was not willing to

18 They are also under closer control from the court as to the dower and *kafāʾa*; the judge is here to protect the interests of the bride.

19 If she does not protest, it will be considered that she has accepted the union, but the Ḥanafīs demand that she must be informed about it. If she swears an oath that she did not know about the contract or that she protested in the presence of a third party when she was informed of it, then her testimony shall be accepted even at a later time and without her having to present further proof.

20 Yushau Sodiq, 'Malik's concept of *maslahah*', 214-31.

accede to her request, since he had already made an agreement with Umaru's family, and he consequently signed the contract over his daughter's protest. She therefore went to the local Sharīᶜa court, supported by an uncle, and demanded that the marriage be annulled. The court referred to the principle that a bride must accept her groom, annulled the marriage, and married her under its own authority to Mahmoud. The father, however, appealed to the state's Sharīᶜa court of appeal, and they reversed the decision. They referred to *jabr*, that Karimatu was required to accept her father's choice. Karimatu then appealed to the federal court of appeal, and they made a Salomonic decision that although the right of *jabr* did in principle exist, her father had in fact given it up when he had asked Karimatu to choose between two suitors. He had then accepted that Karimatu was competent and capable of making her own decision, and must as a consequence accept the choice she had finally made.

Who and how many

Islamic law allows a man to be married to four wives simultaneously. This is established in the Koran and can hardly be rejected within a classical Sharīᶜa framework, although some modernists point to the Koran statement that a man must treat all four 'equally', which they claim is beyond human ability, and that polygamy is therefore implicitly forbidden.[21] But it is only Tunisia and Turkey which has actually banned polygamy. It is, however, not a common occurrence, not least because of the considerable economic charge a second marriage involves. It is primarily a symbol of high status to be able to afford more than one wife. It is probably not too rash to suggest that few women now or in earlier times have ever been very happy at being one of several wives.[22]

21 Less common is a criticism that points to the context of the verse (4:3), which is that polygamy is required *to care for widows and orphans after a war*. Thus it might logically be easily claimed that it is acceptable only in such special circumstances, much like the *mutᶜa* marriage (Chapter 7), but the jurists' argument that a rule of this structural type has to be *ᶜāmm*, general, is normally not disputed.

22 Hanbali law accepts that the wife may write into the marriage contract a clause against the husband taking more wives. This has been accepted into the codification of many modern family laws. However, to include a future divorce into a marriage contract in this fashion is not very common. The

The Sharīᶜa has detailed rules about whom *not* to marry; primarily those to whom one is closely related. Thus a man may not be married to two sisters simultaneously, but there is also ban against any woman who has breastfed him as well as her children or others she has nursed ('milk siblings'). The divide between 'those one may marry' and all others is fundamental to social definition and has enormous consequences for everyday life. While it may be impossible to encounter any person of the opposite sex that 'one may marry', access is free and unhindered for the close family, including 'milk siblings'.

Apart from these absolutes, the Sharīᶜa also requires a certain amount of equality (*kafāʾa*) between the spouses in terms of social status and economy.[23] What this exactly means may vary. The formal criteria posed by the Sharīᶜa are religion (piety; that the spouse should not be known to be a sinner), physical abilities, kinship and money. The religious scholars would clearly give most emphasis to the first of these criteria, but it is probably kinship which is the most important factor, and following that economic equality: A woman has the right to be maintained in 'the manner to which she is accustomed' both in terms of dwellings, the number of servants, and so on. The husband must thus have the means to provide this, and a *qāḍī* may, if he finds (on a request from the family) that this is not the case, dissolve the marriage.

A Muslim man may marry a *dhimmī* (Christian or Jew) woman without her converting, but a Muslim woman cannot marry a non-Muslim man (unless he converts to Islam). This difference is of course based on the conception of the man as the head of the household; a Muslim cannot be placed in a position of subservience under a non-Muslim.[24]

---

duty to treat all wives equally is also true for economic matters, and a wife may go to court if she considers she has not received her due compared to the other wives. She also has the right to have a house separate from that of her co-wife, thus a husband with more than one wife must also be able to acquire several houses.

23 Amelia Zomeño, 'Kafāʾa in the Mālikī school: A *fatwā* from fifteenth-century Fez'; in R. Gleave and E. Kermeli (ed.), *Islamic Law: Theory and Practice*, London 1997, 87-106.

24 This rule was used in the case raised against the Muslim reformer Naṣr Ḥāmid Abū Zayd in Egypt in 1994-6. The radical Islamist opposition claimed that Abū Zayd by his critical study of the Koran had apostasized

Divorce

The Sharīᶜa has, unlike traditional Christianity, always been open to the fact that marriages may have to be dissolved. But this possibility is fundamentally unevenly distributed. The husband has in principle an unlimited access to divorce, while the wife may only 'borrow' this access from the husband, and only under very specific circumstances. Thus one must make a clear distinction between the husband's and the wife's right to divorce.

The man's divorce: ṭalāq

All that is required for a husband to divorce is that he says, 'I divorce you'. This, called *ṭalāq*, is founded in the Koran and cannot be changed, even if a *ḥadīth* says that 'it is the worst thing that God has allowed for Muslims', and such repudiation of the wife is seen as morally reprehensible by jurists and theologians. Thus they have attempted to limit the access to such divorce, without directly challenging the rule itself. This may be seen in the consequences that *ṭalāq* has for the husband, and its categorization into different types.

When the husband has first expressed the formula, it is still reversible. He may not have sexual intercourse with his wife, but has full economic and social responsibilities towards her; she remains living in his house and receives maintenance; if one of them dies the other inherits in the normal fashion. This lasts for a 'waiting period' (*ᶜidda*) of about three months. The husband may at any point in this period change his mind and take the wife back without any formalities.

If he does not take his wife back within this period of *ᶜidda*, the divorce becomes final and irreversible. They have then become fully divorced, and the husband no longer has any

---

from Islam, which in classical law should have led to the death penalty (cf. the previous chapter). But the only part of the Sharīᶜa still in force in Egypt is the family law, and they thus had to pick out this rule to make their case: As Abū Zayd was in their view a non-Muslim, he could not remain married to his (Muslim) wife—in spite of her ardent support of her husband—and the court should therefore divorce them. The argument was accepted in some court instances, but was finally made invalid, although Abū Zayd still decided to go into exile; Kilian Bälz, 'Submitting faith to judicial scrutiny through the family trial: The "Abû Zayd case"', *Die Welt des Islams*, XXXVII, 2, 1997, 135-55.

economic responsibilities towards his wife.[25] However, he may still change his mind and remarry his wife, but this is then a new marriage, and he has to pay another dower and the wife may reject him if she so wishes.

This process may be repeated twice; the husband may divorce the wife temporarily or finally and take her back, respectively without or with a new marriage. But a third divorce draws the line. When he pronounces the divorce formula for a third time, whatever has occurred in between, the divorce is immediate and irreversible, and he is not allowed to marry the same women again. She is banned for him, unless she 'cancels' this ban by having been married to someone else and then be either divorced or widowed from this second marriage. Clearly the intention is to put a damper on any excessive urge to rapidly execute a divorce.

However, these provisions may in fact help to speed up the process rather than slow it down. The husband may repeat the divorce formula three times in succession in a single session, without having to take the wife back between each. He is then 'triply divorced', and the wife has immediately lost her status as a married woman and the right to inheritance from him.[26]

She is, however, still not without certain economic rights. However the divorce has occurred, reversible, irreversible or triply, she will always enter the waiting period from the moment the first divorce formula was uttered. She may in this period not marry any other man, but keeps the right to live in her former husband's house.[27] It is also customary for a husband to pay a particular present, *mut*ᶜ*a*,[28] to the wife at the divorce, this may

25 Unless they have small children; he must then pay both maintenance for the children and a 'caretaker wage' for their mother (or whoever actually takes care of them) until the children have reached a certain age, cf. below.

26 The jurists consider this practice morally reprehensible and discourage it, but do allow its legality.

27 The husband and wife may live together when the divorce is revocable, since any sexual cohabitation would then automatically mean that the divorce is cancelled, which the court favours. But they cannot live in the same house when the divorce is irrevocable. The husband must then either move out or find other housing for his wife for the ᶜ*idda* period. All schools (except the Ḥanbalīs) consider it is his obligation to provide the housing, however, and the Ḥanafīs also say he must pay maintenance in the waiting period; the two other schools only if the woman is pregnant.

28 Not to be confused with the time-limited marriage accepted by the Shīᶜīs. This is just a coincidental similarity of two terms with different origin. Cf.

equal a third of the dower. The schools differ as to economic maintenance in the waiting period. The Ḥanafī school says that the husband must pay her full maintenance throughout the *ᶜidda* period whatever the situation, while the other schools say that this obligation is ended when the divorce has become irreversible, that is to say immediately in the case of a triple divorce.[29]

Each party takes their property out of the marriage if it has been dissolved by *ṭalāq*. The husband thus normally keeps the house. But any deferred dower there may be will then also fall due for payment. This in many cases may be just a small sum, but in others a considerable amount. This deferred dower, which was agreed when the marriage contract was signed, thus functions partly as a economic guarantee for a woman who may in this way lose her home and her house, but can also be a protection against rash use of the right to *ṭalāq*. A husband in this position may thus wish to seek a different solution than divorce, in spite of his absolute right to repudiate his wife.

A *ṭalāq* is only based on the husband's statement, and according to the Sharīᶜa does not need to be presented or confirmed in court, although it is quite common to do so in order to substantiate the economic settlements involved.

The wife's divorce by agreement: khulᶜ

A wife may also seek divorce, but she can only get it as a 'reflection' of the husband's absolute right. She may ask her husband to dissolve the marriage, in exchange for giving up the economic rights she is accorded by the *ṭalāq* rules. If the husband accepts, it will then became a settlement between them that needs no further confirmation from other parties (although it is very common to go to a judge to have the agreement formally registered). It is up to the two spouses to decide what kind of compensation the wife gives up, but the normal arrangement is that she renounces her right to the dower, or at least any deferred

---

also Rosen, *Justice of Islam*, 16.

29 Cf. more on the length of the *ᶜidda* period below. Three of the schools (and the Shīᶜīs) believe that a triple irreversible divorce pronounced on the deathbed (with the obvious intention of depriving the wife of inheritance) is to be disregarded, but some Shāfiᶜīs claim that it is in fact valid and the wife is then dispossessed of inheritance; Bakhtiar, *Encyclopedia of Islamic Law*, 529.

dower that may remain unpaid, and also frees him from paying maintenance during the *ᶜidda* period. The arrangement may also include changed provisions for any children that may have been born in the marriage and that the husband is normally required to provide for.

Such a divorce by agreement is called *khulᶜ*,[30] and it is evident that while it gives the woman the possibility to take the initiative, it is actually more beneficial for the husband in economic terms. It is therefore not uncommon that a husband will, when a marriage is in trouble, try to make the wife initiate a *khulᶜ* deal, while she will try to make him pronounce the *ṭalāq* that gives her a greater economic benefit.[31] A *khulᶜ* is considered an immediate and irreversible single divorce (the wife will immediately lose the right to inherit, but the spouses may change their minds and remarry without the wife having to go through an 'intermediary' marriage).

The frequency of such *khulᶜ* arrangements will have varied, but a modern study suggests that perhaps a third of all divorces are in the form of a *khulᶜ*.[32]

30 Ḥanafī law only uses the term *khulᶜ* if the wife actually pays a sum to the husband; they call it *ṭalāq ᶜalā 'l-ibrāᵓ* when she only renounces rights that the law gives her (maintenance under *ᶜidda*, deferred dower); Shaham, *Family and the Courts*, 103. This distinction has little practical consequence, but shows that *khulᶜ* is in fact only a form of *ṭalāq* by mutual agreement.

31 E.g. by claiming that the husband has pronounced a *ṭalāq* just to her or before a witness. This is linked to the Ḥanafī school's very strict understanding that it is the wording and not the intention of a statement that is taken into account. Thus if a man should make an oath on his marriage—'if I have not finished this work by tomorrow, let my wife be divorced from me!'—and the condition is fulfilled (he was not able to finish the work in time), then he is in fact divorced by his first statement, even if he later protests that this was just a figure of speech, not an actual intention to divorce her. Such oaths were sometimes used as a surety for a third party, e.g. when making loans: 'I shall pay you back, if not, then let me be divorced!', but also a method to control the wife: If she does not do what he says, then she will be automatically divorced from him. Of course, this could backfire if the wife were to consider this preferable to a continued marriage.

32 Rosen, *Justice of Islam*, 104. His study concerns modern-day Morocco. Mir-Hoseini notes from Iran that around one half of all registered divorces are in the form of *khulᶜ*; *Marriage on Trial*, 82.

Judicial divorce, fasād, taṭlīq

If a man is not willing or able to make a *khulᶜ* agreement, the wife has no other recourse than to go to the court and ask a judge to dissolve the marriage over his protests. This takes the form that the judge puts himself in the man's place and performs a triple irreversible *ṭalāq* in his place. All schools permit this in one form or another, but the conditions under which they allow it vary widely.

The Ḥanafī school is the most restrictive, putting as it does great emphasis on wording and formalities. They actually only accept an 'annulment' (*faskh* or *fasād*) by a judge, not divorce per se: That is, he may only dissolve the marriage if the original contract contained some formal errors or was not fulfilled, so that he can declare the contract invalid.[33] But there are not many causes that can lead to this. One possible stratagem is to refer to the sexual intercourse which is a right for both spouses in any marriage. The wife may petition for annulment if the husband is not able to fulfil this duty, that is in case of permanent impotence. But this will need to be proved, in practice only through the husband admitting to this weakness.

The Shāfiᶜī and Ḥanbalī schools take a more lenient position. They are also fairly restrictive, but accept more conditions that may allow a court to dissolve an established marriage. They consider the husband's prolonged absence a cause for *faskh*, divorce through annulment, if he has not provided for the wife's economic maintenance. Thus for example if he has left the country and he either did not leave any provisions for her, or the money ran out while he was away and he cannot be located. The Ḥanafī rules do not allow a marriage to be dissolved on this basis, because it is only the husband himself who can pronounce the *ṭalāq* or accept a *khulᶜ*. The Shāfiᶜī school, however, accepts that the court may dissolve such a marriage so that the woman gains the freedom to remarry and thus secure the survival of herself and her children.

The Ḥanafī court has often accepted that this is a real weakness in their law, which has led to unacceptable hardship for women who through no fault of their own have lost their only

33 Also if the court believes the contract does not conform sufficiently to the *kafāʾa* of the two, cf. above.

realistic provider. When Ḥanafī and Shāfiᶜī judges have worked in the same court, this has on occasion made them come to a tacit understanding: If such a case came before a Ḥanafī judge he would often excuse himself and let such cases go before his Shāfiᶜī colleague. The latter could then dissolve the marriage according to his school and the Ḥanafī judge would later accept this decision on the basis of reciprocal acceptance of verdicts made by the other schools.[34]

The Mālikī court has both in theory and in practice gone far beyond the other two, by accepting that a judge may take the place of a husband even when he is present and available, and by accepting a general term of 'damage' (*ḍarar*) as a basis for such judicial divorce (*taṭlīq*). The damage to the wife that can lead to divorce may be of various kinds: physical (a husband mistreating his wife, for example, is a clear basis for divorce); economic (the husband does not fulfil his duties to provide for the family); or even 'mental'. Thus the classical Mālikī rules may if the judge so decides, go very far in the direction of a modern conception of judicial divorce for 'incompatibility'. The judge has a very wide latitude for personal discretion in how he sees each case, so there may have been considerable variance in how these rules were applied, although the basic rules were the same.

Studies made of divorce cases in different regions over the last three centuries show, however, that judges appear surprisingly often to listen to the wife more than the husband.[35] The rules are clearly heavily weighed in favour of the husband, with his unlimited access to *ṭalāq*. But it would appear that judges, at least to some extent, realize this imbalance and try to compensate

34 Tucker, *In the House of the Law*, 84, from seventeenth- and eighteenth-century Syria. But the Ottoman sultan had already forbidden this procedure in the 1550s, so it must have been a controversial adaptation; Imber, *Ebu's-Su'ud*, 187. Cf. a similar practice in nineteenth-century Egypt, where the women mostly went to Ḥanbalī judges to obtain a divorce if the husband had left them, or in case of physical mistreatment; Shaham, *Family and the Courts,* 118. In fact, this possibility of going to each schools' idiosyncratic rules when necessary 'for the benefits of society' may well have been the reason the system of four chief judges, and thus parallel systems of law in one city, was established by the Mamluks; Rapoport, 'Legal diversity in the age of *taqlīd*', 216–17.

35 E.g. Tucker, *In the House of the Law*; Mir-Hoseini, *Marriage on Trial*, and Shaham, *Family and the Courts.*

by letting the wife be considered more credible in the individual cases that come before them, giving her the benefit of the judgement as far as that can be done within the framework of the law's regulations.[36]

Thus we see that divorce cases often end up in court even if the husband according to the classical law does not need any court acceptance of his *ṭalāq*. This is of course the case if the husband believes he can avoid his economic obligations by taking the case to court and blaming his wife for the divorce.[37] It appears that taking such cases to court is often a strategy chosen by husband or wife in a larger and longer family conflict (which may involve the extended families on both sides), and thus often a struggle between maintenance duties and 'obstinacy': The husband claims the conflict started when the wife left the marital home and returned to her parents—thus he has no economic obligation towards her—while she claims that he never paid her the money that the law requires him to and hence had no other option than to return to her family. The court will often go to great lengths to try to reunite the parties in such cases, because the preservation of a marriage is considered to be absolutely preferable, if it is possible. So it will try to establish settlement agreements (*ṣulḥ*) as a compromise between the husband and the wife, or (often in Mālikī court) establish a group of middlemen, often relatives from both sides, who try to negotiate a solution.[38] It is only when these give up because the conflict is irresolvable that the court will accept a divorce.

36 It is of course most often women who go to court, as only they need the court's aid to obtain a divorce. But the husband may also prefer to go to court rather than just pronounce a *ṭalāq*. If he can get the court to support his claim that it is the wife's fault that the marriage has broken down, by her leaving the house or other unacceptable behaviour, he may get the court to to decide that she has to carry the consequences and free the man from his economic obligations that the divorce normally places on him.

37 It is in any case normal to register a *ṭalāq* formally in order to confirm that the wife has received what is owed to her.

38 Layish, *Divorce*, 123-4. If the judge believes the wife to be guilty, he could according to Egyptian law force her to a 'house of obedience' (*bayt al-ṭā*ᶜ*a*), but it is doubtful if this can be supported by actual Sharīᶜa rule; Shahām, *Family and the Courts*, 73 & 95-6, and *EI* (2), 'Nikāḥ'.

Children

A child born to a married couple is always considered to be the husband's child, and goes into his kinship line, not that of the mother. A man may also accept the paternity of a child born out of wedlock, who will also then enter his kinship line. A husband may, on the other hand, reject the paternity of a child born by his wife. He can do this by making an oath to that effect immediately after the birth. If the wife makes a contrary oath that the husband is the father, the child is considered to be of unknown parentage and enters the kinship line of the mother.[39] Such a *li*ᶜ*ān* declaration is considered to be equivalent to a single irrevocable divorce.

However, the law will go to great lengths to consider a child as legally conceived, far beyond what is known to be possible by medical knowledge. The Sharīᶜa says that a pregnancy may last as little as six months and as long as two years or longer.[40] A child that is born two years after the husband has left the country may thus—unless he chooses to reject it and his wife in a *li*ᶜ*ān* declaration—legally and without problem be considered his.

The same legal tolerance concerns the ᶜ*idda*, the wife's 'waiting period' after a divorce or the husband's death. The wife cannot remarry in this period, but the ex-husband has to pay for her maintenance. This period is limited to three menstruation cycles, that is normally around three months in length.[41] But it is

39 This is a method to solve disputed paternity cases, and is exempt from the *ḥudūd* rule on *qadhf* (cf. the previous chapter). Although the husband in this case is actually accusing his wife of adultery, he need not bring four witnesses, and neither his wife nor he is to be sentenced to the *ḥudūd* punishments for adultery or false accusation respectively. If a child is on the other hand born less than six months after a divorce, the ex-husband is always to be considered the father on the basis of the wife's assertion of this. He cannot in this case deny the paternity.

40 According to Ḥanafī law. This period may also in some cases last much longer, thus it is after a 'reversible' divorce unlimited, unless the mother has reported that the ᶜ*idda* period is over, which is then only established on her own statement to that effect; Shaham, *Family and the Courts*, 155. Such over-long assumptions of pregnancy, originally based on unifying two Koran verses (21:14 and 46:15), thus merges with the idea of 'dormant pregnancy' (cf. the previous chapter; also Bakhtiar, *Encyclopedia of Islamic Law*, 455-8).

41 Unless the wife is pregnant, in that case for forty days after the child is

up to the woman herself to report this, and her word should be accepted without question. The law accepts that one menstruation cycle may last more than a year, so the divorcee may, if she has problems finding a new husband, keep this *ᶜidda* period, during which she is her ex-husband's charge, going for several years.[42]

The father has full economic responsibility for the maintenance of his children, even after a divorce. The mother has the right and duty to keep the children after a divorce until they reach a certain age, normally seven years for boys and nine years for girls.[43] The father must pay the mother for their maintenance throughout this period, and must also pay her directly a certain amount, a 'caretaker wage', as long has she has this responsibility.[44] When the required age has been reached the children will normally move to their father, but they may, if both parties agree, remain with their mother, but then at her cost and expense.[45]

---

born; or she has stopped menstruating, if so precisely three months. The *ᶜidda* period for widows is four months and ten days. The aim of this period is to avoid disputes of paternity, but also, as the rule includes non-menstruating women, clearly to ascertain the maintenance of women without other income for a reasonable period to search for a new husband or other manner of securing her support.

42 This is particular for the Ḥanafī law, which gives the divorcee full *nafaqa* throughout the period. Mālikī and Shāfiᶜī laws does not give her *nafaqa*, only the right to remain in the house, so she has less of a motive to prolong the period here. Ottoman and modern laws tend to put a maximum for the period, so that a woman may not demand *ᶜidda* for more than e.g. nine months or a year. The Mālikīs also accept, in case of doubt, that a woman may be examined by other women for this purpose. The other schools do not accept this.

43 Or alternatively nine years for boys and twelve for girls, according to other views.

44 Unless she marries a 'stranger', one outside the family from whom the daughters 'are not prevented from marriage'. If she does, the father may take the children, or rather let another female relative care for them, as the mother's mother. She will then be the one who has the right to the economic support from the father.

45 If the father dies while the children are minors, the guardianship formally passes to the father's father. But the mother may in some cases take over this role, in particular if the father has indicated so on his deathbed. If so, she may take all decisions concerning them until they are adult, just as the father would have. She is only exempt from the economic liability, her maintenance and that of the children are to be taken from the children's capital (their inheritance) if they have such, otherwise it falls on their father's father and his family; Tucker, *In the House of the Law*, 142.

Sons remain the economic charges of their fathers until they acquire gainful employment, daughters until they are married. Daughters that are divorced or widowed will again become the economic responsibility of their closest live male relative, father, brother or son, until their remarriage.[46]

These are of course all formulaic rules that are used by the court in case of disputes. The reality of division of responsibility, care for their children and details surrounding these will in most cases be decided by the parents and the extended family from case to case according to what suits the particular situation best, and these rules will only become relevant if the parties fail to reach an agreement.

Inheritance

The inheritance laws are normally also included under family law. These rules are, particularly in Sunnī law, unbelievably complex; a saying states that 'one half of all knowledge in the world concerns the rules of inheritance'. We can thus only include a few main points regarding of how an estate is to be divided.

A person may give one third of his wealth to whomever he wants as a testamentary bequest (*waṣīya*). However, he may not give it to someone who inherits from him according to the fixed rules; thus he cannot use a bequest to change the relative division between his kinsfolk. The same applies to gifts that he has given while he was ill and it was evident that his death was approaching.

The remaining parts of his estate are divided among his relatives. They fall into two groups: on the one hand, those that are mentioned in the Koran—the 'koranic heirs' (*farāʾiḍ*); on the other, everyone else (*ʿaṣaba*). The koranic heirs each receive one fixed share of the estate, according to what the Koran specifies for them, while the rest share the remainder. The father's (agnatic) side is favoured in this last group, relatives on the

46 Irrespective of her own income, or at least formally. The father's economic responsibility is incidentally 'on behalf of the child'; any capital the children may have independently from the father's may be used for their maintenance.

mother's (cognatic) side will generally only receive anything if there are no other male heirs. How large a fraction each category of relatives receives depends on how may other relatives there are; it is formulated such that a close relative will 'expel' from the inheritance a more remote. As the koranic heirs get fixed shares and the rest share the remainder, it may often be more profitable to belong to the latter group.

The koranic heirs are, summarized briefly, the spouse, the parents (and father's parents) and sisters. Sons, however, are not Koranic heirs, they are among those who take the 'remainder'. Daughters are koranic heirs if there are no sons, but if there are both sons and daughters they are both residual heirs and share half of the estate, each daughter receiving one half of what each son gets.

We may indicate the most important beneficiaries thus:

Koranic heirs, in fractions of the total estate

Daughters: 1/2 if there is only one daughter, 2/3 if there is more than one.

Father: 1/6; he is also a residual heir.

Mother: 1/6 if she has other children (who also inherit), otherwise 1/3.

Sisters: As daughters, 1/2 or 2/3, if there are no children. Otherwise they are residual heirs, or get nothing.

Spouse: A widower gets 1/2 from his wife, or 1/4 if there are any children. A widow gets half of this, 1/4 or 1/8 if there are children. If there is more than one widow, they share this fraction equally.

Half-brothers and sisters, grandparents and grandchildren may also be koranic heirs under certain conditions (thus if the closest link, parents and children, are no longer alive).

Residual heirs, in order of priority

1. Male relatives,[47] descending (sons, then sons' sons).
2. Male relatives ascending (fathers, then father's brother, father's father, father's father's brother).
3. Brothers and brothers' sons (full brother, half brother on

47 In every case here: on the father's side.

father's side, full brother's sons, half brother's sons).
4. Father's brothers' sons, in the same way.

Female residual heirs receive half of the entitlement of their male counterparts; if a full brother's son is to inherit, then a full brother's daughter will inherit half of what he receives, and so on (two thirds and one third of their joint share, if there is only one of each sex).[48]

These complex rules, of which we have only given the most general indications, are of course attempts at reaching an equitable division; for instance that a widow will herself receive more if she does not have a son who may provide for her. That women do inherit, but less than men, evidently aims for a balance between the acceptance that women are independent economic actors with their own property against the expectation that widows and daughters will become married and provided for and enter the kin of their (new) husbands. The children of daughters will thus not inherit anything from their mother's father, because they are not part of his family, only of their father's.[49]

Thus the inheritance rules try as far as possible to keep property within the kinline of the deceased. But one result of these rules is that the inheritance is divided into many small fractions. This is particularly a problem when applied to agricultural property, which may be divided into successively tinier plots by each generation of inheritance, as each heir will receive perhaps one fifth or one tenth of the land of the previous generation. It will therefore often be the case that the formal inheritance rules are quietly ignored by the family so that the land is maintained in at least minimally workable units. A formal way of keeping land together will be discussed in the next chapter.

48 These are the main rules in the four Sunnī schools. The Shīᶜīs follow them as for the koranic shares, but differ systematically in the division among the residual heirs, in particular in that they do not make a difference between the father's and mother's side, and have a simpler system of division overall; cf. also Chapter 7. Cf. also the *waqf* rules that are often defined so that daughters should be included, and often with equal shares to the sons, but that their children again and further descendants are fully excluded (next chapter)

49 Cf. also the *waqf* rules that are often defined so that daughters should be included, and often with equal shares to the sons, but that their children again and further descendants are fully excluded (next chapter)

These complicated rules are thus not necessarily always followed, at least not into their minutest details. If a conflict arises between the heirs and is taken to court, the judge will make a formal and full calculation according to the Sharīᶜa rules (as these are still accepted law in such matters in most states), but no one will intervene if the heirs reach an agreement amongst themselves in some other way. This may be in order to keep land together, but we may also see that women often do not demand their formal rights in regards to close relatives. A widow may for example ignore her right to her share if the money is instead given to her son.[50] It may be more important for her to keep a good relationship with her son, who is to take care of her in her old age, than to insist on her economic rights in the inheritance. The rules of inheritance must thus be seen more as a framework that *may* be used, particularly if there are possible conflicts or if remote relatives are involved, when the informal network is less likely to provide a solution that is satisfactory.

Modern adaptations

What we have described so far in this chapter are the basic classical Sharīᶜa rules in the fields of family and personal law. They are thus rules that have been practised in most Muslim countries (and still are), more than any other part of the Sharīᶜa. But this does not mean that the modern states have not tried, in the colonial or post-colonial period, to amend and modernize these laws, even if only moderately. Sometimes such changes have had the support of the Sharīᶜa jurists or Sharīᶜa courts. A general tendency of such modernizations are to involve the courts and public registration into family matters that in the classical system are only private arrangements between the parties involved.

Thus the major change is that the family laws are fully or partly codified in almost every Muslim state today. Only Saudi Arabia (and to some extent Egypt and some emirates[51]) maintain a uncodified Sharīᶜa in family law. Among the areas where many

50 Moors, *Women, Property and Islam*, 59-65.

51 Bahrain, Oman, Qatar and the UAE; Abdullahi al-Na'im (ed.), *Islamic Family Law in a Changing World: A Global Resource Book*, London 2002.

or most modern states have tried to adapt the Sharīᶜa rules are:
— *Minimum age for marriage*. The Sharīᶜa accepts, as mentioned, that marriage contracts may be made when the parties are still children. Many countries look disfavourably on this and have tried to set a minimum age for marriages and marriage contracts. Some put this at the classical age for sexual maturity, 15 years,[52] while others have put the minimum age at 16 or 18 years.[53] This change has probably been circumvented in many cases, not least in the rural areas where local officials have been willing to ignore that private contracts are made, weddings celebrated and couples moved in together at lower ages. Consequently the marriages are not officially registered or only when the required age is reached. The only result in such cases is that the couples lose the protection that a formally registered marriage provides them: if a conflict arises, they cannot go to court to seek solutions for a marriage that has no official existence. Perhaps for this reason, several countries (e.g. Syria, Iraq, Israel) allow the court to accept marriages at an earlier age than that codified.
— *The father's* jabr *right.* By banning child marriages, the states have also reduced the problem of *jabr*, the father's right to make a marriage contract without seeking his daughter's consent. The reason for this right was that a minor daughter could not accept or reject such a contract; that is no longer relevant if the minimum age of marriage is the same as or higher than the age of adulthood. Some countries, such as Algeria, have disposed of the *jabr* right altogether.[54] They also accept the Ḥanafī rule that a woman may be her own guardian and contract her own marriage

52 Thus, for girls, Yemen, Jordan, and Morocco before the recent changes; Kuwait, Lebanon (Shīᶜīs), Iran and Sudan say 'puberty', specified in Lebanon and Iran at 9 (if the court agrees), Kuwait at 15; *ibid.* For the recent changes in Moroccan family laws, see Léon Buskens, 'Recent debates on family law reform in Morocco: Islamic law as politics in an emerging public sphere', *Islamic Law and Society*, X, 1, 2003, 70-131.

53 The Algerian law of 1984 set 21 years for men and 18 for women; Ruth Mitchell, 'Family law in Algeria before and after the 1404/1984 family code'; in Gleave and Kermeli, *Islamic law*, 194-204. Iraq has 18 for both sexes, Libya 20 for both; al-Na'im, *Islamic Family Law*.

54 Also Iraq, Yemen, Egypt, and Libya; al-Na'im, *op.cit. Jabr* has also been limited in Morocco; Mir-Hoseini, *Marriage on Trial*, 26. Other countries such as Syria and Jordan have abolished it by raising the minimum age for marriage; *EI* (2), 'Nikāḥ'.

without her *walī*'s approval, but the judge may still dissolve such marriages if he decides they are against the woman's own interests. However, the laws more commonly discuss the opposite issue; whether a father has the right to refuse a daughter's choice. Most countries do allow a *walī* such a right if the girl has not reached maturity, [55] but several allow the court to overturn such a rejection.

— *Limitations on polygamy.* While Tunisia has abolished polygamy outright, neighbouring Algeria has kept the rule, but limited it to a few specific cases, as when the first wife is seriously ill or barren. Several other countries require a court's acceptance for a second marriage.[56] The husband may also need the acceptance of his first wife to remarry, otherwise she may obtain a divorce on this basis.[57] Several countries have also, building on an Ottoman model, tried to implement 'standard contracts' for marriages that state, for example, that a first wife has the right to get a divorce if the husband takes a second wife.[58]

— *Limitations on* ṭalāq. The most common way to deal with *ṭalāq* is also to maintain the principle, but add that the husband must—contrary to the classical rules—present such a repudiation to a judge, who may demand that the husband pays extra compensation to the wife if he finds the reason unsatisfactory. A divorce that is not registered at the court is in some countries illegal, but still valid.[59] Algeria has also introduced a reconciliation period of

55 Thus Iraq, Iran, Libya, Syria, and Tunisia. Tunisia also requires the mother to agree if the girl has not reached maturity. Some countries, thus Algeria, Jordan and Kuwait, say or imply that a *walī*'s acceptence is always required for a first marriage, but not for a second; al-Na'im, *Islamic Family Law*.

56 Thus Syria, Iraq, also the former South Yemen. Iraq abolished polygamy after the 1959 revolution, but reintroduced it in part in 1963; *EI* (2), 'Nikāḥ', and al-Na'im, *Islamic Family Law*.

57 Thus in Pakistan. Egypt says the husband must notify the first wife, while Libya requires the wife's acceptance in writing (or the court's approval); al-Na'im, *Islamic Family Law*.

58 As Jordan, Syria, Iraq and Kuwait; Iran introduced such as well, but have not made such standard contracts compulsory after the revolution; Schirazi, *Constitution of Iran*, 215-19. Such a standard contract could also state e.g. that the wife has the right to seek employment without the husband's further approval.

59 That is, the husband may be imprisoned, but the wife is still divorced from him, thus Israel, similarly in Iran and Lebanon; al-Na'im, *Islamic Family*

three months (that is, comparable to the *ᶜidda* period).[60]

A similar development took place in revolutionary Iran.[61] The family laws were first changed under the Shah in 1967, and included a provision that the husband's *ṭalāq* had to be presented to court, and that the court had the right to grant a judicial divorce if the marriage was 'in ruins', or if the husband took more wives. This 'shah law' was abolished soon after the 1979 revolution. But following strong protests from Iranian women a new law was introduced soon after, in 1982. It reintroduced most of the reforms of the 1967 law and in addition gave divorced women the right to ask for half of what the husband had earned during the marriage, a concept that had been quite unknown to the Sharīᶜa.[62]

— *Extending women's right to divorce*. One method that is used to increase a wife's options in seeking divorce is a so-called 'judicial *khulᶜ*'. Classical *khulᶜ* is based on an agreement between husband and wife. This has in modern countries been transferred to the court, so that a judge can accept a *khulᶜ* agreement on behalf of the husband, against his protests, when the court finds sufficient grounds for it.[63] This differs from the classical judicial divorce in that the wife here renounces or is deprived of the economic rights she normally has on divorce. It is up to the court

---

Law, see also Layish, 'The Transformation of the Sharīᶜa', 92

60 They also, interestingly, limited the Mālikī school's liberal criteria of what qualifies for judicial divorce. The aim was thus probably to make the law similar to a 'unified view' of the four schools. These Algerian laws have also some background in the French colonial laws.

61 Schirazi, *Constitution of Iran*, 215-19, and Mir-Hoseini, *Marriage on Trial*, 54-8.

62 Or in other Muslim countries. This did not apply if the court found that the woman was in any way responsible for the collapse of the marriage. The law was very controversial, and was amended on some points in 1992, but those elements referred to here remained in force. However, such cases were in 1979 transferred to 'special' courts manned by Sharīᶜa judges, so that there was some tension between their views and the law code; Mir-Hoseini, *Marriage on Trial*, 24.

63 Lucy Carroll, 'Qurʾān 2:229: "A Charter granted to the wife"? Judicial *khulᶜ* in Pakistan', *Islamic Law and Society*, III, 1, 1996, 91-126. Pakistan already had in 1939 a civil law that gave the court wide liberty in granting divorce, based more on Mālikī than the Ḥanafī law prevalent in Pakistan. In effect this new law was, according to Carroll, not necessarily an improvement for the women: By primarily granting such judicial *khulᶜ* in cases where a 'civil' divorce would have been possible, the court awarded the woman fewer economic rights than the previous law had done.

to decide what she must give up, but the normal situation is that she returns the full dower. But, as this is a new arrangement, the court or the legislator may also impose new conditions that must be fulfilled for such a *khul*ᶜ to be possible, so that it may circumvent the very limited criteria that in particular the Ḥanafī school lays down for judicial divorce. This has thus been proposed or implemented in Ḥanafī-dominated countries such as Pakistan and Egypt.[64]

64 More countries have also introduced civil laws which regulate *nafaqa*, the size of the dower, and some other of the economic relations involved in family matters, primarily to achieve standardization; *EI* (2), 'Nikāḥ'.

16

ECONOMY, TAXES AND PROPERTY

The Sharīᶜa, being a law formed in a society based on agriculture and trade, includes an extensive set of rules regulating economic matters. As such relations often required a stable basis that all parties to a transaction knew and could rely on, it is to be expected that these rules were practised, at least as a reference in case of conflicts. They were in the Ottoman period to a large degree replaced by *kanun* laws, but were still important into the modern period. However, as international trade became important in the Muslim world, Western-based legal systems took precedence more and more, such that the Sharīᶜa rules were limited to a smaller and smaller section of economic life from the nineteenth century onwards.

We do not have the space to give a systematic presentation of economic law,[1] but we can present a few topics that may be of interest. The basic concept that we can see reflected in many aspects of Islamic law is that of contract (*ᶜaqd*), the voluntary agreement between two parties to exchange goods or commodities.[2] Such an exchange may imply a loss or a profit for either party. This is both acceptable and promoted in Islamic thought as long as it is known at the time of the exchange. However, Islamic law puts great emphasis on avoiding unlawful benefits, usury, in commercial exchanges, and the main deciding element in determining lawfulness is time. It is this factor that has led to the most distinctive difference existing between Islamic and Western eco-

1 Joseph Schacht gives an overview of the main elements of contracts, economic liabilities etc. in *Introduction*, 134-60. Cf. also Doi, *Sharīᶜah*, 348-405, and Tilman Nagel, *Das islamische Recht*, Westhofen 2001, 73-82.

2 Rent or hire—the exchange of temporary possession for an agreed compensation—also falls under the general heading of commercial exchange, but with its own separate rules, to be discussed below. A contract may state that the object bought or sold is to be delivered at a later date (*salam*), but such staggered exchanges are hemmed in by specific restrictions, to make sure they do not conflict with the rules against *ribā*, below. The Sharīᶜa also has extensive rules on illegal exchanges, e.g. with forbidden or impure commodities.

nomic law. This is the Islamic ban on receiving or giving interest on capital.[3]

The ban on interest is based on a Koran verse that condemns *ribā* (2:225-9 i.a.), an expression whose origin is unknown, but is normally understood to mean 'usury'. The jurists have generalized it to cover all kinds of interest, that is to lend capital and at a later time have it returned with an addition. This is placed in the context of other Koran verses that ban gambling with money and similar games,[4] and which in law is linked to 'risk' (*gharar*). Transactions based on uncertainty or risk are not allowed, so the commodity that is exchanged should be known in value and quantity at the moment the transaction is made. That will for example mean that it is forbidden to sell the fruit on the trees before it is ripe, because the buyer does not know if all the fruit will ripen or what its weight will be.[5] That is a risk the Sharīᶜa does not allow him to take. A long list of rules for trade in agricultural and other commodities whose value changes with time follows the same principle: You cannot exchange one amount of a commodity with a different amount of the same commodity (that would be *ribā*),[6] nor a commodity in one form (unripe, dried) with the same commodity in another form (ripe, fresh).

That does not of course preclude all kinds of economic risk. Any investment in trade or productivity involves a certain amount of risk. But that is then shared equally between the investors or participants, and the division of the risk can be decided in advance, something that does not apply for a buyer of a commodity that does not exist at the time of purchase. This principle created a logical problem in the modern period, when insurance became possible. Some claim that insurance must be banned under the Sharīᶜa, because the person who pays an insurance policy does not know in advance whether he will benefit from the

3 There is some disagreement on whether this is an absolute ban, but it is normally seen as that.

4 Koran 5:90-1; cf. also Chapter 4.

5 Doi, *Sharīᶜah*, 359-62. See also Weiss, *Spirit of Islamic Law*, 161-2.

6 So if you buy a gold necklace with gold coins, you can only pay the exact same amount (in weight) as the necklace contains, with nothing extra for the labour. However, you may pay a higher price if you pay with silver coins, as you are then paying with a different commodity; Schacht, *Introduction*, 154.

payment or not; that is to say, he pays for something (the possible future reimbursement) the existence of which is as yet unknown. Others, however, claim that insurance is a way to reduce the risk of accidents or other misfortune, and that this must be in line with the intent of the Sharīᶜa. The negative attitude first present among the scholars has increasingly given way to the view that this is a social good as long as the policy is to the benefit of the one taking out the insurance, but there is still some scepticism regarding making commercial profit on insurance, that is, on other people's risk.[7]

Islamic banking

This topic is linked to a number of initiatives that Muslims, in particular pious or activist Muslims, have taken to adapt the ban on interest to modern capital management. A modern economic system is inconceivable without a functioning banking system, so the challenge is to relate Muslim economies to a global banking system that is based on interest. One solution is to simply consider this as one of this world's imperfections and disregard the ban on interest. That is the case in Kuwait, where we have seen they make a general exception from the Sharīᶜa on this issue, and this has probably been the most common attitude as modern banking has developed and spread in the Muslim world.

But some have lately tried to find alternatives whereby they may manage capital while remaining within the letter of the Sharīᶜa. This is known as 'Islamic banking', and has spread to a number of Muslim countries as an alternative to the practices of traditional or state-run banks.[8] They use a number of techniques

7 Skovgaard, *Defining Islam*, 335-73, also Layish and Warburg, *Reinstatement of Islamic Law*, 209-10.

8 Such Islamic banks (often named this way, e.g., 'Islamic Bank of …') are mostly private and linked to Islamic organizations. They thus often have a reputation for being uncorrupt and efficient, in contrast to the state-run banks. Thus they have often found support on this basis as much as on the basis of their following the Sharīᶜa to a letter. However, this means that when these banks turn out to be less than successful—not least because the system itself is partly similar to that on which pyramid selling is based; they can only function well if there is a continuous surplus of new deposits —the support may quickly fade away.

and adaptations of concepts from the Sharīʿa's rules on trade, some of which are only a camouflage for taking interest while avoiding the name, but also in the process changing the way the banks function.

The central element is that the bank and the customer enter into some form of partnership, where they share a risk, instead of the customer either paying or receiving an interest rate that is determined in advance. There are three main methods for this:[9]

— *Muḍāraba*, or 'sleeping partnership', is the most ideal way for an Islamic bank to give a 'loan'. Rather than the customer borrowing a sum of money to invest in an enterprise and later repaying that with a fixed surplus, the bank may participate in the enterprise. In this 'partnership' the bank participates with the capital (the loan), while the customer puts in his labour and competence. Then the two parties share the profit that the enterprise has produced over a particular period of time, at the end of which the bank receives its part, which includes its original investment, and the customer takes the remainder of the profit.

The same principle runs in reverse for deposits in the bank. It is in this case the customer that 'invests' in the bank, and after a specified time receives his part of the bank's profits. This surplus on the capital (the deposit) does not have a predetermined rate, so the customer does not know how much he will receive every year. But the deposit itself is normally guaranteed, so he does not risk losing the money he deposited.

This refers to savings or investment accounts. Islamic banks also have normal current accounts for immediate use, as other modern banks, but they are normally without any interest or surplus paid to the customer, but also without any fees paid by him.

— *Mushāraka* is another investment form, where two or more partners (the bank and the customer, thus as a 'limited company') each invest their share in an enterprise, and then share the profit in a pre-established manner; thus a more direct support from the bank to an enterprise.

9 Endre Stiansen, 'Islamic banking in the Sudan: Aspects of the laws and the debate', in Stiansen and Jane I. Guyer (ed.), *Credit, Currencies and Culture: African Financial Institutions in Historical Perspective*, Uppsala 1999, 100-17, and Timur Kuran, 'The economic system in contemporary Islamic thought: interpretation and assessment', *International Journal of Middle Eastern Studies*, XVIII, 2, 1986, 149-58.

— *Murābaḥa*, a sales agreement, is one of the most dubious methods to avoid the ban on interest, but also by far the most common. The theory is that the bank buys an object from the customer at a determined price, and then later sells the object back to him for a higher price. The bank does not need to take delivery of the object, and purchase price, sales price and time period are all determined in advance. It is thus a *ḥīla*, a legal fiction which covers that this is actually a loan against interest: the bank gives the customer a sum of money, and later receives it back with an addition that is decided in advance. Still this form of loan is accepted as a part of the Islamic banking system.

These Islamic banks were established particularly in the Gulf countries in the 1970s, either privately or with state support, but have spread to many other countries.[10] Three countries have made them into public policy: Pakistan, Iran and Sudan. Interest is forbidden in all banks in these three countries, so they are required to organize deposits and loans, primarily according to the *muḍāraba* principle. Islamic banks in other countries are mostly private, and often linked to Islamist currents, often also financed by rich investors from the Gulf.

The system thus works, but has evident weaknesses. The most important is perhaps that many of these countries suffer from severe inflation. An interest-giving bank can compensate for this by raising the interest rate, but this is not possible in a system where the income is to accrue from the profits of an enterprise. Another problem is that this system assumes that loans are given to profit-giving activities. A loan to cover the customer's consumption does not give any profit that can be shared. Some suggest that such loans must then be given without any demands of remuneration beyond the amount loaned. But this will be particularly problematic in an inflation-driven economy, so other solutions will have to be found. It is thus unclear to what extent these Islamic banks will be forced into functioning in the same way as traditional ones, perhaps only with a cosmetic name change to avoid calling what it is given and taken 'interest'.

10 In some Gulf countries Islamic banks could get tax exemption which made them more competitive against normal banks.

Ḥawāla

Another function of banks is to transmit money, what we know as giro or bank transfers: Peter who has $100 in his bank sends to John a statement that he may withdraw this amount in the same or co-operating bank, to cover a debt that Peter has to John. Muslim societies, which from the earliest times carried out trade over huge distances, had a similar system that has partly been private and informal, and which still functions in situations where the banks are not trusted or functional. It is called *ḥawāla*, change or exchange, and is regulated in the Sharīᶜa.[11]

The principle is this: Zayd, a man of means who lives in Timbuktu, owes the trader ᶜAmr 1,000 dirham. Rather than paying him the money, he gives him a written note saying, 'You, Ḥasan of Cairo, owe me, Zayd, 1,000 dirham. Please gives this amount to ᶜAmr'. ᶜAmr can then travel to Cairo with this piece of paper rather than carrying any money, thereby avoiding being robbed by thieves for his capital along the way. In Cairo, he receives the money from Ḥasan in return for Zayd's declaration. Ḥasan will then reduce the amount he owes Zayd by 1,000 dirham, or—if he actually does not owe him anything—establish a new credit of 1,000 dirham, to be repaid in another later transaction going in the other direction. Thus the trader may even send money without travelling himself; ᶜAmr can purchase this declaration from the financier Zayd in Timbuktu and then send the paper with a traveller to his cousin in Cairo, who then 'withdraws' the money from Ḥasan.[12]

This system is based on trust between the parties involved, in particular between the financiers Zayd and Ḥasan, and of course on the existence of enough commerce between the towns involved that the sums equal out over time. It was a very common form of transaction, and such lines of trust could be strengthened

11 Schacht, *Introduction*, 148-9, and Doi, *Sharīᶜah*, 359.

12 This system is in extensive usage today, in particular where the banks have ceased to function, as in Somalia; it is the most common way for Somalis abroad to send money home. This has in very recent years led to US and European suspicion that it is used to finance Islamist groups, or to launder money from organized crime. The problem is of course that the system is informal and that governments tend to be worried about transactions they cannot control. *Ḥawāla* is also used in many other Muslim countries as a private alternative to a bureaucratic, expensive and perhaps corrupt or quite simply capital-deficient banking system.

either by kinship or by other types of network, such as Sufi brotherhoods or other links that joined the parties involved.

Taxes

We have so far discussed rules that are either practised or are at least attempts at adapting legal practices to an Islamic ideal. But it is not difficult to see economic areas where the Islamic ideals have had little or no relation to what actually transpired. Here it is the jurists who have by various intricate stratagems tried to make practice fit a theory that became further and further removed from its origin, while at the same time never quite caught up with the reality on the ground. The most evident example of this is perhaps the Sharīᶜa's relation to taxation.

The Muslim rulers were of course in need of income from the start, and imposed taxes more or less according to need without much consideration of the rules for proper taxation that was under formulation in the Sharīᶜa. They may at best have used the names of the Sharīᶜa's taxation scheme, but changed its content and extent to what they required and what the economy at any moment could support.

However, the early jurists were still serious in their endeavours to establish what the imam or sultan could justly collect, and works on taxation are among the earliest legal works we have.[13] However, there was little development from these early works (written probably mostly in the ninth century) until the eighteenth century, when some jurists took up the effort to give an ideological justification for the taxes that the sultans of that time were actually imposing. They created a set of concepts that were apparently based on the early works and formulated so that the current taxes of their time should appear as the realization of that system. But what they came up with was in reality neither in conformity with the original categories nor with the actual practices of their own time. Thus this became a third, intermediary level in the abstraction, which makes it even more complicated to decide what is 'really' the Islamic law of taxation.

13 Such as *Kitāb al-Kharāj* by Abū Yūsuf, one of the founders of the Ḥanafī school, but several other early authors wrote similar works; Calder, *Studies*, 105-60.

But if we are to distil some of the basic elements from the Islamic tax laws, without going too far into detail of what was and was not practised at each particular epoch, we may divide them into two; religiously based taxes and taxes on land.

In the Islamic state Muslims must pay a tax, *zakāt*, from which non-Muslims are exempt, while the latter (the *dhimmīs*) on the other hand pay a tax, *jizya*, that is for them alone.[14] The *zakāt* or charity tax is a religious duty and one of the five 'pillars' of the Islamic faith. It is a property tax that is paid on 'productive property', that is such commodities or possessions that may generate income: capital in the form of gold and silver (the monetary metals),[15] trade goods, some agricultural products[16] and domestic animals,[17] but not fixed property. The poor, who are to receive charity from the *zakāt* do of course not have to pay this tax. While the Sunnī schools have slightly differing rules in how the *zakāt* should be calculated, the Shīᶜīs say that one should pay one fifth of all income from trade (*khums*).

The rules for how the *zakāt* money should be spent are clear: it should go to the poor and to religious purposes. Some therefore say that it is the religious scholars who must take care of collecting and disposing of this tax. This is particularly clear in Shīᶜī practice, where the *khums* amount may be considerable; this goes directly to the *ᶜulamāᵓ* and ensures their economic independence from the state. In so far as the *zakāt* has been a separate tax in Sunnī countries, it has mostly been the state that has collected and used the money without too much interference from outsiders regarding how this was done. *Zakāt* has in the modern period in

14 According to Ḥanafī, Shāfiᶜī and Ḥanbalī law. The Mālikīs and the Shīᶜīs also impose *zakāt* on *dhimmīs*.

15 Beyond a reasonable minimum. The rate is just over two per cent. The Shīᶜīs say today that one should pay *khums* (20 per cent) on all profit that one gains in currency over a year (that is, all expansion of the capital), while the Sunnī schools limit *zakāt* to what is owned in the metals gold and silver; *EI* (2), 'Zakāt', and Calder, 'Khums' and 'Zakāt'.

16 With a different percentage depending on whether the products are grown on naturally or artificially irrigated land (lower in the latter case). The schools have different rules for what kind of products generate *zakāt*, but the average rate is about one tenth of what has ever been produced.

17 Camels, cattle, goats and sheep, but not horses or donkeys; that is, those animals that 'produce' saleable commodities such as wool, meat or milk.

some countries been collected as part of the regular state taxes.[18] In other cases, private Islamic or semi-state bodies may request *zakāt* as voluntary contributions from the believers for welfare purposes such as private schools, health care and similar.

Jizya is a poll tax[19] which denotes the *dhimmī*'s acceptance of Muslim rule. It is a condition for non-Muslims receiving the protection granted by the Sharīᶜa—in fact, for their being allowed to live in the Muslim state at all—that they pay *jizya* to the sultan. The exact form of this tax was not initially clear. It was in the early period often confused with the land tax *kharāj*, and the early caliphs were faced with the economic consequences of Christians converting to Islam and thus escaping the *jizya*. The two taxes were therefore later clearly separated from each other, and *jizya* made into a pure tax on persons, for example put at two dinars a year for each adult free male.[20]

Land tax and property rights

Thus both the Muslim *zakāt* and the non-Muslim *jizya* came to be imposed on individuals. Two other types of taxes were put on land, and their history is closely linked to the development of agriculture, and in particular to how the ownership of land property was conceived; if the peasant who cultivated the land owned it, or rented it, or was hired as a labourer on another man's land. Unfortunately all these concepts are mixed together in something that looks like complete chaos, where the main principle appears to be that one party cultivated the land and one or

18 Saudi Arabia, Libya, Yemen, Malaysia, Pakistan and Sudan; *EI* (2), 'Zakāt'. Each of these countries has its own rules for size, collection and distribution of the tax, but some, such as Libya, set aside a particular percentage for the poor; others (Yemen) let the believers distribute part of the *zakāt* privately. Malaysia replaces the *zakāt* with a tax of a similar size for non-Muslim citizens.

19 A tax paid according to the number of individuals, not income or economic activity.

20 Thus in Egypt from the Abbasid period and later; *EI* (2), 'Djizya'. The tax was not imposed on women, children, the elderly or slaves, and only on residents, not travellers (such as Christian traders). Of course, any tax that was imposed on non-Muslims could be called *jizya*, whatever its size or shape. This was an important potential source of income for the rulers in the first centuries when the Christians were in the majority in Egypt, Syria and Andalus, but it lost much of its importance as the Muslims came to constitute the vast majority in these lands.

more others expropriated a part of its income, while the legal issues of what was actually owned seems to have been of less immediate importance. Thus, it would appear that most of these terms are used interchangeably in the sources without much care.

However, if we go to the theory as it was expounded in the ninth century, we will find that it involved two clear categories, *ᶜushr*, 'dime' and *kharāj*, 'tribute'. The distinction was, as with *zakāt* versus *jizya*, based on religion: Muslims paid *ᶜushr*, non-Muslims paid *kharāj*, which should thus be a higher rate.

This was based on the history of the Muslim conquest of Syria, Iraq and Iran in the seventh century.[21] There were then two categories of land. One was that of owners who had accepted the new rulers and declared their obedience as *dhimmīs*. They were allowed to keep their land, against payment of a *kharāj* tribute to the state. Other land did not have legitimate users, either because it was plantation land owned by the former rulers or because the owners had been killed in battle against the Muslims. The caliph took this land and shared it out to the conquering Muslims, against payment of a fee of one tenth of the produce, a 'dime' or *ᶜushr*.

Both types of land were owned by their users and the difference lay only in the owner's religion, Muslim or non-Muslim. However, the caliph soon faced the problem that many *dhimmīs* converted to Islam, or sold their land to Muslim owners. That would mean that the income would drop if the tax was to continue to follow the owner's religion and thus be reduced to the lower *ᶜushr* rate. So it was soon decided that this was not practical. The two types of tax were instead fixed to the land, not to the users: A Muslim who bought *kharāj* land from a Christian still had to pay *kharāj*, irrespective of his own beliefs.[22] The religious dimension was thus soon lost, and the two became quite simply two different types of agricultural land with different tax rates.[23]

21 Baber Johansen, *The Islamic Law on Land Tax and Rent: The Peasants' Loss of Property Rights as Interpreted in the Hanafite Legal Literature of the Mamluk and Ottoman Periods*, London 1988, and Imber, *Ebu's-Su'ud*, 115-22.

22 This was only true in this direction. *ᶜUshr* land that in some ways fell under the criteria for *kharāj*, e.g. if a non-Muslim acquired it, was reclassified to *kharāj* for eternity.

23 Thus the distinction came to fade away in practical use; an author could write '*kharāj*, that is *ᶜushr*' as the two terms were synonymous; a tax

The transition was more marked as far as the conception of ownership was concerned. The users, who had been considered owners of their land, were increasingly seen as peasants or sharecroppers who cultivated someone else's land, either that of an absentee landowner, the state or other notables. This seems to have happened gradually, as part of a reduction of the peasant's status in society, not through any sudden or conscious decision to change land ownership.

One way this could often happen was, from the tenth century onwards, through the process of tax collection. The sultan could give a trusted solider or follower the privilege of collecting land tax from a certain area or region. This 'tax lord', *muqāṭa*ᶜ,[24] was then allowed to keep a part of what he collected as his income. It was, formally, still the peasant who paid the tax: the tax lord only collected it and passed it on.[25] But in reality this appeared to be more and more like two different processes: the peasant's payment to the lord came to be seen as a rent for being allowed to farm, while the tax lord's payment of taxes to the sultan became a separate relation between the lord and his ruler; the sultan was no longer concerned with the relation between peasant and tax lord. The lord could sell or inherit this right to collect money, so that one person could accumulate larger and larger 'taxation rights'. Thus they could develop into large agricultural units that the lord passed on to his descendants, and he became a landlord whose

---

which only varied according to region and type of land.

24 The system was called *iqṭā*ᶜ or 'tax farming'. Its form changed over time; it was in one period a form of wages for the soldiers who then collected the taxes over a region that was not strictly delimited; *EI* (2), 'Iḳṭāᶜ'. The system was called *iltizām* in the Ottoman period, and this became the most common term; a related purely Ottoman system of allotting land was *ṭimar*. It was probably only in the Ottoman period that the *iqṭā*ᶜ*/iltizām* system as we know it was fully developed. It was mostly abolished in the course of the nineteenth century.

25 Or in advance; thus the tax lord first paid the sultan a fixed amount for his domain, and then collected the money from the peasants afterwards; *EI* (2), 'Mültezim'. The tax lord could in some periods decide for himself how much he wanted to take from the peasants, and any peasant who was not able to pay was not allowed to leave the property; thus a form of bondage. The sultan later demanded the right to confirm such changes in the rate, or could be subject to a legal establishment of 'fair rent'. A tax lord who could not pay his duty to the sultan was dispossessed of his land, which was then given out to another tax lord; Imber, *Ebu's-Su'ud*, 126.

land was cultivated by dependant peasants.

But each plot of land could also pass in inheritance from a user (peasant) to his descendants, and he could sell it to others, apparently without asking his landlord's permission. This was explained so that it was the 'right to use the land', not the ownership itself, that the peasant sold (while what the tax lord had sold had been the 'right to tax the land').

The Ottoman period saw a further twist. The sultan now declared that all land was in fact state land, *miri* land.[26] This was again not based on any juridical basis, but only a result of how the land was viewed in society at that time, and on the sultan's power to make such a declaration. Thus it was up to the jurists to try to find some legal justification for this view. They did this by going back to the original meaning of *ᶜushr* and *kharāj*, which was that the caliph had handed out certain areas of land to his followers.

There had at that time also existed fallow or unused land where the original owner was still alive or not officially declared dead. The caliph had also shared this land out to new users as *ᶜushr* or *kharāj* land, but he could not give them the ownership right, as the owner still legally existed. So what he had distributed was only the right to use the land. The legal owners must, however, have disappeared since that time, and it was the community, represented by the sultan, who had thus inherited the legal ownership of this land. And, said the jurists, this must have transpired for all land at some point or other in the many centuries that had followed. Thus all land must at some point have lain fallow at which point the sultan had acquired and kept the ownership rights, while the right to use had been given to new users—unless the current owners or users could present documentary proof to the contrary. Most land had by this time in any case become *iqṭāᶜ* land, and the tax lords had certainly received their privileges form the sultan.

This legal discussion did not have all that much importance for the actual users, the peasants. In both cases the sultan demanded his taxes from the tax lord / landlord, and he took his income

26 The sultan Mehmed II made such a declaration for all land in the empire in 1470. The only way to avoid this was to present legal proof of original ownership, which few could for land that had been in the family for centuries. For *waqf* land, see below; Johansen, *Islamic Law on Land Tax and Rent*, 81, and Imber, *Ebu's-Su'ud*, 120.

from the peasants, whatever name it had. As long as he was allowed to cultivate the land, and his sons could inherit it from him, it was less important for the peasant whether it was the 'ownership' or 'right to use' that he disposed over. What mattered for him was his exact relation to his landlord (the *muqāṭaʿ*).

This could be of two different kinds. Either the peasant was a *tenant*, who rented the land from the landlord and paid a fixed rent for it, or he was a *sharecropper*, who had [in theory] been placed on the land by the landlord in order to cultivate it and kept one portion of the produce as his income. The difference thus lay in how the payment was calculated: the rent paid by the tenant was independent of the size of each year's crop, while that paid by the sharecropper was relative to the crop. So it could, in a good year, be more profitable to be a tenant, as the surplus over the expected produce was his alone, while it would be preferable to be a sharecropper in a bad year, as the landlord and peasant then shared the deficit below the expected yield.[27] Evidently the key factor was how much the sharecropper was expected to give; this could vary from one piece of land to the next, but the most common was probably one half of the produce for either party.[28]

The landlord need not be a person. A large part of the agricultural land was linked to *waqf* endowments (see below), either as land directly owned by mosques or other religious institutions, or as land being administered by *qāḍī*s on behalf of other *waqf*s. All of this was cultivated by peasants as sharecroppers or tenants. It was the profits it yielded that kept the mosques and religious scholars alive or was given to the needy who were the beneficiaries of the *waqf* grant.

27 The agreement could also specify that the peasant had rented animals, seed grain etc. for a fixed amount, so that a sharecropper could also come into deficit and have debt to the landlord in the same way as a tenant. The contract could state that the peasant should do labour for the landlord, but also conversely that the landlord (e.g. a *waqf*) should maintain the house or similar in order, or that the peasant could perform this work at the landlord's expense.

28 This is taken from the modern period in Yemen; William J. Donaldson, *Sharecropping in the Yemen: A Study in Islamic Theory, Custom and Pragmatism*, Leiden 2000, 143-4. It is of course impossible to calculate a general average valid for Muslim history across time and space, but it is fair to assume that the division has varied according to how fertile each plot was.

Both tenancy and sharecropping created problems for the jurists. The Ḥanafīs were of the opinion that land could not be rented or sold, because a plot of land is not an object. They solved this by saying that the rights of usage may, however, be made the object of a contract, and that this may then be sold. The jurists established a 'fair rent' for the land, based partly on custom (*ᶜurf*) of the locality for that type of land. The landlord was not allowed to exceed this fair rent.[29]

Sharecropping was more problematic, since it went against the ban on 'risk'; neither party knew before the harvesting what the payment was going to be. This legal problem could be circumvented by seeing these contracts as a 'partnership' (*muḍāraba*) between the landlord and the peasant, thus the jurists looked carefully at what each party provided for the 'partnership'. The most important types of partnership were *muzāraᶜa* of land that is sown annually, *mughārasa* of land that is not sown (orchards, perennial bushes, etc.), and *musāqā* of irrigated land. The last type is seen by the jurists as a case where the landlord hires the peasant to perform a task, and this is an acceptable partnership. The landlord providing the bushes or trees and the peasant providing the labour, is also acceptable as partnership; they share the risk of a bad year. But if the peasant provides both the labour and the seed for a land that is sown, it cannot be considered an equitable partnership. The *muzāraᶜa* type is therefore disapproved of in most schools, but later Ḥanafīs accepted it under *istiḥsān*; adaptations to practice. The Shāfiᶜīs only accept the last type, *musāqa* of irrigated land. The other schools are less strict. But the reality is probably that all types of contracts were used, even in those areas dominated by the Shāfiᶜī school.

Waqf

One important type of agricultural land was the 'beneficial endowments'. *Waqf, ḥubus, ṣadaqa, rizqa* are different more or less synonymous terms for such endowments.[30] A *waqf* is a gift to

29 Johansen, *Islamic Law on Land Tax and Rent*, 111-13.

30 Tyan, *Histoire*, 375-84, and Yitzhak Reiter, 'Family *waqf* entitlements in British Palestine (1917-1948)', *Islamic Law and Society*, II, 2, 1995, 174-93. Cf. also Randi Deguilhem (ed.), *Le Waqf dans l'espace islamique: outil*

God for the benefit of a charitable purpose. That is, the item that is donated is to belong to God, but whatever it yields goes to the purpose indicated by the donation. Thus a *waqf* is more important if it consists of something that produces a yield of some sort. He who donates such a gift may freely decide what that purpose should be in a *waqf* document (*waqfīya*), and the 'needy' recipient may be whoever or whatever he wishes.

A *waqf* should preferably be an object of lasting value, such as land or buildings, but may also be other things. One may donate a book or a manuscript as *waqf* to a mosque, for the use of students or scholars in the memory of the founder. Money may also be accepted as *waqf*; it should then be used productively in the same way as land, and it was the profit earned from whatever the money was invested in that was given to the beneficiary.[31]

*Waqf*s may be divided into two kinds. One is what we may call 'public *waqf*s', *waqf khayrī*, which are for the benefit of the poor, or more commonly for religious purposes. Mosque buildings are normally themselves *waqf*s, and agricultural land given as *waqf* is the most widespread source of income for the scholars. A *waqf* is eternal: whenever you give something to God, it is for ever. Thus such donations tend to accumulate; new gifts are added to whatever exists from before. They may thus as centuries go by grow into very significant amounts of property, in particular landed property.[32] *Waqf*s may be given by commoners, but it was particularly common that prominent men and families, including governors or sultans, gave such endowments, and often on a very large scale. This was of course a way to establish social status, in addition to the pious purpose.[33]

---

de pouvoir socio-politique, Damascus 1995, and Richard Leeuwen, *Waqfs and Urban Structures: The Case of Ottoman Damascus*, Leiden 1999.

31 Money *waqf*s were not uncontroversial, but they were the most common form of *waqf* in Istanbul in the sixteenth century; Leeuwen, *Waqfs and Urban Structures*, 110.

32 Almost all cultivated land in Syria in the Ottoman period was in the form of *waqf*s (Leeuwen, *Waqfs and Urban Structures*, 162), and this is probably not untypical for most Ottoman regions. Elsewhere, as in parts of Muslim Africa, the *waqf* system is unknown, but other forms of endowments such as *ṣadaqa* may fill the same function.

33 Leeuwen considers that such *waqf*s, by their great economic potential, could be used as economic incentives during economic depressions; *Waqfs and Urban Structures,* 146.

The other type of *waqf* is when the 'needy' are the founder's own family, such as his descendants, *waqf ahlī*. A man may give all or a part of what he owns to his descendants in general or to specified descendants and their line, in perpetuity. Such *waqf*s are often very specific regarding who is and who is not to be included among the beneficiaries, often detailing several generations down.[34] Thus the founder may determine who is to benefit from his property and the income that comes from it in his own lifetime, and who may transfer their rights to their children again. It is typical that female relatives are included in the first generation, while their descendants are excluded.[35] The founder is again quite free to determine how he wants the system to work.

He may, however, not make himself the beneficiary of his own donation. But it is possible to circumvent this by writing 'my father's eldest son and his successors', without mentioning the name. This solution is accepted by the Ḥanafīs, while the Mālikīs and other scholars reject it.

The motivation for setting up a *waqf* may be truly religious, even for a family *waqf*. To transfer the ownership of one's property to God may be rewarded in the hereafter, and it is both a religious and a moral duty to provide for one's own family as much as for the poor and needy.

The *waqf* system may also have two other, more prosaic, effects: The *waqf*s, being the property of God, are exempt from certain taxes.[36] It may thus be a useful way to perform tax

34 *Waqf* rules differ from inheritance in that the latter is divided directly on the basis of relations as they are at the time of death, while a *waqf* may have different rules for successive generations; Aharon Layish, 'The family waqf and the *sharʿī* law of succession in modern times', *Islamic Law and Society*, IV, 3, 1997, 384.

35 See above, Chapter 15.

36 *Waqf* land does however mostly pay *kharāj*, and is in fact the greatest contributor to this tax; Johansen, *Islamic Law on Land Tax and Rent*, 116. The prerequisite for giving something as *waqf* is that one owns it, and if the state has claimed property right of land, as we saw the Ottomans did, the peasant or landlord cannot give it as *waqf*. However, this could be solved by saying that it was not the property right, but the right of *usage*, which the user 'owned', that he gave away, and it was of course usage that provided the proceeds that went to the beneficiaries. (The 'real owner', the sultan, could in that case demand that he had the right to vet such *waqf*s; Imber, *Ebu's-Su'ud*, 120.) But the *kharāj* tax is linked to the land, not to the right of usage.

planning. They are furthermore not subject to the rigorous inheritance laws of the Sharīᶜa, laws that are often practised and put severe limitations on how a person may divide his property among his relatives. Beyond the third that he may give to someone who is *not* in the line of inheritance, he has no influence whatever on how his property is shared out when he is gone. But a donation that is made while he himself is alive is not affected by this. So he may escape the inheritance laws by making the donation as a *waqf* while still alive, and then writing in the *waqfīya* that the income should be shared in the manner he actually wants.

One element here may be to avoid undue division of agricultural plots, which may become impossibly small if they were to be subject to the Sharīᶜa's rules of tiny inheritance fractions. Making them into a *waqf* ensures that the land itself remains unified, while the income is still shared among the relatives.

This need not, however, be the most important motivation.[37] Informal agreements may be just as efficient in avoiding undesired fractioning of the land, by smaller inheritors relinquishing their rights in favour of for example the elder son or whoever they agree should farm the land. The *waqf* system may rather be used to provide for heirs that fall totally outside the Sharīᶜa's inheritance system, such as orphans brought into the family,[38] who are not included in the formal system. But there are evidently may different reasons for and types of *waqf* according to the social context and the customs that exist.

A founder has to nominate a caretaker for the *waqf*, a *mutawallī* who is responsible for its upkeep, so that the beneficiaries gain the best possible benefit from it. If the caretaker finds that the land is no longer productive or optimally exploited, he may exchange it for another (*istibdāl*). This could be an important aspect of the development of *waqf*s, and the Ottoman sultan demanded that all such exchanges should be confirmed by the state as a method to gain control over the *waqf*s.[39]

The founder may nominate himself as caretaker, but is as such under the general supervision of the *qāḍī*, who represents the

37 Reiter, 'Family *waqf* entitlements', 192-3, from Palestine in the nineteenth century.

38 Formal adoption as such is not recognized, as it is considered to be forbidden by K 33:4.

39 Leeuwen, *Waqfs and urban structures,* 108 & 159-62.

community interest. The *qāḍī* should ensure that the wording of the endowment is satisfied and that the beneficiaries actually get the funds they are entitled to, and that the *waqf* is maintained in the best possible way to give profit, and to ensure that buildings are kept up, and that agricultural lands are cultivated for the good of the beneficiaries.

A *qāḍī* may replace a *mutwallī* who does not perform his duties with another at his discretion, even when it is the founder who is the caretaker. The *qāḍī* thus has a real responsibility for the best possible maintenance of the *waqf*, and he may accept changes that are contrary to the wording of the *waqfīya*, if changed conditions make this necessary to improve the yield; such as exchanging land for land or modifying the *waqfīya*'s specifications for how the capital should be used.

As the number of *waqf*s grew, this started to amount to a considerable amount of work. Thus there were already in the tenth century or earlier established specific aides to the *qāḍī* whose task was to supervise the *waqf*s. These were centralized into offices in the main cities or the capitals, but were in principle still manned by qualified *qāḍī*s who had specialized in this line of work. Under the Ottomans and later this administration was appropriated by the state and eventually became centralized directorates. These offices supervised *waqf* properties, which included among many other things those mosques that were held as *waqf*.

Thus it became an important economic and political objective for the state or sultan to keep control over and also limit the size or amount of the *waqf*s. They reduced the state's income, as they were exempt from certain taxes or could otherwise escape the state's control. They also gave the *ᶜulamāʾ* an independent economic basis, which of course made it easier for them to function as a focus of opposition to the sultan, if a conflict were to arise.

There was thus an eternal rivalry between the state and the scholars over the *waqf*s, where the state, when it had the strength, tried to limit and declassify or nationalize *waqf*s. They could impound those that were no longer maintained productively, or try to take direct control over the mosques, furiously opposed by the *ᶜulamāʾ*. The reformer Muḥammad ᶜAlī of Egypt was one of those who were successful in this, when he abolished and redistributed the *iqṭāʾ*, much of which was in the form of *waqf*, and also pulled in those *waqf*s that were undocumented or 'unconfirmed' since they had existed for centuries and both documents and witnesses were long gone and forgotten.[40] However, he was neither the first nor the last ruler to fight over the *waqf*s.

Today almost all public *waqf*s are bureaucratized in the modern nation states, many of them administered by separate ministries (*wizārat al-awqāf*), while some Muslim countries[41] still recognize the family *waqf*s.

40 Afaf Lutfi al-Sayyid Marsot, *Egypt in the Reign of Muhammad Ali*, Cambridge 1984, 44, 143-4, and Delanoue, *Moralistes et politiques musulmans*, 59. About one fifth of all agricultural land in Egypt was then *waqf*.

41 Not, however, Egypt, Syria or Libya among others.

CONCLUSION

The aim of this book is to indicate how the Sharīᶜa has developed out of a dynamic between religion and state, both as to how it was conceived in theory and how it was practised in court. We have suggested that this dynamic is fundamental for understanding both the Sharīᶜa and how Islamic society has changed over time.

We have seen how in the initial period of Islamic history the conception grew that the guidelines of behaviour in the new Muslim society had to be found in God's revelation, as expressed in the Koran and *sunna*. This gave the law a reference and an authority that went beyond the individual town and region. It made the law into a unifying factor for an Islamic world community that quickly fell apart into competeing political entities. The Sharīᶜa and the class of *ᶜulamāʾ* that formulated it was what made it possible to consider this an 'Islamic world' and not just a confusion of petty sultanates ruled by rival princes. It gave the community a common frame of reference so that 'civil society' could function across political boundaries, both in terms of trade and in other ways. The rules for interaction were known and shared across continents and did not change even if one sultan conquered the domains of his neighbour.

The reason the Sharīᶜa could play this unifying role was that it had already at the outset freed itself from the state and political power. But although the law could thus become 'parastatal', the courts could not. The state and the sultan was still the institution that had and must have the monopoly of legitimate use of force, and thus also the application of the laws.

This created a potential split between the law and its court, one belonging to 'civil society', the other to the 'state'. We have seen that this dichotomy was partly expressed in the division of the scholars of law into two categories, or rather two functions, one an 'independent' *muftī*, the other a 'state-appointed' *qāḍī*. Similarly we saw from the early period a split between two types of courts, a 'Sharīᶜa court' or '*qāḍī*'s court' where the letter and procedures of the Sharīᶜa were always dominant, and one or more 'sultan's courts' or '*siyāsa* courts' where the Sharīᶜa was more of an inspiration and general reference that might be ignored if need arose.

This situation also had consequences for the Sharīᶜa. As criminal cases tended to go more and more to the *siyāsa* courts, the Sharīᶜa courts found their most important function as a forum for conflict resolution in private disputes of various kinds. The rules of procedure of the Sharīᶜa made it in many ways badly suited to functioning effectively as a basis for a criminal court, and there was little social pressure to develop those parts of the law to make it more practicable, for example in achieving convictions, as the implementation of criminal law could be filled by separate *siyāsa* courts instead.

We can see this dichotomy already in the early period of the caliphate. As time passed the emphasis in this relationship shifted continuously in favour of the state. In the medieval period the sultans had already started to interfere with the 'civilian' side of the equation by appointing *muftī*s and linking some of them to the courts. The Ottomans took major steps in this direction when they made the *muftī*s, in particular at the higher level, state employees fully integrated into the state, and formulated laws in the form of *kanun* that in effect were state laws independent of the Sharīᶜa. The sultan had thus collected the legal power in his hands. There was no longer any reason to maintain the distinction between Sharīᶜa courts and sultan's courts, and the sultan unified all courts into one, under the authority of the *qāḍī*. The *qāḍī* was now fully the servant of the sultan and both he and the *muftī* had to give verdicts based the *kanun*, which included the Sharīᶜa, but expressed in a form acceptable to the sultan.

Or at least in the central regions, where the power of the sultan was strongest. Earlier practices were maintained to a greater degree in the provinces, not least because there was here a difference between the 'state's *madhhab*', the Ḥanafīya, and 'the people's *maddhab*', that might be Mālikī, Shāfiᶜī or another. That made it more difficult to merge all law into one court.

Thus colonialism and the modern states that followed it did not represent as clear a rupture with the past as one might have supposed. The state remained, as it had been under the Ottomans, the master and final authority for the law, but still allowed elements of the Sharīᶜa to function in various ways. In most Muslim countries there is still both a dichotomy between 'state law' and an independent 'Sharīᶜa' and—as under the medieval *siyāsa*—a merger of them through the incorporation of Sharīᶜa-based rules into the codified laws of the state. The radical Islamists of today are not capable of breaking out of this model. Their answer is simply to expand the influence of the Sharīᶜa rules on the national codified state laws of each country, a *siyāsa* concept where the state defines the Sharīᶜa. Some symbolic rules like the *ḥudūd* and restrictions on women are introduced into their *siyāsa*. But the main body of law may not be dramatically different in those countries such as Iran that have passed through an Islamic 'revolution' and those that have not, be they traditional shaykhdoms like Kuwait or 'modernist' states like Egypt and Jordan. Only Saudi Arabia has maintained a system resembling the classical Sharīᶜa, where it is the *ᶜulamāʾ* and not the king who have legal authority. But this may be an unstable exception to the rule.

Does this mean that the Sharīᶜa has a future? It probably has for as long as many, perhaps most, Muslims see in it an inspiration or a pattern of behaviour. But the fact that it is so flexible also means that it is subject to the dynamics of history. The impetus of the Islamists and their clamour for the Sharīᶜa is of course the result of wider historical and social developments of the last generation. This has made them emphasize the 'anti-modern' elements and understanding of the Sharīᶜa, as an attack on the current 'modernist' and 'immoral' regimes in the Muslim world. If this historical development were to turn in the future, then the content of the Sharīᶜa could also be perceived differently, as it was in the first half of the twentieth century, when there were only few protests against the revisions of the Sharīᶜa-based family laws. The Sharīᶜa is God's eternal law for the Muslims, as expressed in the Revelation and in the legal literature based on it. But it is also and at the same time that which the Muslims believe that the Sharīᶜa should be. This paradox also contains the key to the future of the Sharīᶜa.

GLOSSARY

The following is a compilation of technical terms and concepts used in the text, with the original meaning in the source language (if relevant). The terms are all of Arabic origin when not otherwise indicated (Turk.: Turkish, Pers.: Persian, Ar.: Arabic). The plural form (pl.) or singular (sing.) is also indicated when it differs markedly from the form given. Words noted as synonymous (syn.) or nearly synonymous will often have nuances in technical usage, but may also be used interchangeably in the literature.

adab al-qāḍī	'mirror of judges', literary genre that presents the correct behaviour for *qāḍ*īs. Similar for *muftī*s is *adab al-muftī*.
adnā	lower, less applicable; in *qiyās* the 'inferior' basis for analogy.
agha	Turk. military title (actually 'chief, Ar. *āghā*).
aḥād	*ḥadīth* that does not have *tawātur* (*q.v.*) certainty, or has an *isnād* (*q.v.*) which has only a single chain of transmitters.
Ahl al-ḥadīth	'Traditionists', name for those who promoted *ḥadīth* as the only guideline for Muslim norms (*ahl*: people, group).
Ahl al-raʾy	name for those who promoted established practice as a basis for the law (cf. *raʾy*).
Akhbārīs	legal-theological current in Shīʿism that emphasized *ḥadīth* (*akhbār*, *q.v. khabar*. Opposite: Uṣūlīs).
alkali	Hausa: judge (from *al-qāḍī.*, *q.v. qāḍī*).
ʿamal	work; here: [legal] practice, custom.
amīr, pl. *umarāʾ*	emir, prince (act. 'ruler', from *amara*, to give order).
ʿāmm	general, unrestricted (a rule that is valid for everyone).
amr	(1) matter, thing (pl. *umūr*); (2) order, decree (pl. *awāmir*. Turk. *emr*, *q.v.*).
amr bi'l-maʿrūf wa-nahy ʿan al-munkar	'to order the good [act. known] and deny the illegal [act. rejected]'; the ruler's religious duty and legitimation.
ʿaqd	contract.
ʿāqila	selection; here: 'solidarity group' that shares in the payment of *diya* compensation (*q.v.*) for involuntary manslaughter or bodily harm.
ʿaql	reason.
ʿaṣaba	group, community; relatives on the masculine side. In inheritance cases those who have a right to the 'residue' after the Koranic shares have been subtrac-

	ted (cf. *farā'iḍ*).
asbāb al-nuzūl	'the reasons for the revelation', the context of a Koran verse or *ḥadīth*.
ashrāf	noble, prominent people; descendants of the Prophet (pl. of *sharīf*).
aṣl	origin, root; in *qiyās* the original case that is mentioned in the revelation Text (pl. *uṣūl*, *q.v. far*ᶜ).
awlā	more suitable, in *qiyās* the 'superior' reason for analogy (from *awwal*, first).
āyat Allāh	ayatollah, Shīᶜī high level scholar (act. 'sign of God').
bāᶜith	motive, in *qiyās* the reason behind a rule (syn. *ᶜilla*, *q.v.*).
bāsh-muftī	Turk., (local) chief *muftī*.
bawwāb	doorman.
bayt al-ṭāᶜa	'house of obedience', judicial command of 'disobedient' wives to remain with husband (Egypt).
bey	Turk. military title. E.g. the title of the factual ruler of Tunisia from 1705 (act. *beg*, Ar. *bāy* or *bēk*).
bidᶜa	deviation from the established doctrine (act. 'novelty', may be 'good' [*bidᶜa ḥasana*], but most often used for objects of criticism).
ḍaᶜīf	weak; on *ḥadīth*: uncertain or not trustworthy.
dalāla, pl. *–āt*	indication, sign, meaning deduced from the text of Revelation, cf. *dalīl*.
dalīl,pl. *adilla/dalā'il*	proof, indication, source in the Revelation text for a rule of law. Also used of the 'four sources', Koran, *sunna*, *qiyās* and *ijmāᶜ*. Cf. *dalāla*.
Dār al-iftā'	the office of *Muftī* of Egypt (from 1895).
dār al-islām	the Muslim world; the part of the world where the Muslims hold power (opposite: *dār al-ḥarb*, the world that is at war with the Muslims, *dār al-ṣulḥ*, the world that has made peace treaties with the Muslims).
ḍarar	harm, cf. *ḍarūra*.
ḍarūra	necessity, syn. *ḥāja*.
dey	Turk. military or official title. Used for factual rulers of Algeria and Tunisia in the sixteenth and seventeenth century respectively (act. *dayı*).
dhimmī	protected people, those of the 'people of the book' (*ahl al-kitāb*) who are permanently resident under Muslim rule. Primarily used for Jews and Christians, also includes Zoroastrians and some other religions.
dīwān	collection. Here the (high) council of a sultan or governor, Turk. *divan*. Also used e.g. of the Ottoman tax offices, and of local police courts in some Ottoman provinces.
dīwān khadīwī	the governor's *maẓālim* court (*q.v.*) in nineteenth-

	century Egypt.
diya	'blood money', a monetary compensation for [involuntary] manslaughter or bodily harm, cf. *ṣulḥ*.
ehl-i örf	Turk., local officials (from Ar. *ahl al-^{c}urf*, 'people of custom).
emr	Turk., decree (from Ar. *amr*, *q.v.*).
encümen-i âli	Turk., Ottoman legislative assembly (reformist, 1840s. From Pers. *anjuman*, assembly, Ar. *^{c}ālī*, high).
faqīh, pl. *fuqahāʾ*	jurist, scholar specialised in *fiqh* (*q.v.*). In Iran, 1979, title of the 'Leader', the highest religious-political office in the country.
far^{c}	branch, in *qiyās* the derived case which is 'analogous' to the original (*aṣl*, *q.v.* Pl.: *furu^{c}*, *q.v.*).
farāʾiḍ	duties. Also: those parts of the inheritance that are regulated by the Koranic verses. Also used of the inheritance laws in general (pl. of *farḍ*, *q.v.*).
farḍ	duty. Here what is compulsory for the believer (equal to *wājib*). Pl. *farāʾiḍ*, *q.v.*
—*farḍ ^{c}aynī*	individual duty, that which every Muslim must do.
—*farḍ kifāʾī*	collective duty, that which the community must ensure is done (act. 'sufficient duty'. Also written *farḍ kifāya*.).
fasād	weakness, incorrectness; here, reason for annulling a marriage (thus close to *faskh*, *q.v.*).
fāsiq	grave sinner. A *f.* cannot give testimony in court (cf. *fisq*).
faskh	annulment; here: dissolution of a marriage because of formal errors in the contract or similar (thus near syn. to *fasād*, *q.v.*).
fatwā, pl. *fatāwā*	statement from a *muftī* (*q.v.*), legal opinion.
fetva emini	Turk., the master of a *fetvahane* (*q.v.*).
fetvahane	Turk., '*fatwā* house', the office of a *muftī*.
fiqh	law, the science of law (act. 'deep understanding').
fisq	grave (religious) sin, injustice.
furū^{c}	the science of the rules of law (the 'branches of law', pl. of *far^{c}*, *q.v.* Opposite: *aṣl*).
futyā	the process of issuing a *fatwā* (*q.v.*).
gharar	'risk'; here: in economic transactions.
gharīb	peculiar, unknown: no longer practised.
ghasb	illegitimate appropriation of someone else's property.
ḥadīth, pl. *aḥādīth*	Tradition of the Prophet, a normative statement about something the prophet Muḥammad said or did (*q.v.* *sunna* (2)).
ḥāja	necessity, syn. *ḍarūra*.
ḥakam, *ḥākim*	middle-man, conciliator, arbitrator; judge (general, also in lower or non-Sharī^{c}a courts, 'justice of the

	peace'); (*ḥākim*, 2), ruler (syn. sultan).
halāl	allowed, not forbidden. Also used for allowed food, thus meat slaughtered according to the religiously prescribed rules.
ḥarām	forbidden, sinful (also holy, protected; related to *ḥaram*, holy place; from this *al-Ḥaramayn*, the 'two holy' [cities] Mecca and Medina, and *ḥarīm*, protected area [of a house: the women's domain]).
ḥasan	good (e.g. of the trustworthiness of a *ḥadīth*).
hatt-ı hümayunhatt-ı şerif	Turk., decree from the Ottoman sultan. Here used of the reform programs from 1839 (*hatt-ı şerif-i Gülhane*; from Ar., *khaṭṭ*, plan, *ḥumā*, defenders, *sharīf*, noble).
ḥawādith	'occurrences'; here: time-limited (not eternal) rules of law.
ḥawāla	referral; here: transmission of money by exchange of letters of credit (also generally; cheque, money order).
ḥisba	accounting; here (1) the ruler's duty to 'command the good' (cf. *amr bi'l-ma^{c}rūf*); (2) an individual's right to try a case on behalf of a collective; (3) *siyāsa* court for the 'public sphere', in particular market-related matters.
ḥiyal	trick; here legal fiction (pl. of *ḥīla*).
ḥubus	endowment, syn. *waqf* (*q.v.*).
ḥudūd	The five rules of law that are specified in the Revelation, pl. of *ḥadd*. Act. 'limit', thus 'God's limits for man'.
hujjat al-islām	Shī^{c}ī mid-level scholar (cf. *mujtahid*. Act. 'proof of Islam').
ḥukm, pl. *aḥkām*	rule of law, verdict (act. 'wisdom, justice').
^{c}ibādāt	religious rules and observances, man's relation to God ('obedience to God').
^{c}idda	a wife's 'waiting period' after a marriage has ended by divorce or death, normally three months' duration.
iḥtiyāṭ	caution (in Shī^{c}ism to avoid actions that may be wrong or be against the will of the *imām*).
ijbār	power, compulsion; here: a father's right to marry off a minor daughter without her consent (syn. *jabr*, *q.v.*).
ijmā^{c}	'consensus', what everyone in a group (all Muslims) are in agreement on.
ijtihād	to develop new rules of law (thus '[re-]interpretation of the sources of law'. Act. 'effort').
ikhtilāf	disagreement among scholars ('difference').
ikhtiyār	[free] choice, to draw principles from other schools into one's own conclusion (cf. *takhyīr*, *takhayyur*).

ikhwān	brotherhood; here used for a political-religious movement in Saudi Arabia which lost a civil war in the 1920s (act. 'brothers', pl. of *akh*).
ilḥād	heresy, syn. *zandaqa* (*q.v.* Koranic).
ᶜilla, pl. *ᶜilal*	the 'effective cause' of a rule of law; the general element that lies behind a rule explicated in Revelation.
ᶜilm, pl. *ᶜulūm*	knowledge, science. Divided into two, *ᶜulūm al-dīn*, the religious sciences (*fiqh*, *tafsīr*, *ḥadīth*, *qq.v.*), and *ᶜulūm al-dunyā*, the worldly sciences. Cf. *ᶜulamāʾ*, scientists, (religious) scholars.
iltizām	tax land, Ottoman name for the *iqṭāᶜ* system (*q.v.*).
imām, pl. *aʾimma*	the one who stands in front, leader. (1) [imam] prayer leader; (2) [*imām*] in Shīᶜism: the divinely inspired descendant of the Prophet who should lead the community of Muslims; (3) in Sunnism: ruler, syn. caliph; (4) one of the founders of the four schools of law ('the four *imāms*', *al-aʾimma al-arbaᶜa*).
iqṭāᶜ	tax land, area where a 'tax lord' could collect tax/rent. Not dissimilar to the 'domain' of medieval Europe.
irtidād	apostasy from Islam (syn. *ridda*, *q.v.*).
isnād, pl. *asānīd*	'chain of authority', list of transmitters who told a *ḥadīth* (*q.v.*) from the first eye witness to the time of writing two centuries later.
istibdāl	exchange; here: of the *waqf* property that is mentioned in the *waqfīya* (*q.v.*) for another to improve profitability.
istidlāl	to form rules of law on the basis of 'indications' (*dalīl*), e.g. through *istiḥsān*, *istiṣlāḥ*, *siyāsa* (*qq.v.*).
istiftāʾ	to seek a *fatwā* (*q.v.*).
istiḥsān	to put aside and replace a rule when it would have an unreasonable effect (act. 'to consider something good', cf. *ḥasan*).
istinbāṭ	derivation, uncovering. In *qiyās*, methods to find the *ᶜilla* of a rule.
istiṣḥāb	continuity; the principle that matters should continue in its 'natural course' unless there is a positive reason to change it.
istiṣlāḥ	to formulate a rule on the basis of 'the common good' (*maṣlaḥa*, *q.v.*—Act. to 'consider something good, suitable').
jabr	power, compulsion; here: a father's right to marry off a minor daughter without her consent (syn. *ijbār*, *q.v.*).
jālī	clear, evident.
jamᶜ	to unite, cf. *jāmiᶜ*, in evidence: to find a way in

which both of two conflicting statements may be correct.

jāmi^{c} — unifying; in *qiyās* that which unifies the original and the derived case (other meanings e.g. 'community' or 'Friday' mosque; pl. *jawāmi^{c}*).

jihād — struggle. Act. *jihād fī sabīl Allāh*, struggle for the sake of God. In normal usage, the military struggle of a Muslim community against a non-Muslim enemy. In religion every Muslim's inner struggle with his conscience is considered to be the 'higher' form of *jihād*, while the military struggle is the 'inferior' form.

jināya — illegitimate damage to person or property.

jizya — person (poll) tax on *dhimmīs* (*q.v.*).

kafāʾa — equality; here: between bride a groom, personally and materially.

kāfir, pl. *kāfirūn*, *kuffār* — an infidel (cf. *kufr*, includes Jews and Christians).

kahia — Turk., here: a court for conflicts between Europeans and Muslims in Tunisia (from Pers. *ketkhudā* to Turk. *kāhya*, one of the offices of the *wazīr*).

kalimāt al-kufr — 'words of infidelity', proof of heresy or blasphemy (cf. *kufr*).

kanun — the legal decrees of the Ottoman sultan (Turk., from Ar. *qānūn*, *q.v.*).

kanunname — collection of *kanun* decrees in a book.

Kannuname-i cedit — the last edition of *kanunname*, 1673.

kātib, pl. *kuttāb* — writer, author, secretary. In court: court recorder.

kazasker — the highest official in the Ottoman empire (from Ar. *qāḍī ^{c}askar*, the army's judge, *q.v.*).

khabar, pl. *akhbār* — report, news. (1) Tradition from the Prophet (syn. *ḥadīth*, *q.v.*), in particular in Shī^{c}ism; (2) statement from an expert witness in a trial.

khalīfa, pl. *khulafāʾ* — caliph, the highest political leader of the *umma* (*q.v.*); the Prophet's successor in his earthly role.

kharāj — 'tribute'; tax on land property.

khāṣṣ — specific, limited (a rule that only concerns a particular category).

khediv — Turk., title of the autonomous governor of Egypt 1867-1914 (from Pers. *khidīw*, master).

khul^{c} — divorce initiated by the wife, against economic compensation and with the husbands acceptance.

al-khulafāʾ al-rāshidūn — the four 'rightly-guided' caliphs Abū Bakr, ^{c}Umar, ^{c}Uthmān and ^{c}Alī (632-661).

khums — a fifth; Shī^{c}ī term for the charity tax *zakāt* (*q.v.*).

komiteh — Pers., local revolutionary or neighbourhood committee, Iran 1979.

kufr — unbelief, not to believe in Islam.

lafẓī — literal, word for word (on transmission of *ḥadīth*.

	Opposite: *bi'l-maᶜnā, q.v. maᶜnā*).
liᶜān	divorce on a husband's rejection of the paternity for his wife's child but cannot prove *zinā*.
madhhab, pl. *madhāhib*	school of law, juridical current or legal system (also 'rite'; act. 'method').
madrasa, pl. *madāris*	school, place of learning for *ᶜulamā᾿* (*q.v.*, also *ᶜilm*).
mafhūm	implicit meanings of a Koran verse (act. 'understood').
maghāzī	stories of the Prophet's military campaigns (act. military expeditions; pl. of *maghzāh*, from *ghazw*, raid, hence 'razzia').
maḥākim ahlīya	civil courts (Egypt, 1842).
mahdī	(1) the divinely inspired ruler (in Shīᶜism, the returned twelfth *imām*) that leads the Muslims to the day of Judgement; (2) rebel leader who claims to be this *mahdī* and mobilizes support on that basis.
maḥkama, pl. *mahākim*	court.
mahr	dower.
Majalla	Ottoman Sharīᶜa law, cf. *Mecelle*.
majāz	allegories (in a Koran verse).
majlis	council; (1) the Sultan's or governor's council (cf. *dīwān); (2) local governors siyāsa court (cf. maẓālim).*
majlis al-ᶜulamā᾿	the council of scholars (Egypt, nineteenth century).
makrūh	'disliked' or disapproved of, but not banned.
maᶜnā	meaning. (1) on *ḥadīth* transmission: *bi'l-m.*: by content, not literal [opposite of *lafẓī, q.v.*); (2) basis for a rule (syn. *ᶜilla, q.v.).*
mandūb	recommended, but not compulsory.
manṣūṣ al-ᶜilla	'textual *ᶜilla* [*q.v.*]', an *ᶜilla* that is clearly expressed in a text of Revelation.
maqāṣid	here God's motives for giving the Sharīᶜa (act. goal, intention, pl. of *maqṣid*).
maqṭūᶜ	'cut off', of an *isnād (q.v.)* which has a gap in the chain of transmitters (syn. *munqaṭīᶜ*).
marjaᶜ al-taqlīd	the highest level in the Shīᶜī hierarchy of scholars, syn. *ayāt Allāh al-ᶜuẓmā*, grand ayatollah. Act. 'source for imitation' strictly speaking a general title for Shīᶜī scholas (Pers. *marjaᶜ-e taqlīd*).
muṣḥaf	(material) copy of the Koran.
mashhūr	(1) on *ḥadīth*: well known, accepted; (2) a rule of law that has been generally accepted in a school; the rule that is practised. Often the 'last' version that replaces earlier versions.
maṣlaḥa	here 'the common good' (act. matter, affair, pl. *maṣāliḥ*, also welfare, cf. *istiṣlāḥ*, also *ṣulḥ*).
—*maṣlaḥa mursala*	free *maṣlaḥa*; to build a rule on the common good

	without giving it a basis in a text of Revelation.
matn, pl. *mutūn*	the text of a *ḥadīth* (*q.v.*) after the *isnād* chain (*q.v.*).
mawṣūl	continuous, of an *isnād* (*q.v.*) that has no gap in the chain of transmitters (syn. *mutaṣṣil*).
maẓālim	the ruler's court, court for 'correction of injustices'.
Mecelle	codified Ottoman law from 1873 based on the Sharīᶜa, act. *Mecelle-i ahkâm-ı adliye majalla* (from Ar. *majalla*, book, scroll).
meclis	Turk., council, court, from Ar. *majlis* (*q.v.*).
mehkeme	Turk., (modern) court, from Ar. *maḥkama* (*q.v.*).
The *miḥna*	the 'Inquisition' of scholars launched by the caliph Maʾmūn (833-51).
millet	Turk., (group of) people (from Ar. *milla*), in the Ottoman empire, partly autonomous communities of religious or ethnic minorities.
miri	Turk., public; here: state-owned land, the sultan's property (from Ar. *amīrī*, that of the emir).
muᶜāmalāt	transactions; rules concerning human/ social relations (opposite those between man and God, *ᶜibādāt*, *q.v.* From *ᶜamal*, *q.v.*).
muᶜāwin	assistant, helper.
mubāḥ	neutral, neither recommended nor discouraged.
mubtadiᶜ	s.o. who performs *bidᶜa* (*q.v.*), heterodox.
muḍāraba	'quiet' or limited partnership, the bank invests in a customer's enterprise and receives a part of the profit.
mudarris	teacher.
mudhākara	'*ḥadīth* gathering'; get-together for relating and exchanging *ḥadīth*.
muftī	scholar of law, religious guide, s.o. who issues *fatwā*s (*q.v.*, from *futya*, *q.v.*).
mughārasa	tenancy of land producing more-yearly crops (trees, bushes, etc.).
muḥtasib	judge in the *ḥisba* court (*q.v.*), responsible for the market and public services of a town.
mujtahid	s.o. who can perform *ijtihād* (*q.v.*), in Shīᶜism a jurist on an intermediate or higher level.
—*mujtahid fī 'l-madhhab*	'm. in the school', a *mujtahid* who stays within the methodology of his chosen school.
—*mujtahid muqayyad*	m. who is 'dependent' on his school, who can develop subsidiary, not totally new rules of law (also *m. muntasib*).
—*mujtahid mustaqill*	'independent m.', one who is not bound to any school of law (also *m. muṭlaq*).
mukhtaṣar, pl. *-āt*	book that sums up general rules of law (act. 'abbreviation').
mullā	Shīᶜī religious scholar, mostly at the lower level (village, etc.).

munāẓara — debate between scholars (here: jurists).
munkar — disapproved, in *ḥadīth* a hardly trustworthy transmission.
munqaṭiᶜ — 'cut off', an *isnād* (*q.v.*). that has a gap in the chain of transmitters (syn. *maqṭūᶜ*).
muqallid — s.o. who must accept the *taqlīd* (*q.v.*, i.e. does not have the competence to perform *ijtihād*, *q.v.*).
muqāṭaᶜ, *muqṭaᶜ* — 'tax lord', cf. *iqṭāᶜ*. In the Ottoman period also called *multazim* (cf. *iltizām*).
muqayyad — dependent, limited (a rule that must be understood in light of another rule, a scholar who must stay within an established framework).
murābaḥa — resale with specified markup.
mursal — 'transmitted', a *ḥadīth* where the first link (the eye witness) is not named.
Murshid — Egyptian law based on the Ottoman *Mecelle* (*q.v.* Act. 'guide').
muṣannaf — authored or ordered. Here a *ḥadīth* collection organized according to theme (cf. *taṣnīf*).
musāqā — in tenancy: artificially irrigated land.
musāwī — equivalent, on the same level; in *qiyās*: 'equal' basis for analogy.
mushāra — chamber of judges (cf. *shūrā*. Used in the Mamluk period).
mushāraka — partnership, cooperation.
mushrik, pl. *-ūn* — heathen, polytheist; s.o. who believes in many gods (cf. *shirk*).
musnad — *ḥadīth* collection organized according to *isnād* (*q.v.*) names.
mustaftī — s.o. who seeks a *fatwā* (*q.v.*).
mutᶜa — (1) in Shīᶜism: time-limited marriage; (2) in Sunnism: gift from husband to wife by a divorce (in particular if divorced before the marriage is consummated).
mutarjim — interpreter.
mutaṣṣil — continuous, of an *isnād* (*q.v.*) that has no gap in transmission (syn. *mawṣūl*).
mutawallī — caretaker; here responsible for a *waqf* (*q.v.*).
muṭāwiᶜa — the 'religious police', committees for public morality (Saudi Arabia, twentieth century).
muṭlaq — absolute, free (a rule that can be understood in itself; a scholar who does not need to refer to others).
muzakkī — guarantor for honesty; an officer of the court who evaluates court witnesses (cf. *shāhid*).
muzāraᶜa — tenancy of land that is sown, but not artifically irrigated.
nāʾib — assistant.
al-nāʾib al-ᶜāmm — the 'general representative' of the Shīᶜī *imām*, i.e.

	the collective of scholars; the basis for the authority of the Shīʿī *ʿulamāʾ*.
nāʾib al-qāḍī	assistant judge (institutionalized in Egypt, nineteenth century).
nafaqa	maintenance, a husband's duty to provide for the wife.
naqīb al-ashrāf	official responsible for i.a. the stipends of the *ashrāf* (*q.v.*), those of the Prophet's kin.
naql	transmission.
naqlī	transmitted, in *ijmāʿ*: 'confirming' consensus.
nāshiza	'obstinate', a wife who has left her husband's house without permission.
naskh	abrogation ('replacement') of a earlier Koran verse or *sunna* by a later one. Verb, 'to abrogate': *nasakha*. '*Al-nāsikh wa'l-mansūkh*', 'that which replaces and that which is replaced').
naṣṣ	text, from this: the Text of Revelation, the content of the Koran and sound *ḥadīth* (pl.: *nuṣūṣ*).
niẓām	system, order; here: the king's decree (Saudi Arabia, twentieth century).
Niẓām asāsī	the constitution of Saudi Arabia, 'basic order'.
Nizam-ı cedit	Turk., 'The new order', Ottoman reform decree, 1793 (from Ar. *al-niẓām al-jadīd*).
nizamiye	Turk., court applying the laws of the *tanẓimāt* reforms (*q.v.*, from Ar. *niẓāmīya*).
pasdarān	Pers., *Sipāh-e pasdarān-e enqelāb-e islāmī*: The revolutionary guard (parallel military forces), Iran 1979.
qaḍāʾ	to judge.
qadhf	slander; here: false accusation of *zinā* (*q.v.*), one of the *ḥudūd* crimes.
qāḍī, pl. *quḍāt*	judge in a Sharīʿa court.
—*qāḍī ʿaskar*	the army's judge. In the Ottoman period, the highest-ranking judge in the empire (Turk.; *kazasker*, *q.v.*).
—*qāḍī al-jamāʿa*	chief judge ('the judge of the community'. Used in the Maghreb).
—*qāḍī al-nikāḥ*	'marriage judge', in a separate court (syn. *qāḍī al-ʿaqīd*).
—*qāḍī al-quḍāt*	chief judge ('judge of judges').
qānūn	law; in particular the legal decrees of the Ottoman sultan (Turk. *kanun*, *q.v.*).
qānūnīya	the sultan's *kanun* decrees in general.
qasāma	compensation for killing paid in common by a local community when the perpetrator is unknown.
qaṭʿī	certain, without doubt (on the understanding of a Koran verse or *ḥadīth*).
qawāʿid	fundament, principle (pl. of *qāʿida*). Here (1) the basic principles of the Sharīʿa; (2) literary genre for

	abstraction of the rules of a school to a small number of maxims.
qawl	statement; in a school of law: a (not yet authorized) expression of a rule.
qiṣāṣ	retribution (*lex talio*) for murder or bodily harm.
qiyās	'analogies' drawn from one case (*aṣl*, *q.v.*) to a similar case or general category (*far*ᶜ, *q.v.*) by a specific methodology.
quloghli	Turk., person of mixed Turkish-Arabic descent (Ottoman period).
*ra*ᵓ*y*	(1) established practice in an area (*q.v. sunna* (3)); (2) personal view (as basis for a rule of law); (3) legal procedure (act. 'view', 'opinion'). Meaning (2) most common in later periods, derogatory term as 'personal whims without basis in the Revelation'.
ribā	usurious rent, normally extended to interest in general.
ridda	apostasy from Islam (syn. *irtidād*, *q.v.*).
rijāl	men (pl. of *rajul*); ᶜ*ilm al-rijāl*: the science of *ḥadīth* transmitters (auxiliary science for evaluation of *isnād*s).
risāla	treatise, book, writing. Here a requirement to reach the rank of ayatollah.
riwāyāt	'recensions', variants of an originally orally transmitted work (sing. *riwāya*, act. 'stories').
rizqa	endowment, syn. *waqf* (*q.v.*).
rusum	local custom (Turk., from Ar. 'rules, documents', pl. of *rasm*).
sabab	reason, cause, in *qiyās* the background for a rule (syn. ᶜ*illa*, *q.v.* Pl. *asbāb*, *q.v.*).
sabb al-rasūl	blasphemy, insults against the prophet Muḥammad.
ṣadaqa	endowment, syn. *waqf* (*q.v.*).
ṣadaqa/ṣidqa	charitable gift. Here (1) poor tax, either syn. with *zakāt* (*q.v.*) or a voluntary donation; (2) endowment to God, syn. *waqf* (*q.v.*).
ṣāḥib	master, chief, responsible. From this: *ṣ. al-shurṭa* (police chief), *ṣ al-madīna* (town authority), *ṣ. al-maẓālim* (judge of the *maẓālim* (*q.v.*), court), *ṣ. al-radd* (judge of the 'appeals' court).
ṣaḥīḥ	sound, secure (i.a. of *ḥadīth*). In definite dual, *al-Ṣaḥīḥān*, the two *ḥadīth* collections of al-Bukhārī and Muslim.
salaf	'predecessors', the early generations of Islam (either just the Prophet's generation or the first three generations, including the *ṭābi*ᶜ*ūn* and *ṭābi*ᶜ *ṭābi*ᶜ*ūn*, 'followers').
şeyhül-islam	Turk., chief *muftī*; the highest religious authority in the Ottoman empire (from Ar. *shaykh al-islām*).

shāhid, pl. *shuhūd*	witness, court witness.
shakhṣī	personal, here personal (family) law.
Sharīᶜa	the Islamic law. Here (1) the sum total of the rules of law, as they are known among men, also (2) God's revealed law, the divine element in the rules of law. From *sharᶜ*, Revelation, from it *sharᶜī*, 'Sharīᶜa-an', that related to the Sharīᶜa (cf. *tashrīᶜ*).
shirk	heathendom, polytheism (act. 'to associate' or 'share', here: to associate God with other divinities. Cf. *mushrik*).
shubuhāt	'resemblances'; here: illegalities that resemble legal situations and may be the result of mistakes; extenuating circumstances.
shūrā	consultation or council (e.g. council of scholars or other Muslims, council of judges, *muftī*s, etc.).
Shūrā-ye negahbān	Pers., 'Council of Guardians' (Iran, 1979).
shurṭa	police.
shurūṭ	condition (pl. of *sharṭ*); here: standard formulas for contracts.
sīra, pl. *siyar*	biography (of the Prophet Muḥammad. Act. 'road'; from this 'the path of his life').
siyāsa sharᶜīya	'Sharīᶜa politics'; (1) state rule on the basis of the Sharīᶜa's principles; (2) to judge according to the 'spirit' of the Sharīᶜa unrestricted to its rules of procedure.
siyāsa court	court which judges according to *siyāsa sharᶜīya*, e.g. *shurṭa*, *maẓālim*, *ḥisba* (*qq.v.*) courts; in general: any court that aims to apply the general rules of the Sharīᶜa but is based on a political authority and its definition of the laws.
subaşı	Turk., police.
sukūt	silent, not vocal.
ṣulḥ	peace, compromise; here (1) peace agreement; (2) monetary compensation for intentional homicide or bodily harm instead of retaliation (*qiṣāṣ*, *q.v.*); (3) agreement to solve conflicts of marriage.
sunna	practice. (1) The Sunna: The sum-total of what the Prophet Muḥammad did or authorized, one of the sources of Revelation; (2) a *sunna*, pl. *sunan*, a normative statement of action made by the Prophet or his contemporaries (expressed in *ḥadīth*, *q.v.*); (3) general practice in a location. Also adjectivally, 'this is *sunna*', in conformity with (1).
taᶜdīyat al-ḥukm	'transmission of the rule'. Shīᶜī, related to to Sunnī *qiyās* (*q.v.*).
tafsīr	explanation of the apparent meaning of a Koran verse or *ḥadīth*.
taḥkīm	to solve conflicts, decide between opponents (cf.

ḥākim).

takfīr	to call s.o. an infidel (cf. *kufr*).
takhalluf	to be left behind, underdevelopment.
takhayyur	[free] choice, nearly syn. with *takhyīr*, *ikhtiyār* (*qq.v.*).
takhrīj	to pull out; in a school of law: to construct new rules based on the authority of the founder of the school.
takhyīr	to choose something above something else, cf. *ikhtiyār*, *takhayyur*.
ṭalāq	divorce, a husband's repudiation of his wife.
talfīq	to accept particular rules from other schools; to disregard the schools of law in constructing a law based on Sharīᶜa.
tamṣīr	'Egyptianization'; e.g. of originally European laws.
tanẓīmāt	the Ottoman reform program 1836-78 (act. from *tanẓīm*, organization; from *Nizam-ı cedit* [*al-niẓām al-jadīd*], *q.v.*).
taqīya	caution; in Shīᶜism to hide one's belief from enemies.
taqlīd	to accept as authoritative the views of a (another) scholar.
tarjīḥ	preference; to prefer something to something else.
tasāquṭ	to fall; in evidence: to disregard testimonies when they are contradictory.
tashrīᶜ	to legislate, to formulate rules of law (in the Sharīᶜa or in general. From *sharᶜ*, *q.v.* Sharīᶜa).
taṣnīf	authorship, to organize a work thematically.
taṭbīq	to apply.
taṭlīq	divorce performed by the court (cf. *ṭalāq*, *faskh*, *fasād*).
tawātur	highly frequent, general; a *ḥadīth* that is so widespread that it must be true.
taʾwīl	explanation of the underlying meaning of a Koran verse or *ḥadīth*.
taᶜzīr	punishment, criticism. Here: penalties decided at the judge's own discretion (opposite: *ḥudūd* penalties, *qiṣāṣ*, *qq.v.*).
teftiş	Turk., inspection (from Ar. *taftīsh*).
thābit	believable, solid (on the trustworthiness of a *ḥadīth*).
tilāwa	'dictation', here: the formulation of a Koran verse or *ḥadīth*.
ᶜulamāʾ	the class of scholars; pl. of *ᶜālim*, scholar (*q.v.* *ᶜilm*). Among these, specialists such as *fuqahāʾ* (*q.v.* *faqīh*); *muḥaddithūn*, *ḥadīth* specialists; *mufassirūn*, Koran specialists (*q.v.* *tafsīr*), etc.; also *muftī*s and *qāḍī*s.
umma	the community of Muslims (world community).
ummahāt	the basic works of a school of law (pl. of *umm*,

mother, original).

ᶜuqūbāt punishment; the Sharīᶜa's criminal law (pl. of *ᶜuqūba*). Includes *ḥudūd* and *taᶜzīr* (*qq.v.*).

ᶜurf custom, normal practice (also used: *ᶜāda*, cf. *ᶜamal*, *rusum*).

ᶜushr one tenth; a tax on land, originally for land owned by Muslims.

uṣūl al-fiqh the methodology behind the law (the 'sources of the science of law', pl. of *aṣl*, *q.v.*).

Uṣūlīs legal/theological current in Shīᶜism that emphasized rational law (opponents: Akhbārīs, *q.v.*).

velāyat-e faqīh Pers. theory of state, Iran 1979, 'the rule of the jurist' (from Ar. *wilāyat al-fqqīh*).

wājib required, compulsory. For many syn. with *farḍ* (*q.v.*).

wakīl representative, assistant. Legally: lawyer (modern: *muḥāmī*).

wālī governor.

walī close; here: guardian, a woman's closest male relative (act. *walī al-amr* Also: s.o. who stands close to God, saint, pl. *awliyāʾ*).

waqf endowment (to God).

—*waqf ahlī* family *w.*, for the benefit of relatives or descendants.

—*waqf khayrī* general *w.*, for the benefit of other than the family.

waqfīya document that designates a property as *waqf* (*q.v.*) and defines the conditions for it, who is to benefit, etc.

waṣīya testamentary gift.

waziri Hausa; vizier, the sultan's or emir's 'minister' and most prominent official (from Ar. *wazīr*).

ẓāhir evident, exterior, clear.

ẓāhir al-riwāya the most believable (most evident) reading; a rule of law that is considered to be accepted in a school of law (cf. *mashhūr*).

zakāt the alms tax, one of the five 'pillars' of Islam.

zandaqa heresy, atheism, cf. *zindiq*.

ẓannī assumed, probable (what is not *qaṭīᶜ*, *q.v.*).

zinā fornication, adultery, any illegitimate sexual activity, one of the *ḥudūd* crimes.

zindiq free-thinker, Muslim who in reality has left Islam.

ẓulm oppression (e.g. political), injustice.

BIBLIOGRAPHY

Sources

Most of the sources for classical Islamic law are still available only in Arabic. We have, however, listed below some sources that are available in European languages, for the benefit of the beginner student who is not yet ready to tackle the sources in their original language.

Koran and ḥadīth

The Koran Interpreted, trans. A.J. Arberry, London 1955; Oxford 1998

This is one of the most classic English translations of the Koran, and the one used in this book. Notice, however, that Arberry's numbering of *sūras* may vary slightly from those of other editions of the Koran.

El-Bokhârî, *Les Traditions islamiques*, trans. O. Houdas and W. Marçais, Paris 1903, 1984.

Houdas and Marçais' translation is probably the most reliable into a European language of Bukhārī's *Ṣaḥīḥ*. Like the collections below, however, Bukhārī's work has also been translated into English in India.

Ṣaḥīḥ Muslim; being Traditions of the Sayings and Doings of the Prophet Muhammad, trans. ᶜAbdul Ḥamīd Siddīqī, Lahore 1971-5.

Sunan Abu Dawud, trans. with comm. Ahmad Hasan, New Dehli 1984, 1996.

Sunan ibn-i-Majah, to English by Muhammad Tufail Ansari, Lahore 1993-6.

Sunan Nasāʾī (Arabic-English), trans. into English by Muḥammad Iqbāl Ṣiddiqi, Lahore 1994, 1999.

Basic works in: Ḥanafī law

al-Qudūrī, Aḥmad b. Muḥammad (d. 1086), *Le Statut personnel en droit musulman* [selection from *al-Mukhtaṣar*], trans. G.-H. Bousquet and L. Bercher, Paris 1952

al-Marghīnānī, ᶜAlī b. Abī Bakr (d. 1196), *The Hedaya, Or Guide: A Commentary on the Mussulman Laws,* Lahore 1975 (orig. 4 vols, 1791).

Shāfiᶜī law

al-Shāfiᶜī, Muḥammad b. Idrīs (d. 820), *al-Risāla fī uṣūl al-fiqh: Treatise on the Foundations of Islamic Jurisprudence*, trans. Majid Khadduri, Cambridge 1961.

al-Shīrāzī, Abū Iṣḥāq (d. 1083), *Kitâb et-tanbîh; ou, Le livre de l'admonition touchant la loi musulmane selon le rite de l'Imân ech-Chafé'î*, trans. G.-H. Bousquet, Alger 1949-52.

—, *Kitāb al-Lumaᶜ fi uṣūl al-fiqh - Traité de théorie légale musulmane*, trans. Éric Chaumont, Berkeley 1999.

al-Nawawī, Yaḥyā b. Sharaf (d. 1277), *Minhaj et talibin: A Manual of Muhammadan Law; According to the School of Shafi*, trans. L.W.C. Van Den Berg / E.C. Howard, Lahore 1977.

Mālikī law

Mālik b. Anas (d. 795), *Al-Muwatta of Imam Malik ibn Anas, The First Formulation of Islamic Law,* trans. Aisha Abdurrahman Bewley, London 1989.

al-Qayrawānī, Ibn Abī Zayd (d. 996), *The Risâla: Treatise on Mâlíkî law*, trans. Joseph Kenny, Minna, Nigeria 1992.

Cf. also *A Madinan View: on the Sunnah, Courtesy, Wisdom and History*, trans. Abdassamad Clarke, London 1999. The *Risāla* has been translated many times into French, e.g. *La Risala,* trans. Kawsar Abdel Salaam el-Béheiry, Cairo-Algiers 1988.

Khalīl b. Isḥāq (d. 1365), *Abrégé de la loi musulmane selon le rite de l'imâm Mâlek* [*al-Mukhtaṣar*], trans. G.-H. Bousquet, 4 vols., Algiers 1956-62.

A shorter English translation: *Mâliki law: being a summary from French translations of the Mukhtaṣar of Sîdî Khalîl*, trans. F.H. Ruxton, London 1916, 1980.

Ibn ᶜĀṣim, Muḥammad b. Muḥammad (d. 1427), *Tuhfat al-hukkam, or Gift for the Judges. English Translation of the First Six Hundred Verses* by Bello Muhammad Daura, Zaria 1989.

Also French trans., *al-'Âçimiyya ou Tuḥfat al-ḥukkâm fi nukat al-'uqoûd wa'l-aḥkâm = Le présent fait aux juges touchant les points délicats des contrats et de jugements*, trans. Léon Bercher, Algiers 1958.

Ḥanbali law

Ibn Qudāma, Muwaffaq al-Dīn (d. 1223), *Le Précis de droit d'Ibn Qudāma* [*al-ᶜUmda*], trans. H. Laoust, Beirut 1950.

Ibn Taymīya, Taqī 'l-Dīn (d. 1328), *Ibn Taimiyya on Public and Private Law in Islam; or, Public Policy in Islamic Jurisprudence* [*al-Siyāsa al-sharᶜīya fī iṣlāḥ al-rāʾī wa'l-raʾīya*], trans. Omar A. Farrukh, Beirut 1966.

Cf. also *Le Traité de droit public d'Ibn Taimiya*, trans. Henri Laoust, Beirut 1948.

—, *Public Duties in Islam: The Institution of the Hisba* (*al-Ḥisba fī 'l-islām*), trans. Muhtar Holland, Leicester 1982.

—, *The Madinan Way: the Soundness of the Basic Premises of the School of the People of Madina*, trans. Aisha Bewley, Norwich 2000.

Secondary works

The following bibliography / reading list does not slavishly follow the chapter divisions of this work, but is divided according to the main themes discussed. Evidently many works are relevant for several chapters, but are listed here only once, where they have been most useful for the discussion.

Collected works and general histories

al-Azmeh, Aziz (ed.), *Islamic Law. Social and Historical Contexts*, London 1988.

Bleuchot, Hervé, *Droit musulman,* 2 vols, Paris 2000-2002.
Brunschvig, Robert, *Études d'islamologie*, II: *Droit Musulman*, Paris 1976.
Coulson, Neil J., *A History of Islamic Law*, Edinburgh 1964, 1978.
—, *Conflicts and Tensions in Islamic Jurisprudence,* Chicago 1969.
Gleave, Robert and E. Kermeli (eds), *Islamic Law: Theory and Practice*, London 1997.
Goldziher, Ignaz, *Introduction to Islamic Theology and Law*, Princeton 1981.
Heer, Nicholas (ed.), *Islamic Law and Jurisprudence*, Seattle 1990.
Hurgronje, Chr. Snouck, *Oeuvres choisies*, Leiden 1957.
Johansen, Baber, *Contingency in a Sacred Law: Legal and Ethical Norms in the Muslim* fiqh, Leiden 1999.
Khadduri, Majid and Herbert J. Liebesny (eds), *Law in the Middle East* [vol. 1:] *Origin and Development of Islamic Law*, Washington, DC 1955.
Mallat, Chibli (ed.), *Islam and Public Law*, London 1993.
Nagel, Tilman, *Das islamische recht. Eine Einführung*, Westhofen 2001.
Schacht, Joseph, *An Introduction to Islamic Law*, Oxford 1964.
Turner, Bryan S., *Weber and Islam: A critical Study*, London 1974.
Vermeulen, Urbain and J.M.F: van Reeth (eds), *Law, Christianity and Modernism in Islamic Society: Proceedings of the Eighteenth Congress of the Union Européenne des Arabisants et Islamisants held at the Katholieke Universiteit Leuven (September 3 - September 9, 1996)*, Leuven 1998.
Weiss, Bernard G., *The Spirit of Islamic Law,* Athens, GA 1998.
—, (ed.), *Studies in Islamic Legal Theory*, Leiden 2002.

Reference works used

Bogdan, Michael, *Comparative Law*, Stockholm 1994.
Brockelmann, Carl, *Geschichte der Arabischen Litteratur* (GAL), 2 volumes, 3 supplements, Leiden 1937-49.
Esposito, J. (ed), *The Oxford Encyclopedia of the Modern Islamic World*, New York 1995.
Hodgson, Marshall, *The Venture of Islam*, Chicago 1974.
Makdisi, John, 'Islamic Law Bibliography', *Law Library Journal*, LXXVIII, 1986, 103-89.
Melville, Charles (ed.), *Safavid Persia: The History and Politics of an Islamic Society*, London 1996.
Morgan, David, *Medieval Persia 1040-1797*, London 1988.
Savory, Roger, *Iran under the Safavids*, Cambridge 1980.
Shaban, M.M., *Islamic History*, 2 vols, Cambridge 1971-7.
al-Zwaini, Laila and Rudolph Peters, *A Bibiography of Islamic Law, 1980-1993,* Leiden 1994.

The theory of the law

General overviews

Cook, Michael, *Commanding Right and Forbidding Wrong in Islamic Thought*,

Cambridge 2000.
Hallaq, Wael B., 'Usūl al-fiqh: Beyond Tradition', *Journal of Islamic Studies*, III, 2, 1992, 172-202.
—, *A History of Islamic Legal Theories: An Introduction to Sunnī uṣūl al-fiqh*, Cambridge 1997.
Kamali, Mohammed Hashim, *Principles of Islamic Jurisprudence*, Cambridge 1991.
Johansen, Baber, 'Die sündige, gesunde Amme. Moral und gesetzliche Betimmung (*ḥukm*) im islamischen Recht', *Die Welt des Islams*, XXVIII, 1988, 264-82 (and in *Contingency*, 172-88).

The sources: Koran and ḥadīth

Azami, M.M., *Studies in Early Hadith Literature*, Beirut 1968.
Burton, John, *The Collection of the Qur'ān*, Cambridge 1977.
—, *The Sources of Islamic Law. Islamic Theories of Abrogation*, Edinburgh 1990.
—, 'Law and Exegesis: the Penalty for Adultery in Islam', in G.R. Hawting and Abdul-Kader A. Shareef (eds), *Approaches to the Qur'ān*, London 1993, 269-84.
—, *An Introduction to the Ḥadīth*, Edinburgh 1994.
Guillaume, Alfred, *The Traditions of Islam: An Introduction to the Study of the Hadith Literature*, Oxford 1924 (reprint Beirut 1966).
Hawting, G.R., 'The Role of Qur'ān and ḥadīth in the Legal Controversy about the Rights of a Divorced Woman during her "Waiting Period" (ʿidda)', *Bulletin of the School of Oriental and African Studies*, LII, 3, 1989, 430-45.
Juynboll, G.H.A., *The Authenticity of the Tradition Literature: Discussions in Modern Egypt*. Leiden 1969.
—, *Muslim Tradition, Studies in Chronology, Provenance and Authorship of Early Ḥadīth*, Cambridge 1983.
—, 'Some new ideas on the development of *Sunna* as a technical term in early Islam', *Jerusalem Studies in Arabic and Islam*, X, 1987, 97-118.
—, *Studies on the Origins and Uses of Islamic Ḥadīth*, Aldershot 1996.
Semaan, K.I., 'Al-nāsikh wa-al-mansūkh. Abrogation and its Application in Islam', *Islamic Quarterly*, VI, 1961, 11-29.
Ṣiddīqī, Muḥammad Zubayr, *Ḥadīth Literature: Its Origins, Development, Special Features and Criticism*, Calcutta 1961.

The development: ijtihād, qiyās, ijmāʿ and other sources and principles

Bagby, Ihsan A., 'The Issue of *maṣlaḥah* in Classical Islamic Legal Theory', *International Journal of Islamic and Arabic Studies*, II, 2, 1985, 1-11.
Brunschvig, Robert, 'Le Système de la preuve en droit musulman', *Recueils Soc. Jean Bodin*, XVIII, 1963, 169-86 (and in *Études*, 201-18).
—, 'De la fiction legale dans l'Islam médiéval', *Studia Islamica*, XXXII, 1970, 41-51 (and in *Études*, 335-45).
Goldziher, Ignaz, 'Über iğmâʿ', *Nachrichten, Akademie der Wissenschaften zu*

Göttingen, Göttingen 1916.

Hallaq, Wael B., 'On the Authoritativeness of Sunni Consensus', *International Journal of Middle Eastern Studies*, XVIII, 4, 1986, 427-54.

—, 'Non-analogical Arguments in Sunni Juridical qiyās', *Arabica*, XXXVI, 3, 1989, 286-306.

—, 'Model shurût Works and the Dialectics of Doctrine and Practice', *Islamic Law and Society*, II, 2, 1995, 109-34.

Hasan, Ahmad, 'Early Modes of ijtihād: rāʾy, qiyās and istihsān', *Islamic Studies*, VI, 1967, 47-79.

—, 'The Definition of qiyās in Islamic Jurisprudence', *Islamic Studies*, XIX, 1, 1980, 1-28.

—, 'The Legal Cause in Islamic Jurisprudence: an Analysis of 'illat al-ḥukm', *Islamic Studies*, XIX, 4, 1980, 247-70.

—, 'The Justification of qiyās', *Islamic Studies*, XX, 1981, 201-28.

—, 'The Conditions of Legal Cause in Islamic Jurisprudence', *Islamic Studies*, XX, 4, 1981, 303-42.

—, 'Definition of sabab and its Kinds in Islamic Jurisprudence', *Islamic Studies*, XXI, 3, 1982, 48-60.

—, 'Subject Matter of qiyās', *Islamic Studies*, XXI, 4, 1982, 97-129.

—, 'The Critique of qiyas', *Islamic Studies*, XXII, 3, 1983, 45-69; 4, 1983, 31-55.

—, *The Doctrine of ijmāᶜ in Islam. A Study of the Juridical Principle of Consensus*, Islamabad 1984.

—, 'Methods of Finding the Cause of a Legal Injunction in Islamic Jurisprudence', *Islamic Studies*, XXV, 1, 1986, 11-44.

—, *Analogical Reasoning in Islamic Jurisprudence: A Study of the Juridical Principle of Qiyas*, Delhi 1994.

Heinrichs, Wolfhart P., '*Qawāʾid* as a Legal Genre', in Weiss, *Studies in Islamic Legal Theory*, 365-84

Hourani, Georges F., 'The Basis of Authority of Consensus in Sunnite Islam', *Studia Islamica*, XXI, 1964, 13-60.

Nour, Alhaji A.M., 'Qias as a Source of Islamic Law', *Journal of Islamic and Comparative Law*, V, 1969-76, 18-50.

Omer, A.I., 'The Institution of al-hisba in the Islamic Legal System', *Journal of Islamic and Comparative Law,* X, 1981, 63-76.

Qadri, Moinuddin, 'Traditions of taqlīd and talfīq', *Islamic Culture*, LVII, 2, 1983, 39-61; 3, 1983, 123-45.

Rahman, Fazlur, 'Concepts sunnah, ijtihād and ijmāʾ in the early period', *Islamic Studies*, L, 1962, 5-21.

Shehaby, Nabil, '*ᶜIlla* and *qiyās* in Early Islamic Legal Theory', *Journal of the American Oriental society*, CII, 1982, 27-46.

Turki, Abdel Magid, 'L'ijmâ' ummat al-mu'minîn entre la doctrine et l'histoire', *Studia Islamica*, LIX, 1984, 49-78.

Tyan, Émile, 'Méthodologie et sources du droit en Islam (Istiḥsān, Istiṣlāḥ, Siyāsa šarᶜiyya)', *Studia Islamica*, X, 1959, 79-109.

—, 'La Condition juridique de "l'absent" (mafḳūd) en droit musulman, particulièrement dans le madhab Ḥanafite', *Studia Islamica*, XXXI, 1970, 249-56.

Wakin, Jeanette, *The Function of Documents in Islamic Law*, Albany 1972.
Weiss, Bernard G., 'Interpretation in Islamic Law: The Theory of ijtihād', *American Journal of Comparative Law*, XXVI, 2, 1978.
Ziadeh, Farhat J., 'Integrity (ᶜadālah) in Classical Islamic Law', in Heer, *Islamic Law and Jurisprudence*, 73-93.

The formation of the law

The early development of the law and the four madhhabs

Ansari, Zafar Ishaq, 'Islamic Juristic Terminology before Šāfiᶜī. A Semantic Analysis with Special Reference to Kūfa', *Arabica*, XIX, 1972, 255-300.
Ahmad, Ziauddin, 'Al-Musnad min masāᵓil Aḥmad b. Ḥanbal: An Important Ḥanbali Work', *Islamic Studies*, XX, 2, 1981, 97-110.
Azami, M.M., *On Schacht's Origins of Muhammadan Jurisprudence*, Riyad 1985.
Brockopp, Jonathan E., *Early Mālikī Law: Ibn ᶜAbd al-Ḥakam and his Major Compendium of Jurisprudence*, Leiden 2000.
—, 'Competing Theories of Authority in Early Mālikī texts', in Weiss, *Studies in Islamic Legal Theory*, 3-22.
Calder, Norman, 'Ikhtilâf and ijmâᶜ in Shâfiᶜî's Risâla', *Studia Islamica*, LVIII, 1983, 55-81.
—, *Studies in Early Muslim Jurisprudence*, Oxford 1993.
Crone, Patricia, *Roman, provincial and Islamic law: The origins of the Islamic patronate*, Cambridge 1987.
Crone, Patricia and Martin Hinds, *God's Caliph: Religious Authority in the First Centuries of Islam*, Cambridge 1986.
Doi, ᶜAbdur Raḥmān I., 'The *Muwaṭṭa'* of Imām Mālik on the Genesis of the Sharī'a Law: A Western Scholar's Confusion', *Hamdard Islamicus*, IV, 3, 1981, 27-41.
Dutton, Yasin, 'ᶜAmal vs. Ḥadīth in Islamc Law: The Question of sadl al-yadayn (Holding One's Hands by One's Sides) While Doing the Prayer', *Islamic Law and Society*, III, 1, 1996, 13-40.
—, *The Origins of Islamic law: The Qurᵓan, the Muwaṭṭaᵓ and Madinan ᶜamal*, London 1999.
Fadel, Mohammad Hossam, 'Adjudication in the Mālikī madhhab: A Study of Legal Process in Medieval Islamic Law', Ph.D., University of Chicago 1995.
—, 'The Social Logic of *taqlīd* and the Rise of *mukhataṣar*', *Islamic Law and Society*, III, 2, 1996, 193-233.
—, '"*Istiḥsān* is Nine-Tenth of the Law": The Puzzling Relationship of *uṣūl* to *furūᶜ* in the Mālikī *madhhab'*, in Weiss, *Studies in Islamic Legal Theory*, 161-76.
Fierro, Maribel, 'The Introduction of ḥadīth in al-Andalus (2nd/8th–3rd/9th Centuries)', *Der Islam*, LXVI, 1, 1989, 68-93.
Goitein, S.D., 'The Birth-Hour of Muslim Law? An Essay in Exegesis', *Muslim World*, L, 1, 1960, 23-9.
Hallaq, Wael B., 'Was the Gate of *ijtihād* Closed?', *International Journal of*

Middle Eastern Studies, XVI, 1, 1984, 3-34.
—, 'Was al-Shafiᶜī the Master Architecht of Islamic Jurisprudence?', *International Journal of Middle Eastern Studies*, XXV, 4, 1993, 587-605.
—, 'From *fatwās* to *furūᶜ*: Growth and Change in Islamic Substantive Law', *Islamic Law and Society*, I, 1, 1994, 29-65.
—, *Law and Legal Theory in Classical and Medieval Islam*, Aldershot 1995.
—, 'Iftaᵓ and ijtihad in Sunni Legal Theory: a Develomental Account', in Masud *et al*, *Islamic Legal Interpretation*, 35-6.
—, *Authority, Continuity, and Change in Islamic Law*, Cambridge 2001.
—, 'From Regional to Personal Schools of Law? A Reevaluation', *Islamic Law and Society*, VIII, 1, 2001, 1-26.
—, 'On Dating Malik's *Muwatta'*, *UCLA Journal of Islamic and Near Eastern Law*, I, 1, 2001-2, 47-65.
—, '*Takhrīj* and the Construction of Juristic Authority', in Weiss, *Studies in Islamic Legal Theory*, 317-35.
Halm, Heinz, *Die Ausbreitung der šāfiᶜitischen Rechtsschule von den Anfängen bis zum 8./14. Jahrhundert*, Wiesbaden 1974.
Hasan, Ahmad, 'Al-Shāfiᶜī's role in the Development of Islamic Jurisprudence', *Islamic Studies* (Karachi), V, 3, 1966, 239-73.
Hurvitz, Nimrod, 'Schools of Law and Historical Context: Re-examining the Formation of the Ḥanbalī *madhhab*', *Islamic Law and Society*, VII, 1, 2000, 37-64.
— *The Formation of Ḥanbalism: Piety into Power*, London 2002.
Jackson, Sherman A., *Islamic Law and the State: The Constitutional Jurisprudence of Shihāb al-Dīn al-Qarāfī*, Leiden, 1996.
—, 'Taqlid, Legal Scaffolding and the Scope of Legal Injunctions in Post-formative Theory: *muṭlaq* and *ᶜāmm* in Jurisprudence of Shihāb al-Dīn al-Qarāfī', *Islamic Law and Society*, III, 2, 1996, 165-92.
—, '*Kramer versus Kramer* in a Tenth/Sixteenth Century Egyptian Court: Post-formative Jurisprudence between Exigency and Law', *Islamic Law and Society*, VIII, 1, 2001, 47-51
Johansen, Baber, 'Coutumes locales et coutumes universelles aux sources des règles juridiques en droit musulman hanéfite', *Annales islamologiques*, XXVII, 1993, 29-35 (and in *Contingency*, 163-71).
—, 'Casuistry: between Legal Concept and Social Praxis', *Islamic Law and Society*, II, 2, 1995, 135-56.
Lowry, Joseph, 'Does Shāfiᶜī have a Theory of Four Sources of Law?', in Weiss, *Studies in Islamic Legal Theory*, 23-50.
Makdisi, George, 'The Juridical Theology of Shâfi'î: Origins and Significance of uṣûl al-fiqh', *Studia Islamica*, LIX, 1984, 5-47.
— 'Freedom in Islamic Jurisprudence: Ijtihad, taqlid and academic Freedom', in Makdisi, Dominique Sourdel and Janine Sourdel-Thomine (eds), *La Notion de liberté au Moyen-âge. Islam, Byzance, Occident*, Paris 1985, 79-88.
Mansour, Mansour Hasan, *The Maliki School of Law Spread and Domination in North and West Africa, 8th-14th Centuries*, San Francisco 1995.
Masud, Muhammad Khalid, *Shāṭibī's Philosophy of Islamic Law*, Islamabad 1995.

Melchert, Christopher, 'Religious politices of the caliphs from al-Mutawakkil to al-Muqtadir, A.H. 232-295/A.D. 847-908', *Islamic Law and Society*, III, 3, 1996, 316-42.

—, *The Formation of the Sunni Schools of Law: 9h-10th Centuries C.E.*, Leiden 1997 (orig. Ph.D., University of Pennsylvania 1992).

—, 'How Ḥanafism came to originate in Kufa and traditionalism in Medina', *Islamic Law and Society*, VI, 3, 1999, 318-47.

—, 'Traditionist-jurisprudents and the framing of Islamic Law' *Islamic Law and Society,* VIII, 3, 2001, 383-406.

—, 'Qur'ānic abrogation across the ninth century: Shāfiʿī, Abū ʿUbayd, Muḥāsibī, and Ibn Qutayba', in Weiss, *Studies in Islamic Legal Theory*, 75-98.

Motzki, Harald, 'Der Fiqh des -Zuhrī: die Quellenproblematik', *Der Islam*, LXVIII, 1, 1991, 1-44.

—, 'Quo vadis, Ḥadīṯ-Forschung? Eine kritische Untersuchung von G.H.A. Juynboll: "Nāfiʿ the mawlā of Ibn ʿUmar, and his position in Muslim Ḥadīṯ Literature"', *Der Islam*, LVIII, 1-2, 1996, 40-80 & 193-231.

—, 'The Prophet and the Cat. On dating Mālik's *Muwaṭṭa'* and legal traditions', *Jerusalem Studies in Arabic and Islam*, 22, 1998, 18-83.

—, *The Origins of Islamic Jurisprudence: Meccan Fiqh before the Classical Schools.* Leiden 2001 (trans. of *Die Anfänge der islamischen Jurisprudenz: Ihre Entwicklung in Mekka bis zur Mitte der 2./8. Jahrhundert*, Stuttgart 1991).

—, (ed.), *The Biography of Muḥammad: The Issue of Sources*. Leiden 2000.

Muranyi, Miklos, *Materialien zur malikitischen Rechtsliteratur*, Wiesbaden 1984.

—, *Ein altes Fragment medinensischer Jurizprudenz aus Qairawān: Aus dem Kitāb al-Ḥaǧǧ des ʿAbd al-ʿAzīz b. ʿAbd Allāh b. Abī Salama al-Māǧišūn (st. 164/780-81)*, Stuttgart 1985.

—, *Beiträge zur Geschichte der Ḥadīṯ- und Rechtsgelehrsamkeit der Mālikiyya in Nordafrika bis zum 5. Jh. d.H.: Bio-bibliographische Notizen aus der Moscheebibliotheek von Qairawān*, Wiesbaden 1997.

—, 'Die frühe Rechtslitteratur zwischen Quellen-analyse und Fiktion', *Islamic Law and Society,* IV, 2, 1997, 224-41.

Reinhart, A. Kevin, '"Like the difference between Heaven and Earth": Ḥanafī and Shāfiʿī discussion of *wājib* and *farḍ*', in Weiss, *Studies in Islamic Legal Theory*, 205-34.

Schacht, Joseph, *The Origins of Muhammadan Jurisprudence*, Oxford 1950, 1979.

—, 'Pre-Islamic background and early development of jurisprudence', in Khadduri and Liebesny, *Law in the Middle East*, 28-56.

—, 'Classicisme, traditionalisme et ankylose dans la loi religieuse de l'Islam', in R. Brunschvig and G.E. von Grunebaum (eds), *Classicisme et déclin culturel dans l'histoire de l'islam,* Paris 1957, 141-61.

Schoeler, Gregor, 'Die Frage der schriftlichen oder mündlichen Überlieferung der Wissenschaften im frühen Islam', *Der Islam*, LXII, 2, 1985, 201-30.

—, 'Weiteres zur Frage der schriftlichen oder mündlichen Überlieferung der Wissenschaften im Islam', *Der Islam*, LXVI, 1, 1989, 38-67.

—, 'Mündliche Thora und Ḥadīṯ – Überlieferung, Schreibverbot, Redaktion', *Der Islam*, LXVI, 2, 1989, 213-51.

—, 'Schreiben und Veröffentlichen. Zu Verwendung und Funktion der Schrift in den ersten islamischen Jahrhunderten', *Der Islam*, LXIX, 1, 1992, 1-43.

—, *Charakter und Authentie der muslimischen Überlieferung über das Leben Mohammed*, Berlin 1996.

Sodiq, Yushau, 'Malik's concept of *maslahah* (the consideration of the common good): a critical study of this method as a means of achieving the goals and purposes of Islamic Law with special reference to its application at the *shari'ah* courts in Northern Nigeria', Ph.D., Temple University 1991.

Spectorsky, Susan A., 'Aḥmad ibn Ḥanbal's fiqh', *Journal of the American Oriental Society*, CII, 3, 1982, 461-5.

—, '*Sunnah* in the responses of Isḥāq b. Rāhwayh', in Weiss, *Studies in Islamic Legal Theory*, 51-74.

Tsafrir, Nurit, 'The beginnings of the Ḥanafī school in Isfahan', *Islamic Law and Society*, V, 1, 1998, 1-21

Turki, Abdel Magid, 'La vénération pour Mālik et la physionomie du Mālikisme Andalou', *Studia Islamica*, XXXIII, 1971, 41-65.

—, 'La logique juridique, des origines jusqu'à Shâfi[c]î (Réflexions d'ordre méthodologique)', *Studia Islamica*, LVII, 1983, 31-45.

Vikør, Knut S., '"The Truth about Cats and Dogs": The Historicity of Early Islamic law', *Historisk Tidsskrift* (Oslo), LXXXII, 1, 2003, 1-17.

Wansbrough, John, *Quranic Studies: Sources and Methods of Scriptural Interpretation*, London 1977.

—, *The Sectarian Milieu: Content and Composition of Islamic Salvation History*, Oxford 1978.

Watt, W. Montgomery, 'The closing of the door of iǧtihād', in *Orientalia hispanica, sive studia F M Pareja octogenario dictata edenda curavit J.M. Barral*, Leiden 1974, vol. I, 675-8.

Weiss, Bernard G., *The Search for God's Law. Islamic Jurisprudence in the Writings of Sayf al-Dīn al-Āmidī*, Salt Lake City 1992.

Wheeler, Brannon M., *Applying the Canon of Islam: The Authorization and Maintenance of Interprative Reasoning in Ḥanafī Scholarship,* Albany, NY 1996.

Wiederhold, Lutz, 'Legal doctrines in conflict: the relevance of madhhab boundaries to legal reasoning in the light of an unpublished treatise on taqlīd and ijtihād', *Islamic Law and Society*, III, 2, 1996, 234-304.

—, 'Blasphemy against the Prophet Muḥammad and his companions (*sabb al-rasūl, sabb al-ṣaḥābah*): The introduction of the topic into Shāfi[c]ī legal literature and its relevance for legal practice under Mamluk rule', *Journal of Semitic Studies*, XLII, 1, 1997, 39-70.

Zysow, Ason, 'The economy of certainty: An introduction to the typology of Islamic legal theory', Ph.D., Harvard University 1984.

—, 'Mu[c]tazilism and Māturīdism in Ḥanafī Legal Theory', in Weiss, *Studies in Islamic Legal Theory*, 235-65

Shī[c]ī and Iranian law

Babayan, Katrhyn, 'Sufis, Dervishes and Mullas: The Controversy over Spiritual and Temporal Dominion in Seventeenth-Century Iran', in Melville, *Safavid Persia*, 117-38.

Brunschvig, Robert, 'Les *uṣûl al-fiqh* imâmites à leur stade ancien (Xe et XIe siècles)', in Tawfiq Fahd (ed.), *Le Shî'isme imâmite*, Paris 1970, 201-13 (and in *Études*, 323-34).

Calder, Norman, 'Zakāt in Imāmī Shīᶜī Jurisprudence, from the Tenth to the Sixteenth Century AD', *Bulletin of the School of Oriental and African Studies*, XLIV, 3, 1981, 468-80.

—, 'Khums in Imāmī Shīᶜī Jurisprudence, from the Tenth to the Sixteenth Century AD', *Bulletin of the School of Oriental and African Studies*, XLV, 1, 1982, 39-47.

Dodge, Bayard, 'The Fāṭimid Legal code', *Muslim World*, L, 1960, 30-8.

Fyzee, Asaf A.A., 'Aspects of Fatimid Law', *Studia Islamica*, XXXI, 1970, 81-91.

Gleave, Robert, *Inevitable Doubt: Two Theories of Shīᶜī Jurisprudence*, Leiden 2000.

—, 'Imāmī Shīᶜī Refutations of *qiyās*', in Weiss, *Studies in Islamic Legal Theory*, 267-91.

Hajji, Amin, 'Institutions of Justice in Fatimid Egypt', in Azmeh, *Islamic Law*, London, 1988, 198-214.

Haykel, Bernard A., *Revival and Reform in Islam: The legacy of Muhammad al-Shawkani*, Cambridge 2003.

—, 'Reforming Islam by Dissolving the *madhhab*s: Shawkānī and his Zaydī Detractors in Yemen', in Weiss, *Studies in Legal Theory*, 337-64.

Keddie, Nikki R., 'The Roots of the ulama's Power in Modern Iran', in Keddie (ed.), *Scholars, Saints and Sufis: Muslim Religious Institutions since 1500,* Berkeley, CA 1972, 211-29.

Kohlberg, Etan, 'The Akhbāriyya in Seventeenth and Eighteenth Century Iran', in John Voll and Nehemia Levtzion (eds), *Eighteenth Century Renewal and Reform in Islam*, New York 1987, 133-60.

Litvak, Meir, *Shiᶜi Scholars of Ninenteenth-Century Iraq: The ᶜUlamaᵓ of Najaf and Karbalaᵓ*, Cambridge 1998.

Mallat, Chibli, *The Renewal of Islamic Law, Muhammad Baqer as-Sadr, Najaf and the Shi'i International*, Cambridge 1993.

Mayer, Ann Elizabeth, 'Islamic law as a cure for political law: the withering of an Islamist illusion', in *Mediterranean Politics*, VII, 4, 2002, 117-42.

Modarressi, Hossein, 'Rationalism and Traditionalism in Shî'î Jurisprudence: A Preliminary Survey', *Studia Islamica*, LIX, 1984, 141-58.

Momen, Moojan, *An Introduction to Sh'i Islam*, New Haven, CT 1985.

Mutahharī, Murtaḍā, 'Ijtihād in the Imāmiyyah Tradition', *Al-Tawḥīd*, IV, 1, 1986, 26-48.

Richard, Yann, *Shiᵓite Islam: Polity, Ideology and Creed*, Oxford 1995.

Savory, Roger, 'The Principal Offices of the Safawid State during the Reign of Ismāᶜīl I (907-30/1501-24)', *Bulletin of the School of Oriental and African Studies*, XXIII, 1, 1960, 91-105.

Schirazi, Asghar, *The Constitution of Iran: Politics and State in the Islamic Republic*, London 1997.

Stewart, Devin J., *Islamic Legal Orthodoxy: Twelver Shiite Responses to the*

Sunni Legal System, Salt Lake City 1998.

Other law outside the four schools

Abdallah, Fadel I., 'Notes on Ibn Ḥazm's Rejection of Analogy (qiyās) in Matters of Religious Law', *American Journal of Islamic Social Sciences*, II, 2, 1985, 207-24.

Arnaldez, Roger, 'La Place du Coran dans les *uṣūl-al-fiqh* d'après la *Muḥallā* d'Ibn Ḥazm', *Studia Islamica*, XXXII, 1970, 21-30.

Fierro, Maribel, *La heterodoxia en al-Andalus durante el periodo omeya*, Madrid 1987.

—, 'Vida e obra', in Muḥammad b. Waḍḍāḥ al-Qurṭubī, *Kitāb al-bidaᶜ: (Tratado contra las innovaciones)*, trans. M. Fierro, Madrid 1988, 9-57.

—, 'The Legal Policies of the Almohad Caliphs and Ibn Rushd's *Bidāyat al-mujtahid'*, *Journal of Islamic Studies*, X, 3, 1999, 226-48.

Goldziher, Ignaz, *The Ẓāhirīs: Their Doctrine and their History*, Leiden 1884, 1971.

Linant de Bellefonds, Y., 'Ibn Hazm et le Zahirisme juridique', *Revue algérienne, tunisienne et marocaine de législation et de jurisprudence*, LXXVI, 1, 1960, 1-43.

The law practised in the courts

The muftī, the qāḍī and the courts in classical practice

Cahen, Claude, 'A propos des Shuhūd', *Studia Islamica*, XXXI, 1970, 71-9.

Calder, Norman, 'Al-Nawawi's typology of *muftī*s and its Significance for a General Theory of Islamic Law', *Islamic Law and Society*, III, 2, 1996, 137-64.

Calero Secall, M. Isabel, 'Rulers and qāḍīs: their relationship during the Naṣrid Kingdom', *Islamic Law and Society*, VII, 2, 2000, 235-5.

Escovitz, Joseph H., *The Office of* qâḍî al-quḍât *in Cairo under the Baḥrî Mamlûks*, Berlin 1984.

Hallaq, Wael B., 'Murder in Cordoba: Ijtihâd, iftâʾ and the evolution of substantive law in medieval Islam', *Acta Orientalia*, LV, 1994, 55-83.

Hicks, Stephen C., 'The fuqaha and Islamic Law', *American Journal of Comparative Law*, XXX, suppl., 1982, 1-13.

Lagardère, Vincent, *Histoire et société en occident musulman au Moyen Âge: Analyse du Miᶜyār d'al-Wanšarīsī*, Madrid 1995.

Makdisi, George, *The Rise of Colleges: Institutions of Learning in Islam and the West*, Edinburgh 1981.

Masud, Muhammad Khalid, Brinkley Messick and David S. Powers (eds), *Muftis, Fatwas and Islamic Legal Interpretation*, Cambridge, MA 1996.

Mozaffari, Mehdi, *Fatwa: Violence and Discourtesy*, Aarhus 1998.

Müller, Christian, *Gerichtspraxis im Stadtstaat Córdoba: Zum Recht der Gesellschaft in einer mālikitisch-islamischen Rechtstradition des 5./11. Jahrhunderts*, Leiden 1999.

—, 'Judging with God's law on Earth: Judicial powers of the *qāḍī al-jamāᶜa* of

Cordoba in the fifth/eleventh century', *Islamic Law and Society*, VII, 2, 2000, 159-86.
Powers, David S., 'On judicial review in Islamic law', *Law & Society Review*, XXVI, 2, 1992, 315-41.
—, 'Legal consultation (*futyā*) in medieval Spain', in Mallat, *Islam and Public Law*, 85-106.
— 'Kadijustiz or qāḍī-justice? A paternity dispute from fourteenth-century Morocco', *Islamic Law and Society*, I, 3, 1994, 332-66 (and *Law, Society and Culture*, 23-52).
— *Law, Society and Culture in the Maghrib, 1300-1500*, Cambridge 2002.
Rappaport, Yossef, 'Legal diversity in the age of *taqlīd*: The four chief *qāḍīs* under the Mamluks', *Islamic Law and Society*, X, 2, 2003, 210-28.
Serrano, Delfina, 'Legal practice in an Andalusī-Maghribī source from the twelfth century CE: The *Madhāhib al-ḥukkām fī nawaāzil al-aḥkām*', *Islamic Law and Society*, VII, 2, 2000, 187-234.
Tyan, Émile, *Histoire de l'organisation judiciaire en pays d'islam*, Leiden 1960.
Ziadeh, Farhat J., 'Compelling defendant's appearance at court in Islamic law', *Islamic Law and Society*, III, 3, 1996, 305-15.
Yanagihashi, Hiroyuki, 'The judicial functions of the sulṭān in civil cases according to the Mālikīs up to the sixth/twelfth century', *Islamic Law and Society*, III, 1, 1996, 41-74.

The Ottoman and early modern period

Brunschvig, Robert, 'Justice religieuse et justice laïque dans la Tunisie des Deys et des Beys jusq'au milieu du XIXe siècle', *Studia Islamica*, XXIII, 1965, 27-70 (and in *Études*, 219-69).
Dallal, Ahmad, 'The origins and objectives of Islamic revivalist thought', *Journal of the Americal Oriental Society*, CXIII, 3, 1993, 341-59.
Gerber, Haim, *Economy and Society in an Ottoman City: Bursa, 1600-1700*, Jerusalem 1988.
—, *State, Society and Law in Islam: Ottoman Law in Comparative Perspective*, Albany 1994.
—, *Islamic Law and Culture: 1600-1840*, Leiden 1999.
Heyd, Uriel, 'Some aspects of the Ottoman fetvā', *Bulletin of the School of Oriental and African Studies*, XXXII, 1, 1969, 35-56.
Imber, Colin, 'Why you should poison your husband: A note on liability in Ḥanafī law in the Ottoman Period', *Islamic Law and Society*, I, 2, 1994, 206-16.
—, *Ebu's-Su'ud: The Islamic Legal Tradition*, Edinburgh 1997.
Jennings, Ronald C., 'The office of vekil (wakil) in the 17th century Ottoman Sharia courts', *Studia Islamica*, XLII, 1975, 147-69.
—, 'Limitations of the judicial powers of the Kadi in 17th c. ottman kayseri', *Studia Islamica*, L, 1979, 151-84.
Repp, Richard C., *The Müfti of Istanbul: A Study in the Development of the Ottoman Learned Hierarchy*, London 1986.
—, 'Qānūn and sharīʿa in the Ottoman context', in Azmeh, *Islamic Law*, 124-45.

Developments in the nineteenth century

Ageron, Charles-Robert, *Modern Algeria: A History from 1830 to the Present*, London 1991 (trans. from *Histoire d'Algérie contemporaine*, Paris 1964-90).

Christelow, Allan, *Muslim Law Courts and the French Colonial State in Algeria*, Princeton 1985.

—, 'The transformation of the Muslim court system in Colonial Algeria', in Azmeh, *Islamic Law*, London 1988, 215-30.

Delanoue, Gilbert, *Moralistes et politiques musulmans dans l'Égypte du XIXe siècle (1798-1882)*, Cairo 1982.

Doughty, Charles M., *Travels in Arabia Deserta*, London 1888 (reprint 1924).

Hourani, Albert, *Arabic Thought in the Liberal Age 1798-1939*, Oxford 1962.

—, 'How should we write the history of the Middle East?', *International Journal of Middle Eastern Studies*, XXIII, 2, 1991, 125-36.

Kerr, Malcolm, *Islamic Reform, The Political and Legal Theories of Muḥammad ᶜAbduh and Rashīd Riḍā*, Los Angeles 1966.

Layish, Aharon, *The Mahdi's Legal Methodology and its Application in the Sudan: A Selection from the Mahdi's Documents (1881-1885)*, Jerusalem 1996.

Marsot, Afaf Lutfi al-Sayyid, *Egypt in the Reign of Muhammad Ali,* Cambridge 1984.

Melasuo, Tuomo, 'The problems and contradictions of land conflicts in Algeria', in Bo Utas and Knut S. Vikør (eds), *The Middle East Viewed from the North*, Bergen 1992, 85-92.

O'Fahey, R.S., 'The office of *qāḍī* in Dār Fūr: a preliminary inquiry', *Bulletin of the School of Oriental and Afrian Studies*, XL, 1, 1977, 110-24.

Peskes, Esther, *Muḥammad b. ᶜAbdalwahhāb (1703-92) im Widerstreit: Untersuchungen zur Rekonstruktion der Frühgeschichte der Wahhābīya*, Beirut 1993.

Peters, Rudolph, '*Idjtihād* and *taqlīd* in 18th and 19th century Islam', *Die Welt des Islams*, XX, 3-4, 1980, 131-45.

—, 'The codification of criminal law in nineteenth century Egypt: Tradition or modernization?', in J.M. Abun-Nasr, U. Spellenberg and U. Wanitzek (eds), *Law, Society and National Identity*, Hamburg 1990, 211-25.

—, 'Murder on the Nile: Homicide trials in 19th century Egyptian Shariᶜa courts', *Die Welt des Islams*, XXX, 1990, 98-116.

—, 'Islamic and secular criminal law in nineteenth century Egypt: The role and function of the qadi', *Islamic Law and Society*, IV, 1, 1997, 70-90.

—, 'The infatuated Greek: Social and legal boundaries in ninteenth-century Egypt', *Égypte/Monde arabe*, XXXIV, 2, 1998, 53-65.

Roberson, B.A., 'The emergence of the modern judiciary in the Middle East: Negotiating the mixed courts of Egypt', in Mallat, *Islam and Public Law*, 107-39.

Vikør, Knut S., *Sufi and Scholar on the Desert Edge*, London 1995.

—, *Sources for Sanusī Studies*, Bergen 1996.

Contemporary practises

El-Affendi, Abdelwahab, *Who Needs an Islamic State?*, London 1991.

Botiveau, Bernard, *Loi islamique et droit dans les sociétés arabes,* Paris 1993.

Brown, Daniel W., *Rethinking Tradition in Modern Islamic Thought*, Cambridge 1996.

Coulson, Neil J., 'The state and the individual in Islamic Law', *International and Comparative Law Quarterly*, VI, 1957, 49-60

Krawietz, Birgit, 'Frevelfurcht oder Fortbildung des islamischen Rechts', in Aulis Aarnio *et al.* (eds), *Rechtsnorm und Rechtswirklichkeit. Festschrift für Werner Krawietz*, Berlin 1993, 733-47.

—, 'The weighing of conflicting indicators in Islamic law', in Vermeulen and van Reeth, *Law, Christianity and Modernism in Islamic Society,* 71-4

—, 'Cut and paste in legal rules: Designing Islamic norms with *talfiq*', *Die Welt des Islams*, XLII, 1, 2002, 3-40.

Layish, Aharon, 'The contribution of the modernists to the secularization of Islamic law', *Middle Eastern Studies*, XIV, 1978, 263-77.

—, 'Reforms in Islamic commercial law—Toward a reopening of the gate to ijtihād?', *Asian and African Studies (Haifa)*, XXI, 1987, 221-7.

—, 'The family waqf and the *sharᶜī* law of succession in modern times', *Islamic Law and Society*, IV, 3, 1997, 352-88.

—, 'The Transformation of the Sharīᶜa from Jurists' Law to Statutory Law in the Contemporary Muslim World', *Die Welt des Islams*, XLIV, 1, 2004, 85-113.

Liebesny, Herbert J., 'Judicial systems in the Near and Middle East. Evolutionary development and Islamic revival', *Middle East Journal*, XXVII, 2, 1983.

Lindholm, Tore and Kari Vogt (eds), Islamic Law Reform and Human Rights: Challenges and Rejoinders, Proceedings of the Seminar on Human Rights and the Modern Application of Islamic Law, Oslo 14-15 February 1992, Copenhagen-Oslo, 1993.

Mayer, Ann Elizabeth, 'The Shari'ah: A metodology or a body of substantive rules?', in Heer, *Islamic Law and Jurisprudence*, 177-98.

Peters, Rudolph, 'Islamic law and human rights: A contribution to an ongoing debate', *Islam and Christian-Muslim Relations*, X, 1, 1999, 5-14.

—, 'From Jurists' Law to Statute Law or What Happens when the Shari'a is Codified', *Mediterranean Politics*, VII, 4, 2002, 82-95.

Rosen, Lawrence, *The Anthropology of Justice Law as Culture in Islamic Society*, Cambridge 1989.

—, *The Justice of Islam: Comparative Perspectives on Islamic Law and Society*, London 2000.

Starr, June and Jane F. Collier (eds), *History and Power in the Study of Law: New Directions in Legal Anthropology*, Ithaca, NY 1989.

Vikør, Knut S., 'The Sharīᶜa and the nation state: who can codify the divine law?', in Bjørn Olav Utvik and K.S. Vikør (eds), *The Middle East in a Globalized World*, Bergen 2000, 220-50.

White, Elizabeth H., 'Legal reform as an indicator of women's status in Muslim nations', in Nikki Keddie and Lois Beck (eds), *Women in the Muslim World,* Cambridge, MA 1978, 52-68.

Weichman, Lynn, 'Islamic Law: Stuck with the State?', in A. Huxley (ed.), *Religion, Law and Tradition: Comparative Studies in Religious Law*, London 2002, 61-83.

Zubaida, Sami, *Law and Power in the Islamic World*, London 2003.

Individual countries or regions

Egypt

Oussama, Arabi, 'Intention and method in Sanhūrī's fiqh: Cause as ulterior motive', *Islamic Law and Society*, IV, 2, 1997, 200-23.

Botiveau, Bernard, 'Contemporary reinterpretations of Islamic Law: The case of Egypt', in Mallat, *Islam and Public Law*, 261-77.

Bälz, Kilian, 'Submitting faith to judicial scrutiny through the family trial: The "Abû Zayd case"', *Die Welt des Islams*, XXXVII, 2, 1997, 135-55.

Dupret, Baudouin, 'Sexual morality at the Egyptian bar: Female circumcision, sex change operations and motives for suing', *Islamic Law and Society*, IX, 1, 2002, 42-69.

Hill, Enid, 'Islamic Law as a source for the development of a comparative jurisprudene: theory and pratice in the life and work of Sanhūrī', in Azmeh, *Islamic Law*, London, 1988, 146-97.

Skovgaard-Petersen, Jakob, *Defining Islam for the Egyptian State: Muftis and Fatwas of the Dār al-iftā*, Leiden 1997.

North Africa

al-Ahnaf, Mustafa, Bernard Botiveau and Franck Frégosi (eds), *L'Algérie par ses islamistes*, Paris 1991.

Fluehr-Lobban, Carolyn, *Islamic Law and Society in the Sudan*, London 1987.

Hamdi, Mohamed Elhachmi, *The Politicisation of Islam: A Case Study of Tunisia*, Boulder, CO 1998.

—, *The Making of an Islamic Political Leader: Conversations with Hasan al-Turabi*, Boulder, CO 1998.

Layish, Aharon, *Legal Documents on Libyan Tribal Society in Process of Sedentarization (with an Anthropological Critique by John Davis)*, Vol I, Wiesbaden 1998.

Layish, Aharon and Gabriel R. Warburg, *The Reinstatement of Islamic Law in the Sudan under Numayrī: An Evaluation of a Legal Experiment in the Light of its Historical Context, Methodology and Repercussions*, Leiden 2002.

Mayer, Ann Elizabeth, 'A survey of Islamifying trands in Libyan Law since 1969', *Libyan Studies*, VII, 1975-6, 53-5.

— 'Le droit musulman en Libye à l'âge du "Livre vert"', *Maghreb-Machrek*, 93, 1981, 5-22.

— 'In search of the sacred law: the meandering course of Qadhafi's Legal Policy', in Dirk Vandewalle (ed.), *Qadhafi's Libya, 1969-1994*, New York 1995, 113-37.

Safwat, Safiya, 'Islamic laws in the Sudan', in Azmeh, *Islamic Law*, 231-49.

Stiansen, Endre, 'Islamic banking in the Sudan: Aspects of the laws and the debate', in Stiansen and Jane I. Guyer (eds), *Credit, Currencies and*

Culture: African Financial Institutions in Historical Perspective, Uppsala 1999, 100-17.

Sub-saharan Africa

Anderson, J.N.D., *Islamic Law in Africa*, London 1970.

Bang, Anne K. and Knut S. Vikør, 'A tale of three *shambas*: Shāfiᶜī-Ibāḍī legal cooperation in the Zanzibar Protectorate', *Sudanic Africa*, 10, 1999, 1-26 & 11, 2000, 1-24.

Basri, Ghazali, *Nigeria and Sharīᶜah: Aspirations and Apprehensions*, Markfield 1994.

Kumo, Suleimanu, 'The application of Islamic Law in Northern Nigeria: Problems and prospects', in S. Khalid Rashid (ed.), *Islamic Law in Nigeria: Application and Teaching*, Lagos 1986, 42-51.

—, 'Shari'a under colonialism - Northern Nigeria', in Nura Alkali *et al, Islam in Africa. Proceedings of the Islam in Africa Conference*, Ibadan 1993, 1-22.

Sulaiman, Ibrahim K.R., 'The Sharīᶜah and the 1979 constitution', in S. Khalid Rashid (ed.), *Islamic Law in Nigeria: Application and Teaching*, Lagos 1986, 52-74.

Yusuf, Ahmed Beita, *Nigerian Legal System: Pluralism and Conflict of Laws in the Northern States*, New Dehli 1982.

Turkey

Starr, June, *Dispute and Settlement in Rural Turkey: An Ethnography of Law*, Leiden 1978.

—, *Law as Metaphor, From Islamic Courts to the Palace of Justice*, Albany, NY 1992.

Palestine

Eisenman, Robert H., *Islamic Law in Palestine and Israel, A History of the Survival of Tanzimat and Shari'a in the British Mandate and the Jewish State,* Leiden 1978.

Layish, Aharon, 'The status of the Sharīᶜa in a non-Muslim state: The case of Israel', *Asian and African Studies*, XXVII, 1993.

Taji-Farouki, Suha, 'Islamic state theories and contemporary realities', in Abdel Salam Sidahmed and Anoushiravan Ehteshami (eds), *Islamic Fundamentalism*, Boulder, CO 1996, 35-50.

Gulf countries and Yemen

Ballantyne, Wiliam, 'A reassertion of the sharī'ah: The jurisprudence in Gulf states', in Nicholas Heer (ed.), *Islamic Law and Jurisprudence*, Seattle 1990, 149-60.

—, *Essays and Addresses on Arab Laws*, London 2000.

Brown, Nathan J., *The Rule of Law in the Arab World: Courts in Egypt and the Gulf*, Cambridge 1997.

Buchan, James, 'Secular and religious opposition in Saudi Arabia', in Tim Niblock (ed.), *State, Society and Economy in Saudi Arabia*, London 1982, 106-24.

Al-Farsy, Fouad, *Saudi Arabia: A Case Study in Development*, London 1982.

Habib, John S., *Ibn Sau'd's Warriors of Islam: The Ikhwan of Najd and their Role in the Creation of the Sa'udi Kingdom*, Leiden 1978.

Lackner, Helen, *A House Built on Sand: A Political Economy of Saudi Arabia*, London 1978.

Messick, Brinkley, *The Calligraphic State: Textual Domination and History in a Muslim Society*, Berkeley, CA 1996.

Mühlböck, M.F., 'Modernization and traditonalism in the legislation of Kuwait', in Vermeulen and van Reeth, *Law, Christianity and Modernism in Islamic Society,* 87-95.

Niblock, Tim, 'The Saudi Arabian Political System', in Niblock (ed.), *State, Society and Economy in Saudi Arabia*, London 1982, 75-105.

Steinberg, Guido, *Religion und Staat in Saudi-Arabien. Die wahhabitischen Gelehrten 1902-1953*, Würzburg 2002.

Vogel, Frank E., *Islamic Law and Legal Systems: Studies of Saudi Arabia*, Leiden 2000.

Würth, Anna, 'A Sana'a court: The court, the family, and the ability to negotiate', *Islamic Law and Society*, II, 3, 1995, 320-40.

Pakistan

Carroll, Lucy, 'Qurʾān 2:229: "A charter granted to wife"? Judicial khulᶜ in Pakistan', *Islamic Law and Society*, III, 1, 1996, 91-126.

Hussain, Mir Zohair, 'Islam in Pakistan under Bhutto and Zia-ul-Haqq', in Hussin Mutalib and Taj ul-Islam Hashmi (eds), *Islam, Muslims and the Modern State*, London 1994, 47-79.

Mehdi, Rubya, *The Islamization of the Law in Pakistan*, London 1994.

Some areas of law

General reference works

Bakhtiar, Laleh, *Encyclopedia of Islamic Law: A Compendium of the Views of the Major Schools*, Chicago 1996.

Doi, ᶜAbdur Raḥmān I., *Sharīᶜah : The Islamic Law*, London 1997.

Family law

Buskens, Léon, 'Recent debates on family law reform in Morocco: Islamic law as politics in an emerging public sphere', *Islamic Law and Society*, X, 1, 2003, 70-131.

Layish, Aharon, *Divorce in the Libyan Family: A Study Based on the* sijills *of the* sharīᶜa *Courts of Ajdābiyya and Kufra,* New York / Jerusalem, 1991.

Manek, Mohanlal Dayalji, *Handbook of Mahomedan law (Muslim Personal Law),* Bombay 1961.

Mir-Hosseini, Ziba, *Marriage on Trial: A Study of Islamic Family Law: Iran and Morocco Compared*, London 1997.

Mitchell, Ruth, 'Family law in Algeria before and after the 1404/1984 family code', in Gleave and Kermeli, *Islamic Law*, 194-204.

Moors, Annelies, *Women, Property and Islam, Palestinian Experiences 1920-*

1990, Cambridge 1995.

al-Na'im, Abdullahi (ed.), *Islamic Family Law in a Changing World: A Global Resource Book*, London 2002.

Rappaport, Yossef, 'Matrimonial gifts in early Islamic Egypt', *Islamic Law and Society*, VII, 1, 2000, 1-36.

Shaham, Ron, 'Custom, Islamic Law and Statutory Legislation: Marriage Registration and Minimum Age at Marriage in Egyptian Shari'a Courts', *Islamic Law and Society*, II, 3, 1995, 258-81.

—, *Family and the Courts in Modern Egypt: A Study Based on Decisions by the Sharīᶜa Courts, 1900-1955*, Leiden 1997.

Tucker, Judith E., 'Muftīs and Matrimony: Islamic Law and Gender in Ottoman Syria and Palestine', *Islamic Law and Society*, I, 3, 1994, 265-300.

—, *In the House of the Law: Gender and Islamic Law in Ottoman Syria and Palestine,* Berkeley, CA 1998.

Zomeño, Amelia, 'Kafāᵓa in the Mālikī school: A *fatwā* from fifteenth-century Fez', in Gleave and Kermeli, *Islamic Law*, 194-204.

Economic law

Deguilhem, Randi (ed.), *Le Waqf dans l'espace islamique: outil de pouvoir socio-politique*, Damascus 1995.

Donaldson, William J., *Sharecropping in the Yemen: A Study in Islamic Theory, Custom and Pragmatism*, Leiden 2000.

Johansen, Baber, *The Islamic Law on Land Tax and Rent : The Peasants' Loss of Property Rights as Interpreted in the Hanafite Legal Literature of the Mamluk and Ottoman periods*, London 1988.

—, 'Legal literature and the problem of change: The case of land rent', in Mallat, *Islam and Public Law*, 29-47.

Kuran, Timur, 'The economic system in contemporary Islamic thought: interpretation and assessment', *International Journal of Middle Eastern Studies*, XVIII, 2, 1986, 135-64.

Leeuwen, Richard, *Waqfs and Urban Structures: The Case of Ottoman Damascus*, Leiden 1999.

Reiter, Yitzhak, 'Family *waqf* entitlements in British Palestine (1917-1948), *Islamic Law and Society*, IV, 2, 1997, 174-93.

Criminal law

Haleem, M.A, A.O. Sherif and K. Daniels (eds), *Criminal Justice in Islam: Judicial Procedure in the Sharīᶜa*, London 2003.

Schneider, Irene, 'Imprisonment in pre-classical and classical Islamic Law', *Islamic Law and Society*, II, 2, 1995, 157-73.

INDEX